HENRY BROOKS ADAMS (1838-1918) was the great-grandson of President John Adams; grandson of President John Quincy Adams; and son of Charles Francis Adams, United States Minister to Great Britain. He was graduated from Harvard (1858), did some postgraduate work in Germany, and served as his father's private secretary in London during the Civil War. From 1870-1877 he was assistant professor of history at Harvard and editor of the *North American Review*. Among his books are *The Life of Albert Gallatin, John Randolph, Mont-Saint-Michel and Chartres,* and *The Education of Henry Adams*. He also published two novels (both anonymously), *Democracy* and *Esther*. A collection of his writings, illustrating his skeptical and "dynamic" theory of history, was published in 1919 under the title *The Degradation of the Democratic Dogma*.

GEORGE DANGERFIELD is the author of *The Strange Death of Liberal England, The Era of Good Feelings,* and *Chancellor Robert R. Livingston of New York: 1746-1813*. He has contributed articles and reviews to *American Historical Quarterly, Nation, New Republic, Saturday Review,* and *Harpers,* among others. In 1953 he was awarded a Pulitzer Prize in History.

OTEY M. SCRUGGS teaches history at the University of California, Santa Barbara. He has contributed articles to *Agricultural History, Labor History, Pacific Historical Review, Southwestern Social Science Quarterly,* and *Arizona and the West*. He is now working on a book on American agricultural history (farm labor) in the twentieth century.

History of the United States
During the Administrations of
Jefferson and Madison

Henry Adams

History of the United States

*During the Administrations of
Jefferson and Madison*

Abridged with an Introduction by
George Dangerfield
Otey M. Scruggs

A SPECTRUM BOOK

Prentice-Hall, Inc.

Englewood Cliffs, N. J.

Editors' Note

This book is a volume in the Classics in History Series of works in American history. The titles in the series have been chosen primarily from familiar works that are not easily accessible. In some cases we have also chosen to reprint once influential books that still have intrinsic interest or to create fresh collections of essays or letters that now exist only in scattered or expensive editions.

William E. Leuchtenburg
Bernard Wishy

The division of the *History* into four Parts, and the subdivisions within each Part, have been made by the editors for the convenience of the reader. The numbers in parentheses attached to each section indicate the source in the original nine volume edition by, in order, volume, chapter, and pages. The original spelling and punctuation have been retained wherever possible.

Volume I: Jefferson and *Volume II: Madison,* formerly printed as separate volumes, are here combined under one cover for the first time.

History of the United States

During the Administrations of
Jefferson and Madison

I. JEFFERSON

CONTENTS

VOLUME I

Introduction

Henry Adams' masterpiece, *History of the United States During the Administrations of Jefferson and Madison,* was published in nine volumes between 1889 and 1891; and it is presumed that he began the actual writing of it in 1881. Its three notes are optimism, nationalism, and scientism; tempered by a subtle and sceptical intelligence, they are not strident. Indeed, an American intellectual in the 1880's might have derived all three from the American scene itself; supposing, that is, that he disregarded, as irrelevant or transient, the dullness and corruption of contemporary politics. It would be too much to say that the panic and crash of 1893 changed Adams' attitude towards the American past, present, and future: but we do know that in his presidential "Communication" to the American Historical Association, written from a Mexican retreat in 1894, he called for a science of history which "must be absolute, like other sciences, and must fix with mathematical certainty the path which human society has got to follow." He added that the effects of such a science, upon teaching and upon society, would be *most* disagreeable. He had now set his feet upon the path which led in due course to *The Rule of Phase Applied to History* (1909) and *A Letter to American Teachers of History* (1910)—the effects of which, had anyone taken them seriously, might well have been catastrophic.

There is, however, a distinct relationship between the *History* and the "Communication"; the "Communication" is, as it were, an *ave atque vale* to its great predecessor, now seen as receding into some happier past. At the end of the *History,* for example, Adams could write:

Every serious difficulty which had seemed alarming to the people of the United States had been removed or had sunk from notice in 1816. . . . The continent lay before them, like an uncovered ore bed. They could

1

see, and they could even calculate with reasonable accuracy, the wealth
it could be made to yield. With almost the certainty of a mathematical
formula, knowing the rate of increase of population and of wealth, they
could read in advance their economical history for at least a hundred
years.

Adams' generalizations are often of this "scientific" order; they
are to be taken as challenges, not least as challenges to one's sense
of humor. He is not asking here for an "absolute" science of
history; he is expressing the sceptical hope that the American
people can learn to think scientifically, and the qualified belief
that, if any people can, *they* can. The Adams of the "Communication" had said farewell to this kind of nationalism and this kind of
optimism.

In the *History* Adams attempted to combine the contemporary
view, fathered by the German historian, Leopold von Ranke, that
history should be written "as it actually happened," with the view
held by later historians that their function was to use their knowledge of the present to "predict" the past. The former view was
reflected in Adams' use of quotations from his extensive manuscript
sources to permit the participants on the historical stage to speak
for themselves; the latter in his sometimes subtle, usually penetrating gloss on the quotations.[1] An example is his handling of Burr's
trial. By means of numerous quotations, ranging from short and
broken to lengthy, Adams attempts to bring the reader into the
courtroom at Richmond and to transport him to Monticello to
witness Jefferson's reaction to the Richmond proceedings. With the
end of the trial, however, we return with Adams to the 1880's, from
which vantage point the historian makes the bold, if tenuous
generalization: "The days of Jefferson's power and glory had passed
forever, while those of Marshall had barely begun." Or better, the
generalization, in establishing a link between the 1800's and the
1880's, is merely another assertion of the inevitable triumph of
centralism over particularism, inevitable certainly to the historian
under the influence of the complacent nationalism of the Gilded
Age.

Not surprisingly, since one part was essentially static and the
other dynamic, Adams' method helped lead him into the contradic-

[1] The limitations of space in this edition precluded the retention of Adams'
own footnotes. Those interested in his sources should consult the original, un-
abridged edition. The few notes found in this edition were inserted by the
editors for purposes of identification or clarification.

tions found in the *History*. Thus, in describing another situation involving President Jefferson at the time of the Burr trial, Adams concludes with the tantalizing but unproved statement: "In such a state of mind, and with such a reserve of popular authority, President Jefferson's power found no restraint." Again, however, the present has triumphed over the past: another stone has been placed in Adams' edifice of centralism. If the method helps explain the contradictions in the *History*, it contributes significantly to its vitality and movement. The linear movement of the narrative, which would have become monotonous in a work of such length, is strengthened by the oscillation between quotation and commentary, fact and conjecture, past and present.

Adams had studied and admired Alexis de Tocqueville's *Democracy in America*; he may even have heeded the great Frenchman's warnings about the tendency of democratic historians to disregard the individual's role in history and to fall into a kind of paralyzing determinism. Adams, both as a scientist and also through lack of social data, preferred to think of American individuals as types of character or functions of power; but he does at times confer a brilliant individuality upon these types and functions; and when it comes to Thomas Jefferson, the ambiguous hero of the whole work (which is neither anti-Federalist nor anti-Republican but anti-extremist), he seems to confess (in Tocqueville's words) that "round every man a fatal circle is traced beyond which he cannot pass; but within the wide verge of that circle he is powerful and free."

Tocqueville, at any rate, must be credited with giving Adams his working hypothesis for the *History*: that democracy is inevitable; that it is peaceable; that its movement, if left to itself, is toward centralization; and that, unless it be educated in the higher or abstract sciences, it may sink into mediocrity. The period 1800 to 1815 in American history is particularly suited to the development and testing of this multiple hypothesis; and not less suited to Adams' taste for irony and paradox. The *History*'s central theme is the rise, decline, and renewal of democratic nationalism. How agreeable to begin one's study at the moment when the "revolution" of 1800 had placed the government of the United States at the disposal of men who were theoretically particularists, even nominalists; men, that is to say, who held that the individual States were discrete "nations," and that the Federal Government was a "foreign" government, created solely to maintain commercial relations with the outer world! Such were their views at their most extreme—the views that can still be studied, with profit, in the writings of John

Taylor of Caroline, and still be detected, with pleasure, among the shrill speeches of John Randolph of Roanoke. Needless to say, both precedent and common sense had already greatly modified them for practical purposes. None the less, all good Jeffersonians were men to whom strong central government was presumably anathema. And yet, within five years, President Jefferson was disposing of more power than either of his Federalist predecessors; and doing so with no more than a twinge to his particularist conscience. Only in its battle against the centralizing tendencies of the Supreme Court did the revolution of 1800 live up to its premises; and that battle was fatal to the Jeffersonians. Thus democratic nationalism, like wisdom, was justified of all its children.

The *History* can be seen as falling into four movements. Up to 1805, there is an undisturbed development of nationalism, to which the Louisiana Treaty imparted a vigorous impulse. After 1805 the United States becomes a prey to the warring empires of Great Britain and France; the nationalist movement experiences some violent oscillations but is, on the whole, retarded; and it is brought to a standstill by Jefferson's embargo, the supreme example of peaceful coercion. Between 1809 and 1811, under Madison, nationalism sinks into apathy and imbecility. In 1811 it renews itself, and although in the War of 1812 American democracy (true to its peaceable instinct) puts forth no more energy than is required to do the work, in the end all is well. Democratic nationalism has renewed itself for fresh developments, and the national character has been vindicated. American democracy has produced "a new variety of man."

Whether this variety would be of a higher or a lower order is a problem that Adams leaves (with some confidence perhaps) to the future. He is a little too sceptical to accept the myth of "upward" evolution. Indeed, the interest for the student of his *History* lies in his attempt to order his whole scheme on "scientific" and patriotic lines, without losing his franchise as a sceptical historian. When he was teaching history at Harvard, he said that the questions in his examination papers were usually questions he could not answer himself. And surely an historian's worth can be estimated as much by the questions he raises as by the ones he puts to sleep.

The whole *History,* in spite of the abruptness of some of its assertions, is rather a questioning than a conclusive work. Adams, for example (it was a tribute to his presidential name and his personal charm), had gained admittance to the archives of Madrid and Paris and London, those formidable repositories where so much of the American diplomatic past lay voiceless and moribund. The material with which he emerged was immensely valuable, and considering that he was only one man, he analyzed its immensity with acuteness and brilliance. The diplomatic correspondence of the 1800's traveled slowly across the ocean, settling crises that had often ceased to exist, issuing orders that had often lost their meaning before they arrived. Adams does not treat this diplomatic evidence as exact evidence: to him it represents immediacy, a living state of mind, from which, like a lawyer, he endeavors to coax some approximation of the truth. Nor should the contrasts and contradictions which are built into the structure of his work be considered as dialectical: it was not an Hegelian but an imaginative order that he sought to impose upon the flux of events.

Moreover, he was an eclectic, borrowing what he needed from this system and that. If one is looking for the influences which loom most obviously in his thinking—and which are not always reconciled, but simply set to work—they would appear to be Tocqueville's *Democracy,* Comte's *Positive Philosophy,* and the *First Principles* of Herbert Spencer. In a more extended essay, we would examine others: but the trinity of Tocqueville, Comte, and Spencer may suffice to preside over a limited inquiry—Tocqueville who inspired the working hypothesis, and Comte and Spencer who provided the means for developing and testing this hypothesis.[2]

Even in his last years, when nothing but physics and chemistry would do, Adams retained his respect for Comte, but such references as he has been known to make to Spencer are invariably disparaging. Yet it is quite evident that he had rummaged around in the curious mechanical museum of Spencer's *First Principles* and had retrieved from its assemblage of ingenious but dusty objects something very like a working model. A famous passage from the *History* will serve to explain this.

Travellers in Switzerland who stepped across the Rhine where it flowed from its glacier could follow its course among mediaeval towns and feudal ruins, until it became a highway for modern industry, and at last arrived at a permanent equilibrium in the ocean. American history followed the same course. With prehistoric glaciers and mediaeval feudalism the story had little to do; but from the moment it came within sight of the ocean, it acquired an interest almost painful. A child could find

[2] For Comtist and Spencerian influences upon Adams' thinking the reader is referred to two very able studies: William H. Jordy, *Henry Adams: Scientific Historian* (New Haven: Yale University Press, 1952) and Ernest Samuels, *Henry Adams, The Middle Years* (Cambridge, Mass.: Harvard University Press, 1958).

its way in a river valley, and a hoy could float on the waters of Holland; but science alone could sound the depths of the ocean, measure its currents, foretell its storms, or fix its relations to the system of nature. In a democratic ocean science could see something ultimate. Man could go no further. The atom might move, but the general equilibrium could not change.

This remarkable paragraph refers to Spencer's theory of mechanical evolution, in which human society is seen as ultimately attaining a blessed state of "moving equilibrium," where the individual mind is in perfect harmony with the conditions of its existence. That a moving equilibrium may have been nothing more than bourgeois laissez faire, tricked out in a mechanical halo, seems not to have escaped Adams' acute mind: in the final paragraphs of his *History,* at any rate, he jettisons moving equilibrium. But mechanical progression remains a central impulse in the *History,* although it is only a figurative impulse.

Thus the movement of democracy toward a center—in other words "democratic nationalism"—is, in its undisturbed state, likened to inertia; the popular will or instinct is the energy which sets it in motion; and since the law of inertia is resistance to something, the historian then describes the forces which, separately or in collision, accelerate, deflect, or retard this inertial movement. Obviously this will get him into semantic difficulties of the most baffling kind. When is an energy not an energy? When it is a force? What distinction can be made between democratic, geographic, and demographic inertias? Next question. How can one subsume under the term "force"—unless (like Adams) one delights in paradox—such disparate phenomena as Jefferson's heelless slippers, the sordid commercialism of Spencer Perceval, and the mendacity of Napoleon I?

None the less, as a figurative and dramatic device, mechanical progression works very well. After 1805, as the neutral United States is sucked into the vortex of the Napoleonic Wars, the centralizing movement is subjected to, and tested by, its reaction to the most violent collisions of force. When it tends to slow down, as when it tends to renew itself, this progression can only be described in exaggerated terms, so that the line of the narrative resembles the peaks and declivities in a graph. We have endeavored to arrange our abridgement so that it illustrates this.

Comte had a far more sophisticated and a far more educated mind than Spencer, who was merely erudite, and Comte's influence upon Adams is more difficult to explain. The following quotation may help. Adams had evolved the theory that nationalist energy renews itself in cycles. "A period of about twelve years," he writes, "measured the beat of the pendulum, and already a child could calculate the result of a few more returns." If a child could make the calculation, the calculation itself (as Adams rather more than hints) might well be childish. But suppose one takes this cyclical movement to be a phase, a particular stage in a recurring sequence of movements or changes. Adams had been profoundly impressed by Comte's Law of Three States—the "theological," "metaphysical," and "positive" stages through which all branches of human knowledge and all societies must pass. The period under examination in his *History* could be asked to show, not only recurrence, but also redemption. The United States was passing from a "political" to an "economical" state; it was being relieved from the metaphysics of political dogma and directed towards the realm of positive inquiry.

In an extraordinary passage in Volume IV, Adams compares the wounded and insulted *Chesapeake,* as she limps home to port, to the little *Clermont,* puffing and clanking in triumph up the Hudson. The American people, he says, were not yet so scientifically minded as to combine these two events and see that one era was passing and another dawning. The positivist did not enquire into ultimate causes; he examined only conditions and the relations between conditions: the relation between condition *Chesapeake* and condition *Clermont* would one day be obvious. In the final page of the *History,* Adams asks his famous and ambiguous questions in a mood of Tocquevillean doubt, but with a strong suggestion of Comtist optimism. If the American people can develop a truly scientific or positive character, they will release themselves from the treadmill of mechanical progression. If anyone can, *they* can.

We are not able, in this brief introduction, to dwell on the biographical element in Adams' work. We believe that the great personal tragedy of his wife's death which fell across his life in 1885 is not relevant to the *History*. We doubt that Adams was a frustrated politician, or that if he was, it shows in his work. We think that to be an Adams, with all the family vanity and with two nationalist Presidents roosting in the family tree, was a decided advantage, if an equivocal one. It was certainly a great advantage to have learned at the very top level, in London and in Washington, how men who are not historians behave. We might also assert, and do assert, that Adams' experiences in London, where he watched the Civil War from the forlorn but magic casements of the American Legation, contributed greatly to his anti-British bias in the *History*. He was nothing if not a relativist. The ponderous and shifty Whig government of Palmerston and Russell in the 1860's was easily transmuted backwards into the blank Toryism of the governments of Portland and Perceval in the days of Jefferson. And it is well to remember that for seven years he instructed himself and his Harvard seminarians in institutionalist method, which subjected the documents of the past to a rigorous cross-examination, as if the past were on trial for perjury.

A work such as the *History* is not just the sum of its author's influences and advantages, even if one includes among these advantages the possession of a fine mind and the command of a fine prose, the employment of a responsible method and the use of hitherto untapped archival sources. Something more is needed, if one is to account for its endurance, not only as an admitted masterpiece, but as a masterpiece that can still be studied with profit. The answer would seem to be that Adams had, pre-eminently, an historical imagination: that is to say, an imaginary picture of the past which stood in a methodical relation to something called evidence, but which also had the power to bring into itself as evidence certain ascertained facts which historians had hitherto thought useless or had not known how to use.

We might then describe the *History* as a great political narrative, informed with historical imagination. In these days, a great political narrative has to be more than just political: and it may well be that the peculiar spell which Adams' imagination casts upon its readers is its note of moral scientism. His grandfather, John Quincy Adams, in his great *Report on Weights and Measures* (1821) made a curious relation between the Millennium and the Meter. Henry Adams' thinking was not exactly millennial; nor was he so utilitarian as to suppose that measurements are moral; but, like his grandfather, he believed that morality was measurable. He had succeeded in banishing providence from his universe, but Massachusetts was more stubborn. Even his physical analogies are made to subserve a moral purpose. Thus the Embargo is said to have failed because it could not endure long enough to obey a law of physics— namely, that force must be converted into an equivalent force—but also, in violating this law, it became deceptive and corrupting. Even more extraordinary is his use of the War of 1812, not simply as an impeachment of the "metaphysical" statesmanship of Jefferson, which sacrificed the army to a political dogma; but also, and perhaps more so, as evidence of the scientific and moral superiority of the American character.

Adams tried to justify the War of 1812, *vide* the Battle of Chippewa, on the quasi-Darwinist principle of the struggle for existence and the "laws of nature." He also resorted to Horace's principle (and Tocqueville's) of *dulce et decorum*. Neither exactly satisfied him. What truly satisfied him can be shown in his account of the duel between the *U.S.S. Constitution* and the British *Guerrière*. He made a careful comparison of the proportions of the two frigates, the weight and kind of metal they threw, and the numbers of their respective crews; and he reached the conclusion that the *Constitution* was physically superior in a ratio of ten to seven. But when he estimated the damage inflicted upon the *Guerrière,* and the speed with which it was inflicted, he asserted that the *Constitution's moral* superiority was as ten to two. Inflamed with a disinterested love for their insulted country, the *Constitution's* cannoneers had aimed with extreme precision. "It raised the United States in one half hour," he ends, to our astonishment, "to the rank of a first-class power in the world." The artillery battle at New Orleans was also turned into a decisive example of scientific achievement and moral superiority. But it is in his superb description of the privateer that he presents his most optimistic and moral symbol of the American character: the privateer is a scientific and aesthetic marvel, but it never fights unless it has to. In the long run, science is only moral if it is also peaceable.

In making this abridgement we have endeavored to perform our inevitable mutilations in the spirit of the operating theater, not the *abattoir.* We hope that the *History* has survived: in other words, that we have presented both a useable text and an excursion into historiography. We have been guided by the following considerations. (1) Since the first six chapters of the first volume are not only famous but (which is more unusual) widely read, and since they are available in a separate edition, we have excluded them. (2) Since the emphasis of the narrative is more upon the argument with British aristocracy than with French militarism, we have concentrated upon the former. (3) We have tried to preserve a reasonable continuity. The numbers in parentheses attached to each section indicate the source in the original nine volume edition by, in order, volume, chapter, and pages. (4) We have tried to show how Adam's handled all the important events of the period. (5) We have selected what were for Adams the decisive events rather than events that readers may know better. For example, Adams dutifully wrote at great length about the Burr conspiracy, which he considered to be almost meaningless. On the other hand the trial of Burr was, for

him, the culmination of a long battle between Jefferson and the
Judiciary. (6) We wish to demonstrate Adams' emphatic and characteristic use of generalization, contradiction, and contrast. If we have
succeeded, then the *History* will have emerged as (we believe) Adams
intended it to be: as a challenge from the past to the future, for
generations to come.

George Dangerfield
Otey M. Scruggs

I.

"Full Tide of Successful Experiment"—1801-1805

1.

Pseudo-Revolution

Whether the illusions, so often affirmed and so often denied to the American people, took such forms or not, these were in effect the problems that lay before American society: Could it transmute its social power into the higher forms of thought? Could it provide for the moral and intellectual needs of mankind? Could it take permanent political shape? Could it give new life to religion and art? Could it create and maintain in the mass of mankind those habits of mind which had hitherto belonged to men of science alone? Could it physically develop the convolutions of the human brain? Could it produce, or was it compatible with, the differentiation of a higher variety of the human race? Nothing less than this was necessary for its complete success. . . . (I, vi, 184)

The man who mounted the steps of the Capitol, March 4, 1801, to claim the place of an equal between Pitt and Bonaparte, possessed a character which showed itself in acts; but person and manner can be known only by contemporaries, and the liveliest description was worth less than a moment of personal contact. Jefferson was very tall, six feet two-and-a-half inches in height; sandy-complexioned; shy in manner, seeming cold; awkward in attitude, and with little in his bearing that suggested command. Senator Maclay of Pennsylvania described him in 1790, when he had returned from France to become Secretary of State, and appeared before a Committee of the Senate to answer questions about foreign relations.

"Jefferson is a slender man," wrote the senator; "has rather the air of stiffness in his manner. His clothes seem too small for him. He sits in a lounging manner, on one hip commonly, and with one of his shoulders

13

elevated much above the other. His face has a sunny aspect. His whole
figure has a loose, shackling air. He had a rambling, vacant look, and
nothing of that firm collected deportment which I expected would
dignify the presence of a secretary or minister. I looked for gravity, but
a laxity of manner seemed shed about him. He spoke almost without
ceasing; but even his discourse partook of his personal demeanor. It was
loose and rambling; and yet he scattered information wherever he went,
and some even brilliant sentiments sparkled from him."

Maclay was one of the earliest members of the Republican party,
and his description was not unfriendly. Augustus Foster, Secretary
of the British Legation, described Jefferson as he appeared in 1804:—

"He was a tall man, with a very red freckled face, and gray neglected
hair; his manners good-natured, frank, and rather friendly, though he
had somewhat of a cynical expression of countenance. He wore a blue
coat, a thick gray-colored hairy waistcoat, with a red under-waist-
coat lapped over it, green velveteen breeches with pearl buttons, yarn
stockings, and slippers down at the heels,—his appearance being very
much like that of a tall, large-boned farmer."

In the middle of the seventeenth century the celebrated Cardinal
de Retz formed a judgment of the newly-elected Pope from his
remark, at a moment when minds were absorbed in his election,
that he had for two years used the same pen. "It is only a trifle,"
added De Retz, "but I have often observed that the smallest things
are sometimes better marks than the greatest." Perhaps dress could
never be considered a trifle. One of the greatest of modern writers
first made himself famous by declaring that society was founded
upon *cloth;* and Jefferson, at moments of some interest in his career
as President, seemed to regard his peculiar style of dress as a matter
of political importance, while the Federalist newspapers never
ceased ridiculing the corduroy small-clothes, red-plush waistcoat,
and sharp-toed boots with which he expressed his contempt for
fashion.

For eight years this tall, loosely built, somewhat stiff figure, in
red waistcoat and yarn stockings, slippers down at the heel, and
clothes that seemed too small for him, may be imagined as Senator
Maclay described him, sitting on one hip, with one shoulder high
above the other, talking almost without ceasing to his visitors at
the White House. His skin was thin, peeling from his face on
exposure to the sun, and giving it a tettered appearance. This
sandy face, with hazel eyes and sunny aspect; this loose, shackling

person; this rambling and often brilliant conversation, belonged to the controlling influences of American history, more necessary to the story than three-fourths of the official papers, which only hid the truth. Jefferson's personality during these eight years appeared to be the government, and impressed itself, like that of Bonaparte, although by a different process, on the mind of the nation. In the village simplicity of Washington he was more than a king, for he was alone in social as well as in political pre-eminence. Except the British Legation, no house in Washington was open to general society; the whole mass of politicians, even the Federalists, were dependent on Jefferson and "The Palace" for amusement; and if they refused to go there, they "lived like bears, brutalized and stupefied."

Jefferson showed his powers at their best in his own house, where among friends as genial and cheerful as himself his ideas could flow freely, and could be discussed with sympathy. Such were the men with whom he surrounded himself by choice, and none but such were invited to enter his Cabinet. First and oldest of his political associates was James Madison, about to become Secretary of State, whose character also described itself, and whose personality was as distinct as that of his chief. A small man, quiet, somewhat precise in manner, pleasant, fond of conversation, with a certain mixture of ease and dignity in his address, Madison had not so much as Jefferson of the commanding attitude which imposed respect on the world. "He has much more the appearance of what I have imagined a Roman cardinal to be," wrote Senator Mills of Massachusetts in 1815. An imposing presence had much to do with political influence, and Madison labored under serious disadvantage in the dryness of his personality. Political opponents of course made fun of him. "As to Jemmy Madison—oh, poor Jemmy!—he is but a withered little apple-john," wrote Washington Irving in 1812, instinctively applying the Knickerbocker view of history to national concerns.

"In his dress," said one who knew him, "he was not at all eccentric or given to dandyism, but always appeared neat and genteel, and in the costume of a well-bred and tasty old-school gentleman. I have heard in early life he sometimes wore light-colored clothes; but from the time I first knew him . . . never any other color than black, his coat being cut in what is termed dress-fashion; his breeches short, with buckles at the knees, black silk stockings, and shoes with strings, or long fair topboots when out in cold weather, or when he rode on horseback, of which he was fond. . . . He wore powder on his hair,

which was dressed full over the ears, tied behind, and brought to a
point above the forehead, to cover in some degree his baldness, as may
be noticed in all the likenesses taken of him."

Madison had a sense of humor, felt in his conversation, and detected in the demure cast of his flexile lips, but leaving no trace
in his published writings. Small in stature, in deportment modest
to the point of sensitive reserve, in address simple and pleasing, in
feature rather thoughtful and benevolent than strong, he was
such a man as Jefferson, who so much disliked contentious and
self-asserting manners, loved to keep by his side. Sir Augustus
Foster[1] liked Mr. Madison, although in 1812 Madison sent him out
of the country:—

> "I thought Mr. Jefferson more of a statesman and man of the world
> than Mr. Madison, who was rather too much the disputatious pleader;
> yet the latter was better informed and moreover a social, jovial, and
> good-humored companion, full of anecdote, sometimes rather of a
> loose description, but oftener of a political and historical interest.
> He was a little man with small features, rather wizened when I saw
> him, but occasionally lit up with a good-natured smile. He wore a
> black coat, stockings with shoes buckled, and had his hair powdered,
> with a tail."

The third aristocrat in this democratic triumvirate was Albert
Gallatin, marked by circumstances even more than by the President's choice for the post of Secretary of the Treasury. Like the
President and the Secretary of State, Gallatin was born and bred a
gentleman; in person and manners he was well fitted for the cabinet
table over which Jefferson presided. Gallatin possessed the personal
force which was somewhat lacking in his two friends. His appearance
impressed by-standers with a sense of strength. His complexion was
dark; his eyes were hazel and full of expression; his hair black, and
like Madison he was becoming bald. From long experience, at first
among the democrats of western Pennsylvania and afterward as a
leader in the House of Representatives, he had lost all shyness in
dealing with men. His long prominent nose and lofty forehead
showed character, and his eyes expressed humor. A slight foreign
accent betrayed his Genevan origin. Gallatin was also one of the
best talkers in America, and perhaps the best-informed man in
the country; for his laborious mind had studied America with

[1] Augustus John Foster: British Minister to the United States, 1810-1812.

infinite care, and he retained so much knowledge of European affairs as to fit him equally for the State Department or the Treasury. Three more agreeable men than Jefferson, Madison, and Gallatin were never collected round the dinner table of the White House; and their difference in age was enough to add zest to their friendship; for Jefferson was born in 1743, Madison in 1751, and Gallatin in 1761. While the President was nearly sixty years old, his Secretary of the Treasury had the energy and liberality of forty.

Jefferson was the first President inaugurated at Washington, and the ceremony, necessarily simple, was made still simpler for political reasons. The retiring President was not present at the installation of his successor. In Jefferson's eyes a revolution had taken place as vast as that of 1776; and if this was his belief, perhaps the late President was wise to retire from a stage where everything was arranged to point a censure upon his principles, and where he would have seemed, in his successor's opinion, as little in place as George III would have appeared at the installation of President Washington. The collapse of government which marked the last weeks of February, 1801 had been such as to leave of the old Cabinet only Samuel Dexter of Massachusetts, the Secretary of the Treasury; and Benjamin Stoddert of Maryland, the Secretary of the Navy, still in office. John Marshall, the late Secretary of State, had been appointed, six weeks before, Chief Justice of the Supreme Court.

In this first appearance of John Marshall as Chief Justice, to administer the oath of office, lay the dramatic climax of the inauguration. The retiring President, acting for what he supposed to be the best interests of the country, by one of his last acts of power, deliberately intended to perpetuate the principles of his administration, placed at the head of the judiciary, for life, a man as obnoxious to Jefferson as the bitterest New England Calvinist could have been; for he belonged to that class of conservative Virginians whose devotion to President Washington, and whose education in the common law, caused them to hold Jefferson and his theories in antipathy. The new President and his two Secretaries were political philanthropists, bent on restricting the powers of the national government in the interests of human liberty. The Chief Justice, a man who in grasp of mind and steadiness of purpose had no superior, perhaps no equal, was bent on enlarging the powers of government in the interests of justice and nationality. As they stood face to face on this threshold of their power, each could foresee that the contest between them would end only with life.

If Jefferson and his two friends were the most aristocratic of democrats, John Marshall was of all aristocrats the most democratic in manners and appearance.

"A tall, slender figure," wrote Joseph Story in 1808, "not graceful or imposing, but erect and steady. His hair is black, his eyes small and twinkling, his forehead rather low; but his features are in general harmonious. His manners are plain yet dignified, and an unaffected modesty diffuses itself through all his actions. His dress is very simple yet neat; his language chaste, but hardly elegant; it does not flow rapidly, but it seldom wants precision. In conversation he is quite familiar, but is occasionally embarrassed by a hesitancy and drawling. . . . I love his laugh—it is too hearty for an intriguer; and his good temper and unwearied patience are equally agreeable on the bench and in the study."

The unaffected simplicity of Marshall's life was delightful to all who knew him, for it sprang from the simplicity of his mind. Never self-conscious, his dignity was never affected by his situation. Bishop Meade,[2] who was proud of the Chief Justice as one of his flock, being in a street near Marshall's house one morning between daybreak and sunrise, met the Chief Justice on horseback, with a bag of clover seed lying before him, which he was carrying to his little farm at seedtime. Simple as American life was, his habits were remarkable for modest plainness; and only the character of his mind, which seemed to have no flaw, made his influence irresistible upon all who were brought within its reach.

Nevertheless this great man nourished one weakness. Pure in life; broad in mind, and the despair of bench and bar for the unswerving certainty of his legal method; almost idolized by those who stood nearest him, and loving warmly in return—this excellent and amiable man clung to one rooted prejudice: he detested Thomas Jefferson. He regarded with quiet, unspoken, but immovable antipathy the character and doings of the philosopher standing before him, about to take the oath to preserve, protect, and defend the Constitution. No argument or entreaty affected his conviction that Jefferson was not an honest man. "By weakening the office of President he will increase his personal power," were Marshall's words, written at this time; "the morals of the author of the letter to Mazzei cannot be pure." Jefferson in return regarded Marshall with a repugnance tinged by a shade of some

---

[2] William Meade: third Protestant Episcopal bishop of Virginia.

deeper feeling, almost akin to fear. "The judge's inveteracy is profound," he once wrote, "and his mind of that gloomy malignity which will never let him forego the opportunity of satiating it on a victim."

Another person, with individuality not less marked, took the oath of office the same day. When the Senate met at ten o'clock on the morning of March 4, 1801, Aaron Burr stood at the desk, and having duly sworn to support the Constitution, took his seat in the chair as Vice-President. This quiet, gentlemanly, and rather dignified figure, hardly taller than Madison, and dressed in much the same manner, impressed with favor all who first met him. An aristocrat imbued in the morality of Lord Chesterfield and Napoleon Bonaparte, Colonel Burr was the chosen head of Northern democracy, idol of the wards of New York City, and aspirant to the highest offices he could reach by means legal or beyond the law; for as he pleased himself with saying, after the manner of the First Consul of the French Republic, "Great souls care little for small morals." Among the other party leaders who have been mentioned —Jefferson, Madison, Gallatin, Marshall—not one was dishonest. The exaggerations or equivocations that Jefferson allowed himself, which led to the deep-rooted conviction of Marshall that he did not tell the truth and must therefore be dangerous, amounted to nothing when compared with the dishonesty of a corrupt man. Had the worst political charges against Jefferson been true, he would not have been necessarily corrupt. The self-deception inherent in every struggle for personal power was not the kind of immorality which characterized Colonel Burr. Jefferson, if his enemies were to be believed, might occasionally make misstatements of fact; yet he was true to the faith of his life, and would rather have abdicated his office and foregone his honors than have compassed even an imaginary wrong against the principles he professed. His life, both private and public, was pure. His associates, like Madison, Gallatin, and Monroe, were men upon whose reputations no breath of scandal rested. The standard of morality at Washington, both in private society and in politics, was respectable. For this reason Colonel Burr was a new power in the government; for being in public and in private life an adventurer of the same school as scores who were then seeking fortune in the antechambers of Bonaparte and Pitt, he became a loadstone for every other adventurer who frequented New York or whom the chances of politics might throw into office. The Vice-President wielded power, for he was the certain center of corruption.

Thus when the doors of the Senate chamber were thrown open, and the new President of the United States appeared on the threshold, when the Vice-President rose from his chair, and Jefferson sat down in it, with Aaron Burr on his right hand and John Marshall on his left, the assembled senators looked up at three men who profoundly disliked and distrusted each other. . . . (I, vii, 185-96)

Time, which has laid its chastening hand on many reputations, and has given to many once-famous formulas a meaning unsuspected by their authors, has not altogether spared Jefferson's first Inaugural Address, although it was for a long time almost as well-known as the Declaration of Independence; yet this Address was one of the few State Papers which should have lost little of its interest by age. As the starting point of a powerful political party, the first Inaugural was a standard by which future movements were measured, and it went out of fashion only when its principles were universally accepted or thrown aside. Even as a literary work, it possessed a certain charm of style peculiar to Jefferson, a flavor of Virginia thought and manners, a Jeffersonian ideality calculated to please the ear of later generations forced to task their utmost powers in order to carry the complex trains of their thought.

The chief object of the Address was to quiet the passions which had been raised by the violent agitation of the past eight years. Every interest of the new Administration required that the extreme Federalists should be disarmed. Their temper was such as to endanger both Administration and Union; and their power was still formidable, for they controlled New England and contested New York. To them, Jefferson turned:—

"Let us unite with one heart and one mind," . . . he entreated; "let us restore to social intercourse that harmony and affection without which liberty and even life itself are but dreary things. And let us reflect, that, having banished from our land that religious intolerance under which mankind so long bled and suffered, we have yet gained little if we countenance a political intolerance as despotic, as wicked, and capable of as bitter and bloody persecutions. During the throes and convulsions of the ancient world, during the agonizing spasms of infuriated man seeking through blood and slaughter his long-lost liberty, it was not wonderful that the agitation of the billows should reach even this distant and peaceful shore; that this should be more felt and feared by some than by others; that this should divide opinions as to measures of safety. But every difference of opinion is not a difference of principle. We are all Republicans, we are all Federalists."

The Federalist newspapers never ceased laughing at the "spasms" so suddenly converted into "billows," and at the orthodoxy of Jefferson's Federalism; but perhaps his chief fault was to belittle the revolution which had taken place. In no party sense was it true that all were Republicans or all Federalists. As will appear, Jefferson himself was far from meaning what he seemed to say. He wished to soothe the great body of his opponents, and if possible to win them over; but he had no idea of harmony or affection other than that which was to spring from his own further triumph; and in representing that he was in any sense a Federalist, he did himself a wrong.

> "I know, indeed," he continued, "that some honest men fear that a republican government cannot be strong; that this government is not strong enough. But would the honest patriot, in the full tide of successful experiment, abandon a government which has so far kept us free and firm, on the theoretic and visionary fear that this government, the world's best hope, may by possibility want energy to preserve itself? I trust not. I believe this, on the contrary, the strongest government on earth. I believe it is the only one where every man, at the call of the laws, would fly to the standard of the law, and would meet invasions of the public order as his own personal concern. Sometimes it is said that man cannot be trusted with the government of himself. Can he then be trusted with the government of others? Or have we found angels in the forms of kings to govern him? Let history answer this question!"

That the government, the world's best hope, had hitherto kept the country free and firm, in the full tide of successful experiment, was a startling compliment to the Federalist party, coming as it did from a man who had not been used to compliment his political opponents; but Federalists, on the other hand, might doubt whether this government would continue to answer the same purpose when administered for no other avowed object than to curtail its powers. Clearly, Jefferson credited government with strength which belonged to society; and if he meant to practice upon this idea, by taking the tone of "the strongest government on earth" in the face of Bonaparte and Pitt, whose governments were strong in a different sense, he might properly have developed this idea at more length, for it was likely to prove deeply interesting. Moreover, history, if asked, must at that day have answered that no form of government, whether theocratic, autocratic, aristocratic, democratic, or mixed, had ever in Western civilization lasted long, without change or need of change. History was not the witness to which Republicans could with entire confidence appeal, even against kings.

The Address next enumerated the advantages which America enjoyed, and those which remained to be acquired:—

> "With all these blessings, what more is necessary to make us a happy and prosperous people? Still one thing more, fellow citizens—a wise and frugal government, which shall restrain men from injuring one another, which shall leave them otherwise free to regulate their own pursuits of industry and improvement, and shall not take from the mouth of labor the bread it has earned. This is the sum of good government, and this is necessary to close the circle of our felicities."

A government restricted to keeping the peace, which should raise no taxes except for that purpose, seemed to be simply a judicature and a police. Jefferson gave no development to the idea further than to define its essential principles, and those which were to guide his Administration. Except the Kentucky and Virginia Resolutions of 1798, this short passage was the only official gloss ever given to the Constitution by the Republican party; and for this reason students of American history who would understand the course of American thought should constantly carry in mind not only the Constitutions of 1781 and of 1787, but also the Virginia and Kentucky Resolutions, and the following paragraph of Jefferson's first Inaugural Address:—

> "I will compress them," said the President, "within the narrowest compass they will bear, stating the general principle, but not all its limitations. Equal and exact justice to all men, of whatever state or persuasion, religious or political; peace, commerce, and honest friendship with all nations, entangling alliances with none; the support of the State governments in all their rights, as the most competent administrations for our domestic concerns and the surest bulwarks against antirepublican tendencies; the preservation of the general government in its whole Constitutional vigor, as the sheet anchor of our peace at home and safety abroad; a jealous care of the right of election by the People,—a mild and safe corrective of abuses which are lopped by the sword of revolution where peaceable remedies are

unprovided; absolute acquiescence in the decisions of the majority—
the vital principle of republics, from which there is no appeal but to
force, the vital principle and immediate parent of despotism; a well-
disciplined militia—our best reliance in peace and for the first moments of war, till regulars may relieve them; the supremacy of the civil
over the military authority; economy in the public expense, that labor
may be lightly burdened; the honest payment of our debts, and sacred
preservation of the public faith; encouragement of agriculture, and of
commerce as its handmaid; the diffusion of information, and arraignment of all abuses at the bar of public reason; freedom of religion,
freedom of the press, and freedom of person under the protection of
the *habeas corpus;* and trial by juries impartially selected—these principles form the bright constellation which has gone before us and
guided our steps through an age of revolution and reformation. The
wisdom of our sages and the blood of our heroes have been devoted
to their attainment; they should be the creed of our political faith,
the text of civic instruction, the touchstone by which to try the services
of those we trust; and should we wander from them in moments of
error or alarm, let us hasten to retrace our steps and to regain the
road which alone leads to peace, liberty, and safety."

From the metaphors in which these principles appeared as a constellation, a creed, a text, a touchstone, and a road, the world
learned that they had already guided the American people through
an age of revolution. In fact, they were mainly the principles of
President Washington, and had they been announced by a Federalist President, would have created little remonstrance or surprise. In
Jefferson's mouth they sounded less familiar, and certain phrases
seemed even out of place.

Among the cardinal points of republicanism thus proclaimed to
the world was one in particular, which as a maxim of government
seemed to contradict cherished convictions and the fixed practice
of the Republican party. "Absolute acquiescence" was required "in
the decisions of the majority—the vital principle of republics, from
which there is no appeal but to force, the vital principle and immediate parent of despotism." No principle was so thoroughly
entwined in the roots of Virginia republicanism as that which
affirmed the worthlessness of decisions made by a majority of the
United States, either as a nation or a confederacy, in matters which
concerned the exercise of doubtful powers. Not three years had
passed since Jefferson himself penned the draft of the Kentucky
Resolutions, in which he declared "that in cases of an abuse of the
delegated powers, the members of the general government being
chosen by the people, a change by the people would be the Con-

stitutional remedy; but where powers are assumed which have not
been delegated, a nullification of the act is the rightful remedy; that
every State has a natural right, in cases not within the compact, to
nullify of their own authority all assumptions of power by others
within their limits; that without this right they would be under
the dominion, absolute and unlimited, of whosoever might exercise
this right of judgment for them." He went so far as to advise that
every State should forbid, within its borders, the execution of any
act of the general government "not plainly and intentionally authorized by the Constitution"; and although the legislatures of
Kentucky and Virginia softened the language, they acted on the
principle so far as to declare certain laws of the United States
unconstitutional, with the additional understanding that whatever
was unconstitutional was void. So far from accepting with "absolute
acquiescence" the decisions of the majority, Jefferson and his followers held that freedom could be maintained only by preserving inviolate the right of every State to judge for itself what was, and
what was not, lawful for a majority to decide.

What, too, was meant by the words which pledged the new
Administration to preserve the general government "in its whole
Constitutional vigor?" The two parties were divided by a bottomless
gulf in their theories of Constitutional powers; but until the precedents established by the Federalists should be expressly reversed,
no one could deny that those precedents, to be treated as acts of
the majority with absolute acquiescence, were a measure of the
vigor which the President pledged himself to preserve. Jefferson
could not have intended such a conclusion; for how could he promise to "preserve" the powers assumed in the Alien and Sedition laws,
which then represented the whole vigor of the general government
in fact if not in theory, when he had himself often and bitterly
denounced those powers, when he had been a party to their nullification, and when he and his friends had actually prepared to resist
by arms their enforcement? Undoubtedly Jefferson meant no more
than to preserve the general government in such vigor as in his
opinion was Constitutional, without regard to Federalist precedents; but his words were equivocal, and unless they were to be
defined by legislation, they identified him with the contrary legislation of his predecessors. In history and law they did so. Neither
the Alien nor the Sedition Act, nor any other Federalist precedent,
was ever declared unconstitutional by any department of the general
government; and Jefferson's pledge to preserve that government in

its full Constitutional vigor was actually redeemed with no exception or limitation on the precedents established. His intention seemed to be different; but the sweeping language of his pledge was never afterward restricted or even more exactly defined while he remained in power.

Hence arose a sense of disappointment for future students of the Inaugural Address. A revolution had taken place; but the new President seemed anxious to prove that there had been no revolution at all. A new experiment in government was to be tried, and the philosopher at its head began by pledging himself to follow in the footsteps of his predecessors. Americans ended by taking him at his word, and by assuming that there was no break of continuity between his ideas and those of President Washington; yet even at the moment of these assurances he was writing privately in an opposite sense. In his eyes the past was wrong, both in method and intention; its work must be undone and its example forgotten. His conviction of a radical difference between himself and his predecessors was expressed in the strongest language. His predecessors, in his opinion, had involved the government in difficulties in order to destroy it, and to build up a monarchy on its ruins. "The tough sides of our Argosie," he wrote two days after his inauguration, "have been thoroughly tried. Her strength has stood the waves into which she was steered with a view to sink her. We shall put her on her Republican tack, and she will now show by the beauty of her motion the skill of her builders." "The Federalists," said he at one moment, "wished for everything which would approach our new government to a monarchy; the Republicans, to preserve it essentially republican. . . . The real difference consisted in their different degrees of inclination to monarchy or republicanism." "The revolution of 1800," he wrote many years afterward, "was as real a revolution in the principles of our government as that of 1776 was in its form."

Not, therefore, in the Inaugural Address, with its amiable professions of harmony, could President Jefferson's full view of his own reforms be discovered. Judged by his inaugural addresses and annual messages, Jefferson's Administration seemed a colorless continuation of Washington's; but when seen in the light of private correspondence, the difference was complete. So strong was the new President's persuasion of the monarchical bent of his predecessors, that his joy at obtaining the government was mingled with a shade of surprise that his enemies should have handed to him, without question, the power they had so long held. He shared his fears of monarchy with politicians like William B. Giles,[3] young John Randolph,[4] and many Southern voters; and although neither Madison nor Gallatin seemed to think monarchists formidable, they gladly encouraged the President to pursue a conservative and conciliatory path. Jefferson and his Southern friends took power as republicans opposed to monarchists, not as democrats opposed to oligarchy. Jefferson himself was not in a social sense a democrat, and was called so only as a term of opprobrium. His Northern followers were in the main democrats; but he and most of his Southern partisans claimed to be republicans, opposed by secret monarchists.

The conflict of ideas between Southern republicanism, Northern democracy, and Federal monarchism marked much of Jefferson's writing; but especially when he began his career as President his mind was filled with the conviction that he had wrung power from monarchy, and that in this sense he was the founder of a new republic. Henceforward, as he hoped, republicanism was forever safe; he had but to conciliate the misguided, and give an example to the world, for centralization was only a monarchical principle. Nearly twenty years passed before he woke to a doubt on this subject; but even then he did not admit a mistake. In the tendency to centralization he still saw no democratic instinct, but only the influence of monarchical Federalists "under the pseudo-republican mask."

The republic which Jefferson believed himself to be founding or securing in 1801 was an enlarged Virginia—a society to be kept pure and free by the absence of complicated interests, by the encouragement of agriculture and of commerce as its handmaid, but not of industry in a larger sense. "The agricultural capacities of our country," he wrote long afterward, "constitute its distinguishing feature; and the adapting our policy and pursuits to that is more likely to make us a numerous and happy people than the mimicry of an Amsterdam, a Hamburg, or a city of London." He did not love mechanics or manufactures, or the capital without which they could not exist. "Banking establishments are more dangerous than standing armies," he said; and added, "that the principle of spending money to be paid by posterity, under the name of funding, is but swindling futurity on a large scale." Such theories were republican in the Virginia sense, but not democratic; they had nothing in common with the democracy of Pennsylvania and New England,

[3] William Branch Giles: U. S. Senator from Virginia.
[4] John Randolph of Roanoke: Representative from Virginia.

except their love of freedom; and Virginia freedom was not the same conception as the democratic freedom of the North.

In 1801 this Virginia type was still the popular form of republicanism. Although the Northern democrat had already developed a tendency toward cities, manufactures, and "the mimicry of an Amsterdam, a Hamburg, or a city of London," while the republican of the South was distinguished by his dislike of every condition except that of agriculture, the two wings of the party had so much in common that they could afford to disregard for a time these divergencies of interest; and if the Virginians cared nothing for cities, banks, and manufactures, or if the Northern democrats troubled themselves little about the dangers of centralization, they could unite with one heart in overthrowing monarchy and in effecting a social revolution.

Henceforward, as Jefferson conceived, government might act directly for the encouragement of agriculture and of commerce as its handmaid, for the diffusion of information and the arraignment of abuses; but there its positive functions stopped. Beyond that point only negative action remained—respect for States' rights, preservation of constitutional powers, economy, and the maintenance of a pure and simple society such as already existed. With a political system which would not take from the mouth of labor the bread it had earned, and which should leave men free to follow whatever paths of industry or improvement they might find most profitable, "the circle of felicities" was closed.

The possibility of foreign war alone disturbed this dream. President Washington himself might have been glad to accept these ideas of domestic politics, had not France, England, and Spain shown an unequivocal wish to take advantage of American weakness in arms in order to withhold rights vital to national welfare. How did Jefferson propose to convert a government of judiciary and police into the strongest government on earth? His answer to this question, omitted from the Inaugural Address, was to be found in his private correspondence and in the speeches of Gallatin and Madison as leaders of the opposition. He meant to prevent war. He was convinced that governments, like human beings, were on the whole controlled by their interests, and that the interests of Europe required peace and free commerce with America. Believing a union of European powers to be impossible, he was willing to trust their jealousies of each other to secure their good treatment of the United States. Knowing that Congress could by a single act divert a stream

of wealth from one European country to another, foreign Governments would hardly challenge the use of such a weapon, or long
resist their own overpowering interests. The new President found
in the Constitutional power "to regulate commerce with foreign
nations" the machinery for doing away with navies, armies, and
wars.

During eight years of opposition the Republican party had matured its doctrines on this subject. In 1797, in the midst of difficulties with France, Jefferson wrote:—

> "If we weather the present storm, I hope we shall avail ourselves of
> the calm of peace to place our foreign connections under a new and
> different arrangement. We must make the interest of every nation
> stand surety for their justice, and their own loss to follow injury to us,
> as effect follows its cause. As to everything except commerce, we ought
> to divorce ourselves from them all."

A few months before the inauguration, he wrote in terms more
general:—

> "The true theory of our Constitution is surely the wisest and best,
> that the States are independent as to everything within themselves, and
> united as to everything respecting foreign nations. Let the general gov-
> ernment be reduced to foreign concerns only, and let our affairs be
> disentangled from those of all other nations, except as to commerce,
> which the merchants will manage the better the more they are left free
> to manage for themselves, and our general government may be reduced
> to a very simple organization and a very unexpensive one—a few plain
> duties to be performed by a few servants."

Immediately after the inauguration the new President explained
his future foreign policy to correspondents, who, as he knew, would
spread his views widely throughout both continents. In a famous
letter to Thomas Paine—a letter which was in some respects a true
inaugural address—Jefferson told the thought he had but hinted in
public: "Determined as we are to avoid, if possible, wasting the
energies of our people in war and destruction, we shall avoid impli-
cating ourselves with the Powers of Europe, even in support of
principles which we mean to pursue. They have so many other
interests different from ours that we must avoid being entangled in
them. We believe we can enforce those principles as to ourselves
by peaceable means, now that we are likely to have our public
councils detached from foreign views." A few days later, he wrote

to the well-known Pennsylvania peacemaker, Dr. Logan,[5] and explained the process of enforcing against foreign nations "principles as to ourselves by peaceable means." "Our commerce," said he, "is so valuable to them, that they will be glad to purchase it, when the only price we ask is to do us justice. I believe we have in our own hands the means of peaceable coercion; and that the moment they see our government so united as that we can make use of it, they will for their own interest be disposed to do us justice."

To Chancellor Livingston,[6] in September, 1801, the President wrote his views of the principles which he meant to pursue: "Yet in the present state of things," he added, "they are not worth a war; nor do I believe war the most certain means of enforcing them. Those peaceable coercions which are in the power of every nation, if undertaken in concert and in time of peace, are more likely to produce the desired effect."

That these views were new as a system in government could not be denied. In later life Jefferson frequently asserted, and took pains to impress upon his friends, the difference between his opinions and those of his Federalist opponents. The radical distinction lay in their opposite conceptions of the national government. The Federalists wished to extend its functions; Jefferson wished to exclude its influence from domestic affairs:—

"The people," he declared in 1821, "to whom all authority belongs, have divided the powers of government into two distinct departments, the leading characters of which are foreign and domestic; and they have appointed for each a distinct set of functionaries. These they have made co-ordinate, checking and balancing each other, like the three cardinal departments in the individual States,—each equally supreme as to the powers delegated to itself, and neither authorized ultimately to decide what belongs to itself or to its coparcener in government. As independent, in fact, as different nations, a spirit of forbearance and compromise, therefore, and not of encroachment and usurpation, is the healing balm of such a Constitution."

In the year 1824 Jefferson still maintained the same doctrine, and expressed it more concisely than ever:—

"The federal is in truth our foreign government, which department alone is taken from the sovereignty of the separate States. . . . I recol-

[5] George Logan: Philadelphia Quaker, whose unofficial diplomacy in France provoked the so-called "Logan Act" of 1799.
[6] Robert R. Livingston: former Chancellor of the State of New York, now Minister to France.

lect no case where a question simply between citizens of the same State has been transferred to the foreign department, except that of inhibiting tenders but of metallic money, and *ex post facto* legislation."

These expressions, taken together, partly explain why Jefferson thought his assumption of power to be "as real a revolution in the principles of our government as that of 1776 was in its form." His view of governmental functions was simple and clearly expressed. The national government, as he conceived it, was a foreign department as independent from the domestic department, which belonged to the States, as though they were governments of different nations. He intended that the general government should "be reduced to foreign concerns only"; and his theory of foreign concerns was equally simple and clear. He meant to enforce against foreign nations such principles as national objects required, not by war, but by "peaceable coercion" through commercial restrictions. "Our commerce is so valuable to them that they will be glad to purchase it, when the only price we ask is to do us justice."

The history of his Administration will show how these principles were applied, and what success attended the experiment. . . . (I, vii, 199-217)

After passing the month of April at Monticello, Jefferson was able to rest there during the months of August and September, leaving Washington July 30. During six months, from April to October, he wrote less than was his custom, and his letters gave no clear idea of what was passing in his mind. In regard to his principles of general policy he was singularly cautious.

"I am sensible," he wrote, March 31, "how far I should fall short of effecting all the reformation which reason could suggest and experience approve, were I free to do whatever I thought best; but when we reflect how difficult it is to move or inflect the great machine of society, how impossible to advance the notions of a whole people suddenly to ideal right, we see the wisdom of Solon's remark—that no more good must be attempted than the nation can bear, and that all will be chiefly to reform the waste of public money, and thus drive away the vultures who prey upon it, and improve some little on old routines."

"Levees are done away;" he wrote to Macon;[7] "the first communication to the next Congress will be, like all subsequent ones, by message, to which no answer will be expected; the diplomatic establishment in Europe will be reduced to three ministers; the army is

[7] Nathaniel Macon: U. S. Senator from North Carolina.

undergoing a chaste reformation; the navy will be reduced to the legal
establishment by the last of this month; agencies in every department
will be revised; we shall push you to the utmost in economizing."

His followers were not altogether pleased with his moderation of
tone. They had expected a change of system more revolutionary
than was implied by a pledge to do away with the President's occasional receptions and his annual speech to Congress, to cut off three
second-rate foreign missions, to chasten the army, and to execute a
Federalist law about the navy, or even to revise agencies. John
Randolph wrote, July 18, to his friend Joseph Nicholson, a member
from Maryland: "In this quarter we think that the great work is
only begun, and that without a substantial reform we shall have
little reason to congratulate ourselves on the mere change of men."

The task of devising what Randolph called a substantial reform
fell almost wholly upon Gallatin, who arrived in Washington, May
13, and set himself to the labor of reducing to a system the theories
with which he had indoctrinated his party. Through the summer
and autumn he toiled upon this problem, which the President left
in his hands. When October arrived, and the whole Cabinet assembled at length in Washington, under the President's eye, to prepare
business for the coming session, Gallatin produced his scheme. First,
he required common consent to the general principle that payment
of debt should take precedence of all other expenditure. This axiom
of Republicanism was a party dogma too well settled to be disputed. Debt, taxes, wars, armies, and navies were all pillars of corruption; but the habit of mortgaging the future to support present
waste was the most fatal to freedom and purity. Having fixed this
broad principle, which was, as Gallatin afterward declared, the
principal object of bringing him into office, a harder task remained;
for if theory required prompt payment of the debt, party interest
insisted with still greater energy on reduction of taxes; and the
revenue was not sufficient to satisfy both demands. The customs
duties were already low. The highest *ad valorem* rate was 20 per
cent; the average was but 13. Reduction to a lower average, except
in the specific duties on salt, coffee, and sugar, was asked by no one;
and Gallatin could not increase the rates even to relieve taxation
elsewhere. Whatever relief the party required must come from another source.

The Secretary began by fixing the limits of his main scheme.
Assuming four Administrations, or sixteen years, as a fair allowance
of time for extinguishing the debt, he calculated the annual sum

which would be required for the purpose, and found that $7,300,000 applied every year to the payment of interest and principal would discharge the whole within the year 1817. Setting aside $7,300,000 as an annual fund to be devoted by law to this primary object, he had to deal only with such revenue as should remain.

The net receipts from customs he calculated at $9,500,000 for the year, and from lands and postage at $450,000; or $9,950,000 in all. Besides this sum of less than ten million dollars, internal taxes, and especially the tax on whiskey stills, produced altogether about $650,000; thus raising the income to $10,600,000 or $3,300,000 in excess of the fund set apart for the debt.

If taxation were to be reduced at all, political reasons required that the unpopular excise should come first in order of reduction; but if the excise were abolished, the other internal taxes were not worth retaining. Led by the wish to relieve government and people from the whole system of internal taxation, Gallatin consented to sacrifice the revenue it produced. After thus parting with internal revenue to the amount of $650,000, and setting aside $7,300,000 for the debt, he could offer to the other heads of departments only $2,650,000 for the entire expenses of government. Gallatin expected the army to be supported on $930,000, while the navy was to be satisfied with $670,000—a charge of less than thirty-three cents a head on the white population.

Of all standards by which the nature of Jeffersonian principles could be gauged, none was so striking as this. The highest expenditure of the Federalists in 1799, when preparing for war with France and constructing a navy and an army, was six million dollars for these two branches. Peace with France being made in 1800, the expenses of army and navy would naturally fall to a normal average of about three million dollars. At a time when the population was small, scattered, and surrounded by enemies, civilized and savage; when the Mississippi River, the Gulf region, and the Atlantic coast as far as the St. Mary's were in the hands of Spain, which was still a great power; when English frigates were impressing American seamen by scores, and Napoleon Bonaparte was suspected of having bought Louisiana; when New York might be ransomed by any line-of-battle whip, and not a road existed by which a light fieldpiece could be hauled to the Lakes or to a frontier fort—at such a moment, the people could hardly refuse to pay sixty cents apiece for providing some protection against dangers which time was to prove as serious as any one then imagined them to be. Doubtless the republican theory required the States to protect their own coasts and to enforce order within their own jurisdiction; but the States were not competent to act in matters which concerned the nation, and the immense territory, the Lakes, and the Mississippi and Mobile rivers, belonged within the exclusive sphere of national government.

Gallatin cut down by one half the natural estimate. That he should have done this was not surprising, for he was put in office to reduce debt and taxation, not to manage the army and navy; but he could hardly have expected that all his colleagues should agree with him—yet his estimates were accepted by the Cabinet without serious objection, and adopted as a practical scale of governmental expenditure. Encouraged by the announcement of peace in Europe, the Secretaries of War and of the Navy consented to reduce their establishments to suit Gallatin's plans, until the entire expense of both branches for the future was to be brought within $1,900,000, while Gallatin on his side made some concessions which saved his estimates from error. The army bore the brunt of these economies, and was reduced to about three thousand men. The navy was not so great a sufferer, and its calculated reductions were less certain.

Gallatin's scheme partially warranted the claim which Jefferson in his old age loved to put forward, that he had made a revolution in the principles of the government. Yet apart from the question of its success, its vigor was less extreme than it appeared to be. Doubtless, such excessive economy seemed to relieve government of duties as well as responsibilities. Congress and the Executive appeared disposed to act as a machine for recording events, without guiding or controlling them. The army was not large enough to hold the Indians in awe; the navy was not strong enough to watch the coasts; and the civil service was nearly restricted to the collection and disbursement of revenue. The country was at the mercy of any power which might choose to rob it, and the President announced in advance that he relied for safety upon the soundness of his theory that every foreign country felt a vital interest in retaining American commerce and the use of American harbors. All this was true, and the experiment might be called revolutionary, considering the condition of the world; nevertheless there were shades of difference in the arguments on which it rested. Even Jefferson wavered in asserting the permanence of the system, while Gallatin avowedly looked forward to the time when diminished debt and increasing resources would allow wider scope of action. Viewed from this standpoint, the system was less rigid than it seemed, since a period of not more than five or six years was needed to obtain Gallatin's object. . . . (I, viii, 237-43)

Jefferson's first Annual Message deserved study less for what it contained than for what it omitted. If the scope of reform was to be measured by the President's official recommendations, party spirit was likely to find little excuse for violence. The Message began by announcing, in contrast with the expectations of Republicans, that while Europe had returned to peace the United States had begun a war [with the Barbary Powers], and that a hostile cruiser had been captured "after a heavy slaughter of her men." The Federalist wits made fun of the moral which the President added to soften the announcement of such an event: "The bravery exhibited by our citizens on that element will, I trust, be a testimony to the world that it is not the want of that virtue which makes us seek their peace, but a conscientious desire to direct the energies of our nation to the multiplication of the human race, and not to its destruction." The idea seemed a favorite one with the President, for he next congratulated Congress on the results of the new census, which, he said, "promises a duplication in little more than twenty-two years. We contemplate this rapid growth and the prospect it holds up to us, not with a view to the injuries it may enable us to do to others in some future day, but to the settlement of the extensive country still remaining vacant within our limits, to the multiplications of men susceptible of happiness, educated in the love of order, habituated to self-government, and valuing its blessings above all price."

Just and benevolent as this sentiment might be, Jefferson rarely invented a phrase open to more perversion than when he thus announced his party's "conscientious desire to direct the energies of our nation to the multiplication of the human race." Perhaps his want of a sense of humor prevented his noticing this slip of the tongue which the English language had no precise word to describe; perhaps he intended the phrase rather for a European than for an American audience; in any case, such an introduction to his proposed reforms, in the eyes of opponents, injured their dignity and force. As he approached the reforms themselves, the manner in which he preferred to present them was characteristic. As in his Inaugural Address, he showed skill in selecting popular ground.

"There is reasonable ground of confidence," he said, "that we may now safely dispense with all the internal taxes, . . . and that the remaining sources of revenue will be sufficient to provide for the support of government, to pay the interest on the public debts, and to discharge the principals within shorter periods than the laws or the general expectation had contemplated. War, indeed, and untoward events may change this prospect of things, and call for expenses which the imposts could not meet; but sound principles will not justify our taxing the industry of our fellow citizens to accumulate treasure for wars to happen we know not when, and which might not perhaps happen but from the temptations offered by that treasure."

Assuming that "the States themselves have principal care of our persons, our property, and our reputation, constituting the great field of human concerns," the Message maintained that the general government was unnecessarily complicated and expensive, and that its work could be better performed at a smaller cost.

"Considering the general tendency," it said, "to multiply offices and dependencies, and to increase expense to the ultimate term of burden which the citizen can bear, it behooves us to avail ourselves of every occasion which presents itself for taking off the surcharge, that it never may be seen here that, after leaving to labor the smallest portion of its earnings on which it can subsist, government shall itself consume the residue of what it was instituted to guard."

No one could deny that these sentiments were likely to please a majority of citizens, and that they announced principles of government which, if not new, were seldom or never put into practice on a great scale. . . . (I, ix, 248-51)

The concluding sentences of the Message expressed in a few words the two leading ideas which Jefferson wished most to impress on the people,—his abnegation of power and his wish for harmony:—

"Nothing shall be wanting on my part to inform, as far as in my power, the legislative judgment, nor to carry that judgment into faithful execution. The prudence and temperance of your discussions will promote, within your own walls, that conciliation which so much befriends rational conclusion, and by its example will encourage among our constituents that progress of opinion which is tending to unite them in object and in will. That all should be satisfied with any one order of things is not to be expected, but I indulge the pleasing persuasion that the great body of our citizens will cordially concur in honest and disinterested efforts, which have for their object to

preserve the General and State governments in their constitutional
form and equilibrium; to maintain peace abroad, and order and obedience to the laws at home; to establish principles and practices of administration favorable to the security of liberty and property, and to
reduce expenses to what is necessary for the useful purposes of government."

    . . . (I, ix, 262-63)

Honest as Jefferson undoubtedly was in his wish to diminish
executive influence, the task was beyond his powers. In ability and
in energy the Executive overshadowed Congress, where the Republican party, though strong in numbers and discipline, was so weak
in leadership, especially among the Northern democrats, that the
weakness almost amounted to helplessness. Of one hundred and five
members, thirty-six were Federalists; of the sixty-nine Republicans,
some thirty were Northern men, from whom the Administration
could expect little more than votes. Boston sent Dr. Eustis; from
New York came Dr. Samuel L. Mitchill—new members both; but
two physicians, or even two professors, were hardly competent to
take the place of leaders in the House, or to wield much influence
outside. The older Northern members were for the most part men
of that respectable mediocrity which followed where others led. The
typical Northern democrat of that day was a man disqualified for
great distinction by his want of the habits of leadership; he was
obliged, in spite of his principles, to accept the guidance of aristocrats like the Livingstons, Clintons,[8] and Burrs, or like Gallatin,
Jefferson, John Randolph, and the Smiths,[9] because he had never
been used to command, and could not write or speak with perfect
confidence in his spelling and grammar, or enter a room without
awkwardness. He found himself ill at ease at the President's dinner
table; he could talk only upon subjects connected with his district,
and he could not readily accustom himself to the scale of national
affairs. Such men were thrust aside with more or less civility by
their leaders, partly because they were timid, but chiefly because
they were unable to combine under the lead of one among themselves. The moment true democrats produced a leader of their own,
they gave him the power inherent in leadership, and by virtue of
this power he became an aristocrat, was admitted into the circle of
Randolphs and Clintons, and soon retired to an executive office, a

[8] Clintons: George Clinton, Governor of New York, and his nephew, De Witt
Clinton.
[9] Smiths: Robert Smith, Jefferson's Secretary of the Navy, and his brother,
Samuel Smith, U. S. Senator from Maryland in 1803.

custom house or a marshalship; while the never-failing succession of democratic Congressmen from the North continued to act as before at the command of some aristocratic Virginian or educated gentleman from the city of New York.

Owing to this peculiarity, the Northern democrats were and always remained, in their organization as a party, better disciplined than their opponents. Controlling the political power of New York, New Jersey, and Pennsylvania, they wielded it as they were bid. Their influence was not that of individuality, but of mass; they affected government strongly and permanently, but not consciously; their steady attraction served to deflect the Virginia compass several degrees from its supposed bearings; but this attraction was commonly mechanical. Jefferson might honestly strip himself of patronage, and abandon the receptions of other Presidents; he might ride every day on horseback to the Capitol in "overalls of corduroy, faded, by frequent immersions in soapsuds, from yellow to a dull white," and hitch his horse in the shed—he alone wielded power. The only counterpoise to his authority was to be found among his Southern equals and aristocratic Northern allies, whose vantage ground was in the United States Senate or at the head of State governments; but the machinery of faction was not yet well understood. In the three former Administrations, the House had been the most powerful part of the body politic, and the House was ill-suited for factious purposes. The Senate was not yet a favorite place for party leaders to fortify themselves in power; its debates were rarely reported, and a public man who quitted the House for the Senate was thrown into the background rather than into prominence. In 1803 De Witt Clinton resigned a seat there in order to become mayor of New York. In the same year Theodorus Bailey resigned the other seat, in order to become postmaster of New York, leaving the State unrepresented. While senators had not yet learned their power, representatives were restrained by party discipline, which could be defied only by men so strong as to resist unpopularity. As long as this situation lasted, Jefferson could not escape the exercise of executive influence even greater than that which he had blamed in his predecessors. . . . (I, x, 264-67)

The contradictions in Jefferson's character have always rendered it a fascinating study. Excepting his rival Alexander Hamilton, no American has been the object of estimates so widely differing and so difficult to reconcile. Almost every other American statesman might be described in a parenthesis. A few broad strokes of the brush would paint the portraits of all the early Presidents with this exception, and a few more strokes would answer for any member of their many cabinets; but Jefferson could be painted only touch by touch, with a fine pencil, and the perfection of the likeness depended upon the shifting and uncertain flicker of its semi-transparent shadows. Of all the politicians and writers of that day, none could draw portraits with a sharper outline than Hamilton, whose clear-cut characterizations never failed to fix themselves in the memory as distinctly as his own penetrating features were fixed in Ceracchi's marble or on Trumbull's canvas; and Hamilton's contrasted portraits of Jefferson and Burr, drawn in an often-quoted letter written to Bayard [10] in January, 1801, painted what he believed to be the shifting phase of Jefferson's nature.

"Nor is it true," he said, "that Jefferson is zealot enough to do anything in pursuance of his principles which will contravene his popularity or his interest. He is as likely as any man I know to temporize, to calculate what will be likely to promote his own reputation and advantage; and the probable result of such a temper is the preservation of systems, though originally opposed, which, being once established, could not be overturned without danger to the person who did it. To my mind, a true estimate of Mr. Jefferson's character warrants the expectation of a temporizing rather than a violent system."

Never was a prophecy more quickly realized. . . . (I, x, 277-78)

[10] James Ashton Bayard: Delaware Federalist and U. S. Senator in 1805.

2.

Retrocession of Louisiana

Most picturesque of all figures in modern history, Napoleon Bonaparte, like Milton's Satan on his throne of state, although surrounded by a group of figures little less striking than himself, sat unapproachable on his bad eminence; or, when he moved, the dusky air felt an unusual weight. His conduct was often mysterious, and sometimes so arbitrary as to seem insane; but late years have thrown on it a lurid illumination. Without the mass of correspondence and of fragmentary writings collected under the Second Empire in not less than thirty-two volumes of printed works, the greatness of Napoleon's energies or the quality of his mind would be impossible to comprehend. Ambition that ground its heel into every obstacle; restlessness that often defied common sense; selfishness that eat like a cancer into his reasoning faculties; energy such as had never before been combined with equal genius and resources; ignorance that would have amused a schoolboy; and a moral sense which regarded truth and falsehood as equally useful modes of expression—an unprovoked war or secret assassination as equally natural forms of activity—such a combination of qualities as Europe had forgotten since the Middle Ages and could realize only by reviving the Eccelinos and Alberics of the thirteenth century, had to be faced and overawed by the gentle optimism of President Jefferson and his Secretary of State.

As if one such character were not riddle enough for any single epoch, a figure even more sinister and almost as enigmatical stood at its side. On the famous 18th Brumaire, the 9th November, 1799, when Bonaparte turned pale before the Five Hundred, and retired in terror from the hall at St. Cloud, not so much his brother Lucien, or the facile Sieyès, or Barras, pushed him forward to destroy the republic, but rather Talleyrand,[11] the ex-Bishop of Autun, the For-

[11] Charles Maurice de Talleyrand-Périgord: he has been described by R. R. Palmer as "of an aristocratic lineage almost unbearably distinguished."

eign Secretary of the Directory. Talleyrand was most active in directing the *coup d'état*, and was chiefly responsible for the ruin of France. Had he profited by his exile in America, he would have turned to Moreau[12] rather than to Bonaparte; and some millions of men would have gone more quietly to their graves. Certainly he did not foresee the effects of his act; he had not meant to set a mere soldier on the throne of Saint Louis. He betrayed the republic only because he believed the republic to be an absurdity and a nuisance, not because he wanted a military despotism. He wished to stop the reign of violence and scandal, restore the glories of Louis XIV, and maintain France in her place at the head of civilization. To carry out these views was the work of a lifetime. Every successive government was created or accepted by him as an instrument for his purposes; and all were thrown aside or broke in his hands. Superior to Bonaparte in the breadth and steadiness of his purpose, Talleyrand was a theorist in his political principles; his statecraft was that of the old *régime,* and he never forgave himself for having once believed in a popular revolution.

This was the man with whom Madison must deal, in order to reach the ear of the First Consul. In diplomacy, a more perplexing task could scarcely be presented than to fathom the policy which might result from the contact of a mind like Talleyrand's with a mind like Bonaparte's. If Talleyrand was an enigma to be understood only by those who lived in his confidence, Bonaparte was a freak of nature such as the world had seen too rarely to comprehend. His character was misconceived even by Talleyrand at this early period; and where the keenest of observers failed to see through a mind he had helped to form, how were men like Jefferson and Madison, three thousand miles away, and receiving at best only such information as Chancellor Livingston could collect and send them every month or six weeks,—how were they, in their isolation and ignorance, to solve a riddle that depended on the influence which Talleyrand could maintain over Bonaparte, and the despotism which Bonaparte could establish over Talleyrand?

Difficult as this riddle was, it made but a part of the problem. France had no direct means of controlling American policy. Within the last four years she had tried to dictate, and received severe discipline. If France was a political factor of the first class in Jefferson's mind, it was not because of her armies or fleets, or her almost extin-

[12] Victor Marie Moreau: general, republican, conqueror of the Austrians at Hohenlinden (December 1800), thereafter in opposition to Bonaparte, and eventually banished.

guished republican character, or her supposed friendship for Jefferson's party in its struggle with Anglican federalism. The 18th Brumaire severed most of these sentimental ties. The power which France wielded over American destinies sprang not from any direct French interest or fear of French arms, but from the control which Napoleon exercised over the Spanish government at Madrid. France alone could not greatly disturb the repose of Jefferson; but France, acting through Spain on the hopes and fears of the Southern States, exercised prodigious influence on the Union.

Don Carlos IV reigned at Madrid—a Bourbon, but an ally of the French republic, and since the 18th Brumaire a devoted admirer of the young Corsican who had betrayed the republic. So far as Don Carlos was king of Spain only, his name meant little to Americans; but as an American ruler his empire dwarfed that of the United States. From the sources of the Missouri and Mississippi to the borders of Patagonia, two American continents acknowledged his rule. From the mouth of the St. Mary's, southward and westward, the shores of Florida, Louisiana, Texas, and Mexico were Spanish; Pensacola, Mobile, and New Orleans closed all the rivers by which the United States could reach the gulf. The valley of the Ohio itself, as far as Pittsburg, was at the mercy of the King of Spain; the flour and tobacco that floated down the Mississippi, or any of the rivers that fell into the Gulf, passed under the Spanish flag, and could reach a market only by permission of Don Carlos IV. Along an imaginary line from Fernandina to Natchez, some six hundred miles, and thence northward on the western bank of the Mississippi River to the Lake of the Woods, some fourteen hundred miles farther, Spanish authority barred the path of American ambition. Of all foreign powers Spain alone stood in such a position as to make violence seem sooner or later inevitable even to the pacific Jefferson; and every Southern or Western State looked to the military occupation of Mobile, Pensacola, and New Orleans as a future political necessity.

By a sort of tacit agreement, the ordinary rules of American politics were admitted not to apply to this case. To obtain Pensacola, Mobile, and New Orleans, the warmest States' rights champions in the South, even John Taylor of Caroline[13] and John Randolph of Roanoke, were ready to employ every instrument of centralization. On the Southern and Western States this eagerness to expel Spain from their neighborhood acted like a magnet, affecting all, without

[13] John Taylor of Caroline: Virginian political philosopher; U. S. Senator in 1803.

regard to theories or parties. The people of Kentucky, Tennessee, and Georgia could not easily admit restrictions of any sort; they were the freest of the free; they felt keenly their subjection to the arbitrary authority of a king,—and a king of Spain. They could not endure that their wheat, tobacco, and timber should have value only by sufferance of a Spanish official and a corporal's guard of Spanish soldiers at New Orleans and Mobile. Hatred of a Spaniard was to the Tennesseean as natural as hatred of an Indian, and contempt for the rights of the Spanish government was no more singular than for those of an Indian tribe. Against Indians and Spaniards the Western settler held loose notions of law; his settled purpose was to drive both races from the country, and to take their land.

Between the Americans and the Spaniards no permanent friendship could exist. Their systems were at war, even when the nations were at peace. Spain, France, and England combined in maintaining the old colonial system; and Spain, as the greatest owner of American territory, was more deeply interested than any other power in upholding the rule that colonies belonged exclusively to the mother country, and might trade only with her. Against this exclusive system, although it was one with which no foreign power had the legal right to meddle, Americans always rebelled. Their interests required them to maintain the principles of free-trade; and they persuaded themselves that they had a natural right to sell their produce and buy their home cargoes in the best market, without regard to protective principles. Americans were the professional smugglers of an age when smuggling was tolerated by custom. Occasionally the laws were suddenly enforced, and the American trader was ruined; but in war times the business was comparatively safe and the profits were large. Naturally Americans wanted the right to do always what they did by sufferance as neutrals; and they were bent not only upon gaining foothold on the Gulf of Mexico, but on forcing Spain and England to admit them freely to their colonial ports. To do these two things they needed to do more. That the vast and inert mass of Spanish possessions in America must ultimately be broken up, became the cardinal point of their foreign policy. If the Southern and Western people, who saw the Spanish flag flaunted every day in their faces, learned to hate the Spaniard as their natural enemy, the Government at Washington, which saw a wider field, never missed an opportunity to thrust its knife into the joints of its unwieldy prey. In the end, far more than half the territory of the United States was the spoil of Spanish empire, rarely acquired with perfect propriety. To sum up the story in a single word, Spain had immense influence over the United States; but it was the influence of the whale over its captors,—the charm of a huge, helpless, and profitable victim. . . . (I, xiii, 334-40)

However little admiration a bystander might feel for Napoleon's judgment or morals, no one could deny the quickness of his execution. Within six weeks after the battle of Marengo,[14] without waiting for peace with the United States, England, or Austria, convinced that he held these countries in the hollow of his hand, he ordered Talleyrand to send a special courier to the Citizen Alquier, French minister at Madrid, with powers for concluding a treaty by which Spain should retrocede Louisiana to France, in return for an equivalent aggrandizement of the Duchy of Parma. The courier was at once despatched, and returned with a promptitude and success which ought to have satisfied even the restlessness of Bonaparte. The Citizen Alquier no sooner received his orders than he went to Señor Urquijo, the Spanish Secretary for Foreign Relations, and passing abruptly over the well-worn arguments in favor of retrocession, he bluntly told Urquijo to oppose it if he dared.

" 'France expects from you,' I said to him, 'what she asked in vain from the Prince of Peace. I have dispersed the prejudice which had been raised against you in the mind of the French government. You are today distinguished by its esteem and its consideration. Do not destroy my work; do not deprive yourself of the only counterpoise which you can oppose to the force of your enemies. The Queen, as you know, holds by affection as much as by vanity to the aggrandizement of her house; she will never forgive you if you oppose an exchange which can alone realize the projects of her ambition—for I declare to you formally that your action will decide the fate of the Duke of Parma, and should you refuse to cede Louisiana you may count on getting nothing for that Prince. You must bear in mind, too, that your refusal will necessarily change my relations with you. Obliged to serve the interests of my country and to obey the orders of the First Consul, who attaches the highest value to this retrocession, I shall be forced to receive for the first time the offers of service that will inevitably be made to me; for you may be sure that your enemies will not hesitate to profit by that occasion to increase their strength— already a very real force—by the weight of the French influence; they will do what you will not do, and you will be abandoned at once by the Queen and by us.' "

Urquijo's reply measured the degradation of Spain:

[14] Marengo: here, June 14, 1800, Bonaparte routed the Austrians.

" 'Eh! who told you that I would not give you Louisiana? But we must first have an understanding, and you must help me to convince the King.' "

At this reply, which sounded like Beaumarchais' comedies, Alquier saw that his game was safe. "Make yourself easy on that score," he replied; "the Queen will take that on herself." So the conference ended.

Alquier was right. The Queen took the task on herself, and Urquijo soon found that both King and Queen were anxious to part with Louisiana for their daughter's sake. They received the offer with enthusiasm, and lavished praises upon Bonaparte. The only conditions suggested by Urquijo were that the new Italian principality should be clearly defined, and that Spain should be guaranteed against the objections that might be made by other governments.

Meanwhile Bonaparte reiterated his offer on a more definite scale. August 3, immediately after the interview with Urquijo, Alquier put the first demand on record in a note important chiefly because it laid incidental stress on Talleyrand's policy of restraining the United States:—

"The progress of the power and population of America, and her relations of interest always maintained with England, may and must some day bring these two powers to concert together the conquest of the Spanish colonies. If national interest is the surest foundation for political calculations, this conjecture must appear incontestable. The Court of Spain will do, then, at once a wise and great act if it calls the French to the defence of its colonies by ceding Louisiana to them and by replacing in their hands this outpost of its richest possessions in the New World."

Before this note was written, the First Consul had already decided to supersede Alquier by a special agent who should take entire charge of this negotiation. July 28 he notified Talleyrand that General Berthier, Bonaparte's right hand in matters of secrecy and importance, was to go upon the mission. Talleyrand drafted the necessary instructions, which were framed to meet the fears of Spain lest the new arrangement should cause complications with other powers; and toward the end of August Berthier started for Madrid, carrying a personal letter of introduction from the First Consul to King Charles and the *projet* of a treaty of retrocession drawn by Talleyrand. This *projet* differed in one point from the scheme hitherto put forward, and, if possible, was still more alarming to the United States.

"The French Republic," it ran, "pledges itself to procure for the Duke of Parma in Italy an aggrandizement of territory to contain at least one million inhabitants; the Republic charges itself with procuring the consent of Austria and the other States interested, so that the Duke may be put in possession of his new territory at the coming peace between France and Austria. Spain on her side pledges herself to retrocede to the French Republic the colony of Louisiana, with the same extent it actually has in the hands of Spain, and such as it should be according to the treaties subsequently passed between Spain and other States. Spain shall further join to this cession that of the two Floridas, eastern and western, with their actual limits."

Besides Louisiana and the two Floridas, Spain was to give France six ships of war, and was to deliver the provinces to France whenever the promised territory for the Duke of Parma should be delivered by France to Spain. The two powers were further to make common cause against any person or persons who should attack or threaten them in consequence of executing their engagement.

In the history of the United States hardly any document, domestic or foreign, to be found in their archives has greater interest than this *projet;* for from it the United States must trace whatever legal title they obtained to the vast region west of the Mississippi. The treaties which followed were made merely in pursuance of this engagement, with such variations as seemed good for the purpose of carrying out the central idea of restoring Louisiana to France.

That the recovery of colonial power was the first of all Bonaparte's objects was proved not only by its being the motive of his earliest and most secret diplomatic step, but by the additional evidence that every other decisive event in the next three years of his career was subordinated to it. Berthier hastened to Madrid, and consumed the month of September, 1800, in negotiations. Eager as both parties were to conclude their bargain, difficulties soon appeared. So far as these concerned America, they rose in part from the indiscretion of the French Foreign Office, which announced the object of Berthier's mission in a Paris newspaper, and thus brought on Urquijo a demand from the American minister at Madrid for a categorical denial. Urquijo and Alquier could silence the attack only by denials not well calculated to carry conviction. This was not all. Alquier had been told to ask for Louisiana; Berthier was instructed to demand the Floridas and six ships of war in addition.

The demand for the Floridas should have been made at first, if Bonaparte expected it to be successful. King Charles was willing to give back to France a territory which was French in character, and had come as the gift of France to his father; but he was unwilling to alienate Florida, which was a part of the national domain. Urquijo told Berthier that "for the moment the King had pronounced himself so strongly against the cession of any portion whatever of Florida as to make it both useless and impolitic to talk with him about it"; but he added that, "after the general peace, the King might decide to cede a part of the Floridas between the Mississippi and the Mobile, on the special demand which the First Consul might make for it." Berthier was embarrassed, and yielded.

Thus at last the bargain was put in shape. . . . (I, xiv, 363-69)

On the last day of September, 1800, Joseph Bonaparte[15] signed the so-called Treaty of Morfontaine, which restored relations between France and the United States. The next day, October 1, Berthier signed at San Ildefonso the treaty of retrocession, which was equivalent to a rupture of the relations established four-and-twenty hours earlier. Talleyrand was aware that one of these treaties undid the work of the other. The secrecy in which he enveloped the treaty of retrocession, and the pertinacity with which he denied its existence showed his belief that Bonaparte had won a double diplomatic triumph over the United States. . . . (I, xiv, 370)

The story of Toussaint Louverture[16] has been told almost as often as that of Napoleon, but not in connection with the history of the United States, although Toussaint exercised on their history an influence as decisive as that of any European ruler. His fate placed him at a point where Bonaparte needed absolute control. St. Domingo was the only center from which the measures needed for rebuilding the French colonial system could radiate. Before Bonaparte could reach Louisiana he was obliged to crush the power of Toussaint. . . . (I, xv, 378)

Gentle and well-meaning in his ordinary relations, vehement in his passions, and splendid in his ambition, Toussaint was a wise,

---

[15] Joseph Bonaparte: Napoleon Bonaparte's elder brother, successively King of Naples (1806) and King of Spain (1807).

[16] Toussaint Louverture or L'Ouverture: Santo Domingan slave, whom the French made general-in-chief of the whole island in 1797. In 1801, he threw off all allegiance to France.

though a severe, ruler so long as he was undisturbed; but where his own safety or power was in question he could be as ferocious as Dessalines[17] and as treacherous as Bonaparte. In more respects than one his character had a curious resemblance to that of Napoleon— the same abnormal energy of body and mind; the same morbid lust for power, and indifference to means; the same craft and vehemence of temper; the same fatalism, love of display, reckless personal courage, and, what was much more remarkable, the same occasional acts of moral cowardice. One might suppose that Toussaint had inherited from his Dahomey grandfather the qualities of primitive society; but if this was the case, the conditions of life in Corsica must have borne some strong resemblance to barbarism, because the rule of inheritance which applied to Toussaint should hold good for Bonaparte. The problem was the more interesting because the parallelism roused Napoleon's anger, and precipitated a conflict which had vast influence on human affairs. Both Bonaparte and Louverture were the products of a revolution which gave its highest rewards to qualities of energy and audacity. So nearly identical were the steps in their career, that after the 18th Brumaire Toussaint seemed naturally to ape every action which Bonaparte wished to make heroic in the world's eyes. There was reason to fear that Toussaint would end in making Bonaparte ridiculous; for his conduct was, as it seemed to the First Consul, a sort of Negro travesty on the consular *régime*. . . . (I, xv, 382-83)

Rarely has diplomacy been used with more skill and energy than by Bonaparte, who knew where force and craft should converge. That in this skill mendacity played a chief part need hardly be repeated. Toussaint was flattered, cajoled, and held in a mist of ignorance, while one by one the necessary preparations were made to prevent his escape; and then, with scarcely a word of warning, at the First Consul's order the mist rolled away, and the unhappy Negro found himself face to face with destruction. The same ships that brought news of the preliminary treaty signed at London brought also the rumor of a great expedition fitting at Brest and the gossip of creole society in Paris, which made no longer a secret that Bonaparte meant to crush Toussaint and restore slavery at St. Domingo. Nowhere in the world had Toussaint a friend or a hope except in himself. Two continents looked on with folded arms, more and more interested in the result, as Bonaparte's ripening

---

[17] Jean Jacques Dessalines: followed Toussaint as ruler of Santo Domingo; assassinated in 1806.

schemes began to show their character. As yet President Jefferson
had no inkling of their meaning. The British government was somewhat better informed, and perhaps Godoy[18] knew more than all the
rest; but none of them grasped the whole truth, or felt their own
dependence on Toussaint's courage. If he and his blacks should
succumb easily to their fate, the wave of French empire would roll
on to Louisiana and sweep far up the Mississippi; if St. Domingo
should resist, and succeed in resistance, the recoil would spend its
force on Europe, while America would be left to pursue her democratic destiny in peace.

Bonaparte hurried his preparations. The month of October, 1801,
saw vast activity in French and Spanish ports, for a Spanish squadron accompanied the French fleet. Not a chance was to be left for
Toussaint's resistance or escape. . . . (I, xv, 390-91)

Livingston landed at Lorient November 12 . . . and . . . was
presented to the First Consul in the diplomatic audience of December 6. Caring nothing for Toussaint and much for France, Livingston did not come prepared to find that his own interests were the
same with those of Toussaint, but already by December 30 he wrote
to Rufus King: "I know that the armament, destined in the first
instance for Hispaniola, is to proceed to Louisiana provided Toussaint makes no opposition." . . . (I, xv, 392)

. . . The immense fleet, with an army of ten thousand men and
all their equipments, arrived in sight of St. Domingo at the close of
January, 1802. Toussaint was believed to have watched them from a
lookout in the mountains while they lay for a day making their
preparations for combined action. Then Leclerc[19] sailed for Cap
Français, where Christophe commanded. After a vain attempt to
obtain possession of the town as a friend, he was obliged to attack.
February 5, Christophe set the place in flames, and the war of races
broke out.

The story of this war, interesting though it was, cannot be told
here. Toussaint's resistance broke the force of Bonaparte's attack.
Although it lasted less than three months, it swept away one French
army, and ruined the industry of the colony to an extent that required years of repair. Had Toussaint not been betrayed by his own
generals, and had he been less attached than he was to civilization

[18] Manuel de Godoy, Duke of Alcudia and Prince of the Peace: formerly the
Queen's lover, he was now first Minister to King Carlos IV of Spain.

[19] Charles V. Leclerc: General, husband of Bonaparte's sister Pauline.

RETROCESSION OF LOUISIANA

and despotic theories of military rule, he would have achieved a personal triumph greater than was won by any other man of his time. . . . (I, xv, 393-94)

Jealous of Toussaint's domination, and perhaps afraid of being sent to execution like Moyse—the best general officer in their service—for want of loyalty to his chief, Christophe,[20] after one campaign, April 26, 1802, surrendered his posts and forces to Leclerc without the knowledge and against the orders of Toussaint. Then Louverture himself committed the fatal mistake of his life, which he of all men seemed least likely to commit—he trusted the word of Bonaparte. May 1, 1802, he put himself in Leclerc's hands in reliance on Leclerc's honor. . . . (I, xv, 395)

The First Consul's orders to Leclerc were positive, precise, and repeated. "Follow exactly your instructions," said he, "and the moment you have rid yourself of Toussaint, Christophe, Dessalines, and the principal brigands, and the masses of the blacks shall be disarmed, send over to the continent all the blacks and mulattoes who have played a *role* in the civil troubles. . . . Rid us of these gilded Africans, and we shall have nothing more to wish." With the connivance and at the recommendation of Christophe, by a stratagem such as Bonaparte used afterward in the case of the Duc d'Enghien[21] and of Don Carlos IV, Toussaint was suddenly arrested, June 19, 1802, and hurried on shipboard. Some weeks later he was landed at Brest; then he disappeared. Except a few men who were in the secret, no one ever saw him. Plunged into a damp dungeon in the fortress of Joux, high in the Jura Mountains on the Swiss frontier, the cold and solitude of a single winter closed this tropical existence. April 7, 1803, he died forgotten, and his work died with him. Not by Toussaint, and still less by Christophe or Dessalines, was the liberty of the blacks finally established in Haiti, and the entrance of the Mississippi barred to Bonaparte. . . . (I, xv, 396-97)

Although the retrocession of Louisiana to France had been settled in principle by Berthier's treaty of Oct. 1, 1800, six months

[20] Henri Christophe: Negro general, later President (1807) and King (1812) of Haiti.

[21] Louis Antoine Henri de Bourbon Condé, Duc D'Enghien: In March 1804, on Bonaparte's orders, he was kidnapped from his Baden residence, and tried and executed in France on an implausible charge of conspiracy. Since he was a pretender to the throne, his death permitted Bonaparte to establish himself as a revolutionary, or regicide, Emperor.

before Jefferson came into office, the secret was so well kept that
Jefferson hardly suspected it. He began his administration by antici-
pating a long period of intimate relations with Spain and France.
In sending instructions to Claiborne as governor of the Mississippi
Territory,—a post of importance, because of its relations with the
Spanish authority at New Orleans,—President Jefferson wrote pri-
vately,—

"With respect to Spain, our disposition is sincerely amicable, and
even affectionate. We consider her possession of the adjacent country
as most favorable to our interests, and should see with an extreme pain
any other nation substituted for them."

Disposed to be affectionate toward Spain, he assumed that he
should stand in cordial relations with Spain's ally, the First Consul.
Convinced that the quarrels of America with France had been arti-
ficially created by the monarchical Federalists, he believed that a
policy of open confidence would prevent such dangers in the future.
The First Consul would naturally cultivate his friendship, for every
Federalist newspaper had for years proclaimed Jefferson as the
head of French influence in America, and every Republican newspaper had branded his predecessors as tools of Great Britain. In
spite of the 18th Brumaire, Jefferson had not entirely lost faith in
Bonaparte, and knew almost nothing of his character or schemes.
At the moment when national interest depended on prompt and
exact information, the President withdrew half his ministers from
Europe, and paid little attention to the agents he retained. He took
diplomatic matters into his own hands, and meant to conduct them
at Washington with diplomatists under his personal influence,—a
practice well suited to a power superior in will and force to that
with which it dealt, but one which might work badly in dealing
with Bonaparte. . . . (I, xvi, 403-404)

By the spring of 1802 Jefferson became alive to the danger. He
then saw what was meant by the French expedition against Toussaint. . . . (I, xvi, 406)

3.

"Peace Is Our Passion"

Chancellor Livingston reached France about November 10, 1801, just in time to see Leclerc's expedition sail. He was met by private assurances that Louisiana and the Floridas had been bought by France, and he went to Talleyrand with inquiries. The imperturbable Talleyrand looked him in the face and denied the fact. "It had been a subject of conversation," he said, "but nothing concluded." At that moment Rufus King[22] was sending from London the text of Lucien Bonaparte's[23] treaty, dated eight months before, which fixed the details of the retrocession. President Jefferson received at the same instant Talleyrand's explicit denial and the explicit proof that Talleyrand was trying to deceive him. Jefferson soon satisfied himself that Talleyrand's conduct rested on a system; and he became angrier with every act of the French foreign minister. Livingston, naturally somewhat suspicious and fretful, soon became restive under the treatment he received; for his notes and remonstrances were left equally without answer or attention, whether they related to Louisiana or to the debts due by the Government of France to American citizens. As Livingston grew hot, . . . Madison became irritable, and by the month of May had reached the point of saying that if such conduct should continue, "the worst events are to be apprehended."

The President himself then intervened. A French gentleman, Dupont de Nemours,[24] happened to be in the United States on the point of returning to France. Dupont's name was then as well and honorably known in France as that of his descendents was to become in the annals of the United States. To him Jefferson turned as a medium of unofficial communication with the First Consul. He enclosed to Dupont a letter addressed to Livingston on the Louisi-

[22] Rufus King: New York Federalist, Minister to Great Britain, 1796-1803.
[23] Lucien Bonaparte: a younger brother, Ambassador to Spain in 1800.
[24] Victor Marie Dupont de Nemours: later associated with his brother, Éleuthère Irénée, in the latter's powder works in Delaware.

ana affair, which he requested Dupont to read, and, after reading, to seal.

"I wish you to be possessed of the subject," he wrote, "because you may be able to impress on the Government of France the inevitable consequences of their taking possession of Louisiana; and though, as I here mention, the cession of New Orleans and the Floridas to us would be a palliation, yet I believe it would be no more, and that this measure will cost France, and perhaps not very long hence, a war which will annihilate her on the ocean, and place that element under the despotism of two nations,—which I am not reconciled to the more because my own would be one of them."

This idea was still more strongly expressed in the enclosure to Livingston, which Dupont was to read, in order that he might communicate its sense to Bonaparte:—

"The day that France takes possession of New Orleans fixes the sentence which is to restrain her forever within her low-water mark. It seals the union of two nations, who in conjunction can maintain exclusive possession of the ocean. From that moment we must marry ourselves to the British fleet and nation. . . . Will not the amalgamation of a young and thriving nation continue to that enemy the health and force which are at present so evidently on the decline? And will a few years' possession of New Orleans add equally to the strength of France?"

Dupont was to impress on the First Consul the idea that if he should occupy Louisiana, the United States would wait "a few years," until the next war between France and England, but would then make common cause with England. Even a present cession of New Orleans and the Floridas to the United States, though it would remove the necessity of an immediate advance to England, would not prevent the risk of a quarrel with France, so long as France should hold the west bank of the Mississippi. To obviate such a quarrel was the object of Dupont's unofficial mission. "If you can be the means of informing the wisdom of Bonaparte of all its consequences, you have deserved well of both countries." . . . (I, xvi, 409-11)

The seizure of Toussaint and his disappearance from the island, which occurred as Jefferson wrote this letter, overthrew its hopeful theories; but before long, reports began to arrive in the United States that Leclerc had met with a new disaster, so terrible as to surpass the horrors even of St. Domingo history. The first French army, of seventeen thousand men, had been consumed in the task of subjecting the Negroes. A second army was next swept away by yellow fever. In the middle of September, 1802, Leclerc wrote to the First Consul that of 28,300 men sent to St. Domingo, 4,000 remained fit for service. "Add to our losses that of 5,000 sailors, and the occupation of St. Domingo has cost us till now 24,000 men, and we are not yet definitely masters of it." He was depending on Toussaint's generals and army for his support against an insurrection of the laborers, who were maddened by the rumor that slavery had been restored at Guadeloupe, and was soon to be reestablished at St. Domingo. Nothing could be more discouraging than Leclerc's letters:—

"I have no false measure to reproach myself with, Citizen Consul; and if my position, from being a very good one, has become very bad, it is necessary to blame here only the malady which has destroyed my army, the premature re-establishment of slavery at Guadeloupe, and the newspapers and letters from France, which speak only of slavery. Here is my opinion on this country. We must destroy all the Negroes in the mountains, men and women, keeping only infants less than twelve years old; we must also destroy half those of the plain, and leave in the colony not a single man of color who has worn an epaulette. Without this the colony will never be quiet; and at the beginning of every year, especially after murderous seasons like this, you will have a civil war, which will shake your hold on the country. In order to be master of St. Domingo, you must send me twelve thousand men without losing a single day."

Besides these 12,000 men and $1,200,000 in specie, Leclerc required 5,000 more men in the following summer. "If you cannot send the troops I demand, and for the season I point out, St. Domingo will be forever lost to France." . . . (I, xvi, 414-16)

News of Leclerc's death, November 1, 1802, and of the hopelessness of Bonaparte's schemes against St. Domingo, reached the Government at Washington nearly at the same time with other news which overshadowed this. The people of the United States expected day by day to hear of some sudden attack, from which as yet only the dexterity of Godoy and the disasters of Leclerc had saved them. Although they could see only indistinctly the meaning of what had taken place, they knew where to look for the coming stroke, and in such a state of mind might easily exaggerate its importance. A few days before Congress met, the Western post brought a despatch from Governor Claiborne[25] at Natchez announcing that the Spanish Intendant, Don Juan Ventura Morales, had forbidden the Americans to deposit their merchandise at New Orleans, as they had a right to do under the treaty of 1795. . . . (I, xvi, 418)

According to the explanation given by Morales to Laussat, the new French prefect whom Bonaparte sent to receive possession of Louisiana, the Spaniard acted on his own responsibility, in what he believed to be the interests of the colony, and within the stipulations of the treaty. Thinking that the retrocession offered a chance, which might never recur, for reopening a question which had been wrongly decided, Morales, defying the opposition and even the threats of Governor Salcedo, proclaimed the right of deposit to be at an end. He reasoned that Spain as a result of peace with England had shut her colonial ports to strangers, and this measure, so far as it included Louisiana, was illusory so long as the right of deposit should exist. The right had been granted for three years from 1795; and if the practice had been permitted to continue after these three years expired, it might have been owing, not to the treaty, but to the general privileges granted to neutrals during the war; and as for the Americans, it was their own fault not to have looked more carefully to their rights at the close of the three years, when they should have secured the continuation or the promised substitute. As Spain was about to lose Louisiana in any case, Morales remarked that she need not trouble herself about the quarrel he was making with the United States; while the French republic took Louisiana as it actually stood under the treaties, and ought therefore to be glad of whatever improved the actual situation, or opened the path to negotiations more advantageous. This view of the matter, as Morales presented it, was the more interesting because it was in the spirit of Talleyrand's plans, and reversed Godoy's policy.

The rumor that Spain had closed the Mississippi roused varied sensations as it spread eastward. Tennessee and Kentucky became eager for war. They knew that Morales's act was a foretaste of what they were to expect from France; and they might well ask themselves how many lives it would cost to dislodge a French army once fortified on the lower Mississippi. The whole power of the United

[25] William Charles Coles Claiborne: of Tennessee, appointed Governor of Mississippi Territory in 1801

States could not at that day, even if backed by the navy of England, have driven ten thousand French troops out of Louisiana. On the contrary, a vigorous French officer, with a small trained force and his Indian allies, could make Claiborne uneasy for the safety of his villages at Natchez and Vicksburg. No one could foresee what might be the effect of one or two disastrous campaigns on the devotion of the Western people to the Government at Washington. The existence of the Union and the sacrifice of many thousand lives seemed, in the opinion of competent judges, likely to be risked by allowing Bonaparte to make his position at New Orleans impregnable.

The New England Federalists were satisfied that President Jefferson must either adopt their own policy and make war on France, or risk a dissolution of the Union. They had hardly dared hope that democracy would so soon meet what might prove to be its crisis. They too cried for war, and cared little whether their outcry produced or prevented hostilities, for the horns of Jefferson's dilemma were equally fatal to him. All eyes were bent on the President, and watched eagerly for some sign of his intentions. . . . (I, xvi, 420-22)

The essence and genius of Jefferson's statesmanship lay in peace. Through difficulties, trials, and temptations of every kind he held fast to this idea, which was the clew to whatever seemed inconsistent, feeble, or deceptive in his administration. Yielding often, with the suppleness of his nature, to the violence of party, he allowed himself to use language which at first sight seemed inconsistent, and even untruthful; but such concessions were momentary: the unswerving intent could always be detected under every superficial disguise; the consistency of the career became more remarkable on account of the seeming inconsistencies of the moment. He was pliant and yielding in manner, but steady as the magnet itself in aim. His manoeuvres between the angry West and the arbitrary First Consul of France offered an example of his political method. He meant that there should be no war. While waiting to hear the result of Monroe's[26] mission he wrote to an English correspondent a letter which expressed his true feelings with apparent candor:—

"We see . . . with great concern the position in which Great Britain is placed, and should be sincerely afflicted were any disaster to deprive

[26] James Monroe, just retired as Governor of Virginia, was appointed, January 1803, Minister Plenipotentiary to assist Livingston in Paris and Charles Pinckney in Madrid. The main purpose of this appointment was to quiet the war fever in the West.

mankind of the benefit of such a bulwark against the torrent which
has for some time been bearing down all before it. But her power and
prowess by sea seem to render everything safe in the end. Peace is our
passion, and wrongs might drive us from it. We prefer trying *every*
other just principle, right and safety, before we would recur to war."

. . . (I, xvii, 445-46)

4.

Louisiana Purchase

Madison wrote the instructions.[27] If the French government, he said, should meditate hostilities against the United States, or force a war by closing the Mississippi, the two envoys were to invite England to an alliance, and were to negotiate a treaty stipulating that neither party should make peace or truce without consent of the other. Should France deny the right of deposit without disputing the navigation, the envoys were to make no positive engagement, but should let Congress decide between immediate war or further procrastination.

At no time in Talleyrand's negotiations had the idea of war against the United States been suggested. Of his intentions in this respect alone he had given positive assurances. Above all things both he and the First Consul feared a war with the United States. They had nothing to gain by it. Madison's instructions therefore rested on an idea which had no foundation, and which in face of the latest news from Europe was not worth considering; yet even if intended only for use at home, the instructions were startling enough to warrant Virginians in doubting their authenticity. The late Administration, British in feeling as it was supposed to be, had never thought an alliance with England necessary even during actual hostilities with France, and had not hesitated to risk the chances of independent action. Had either of Jefferson's predecessors instructed American ministers abroad, in case of war with France, to bind the United States to make no peace without England's consent, the consequence would have been an impeachment of the President, or direct steps by Virginia, Kentucky, and North Carolina, as in 1798, tending to a dissolution of the Union. Such an alliance, offensive and defensive, with England contradicted every principle established by President Washington in power or professed by Jefferson

---

[27] I.e., new instructions to Monroe and Livingston, of April 18 and 20, 1803.

in opposition. If it was not finesse, it was an act such as the Republicans of 1798 would have charged as a crime.

While Madison was writing these instructions, he was interrupted by the Marquis of Casa Yrujo,[28] who came in triumph to say that his Government had sent out a brigantine especially to tell the President that the right of deposit would be restored and continued till another agreement or equivalent place could be fixed upon. Yrujo was instructed to thank the President for his friendly, prudent, and moderate conduct during the excitement. He sent to New Orleans the positive order of King Charles IV to the Intendant Morales, that the right of deposit should be immediately restored; the western people were told that their produce might go down the river as before, and thus the last vestige of anxiety was removed. In face of this action by Godoy, and of the war evidently at hand between France and England, the success of the peace policy was assured. These events in some degree explained the extraordinary nature of the new instructions of April, 1803. . . . (II, i, 2-4)

The news that Leclerc was dead, that his army was annihilated, St. Domingo ruined, and the Negroes more than ever beyond control, reached Paris and was printed in the "Moniteur" January 7, 1803, in the same active week when Bernadotte, Laussat,[29] and Victor were ordered from France to America, and Monroe was ordered from America to France. Of all the events of the time, Leclerc's death was the most decisive. The colonial system of France centered in St. Domingo. Without that island the system had hands, feet, and even a head, but no body. Of what use was Louisiana, when France had clearly lost the main colony which Louisiana was meant to feed and fortify? The new ruler of France was not unused to failure. More than once he had suddenly given up his dearest plans and deserted his oldest companions when their success was hopeless. He had abandoned Paoli and Corsica with as little compunction as afterward he abandoned the army and the officers whom he led to Egypt. Obstinate in pursuing any object which led to his own advancement, he was quick to see the moment when pursuit became useless; and the difficulties that rose in his path toward colonial empire were quite as great as those which had driven him to abandon

[28] Carlos Martinez d'Yrujo, Marques de Casa Yrujo: Spanish Minister to the United States.
[29] Pierre-Clement Laussat was the only one of this trio to reach America. As Colonial Prefect, after a three week rule in New Orleans, he surrendered Louisiana (December 20, 1803) to the United States.

Corsica and Egypt. Not only had the island of St. Domingo been ruined by the war, its plantations destroyed, its labor paralyzed, and its population reduced to barbarism, so that the task of restoring its commercial value had become extremely difficult; but other and greater objections existed to a renewal of the struggle. The army dreaded service in St. Domingo, where certain death awaited every soldier; the expense was frightful; a year of war had consumed fifty thousand men and money in vast amounts, with no other result than to prove that at least as many men and as much money would be still needed before any return could be expected for so lavish an expenditure. In Europe war could be made to support war; in St. Domingo peace alone could but slowly repair some part of this frightful waste.

Leclerc was succeeded at St. Domingo by General Rochambeau, a son of the Comte de Rochambeau, who twenty years before had commanded the French corps which enabled Washington to capture Cornwallis at Yorktown. A brave officer, but known to be little fit for administration, Rochambeau was incompetent for the task that fell on him. Leclerc had warned the Government that in case of his own retirement he had no officer fit to replace him—least of all Rochambeau, who was next in rank. Rochambeau wrote to inform the First Consul that 35,000 men must be sent to save the island. Without a new commander-in-chief of the highest ability, a new army was useless; and meanwhile Rochambeau was certain to waste the few thousand acclimated soldiers who should form its nucleus.

The First Consul found himself in a difficult and even dangerous situation. Probably the colonial scheme had never suited his tastes, and perhaps he had waited only until he should be firm in power in order to throw off the tutelage of Talleyrand; but the moment had arrived when his tastes coincided with policy. A second failure at St. Domingo would destroy his own credit, and disgust both the army and the public. Abandonment of the island was equally hazardous; for it required the abandonment of French traditions and a confession of failure. Retirement from St. Domingo was impossible, except under cover of some new enterprise; and as Europe stood, no other enterprise remained for France to undertake which would not lead her armies across the Rhine or the Pyrenees. For this undertaking Bonaparte was not yet ready; but even had he been so, it would have offered no excuse for abandoning the colonies. The ocean would still have been open, and St. Domingo within easy reach.

Only one resource remained. Bonaparte told no one his plans;

but he was not a man to hesitate when decision was needed. From
the day when news of Leclerc's death arrived, during the first week
of January, 1803, the First Consul brooded over the means of
abandoning St. Domingo without appearing to desert intentionally
a policy dear to France. Talleyrand and Decrès[30] were allowed to go
on as before; they gave instructions to Bernadotte, and hurried the
preparations of Victor, whom the ice and snow of Holland and the
slowness of the workmen held motionless; they prepared a reinforce-
ment of fifteen thousand men for Rochambeau, and Bonaparte gave
all the necessary orders for hastening the departure of both expeditions. As late as February 5, he wrote to Decrès that fifteen thousand
men had been, or were about to be, sent to St. Domingo and that
fifteen thousand more must be ready to sail by the middle of August.
Yet his policy of abandoning the colonial system had been already
decided; for on January 30 the "Moniteur" produced Sebastiani's[31]
famous Report on the military condition of the East,—a publication
which could have no other object than to alarm England. . . .
(II, i, 13-17)

England at once took Sebastiani's Report as a warning, and
began to arm. February 20 Bonaparte sent to the Corps Législatif
his Annual Report, or Message, which spoke of Great Britain in
language that could not be disregarded; finally, March 12, Livingston saw a melodramatic spectacle which transfixed him with surprise and excitement. The scene was at Madame Bonaparte's drawing room; the actors were Bonaparte and Lord Whitworth, the
British ambassador. "I find, my Lord, your nation want war again!"
said the First Consul. "No, sir," replied Whitworth; "we are very
desirous of peace." "I must either have Malta or war!" rejoined
Bonaparte. Livingston received these words from Lord Whitworth
himself on the spot; and returning at once to his cabinet, wrote to
warn Madison. Within a few days the alarm spread through Europe,
and the affairs of St. Domingo were forgotten.

Bonaparte loved long-prepared transformation scenes. Such a
scene he was preparing, and the early days of April, 1803, found
the actors eagerly waiting it. All the struggles and passions of the
last two years were crowded into the explosion of April. At St.
Domingo, horror followed fast on horror. Rochambeau, shut in
Port au Prince—drunken, reckless, surrounded by worthless men
and by women more abandoned still, wallowing in the dregs of the

[30] Denis Decrès: Admiral, Minister of Marine.
[31] Horace Francois Bastien Sebastiani: Colonel and French diplomat in Egypt.

former English occupation and of a half-civilized Negro empire—
waged as he best could a guerilla war, hanging, shooting, drowning,
burning all the Negroes he could catch; hunting them with fifteen
hundred bloodhounds bought in Jamaica for something more than
$100 each; wasting money, squandering men; while Dessalines and
Christophe massacred every white being within their reach. To
complete Bonaparte's work, from which he wished to turn the
world's attention, high among the Jura Mountains, where the ice
and snow had not yet relaxed their grip upon the desolate little
fortress and its sunless basement, in which for months nothing but
Toussaint's cough had been heard, Commander Amiot wrote a
brief military Report to the Minister of Marine: "On the 17th
[April 7], at half-past eleven o'clock of the morning, on taking him
his food, I found him dead, seated on his chair near his fire." According to Tavernier, doctor of medicine and *chirurgien* of Pontar-
lier, who performed the autopsy, pleuro-pneumonia was the cause
of Toussaint's death.

Toussaint never knew that St. Domingo had successfully resisted
the whole power of France, and that had he been truer to himself
and his color he might have worn the crown that became the play-
thing of Christophe and Dessalines; but even when shivering in
the frosts of the Jura, his last moments would have glowed with
gratified revenge, had he known that at the same instant Bonaparte
was turning into a path which the Negroes of St. Domingo had
driven him to take, and which was to lead him to parallel at St.
Helena the fate of Toussaint himself at the Château de Joux. In
these days of passion, men had little time for thought; and the last
subject on which Bonaparte thereafter cared to fix his mind was
the fate of Toussaint and Leclerc. That the "miserable Negro," as
Bonaparte called him, should have been forgotten so soon was not
surprising; but the prejudice of race alone blinded the American
people to the debt they owed to the desperate courage of 500,000
Haitian Negroes who would not be enslaved. . . . (II, i, 18-21)

Easter Sunday, April 10, 1803, arrived, and Monroe was leaving
Le Havre for Paris, when Bonaparte, after the religious ceremonies
of the day at St. Cloud, called to him two of his ministers, of whom
Barbé-Marbois[32] was one. He wished to explain his intention of
selling Louisiana to the United States; and he did so in his peculiar
way. He began by expressing the fear that England would seize

[32] Francois de Barbé-Marbois: Minister of Finance. During the American Revolution, he had been Secretary of Legation, under Luzerne, at Philadelphia.

Louisiana as her first act of war. "I think of ceding it to the United States. I can scarcely say that I cede it to them, for it is not yet in our possession. If, however, I leave the least time to our enemies, I shall only transmit an empty title to those republicans whose friendship I seek. They ask of me only one town in Louisiana; but I already consider the colony as entirely lost; and it appears to me that in the hand of this growing power it will be more useful to the policy, and even to the commerce, of France than if I should attempt to keep it."

To this appeal the two ministers replied by giving two opposite opinions. Marbois favored the cession, as the First Consul probably expected him to do; for Marbois was a republican who had learned republicanism in the United States, and whose attachment to that country was secured by marriage to an American wife. His colleague, with equal decision, opposed the scheme. Their arguments were waste of breath. The First Consul said no more, and dismissed them; but the next morning, Monday, April 11, at daybreak, summoning Marbois, he made a short oration of the kind for which he was so famous:—

"Irresolution and deliberation are no longer in season; I renounce Louisiana. It is not only New Orleans that I cede; it is the whole colony, without reserve. I know the price of what I abandon. I have proved the importance I attach to this province, since my first diplomatic act with Spain had the object of recovering it. I renounce it with the greatest regret; to attempt obstinately to retain it would be folly. I direct you to negotiate the affair. Have an interview this very day with Mr. Livingston."

The order so peremptorily given was instantly carried out; but not by Marbois. Talleyrand, in an interview a few hours afterward, startled Livingston with the new offer.

"M. Talleyrand asked me this day, when pressing the subject, whether we wished to have the whole of Louisiana. I told him no; that our wishes extended only to New Orleans and the Floridas; that the policy of France, however, should dictate (as I had shown in an official note) to give us the country above the River Arkansas, in order to place a barrier between them and Canada. He said that if they gave New Orleans the rest would be of little value, and that he would wish to know 'what we would give for the whole.' I told him it was a subject I had not thought of, but that I supposed we should not object to twenty millions [francs], provided our citizens were paid. He told me that this was too low an offer, and that he would be glad if I would reflect upon it and tell him tomorrow. I told him that as Mr. Monroe would be in town in two days, I would delay my further offer until I had the pleasure of introducing him. He added that he did not speak from authority, but that the idea had struck him."

The suddenness of Bonaparte's change disconcerted Livingston. For months he had wearied the First Consul with written and verbal arguments, remonstrances, threats,—all intended to prove that there was nothing grasping or ambitious in the American character; that France should invite the Americans to protect Louisiana from the Canadians; that the United States cared nothing for Louisiana, but wanted only West Florida and New Orleans—"barren sands and sunken marshes," he said; "a small town built of wood; . . . about seven thousand souls"; a territory important to the United States because it contained "the mouths of some of their rivers," but a mere drain of resources to France. To this rhapsody, repeated day after day for weeks and months, Talleyrand had listened with his imperturbable silence, the stillness of a sceptical mind into which such professions fell meaningless; until he suddenly looked into Livingston's face and asked: "What will you give for the whole?" Naturally Livingston for a moment lost countenance.

The next day, Tuesday, April 12, Livingston, partly recovered from his surprise, hung about Talleyrand persistently, for his chance of reaping alone the fruit of his labors vanished with every minute that passed. Monroe had reached St. Germain late Monday night, and at one o'clock Tuesday afternoon descended from his postchaise at the door of his Paris hotel. From the moment of his arrival he was sure to seize public attention at home and abroad. Livingston used the interval to make one more effort with Talleyrand:—

"He then thought proper to declare that his proposition was only personal, but still requested me to make an offer; and upon my declining to do so, as I expected Mr. Monroe the next day, he shrugged up his shoulders and changed the conversation. Not willing, however, to lose sight of it, I told him I had been long endeavoring to bring him to some point, but unfortunately without effect; and with that view had written him a note which contained that request. . . . He told me he would answer my note, but that he must do it evasively, because Louisiana was not theirs. I smiled at this assertion, and told him that I had seen the treaty recognizing it. . . . He still persisted that they had it in contemplation to obtain it, but had it not."

An hour or two afterward came a note from Monroe announcing that he would wait upon Livingston in the evening. The two American ministers passed the next day together, examining papers and preparing to act whenever Monroe could be officially presented. They entertained a party at dinner that afternoon in Livingston's apartments, and while sitting at table Livingston saw Barbé-Marbois strolling in the garden outside. Livingston sent to invite Marbois to join the party at table. While coffee was served, Marbois came in and entered into conversation with Livingston, who began at once to tell him of Talleyrand's "extraordinary conduct." Marbois hinted that he knew something of the matter, and that Livingston had better come to his house as soon as the dinner company departed. The moment Monroe took leave, Livingston acted on Marbois's hint, and in a midnight conversation the bargain was practically made. Marbois told a story, largely of his own invention, in regard to the First Consul's conduct on Easter Sunday, three days before. Bonaparte mentioned fifty million francs as his price for Louisiana; but as Marbois reported the offer to Livingston, Bonaparte said: "Well! you have charge of the Treasury. Let them give you one hundred millions of francs, and pay their own claims, and take the whole country." The American claims were estimated at about twenty-five millions, and therefore Marbois's price amounted to at least one hundred and twenty-five million francs.

Yet twenty-four or twenty-five million dollars for the whole west bank of the Mississippi, from the Lake of the Woods to the Gulf of Mexico, and indefinitely westward, was not an extortionate price, especially since New Orleans was thrown into the bargain, and indirect political advantages which could not be valued at less than the cost of a war, whatever it might be. Five million dollars were to be paid in America to American citizens, so that less than twenty millions would come to France. Livingston could hardly have been blamed for closing with Marbois on the spot, especially as his instructions warranted him in offering ten millions for New Orleans and the Floridas alone; but Livingston still professed that he did not want the west bank. "I told him that the United States were anxious to preserve peace with France; that for that reason they wished to remove them to the west side of the Mississippi; that we would be perfectly satisfied with New Orleans and the Floridas, and had no disposition to extend across the river; that of course we would not give any great sum for the purchase. . . . He then pressed me to name the sum." After a little more fencing, Marbois dropped at once from one hundred millions to sixty, with estimated claims to the amount of twenty millions more. "I told him that it was vain to ask anything that was so greatly beyond our means; that true policy would dictate to the First Consul not to press such a demand; that he must know it would render the present government unpopular." The conversation closed by Livingston's departure at midnight with a final protest: "I told him that I would consult Mr. Monroe, but that neither he nor I could accede to his ideas on the subject." Then he went home; and sitting down to his desk wrote a long despatch to Madison, to record that without Monroe's help he had won Louisiana. The letter closed with some reflections:—

"As to the quantum, I have yet made up no opinion. The field open to us is infinitely larger than our instructions contemplated, the revenue increasing, and the land more than adequate to sink the capital, should we even go the sum proposed by Marbois—nay, I persuade myself that the whole sum may be raised by the sale of the territory west of the Mississippi, with the right of sovereignty, to some Power in Europe whose vicinity we should not fear. I speak now without reflection and without having seen Mr. Monroe, as it was midnight when I left the Treasury Office, and it is now near three o'clock. It is so very important that you should be apprised that a negotiation is actually opened, even before Mr. Monroe has been presented, in order to calm the tumult which the news of war will renew, that I have lost no time in communicating it. We shall do all we can to cheapen the purchase; but my present sentiment is that we shall buy."

. . . (II, ii, 26-32)

A fortnight passed after Monroe's arrival without advancing matter a step. This period of inaction seems to have been broken by the First Consul. April 23 he drew up a "*Projet* of a Secret Convention," which he gave to Marbois and which set forth that to prevent misunderstandings about the matters of discussion mentioned in Articles II and V of the Morfontaine treaty, and also to strengthen friendly relations, the French republic was to cede its rights over Louisiana; and "in consequence of the said cession, Louisiana, its territory, and its proper dependencies shall become part of the American Union, and shall form successively one or more States on the terms of the Federal Constitution"; in return the United States were to favor French commerce in Louisiana, and give it all the rights of American commerce, with perpetual *entrepôts* at six points on the Mississippi, and a corresponding perpetual right of navigation; further, they were to assume all debts due to American citizens under the treaty of Morfontaine; and, finally, were to pay a hundred million francs to France. With this *projet* Marbois went by appointment, at two o'clock, April 27, to Monroe's lodgings, where the three gentlemen had an informal meeting, of which no other record is known to exist than Monroe's memoranda. Monroe himself was too unwell to sit at the table, and reclined on a sofa throughout the discussion. Marbois produced Bonaparte's *projet,* and after admitting that it was hard and unreasonable, presented a substitute of his own which he thought the First Consul would accept.

Livingston tried to give precedence to the claims; he wanted to dispose of them first, in case the cession should fail; but after pressing the point as far as he could, he was overruled by Monroe, and Livingston took Marbois's project for consideration. The two American commissioners passed a day in working over it. Livingston drafted a claims convention, and it was drawn, as he thought, "with particular attention." Monroe thought differently. "My colleague took Mr. Marbois's project with him, and brought me one, very loosely drawn, founded on it." Monroe made a draft of his own which was certainly not creditable to his legal or diplomatic skill, and which began by adopting an oversight contained in Bonaparte's draft, according to which the cancelled Article II of the treaty of Morfontaine was made a foundation of the new convention. "We called on Mr. Marbois the 29th, and gave him our project, which was read to him and discussed. We proposed to offer fifty millions to France, and twenty millions on account of her debt to the citizens of the United States, making seventy in the whole." Marbois replied that he would proceed only on the condition that eighty millions were accepted as the price. Then at last the American commissioners gave way; and with this change Marbois took their *projet* for reference to the First Consul the next morning.

The 30th of April was taken by Marbois for consultation with the First Consul. May 1 Monroe was presented at the Tuileries, and dined there with Livingston; but Bonaparte said nothing of their business, except that it should be settled. The same evening the two envoys had a final discussion with Marbois. "May 2, we actually signed the treaty and convention for the sixty million francs to France, in the French language; but our copies in English not being made out, we could not sign in our language. They were however prepared, and signed in two or three days afterward. The convention respecting American claims took more time and was not signed till about the 8th or 9th." All these documents were antedated to the 30th April.

The first object of remark in this treaty was the absence of any attempt to define the property thus bought and sold. . . . (II, ii, 40-43)

One point alone was fixed,—the Floridas were not included in the sale; this was conceded on both sides. In his first conversation with Marbois, Livingston made a condition that France should aid him in procuring these territories from Spain. "I asked him, in case of purchase, whether they would stipulate that France would never possess the Floridas and that she would aid us to procure them, and relinquish all right that she might have to them. He told me that she would go thus far." Several days later, Marbois repeated this assurance to Monroe, saying that the First Consul authorized him, besides offering Louisiana, "to engage his support of our claim to the Floridas with Spain." Yet when the American commissioners tried to insert this pledge into the treaty, they failed. Bonaparte would give nothing but a verbal promise to use his good offices with Spain.

Besides the failure to dispose of these two points, which were in reality but one, the treaty contained a positive provision, Article III, taken from Bonaparte's *projet*, with slight alteration, that "the inhabitants of the ceded territory shall be incorporated in the Union of the United States, and admitted as soon as possible, according to the principles of the Federal Constitution, to the enjoyment of all the rights, advantages, and immunities of citizens of the United States." On republican principles of the Virginian school, only the States themselves could by a new grant of power authorize such an incorporation. Article III violated Madison's instructions, which forbade the promise. "To incorporate the in- habitants of the hereby-ceded territory with the citizens of the United States," said these instructions, "being a provision which cannot now be made, it is to be expected, from the character and policy of the United States, that such incorporation will take place without unnecessary delay." The provision, which Madison said could not be made, was nevertheless made by Livingston and Monroe. . . . (II, ii, 44-45)

The annexation of Louisiana was an event so portentous as to defy measurement; it gave a new face to politics, and ranked in historical importance next to the Declaration of Independence and the adoption of the Constitution,—events of which it was the logical outcome; but as a matter of diplomacy it was unparalleled, because it cost almost nothing. . . . (II, ii, 49)

When Livingston set his name to the treaty of cession, May 2, 1803, he was aware of the immense importance of the act. He rose and shook hands with Monroe and Marbois. "We have lived long," said he; "but this is the noblest work of our lives." This was said by the man who in the Continental Congress had been a member of the committee appointed to draft the Declaration of Independence; and it was said to Monroe, who had been assured only three months before, by President Jefferson of the grandeur of his destinies in words he could hardly have forgotten: "Some men are born for the public. Nature, by fitting them for the service of the human race on a broad scale, has stamped them with the evidences of her destination and their duty." Monroe was born for the public, and knew what destiny lay before him, while in Livingston's mind New York had thenceforward a candidate for the Presidency whose claims were better than Monroe's. In the cup of triumph of which these two men then drank deep, was yet one drop of acid. They had been sent to buy the Floridas and New Orleans. They had bought New Orleans; but instead of Florida, so much wanted by the Southern people, they had paid ten or twelve million dollars for the west bank of the Mississippi. The negotiators were annoyed to think that having been sent to buy the east bank of the Mississippi, they had bought the west bank instead; that the Floridas were not a part of their purchase. Livingston especially felt the disappointment, and looked about him for some way to retrieve it.

Hardly was the treaty signed, when Livingston found what he sought. He discovered that France had actually bought West Florida without knowing it, and had sold it to the United States without being paid for it. . . . (II, iii, 67-68)

The reasoning on which he rested this change of opinion was in substance the following: France had, in early days, owned nearly all the North American continent, and her province of Louisiana had then included Ohio and the watercourses between the Lakes and the Gulf, as well as West Florida, or a part of it. This possession lasted until the treaty of peace, Nov. 3, 1762, when France ceded to England not only Canada, but also Florida and all other possessions east of the Mississippi, except the Island of New Orleans.

Then West Florida by treaty first received its modern boundary at the Iberville. On the same day France further ceded to Spain the Island of New Orleans and all Louisiana west of the Mississippi. Not a foot of the vast French possessions on the continent of North America remained in the hands of the King of France; they were divided between England and Spain.

The retrocession of 1800 was made on the understanding that it referred to this cession of 1762. The province of Louisiana which had been ceded was *retro*-ceded, with its treaty-boundary at the Iberville. Livingston knew that the understanding between France and Spain was complete; yet on examination he found that it had not been expressed in words so clearly but that these words could be made to bear a different meaning. Louisiana was retroceded, he perceived, "with the same extent that it now has in the hands of Spain, and that it had when France possessed it, and such as it should be according to the treaties subsequently entered into between Spain and other States." When France possessed Louisiana it included Ohio and West Florida; no one could deny that West Florida was in the hands of Spain; therefore Bonaparte, in the absence of negative proof, might have claimed West Florida, if he had been acute enough to know his own rights, or willing to offend Spain—and as all Bonaparte's rights were vested in the United States, President Jefferson was at liberty to avail himself of them. . . . (II, iii, 70-71)

If Jefferson's favorite phrase was true—that the Federalist differed from the Republican only in the shade more or less of power to be given the Executive—it was hard to see how any President could be more Federalist than Jefferson himself. A resolution to commit the nation without its knowledge to an indissoluble British alliance, was more than Washington would have dared take; yet this step was taken by the President, and was sustained by Madison, Gallatin, and Robert Smith as fairly within the limits of the Constitution. In regard to another stretch of the treaty-making power, they felt with reason the gravest doubts. When the President and Cabinet decided early in January, 1803, to send Monroe with two million dollars to buy New Orleans and Florida, a question was instantly raised as to the form in which such a purchase could be constitutionally made. Attorney General Lincoln[33] wished to frame the treaty or convention in such language as to make France appear not as adding new territory to the United States, but as extending already existing territory by an alteration of its boundary. He urged

[33] Levi Lincoln: Massachusetts Jeffersonian, Attorney-General 1801-1804.

this idea upon the President in a letter written the day of Monroe's nomination to the Senate.

> "If the opinion is correct," said he, "that the general government when formed was predicated on the then existing *United* States, and such as could grow out of them, and out of them only; and that its authority is constitutionally limited to the people composing the several political State societies in that Union, and such as might be formed out of them—would not a direct independent purchase be extending the executive power farther, and be more alarming, and improvable by the opposition and the Eastern States, than the proposed indirect mode?"

Jefferson sent this letter to Gallatin, who treated it without favor.

> "If the acquisition of territory is not warranted by the Constitution," said he, "it is not more legal to acquire for one State than for the United States. . . . What could, on his construction, prevent the President and Senate, by treaty, annexing Cuba to Massachusetts, or Bengal to Rhode Island, if ever the acquirement of colonies should become a favorite object with governments, and colonies should be acquired? But does any constitutional objection really exist? . . . To me it would appear, (1) that the United States, as a nation, have an inherent right to acquire territory; (2) that whenever that acquisition is by treaty, the same constituted authorities in whom the treaty-making power is vested have a constitutional right to sanction the acquisition."

Gallatin not only advanced Federal doctrine, but used also what the Virginians always denounced as Federalist play on words. "The United States as a nation" had an inherent right to do whatever the States in union cared to do; but the Republican party, with Jefferson, Madison, and Gallatin at their head, had again and again maintained that the United States *government* had the inherent right to do no act whatever, but was the creature of the States in union; and its acts, if not resulting from an expressly granted power, were no acts at all, but void, and not to be obeyed or regarded by the States. No foreigner, not even Gallatin, could master the theory of Virginia and New England, or distinguish between the nation of States in union which granted certain powers, and the creature at Washington to which these powers were granted, and which might be strengthened, weakened, or abolished without necessarily affecting the nation. Whether the inability to grasp this distinction was a result of clearer insight or of coarser intelligence, the face was the same; and on this point, in spite of his speech on the Alien and Sedition Acts, Gallatin belonged to the school of Hamilton, while both were of one mind with Dallas.[34] The chief avowed object of Jefferson's election had been to overthrow the reign of this school. No Virginian could be expected within two short years to adopt the opinions of opponents who had been so often branded as "monocrats," because of acting on these opinions. Although the Attorney General's advice was not followed, the negotiation for New Orleans was begun on the understanding that the purchase, if made, would be an inchoate act which would need express sanction from the States in the shape of an amendment to the Constitution.

There the matter rested. At the moment of Monroe's appointment, the President, according to his letters, had little hope of quick success in the purchase of territory. His plan was to "palliate and endure," unless France should force a war upon him; the constitutional question could wait, and it was accordingly laid aside. Yet the chief ambition of Southern statesmen in foreign affairs was to obtain the Floridas and New Orleans; and in effecting this object they could hardly escape establishing a serious precedent. Already Jefferson had ordered his ministers at Paris to buy this territory, although he thought the Constitution gave him no power to do so; he was willing to increase the national debt for this purpose, even though a national debt was a "mortal canker"; and he ordered his minister, in case Bonaparte should close the Mississippi, to make a permanent alliance with England, or in his own words to "marry ourselves to the British fleet and nation," as the price of New Orleans and Florida. Jefferson foresaw and accepted the consequences of the necessity; he repeatedly referred to them and deprecated them in his letters; but the territory was a vital object, and success there would, as he pointed out, secure forever the triumph of his party even in New England. . . . (II, iv, 77-81)

Coldly as his ideas were received in the Cabinet, Jefferson did not abandon them. Another month passed, and a call was issued for a special meeting of Congress October 17, to provide the necessary legislation for carrying the treaty into effect. As the summer wore away, Jefferson imparted his opinions to persons outside the Cabinet. He wrote, August 12, to Breckinridge[35] of Kentucky a long and

[34] Alexander James Dallas: Pennsylvania lawyer, commissioned in 1801 United States District Attorney for the Eastern District of Pennsylvania.
[35] John Breckinridge: U. S. Senator from Kentucky.

genial letter. Congress, he supposed, after ratifying the treaty and paying for the country, "must then appeal to *the nation* for an additional article to the Constitution approving and confirming an act which the nation had not previously authorized. The Constitution has made no provision for our holding foreign territory, still less for incorporating foreign nations into our Union. The Executive, in seizing the fugitive occurrence which so much advances the good of their country, have done an act beyond the Constitution. The Legislature, in casting behind them metaphysical subtleties and risking themselves like faithful servants, must ratify and pay for it, and throw themselves on their country for doing for them unauthorized what we know they would have done for themselves had they been in a situation to do it."

Breckinridge—whose Kentucky Resolutions, hardly five years before, declared that unconstitutional assumptions of power were the surrender of the form of government the people had chosen, and the replacing it by a government which derived its powers from its own will—might be annoyed at finding his principles abandoned by the man who had led him to father them; and surely no leader who had sent to his follower in one year the draft of the Kentucky Resolutions could have expected to send in another the draft of the Louisiana treaty. "I suppose they must then appeal to *the nation*" were the President's words; and he underscored this ominous phrase. "We shall not be disavowed by the nation, and their act of indemnity will confirm and not weaken the Constitution by more strongly marking out its lines." The Constitution, in dealing with the matter of amendments, made no reference to the nation; the word itself was unknown to the Constitution, which invariably spoke of the *Union* wherever such an expression was needed; and on the Virginia theory Congress had no right to appeal to the nation at all, except as a nation of States, for an amendment. The language used by Jefferson was the language of centralization, and would have been rejected by him and his party in 1798 or in 1820.

On the day of writing to Breckinridge the President wrote in a like sense to Paine; but in the course of a week despatches arrived from Paris which alarmed him. Livingston had reason to fear a sudden change of mind in the First Consul, and was willing to hasten the movements of President and Congress. Jefferson took the alarm, and wrote instantly to warn Breckinridge and Paine that no whisper of constitutional difficulties must be heard:—

"I wrote you on the 12th instant on the subject of Louisiana and the constitutional provision which might be necessary for it. A letter received yesterday shows that nothing must be said on that subject which may give a pretext for retracting, but that we should do *sub silentio* what shall be found necessary. Be so good, therefore, as to consider that part of my letter as confidential."

He gave the same warning to his Cabinet: "I infer that the less we say about constitutional difficulties the better; and that what is necessary for surmounting them must be done *sub silentio*."

He then drew up a new amendment, which he sent to the members of his Cabinet. The July draft was long, elaborate, and almost a new Constitution in itself; the August draft was comparatively brief. "Louisiana as ceded by France to the United States is made a part of the United States. Its white inhabitants shall be citizens, and stand, as to their rights and obligations, on the same footing with other citizens of the United States in analogous situations." The whole country north of the Arkansas River was reserved for Indians until another amendment should be made; and as an afterthought Florida was to be admitted as a part of the United States "whenever it may be rightfully obtained."

These persistent attempts to preserve his own consistency and that of his party were coldly received. Jefferson found himself alone. Wilson Cary Nicholas, a prominent supporter of the Virginia Resolutions in 1798 and a senator of the United States in 1803, had a long conversation with the President, and in the early days of September wrote him a letter which might have come from Theodore Sedgwick[36] or Roger Griswold[37] in the days of Jay's treaty, when Federalist notions of prerogative ran highest.

"Upon an examination of the Constitution," wrote Nicholas, "I find the power as broad as it could well be made (Sect. 3, Art. IV), except that new States cannot be formed out of the old ones without the consent of the *State* to be dismembered; and the exception is a proof to my mind that it was not intended to confine the Congress in the admission of new States to what was then the territory of the United States. Nor do I see anything in the Constitution that limits the treaty-making power, except the general limitations of the other powers given to the government, and the evident objects for which the government was instituted."

[36] Theodore Sedgwick: Federalist, Judge of the Supreme Court of Massachusetts.
[37] Roger Griswold: Federalist, now Representative from Connecticut.

Had Nicholas reasoned thus in 1798 he would have been a Federalist, as he seemed conscious, for he went on to say: "I am aware that this is to us delicate ground, and perhaps my opinions may clash with the opinions given by our friends during the discussion of the British treaty." Nevertheless he argued that if this treaty was unconstitutional, all other treaties were open to the same objection, and the United States government in such a case could make no treaty at all. Finally, he begged the President to avoid giving an opinion on the subject: "I should think it very probable if the treaty should be declared by you to exceed the constitutional authority of the treaty-making power, it would be rejected by the Senate, and if that should not happen, that great use would be made with the people of a wilful breach of the Constitution."

Such reasoning in the mouths of Virginia Republicans, who had asked and gained office by pledging themselves to their people against the use of implied powers, marked a new epoch. From them the most dangerous of all arguments, the *reductio ad absurdum*, was ominous. What right had they to ask whether any constitutional grant was less complete than the people might have wished or intended? If the Constitution were incomplete or absurd, not the government, but the people of the States who had made it were the only proper authority to correct it. Otherwise, as Nicholas had so often pointed out, their creature would become their tyrant, as had been the law of politics from the beginning.

Jefferson was distressed to find himself thus deserted by his closest friends on an issue which he felt to be vital. The principle of strict construction was the breath of his political life. The Pope could as safely trifle with the doctrine of apostolic succession as Jefferson with the limits of Executive power. If he and his friends were to interpret the treaty-making power as they liked, the time was sure to come when their successors would put so broad an interpretation on other powers of the government as to lead from step to step, until at last Virginia might cower in blood and flames before the shadowy terror called the war power. With what face could Jefferson then appear before the tribunal of history, and what position could he expect to receive?

All this he felt in his kindly way; and with this weight on his mind he wrote his reply to Nicholas. Beginning with the warning that Bonaparte could not be trusted, and that Congress must act with as little debate as possible, particularly as respected the constitutional difficulty, he went on:—

"I am aware of the force of the observations you make on the power given by the Constitution to Congress to admit new States into the Union without restraining the subject to the territory then constituting the United States. But when I consider that the limits of the United States are precisely fixed by the treaty of 1783, that the Constitution expressly declares itself to be made for the United States, . . . I do not believe it was meant that [Congress] might receive England, Ireland, Holland, etc., into it,—which would be the case on your construction. . . . I had rather ask an enlargement of power from the nation, where it is found necessary, than to assume it by a construction which would make our powers boundless. Our peculiar security is in the possession of a written Constitution. Let us not make it a blank paper by construction. I say the same as to the opinion of those who consider the grant of the treaty-making power as boundless. If it is, then we have no Constitution."

From the Virginia standpoint nothing could be better said. Jefferson in this letter made two points clear: the first was that the admission of Louisiana into the Union without express authority from the States made blank paper of the Constitution; the second was that if the treaty-making power was equal to this act, it superseded the Constitution. He entertained no doubts on either point, and time sustained his view; for whether he was right or wrong in law, the Louisiana treaty gave a fatal wound to "strict construction," and the Jeffersonian theories never again received general support. In thus giving them up, Jefferson did not lead the way, but he allowed his friends to drag him in the path they chose. The leadership he sought was one of sympathy and love, not of command; and there was never a time when he thought that resistance to the will of his party would serve the great ends he had in view. The evils which he foresaw were remote: in the hands of true Republicans the Constitution, even though violated, was on the whole safe; the precedent, though alarming, was exceptional. So it happened that after declaring in one sentence the Constitution at an end if Nicholas had his way, Jefferson in the next breath offered his acquiescence in advance:—

"I confess I think it important in the present case to set an example against broad construction by appealing for new power to the people. If, however, our friends shall think differently, certainly I shall acquiesce with satisfaction, confiding that the good sense of our country will correct the evil of construction when it shall produce ill effects."

With these words Jefferson closed his mouth on this subject forever. . . . (II, iv, 84-91)

Nothing could be more interesting than to see the discomfort with which the champions of States' rights tossed themselves from one horn to the other of the Federalist dilemma. The Federalists cared little on which horn their opponents might choose to impale themselves, for both were equally fatal. Either Louisiana must be admitted as a State, or must be held as territory. In the first case the old Union was at an end; in the second case the national government was an empire, with "inherent sovereignty" derived from the war and treaty-making powers,—in either case the Virginia theories were exploded. The Virginians felt the embarrassment, and some of them, like Nicholas, tried to hide it in a murmur of words and phrases; but the Republicans of Kentucky and Tennessee were impatient of such restraint, and slight as it was, thrust it away. The debate was closed by Senator Cocke of Tennessee, who defied opposition. "I assert," said he, "that the treaty-making powers in this country are competent to the full and free exercise of their best judgment in making treaties without limitation of power."

On this issue the vote was taken without further discussion, and by twenty-six to five the Senate passed the bill.[38] Pickering of Massachusetts, Tracy and Hillhouse of Connecticut, and the two senators Wells and White from Delaware, were alone in opposition.

The result of these debates in the Senate and House decided only one point. Every speaker, without distinction of party, agreed that the United States government had the power to acquire new territory either by conquest or by treaty; the only difference of opinion regarded the disposition of this territory after it was acquired. Did Louisiana belong to the central government at Washington, or to the States? The Federalists maintained that the central government, representing the States in union, might, if it pleased, as a consequence of its inherent sovereignty, hold the rest of America in its possession and govern it as England governed Jamaica or as Spain was governing Louisiana, but without the consent of the States could not admit such new territory into the Union. The Republicans seemed rather inclined to think that new territory acquired by war or conquest would become at once a part of the general territory mentioned in the Constitution, and as such might be admitted by Congress as a State, or otherwise disposed of as the general welfare might require, but that in either case neither the

[38] *I.e.*, a Bill to carry the Louisiana Treaty into effect.

people nor the States had anything to do with the matter. At
bottom, both doctrines were equally fatal to the old status of the
Union. In one case the states, formed or to be formed, east of the
Mississippi had established a government which could hold the
rest of the world in despotic control, and which bought a foreign
people as it might buy cattle, to rule over them as their owner; in
the other case, the government was equally powerful, and might
besides admit the purchased or conquered territory into the Union
as States. The Federalist theory was one of empire, the Republican
was one of assimilation; but both agreed that the moment had
come when the old Union must change its character. Whether the
government at Washington could possess Louisiana as a colony or
admit it as a State, was a difference of no great matter if the cession were to hold good; the essential point was that for the first
time in the national history all parties agreed in admitting that
the government could govern. . . . (II, v, 112-15)

5.

Jefferson Triumphant

From every point of view, . . . the Louisiana purchase possessed an importance not to be ignored. Even in 1804 the political consequences of the act were already too striking to be overlooked. Within three years of his inauguration Jefferson bought a foreign colony without its consent and against its will, annexed it to the United States by an act which he said made blank paper of the Constitution; and then he who had found his predecessors too monarchical, and the constitution too liberal in powers—he who had nearly dissolved the bonds of society rather than allow his predecessor to order a dangerous alien out of the country in a time of threatened war—made himself monarch of the new territory, and wielded over it, against its protests, the powers of its old kings. Such an experience was final; no century of slow and half-understood experience could be needed to prove that the hopes of humanity lay thenceforward, not in attempting to restrain the government from doing whatever the majority should think necessary, but in raising the people themselves till they should think nothing necessary but what was good.

Jefferson took a different view. He regarded, or wished to regard, the Louisiana treaty and legislation as exceptional and as forming no precedent. While he signed the laws for governing the territory, he warmly objected to the establishment of a branch bank of the United States at New Orleans. "This institution is one of the most deadly hostility existing against the principles and form of our Constitution," he wrote to Gallatin; "ought we to give further growth to an institution so powerful, so hostile?" Gallatin was clear that the business of the Treasury required such aid, and Jefferson again acquiesced. Gallatin was also allowed and encouraged to enforce the restrictions on the importation of slaves into Louisiana. "It seems that the whole Cabinet," wrote the French *chargé* to his government, "put the utmost weight on this prohibition. Mr. Jefferson is earnestly bent on maintaining it, and his Secretary of the Treasury takes the severest measures to insure its execution."

As though the annexation of Louisiana alone made not enough change in the old established balances of the Constitution, Congress took up another matter which touched the mainspring of the compact. A new Presidential election was at hand. The narrow escape of 1800 warned the party in power not again to risk society by following the complicated arrangements of 1788. In the convention which framed the Constitution no single difficulty was more serious than that of compromising the question of power between the large and small States. Delaware, New Jersey, Rhode Island, Maryland, and Connecticut were well aware that the large States would take the lion's share of power and patronage; they knew that except by accident no citizen of theirs could ever reach the Presidency; and as accident alone could give the small States a chance, accident was to them a thing of value. Whatever tended to make their votes decisive was an additional inducement with them to accept the Constitution. The Vice-presidency, as originally created, more than doubled their chance of getting the Presidency, and was invented chiefly for this purpose; but this was not all. As the number of electoral votes alone decided between President and Vice-president, a tie vote was likely often to occur; and such a tie was decided by the House of Representatives, where another bribe was intentionally offered to the small States by giving the election to the State delegations voting as units, so that the vote of Delaware weighed as heavily as the vote of Pennsylvania.

The alarm caused by Burr's rivalry with Jefferson in February, 1801, satisfied the Republican party that such a door to intrigue ought not to be left open. October 17, 1803, before the Louisiana treaty was taken up, an amendment to the Constitution was moved by friends of the Administration in the House. This, which took shape at length as the Twelfth Amendment, obliged the members of the electoral college to distinguish in their ballots the persons voted for as President and Vice-president.

Slight as this change might appear, it tended toward centralizing powers hitherto jealously guarded. It swept away one of the checks on which the framers had counted to resist majority rule by the great States. Lessening the influence of the small States, and exaggerating the office of President by lowering the dignity of Vice-

president, it made the processes of election and government
smoother and more efficient,—a gain to politicians, but the result
most feared by the States' rights school. The change was such as
Pennsylvania or New York might naturally want; but it ran counter
to the theories of Virginia Republicans, whose jealousy of Executive influence had been extreme. . . . (II, vi, 130-33)

The annexation of Louisiana, the constitutional amendment in
regard to the Vice-presidency, the change of financial practices
foreshadowed by the Mediterranean Fund,[39] were signs of reaction
toward nationality and energy in government. Yet the old prejudices
of the Republican party had not yet wholly lost their force. Especially the extreme wing, consisting of men like John Randolph and
W. B. Giles, thought that a substantial reform should be attempted.
Increase of power encouraged them to act. The party, stimulated
by its splendid success and irresistible popularity, at length, after
long hesitation, prepared for a trial of strength with the last rem-
nant of Federalism,—the Supreme Court of the United States. . . .
(II, vii, 142)

Precisely as the House, by the President's invitation, was about
to impeach Judge Pickering,[40] the Supreme Court, through the
Chief-Justice's mouth, delivered an opinion which could be regarded in no other light than as a defiance. Chief Justice Marshall's
own appointment had been one of those made by the last President
between Dec. 12, 1800, and March 4, 1801, which Jefferson called
an "outrage on decency," and which, except as concerned life offices, he held to be "nullities." His doctrine that all appointments
made by a retiring President were nullities, unless made with the
consent of the President elect, rested on the argument that the
retiring President was no longer selecting his own but his successor's
agents. Perhaps it involved also the favorite idea that the election
of 1800 was something more than a change of Presidents,—that it
was a real revolution in the principle of government. Any theory
was sufficient for the Executive, but executive theories did not
necessarily bind the Judiciary. Among the nominations which, like
the appointment of Marshall, were obnoxious to Jefferson, was that
of William Marbury as justice of the peace for five years for the

[39] The "Mediterranean Fund" was embodied in a Bill (March 1804) to increase
the naval force and enlarge expenses in the Mediterranean.

[40] John Pickering: Federalist, Federal District Judge in New Hampshire, impeached as unfit (he was effectually insane) and removed March 12, 1804.

District of Columbia. The nomination was sent to the Senate March 2, 1801, and was approved the next day, a few hours before Jefferson took his oath of office. The commission, regularly made out, signed by the President, countersigned by John Marshall the acting Secretary of State, and duly sealed, was left with other documents on the table in the State Department, where it came into the possession of Attorney General Lincoln, acting as President Jefferson's Secretary of State. Jefferson, having decided that late appointments were nullities, retained Marbury's commission. Marbury, at the December term of 1801, moved the Supreme Court for a Rule to Secretary Madison to show cause why a mandamus should not issue commanding him to deliver the document. The Rule was duly served, and the case argued in December, 1801; but the Judiciary Act[41] having suspended for fourteen months the sessions of the Supreme Court, the Chief Justice did not deliver his opinion until Feb. 24, 1803.

The strongest admirers of Marshall admitted that his manner of dealing with this case was unusual. Where a judgment was to turn on a question of jurisdiction, the Court commonly considered that point as first and final. In the case of Marbury the Court had no original jurisdiction, and so decided; but instead of beginning at that point and dismissing the motion, the Court began by discussing the merits of the case, and ruled that when a commission had been duly signed and sealed the act was complete, and delivery was not necessary to its validity. Marbury's appointment was complete; and as the law gave him the right to hold for five years, independent of the Executive, his appointment was not revocable: "To withhold his commission, therefore, is an act deemed by the Court not warranted by law, but violative of a legal vested right."

This part of the decision bore the stamp of Marshall's character. The first duty of law, as he understood it, was to maintain the sanctity of pledged word. In his youth society had suffered severely from want of will to enforce a contract. The national government, and especially the judiciary, had been created to supply this want by compelling men to perform their contracts. The essence of the opinion in Marbury's case was that the Executive should be held to the performance of a contract, all the more because of his personal repugnance. Marshall ruled that Marbury had to his com-

[41] The Judiciary Act of April 29, 1802: This Act replaced the (Federalist) Judiciary Act of February 27, 1801, which increased the number of federal courts (incidentally allowing President Adams to fill them with Jefferson's opponents) and which was repealed on March 3, 1802.

mission a vested legal right of which the Executive could not deprive him; and although the Court could not intermeddle with the prerogatives of the Executive, it might and would command a head of department to perform a duty not depending on Executive discretion, but on particular Acts of Congress and the general principles of law. The mandamus might issue, but not from the Supreme Court, which had appellate jurisdiction only. In other words, if Marbury chose to apply for the mandamus to Judge Cranch and the District Court, he might expect the success of his application.

The decision in Marbury's case naturally exasperated Jefferson; but the chief-justice knew the point beyond which he could not go in asserting the jurisdiction of his court, and was content to leave the matter as it stood. Marbury never applied for the mandamus in the court below. The opinion in the case of Marbury and Madison was allowed to sleep. . . . (II, vii, 144-47)

As the year 1804 began, with Louisiana annexed, the Electoral Amendment secured, and the impeachments in prospect, the Federalists in Congress wrought themselves into a dangerous state of excitement. All agreed that the crisis was at hand; democracy had nearly reached its limit; and, as Justice Chase said from the bench, peace and order, freedom and property, would soon be destroyed. They discussed in private what should be done; and among the New Englanders almost all the men of weight were found to favor the policy of at least saving New England. Of the six Federalist senators from the Eastern States,—Plumer and Olcott of New Hampshire, Pickering and Adams[42] of Massachusetts, Tracy and Hillhouse of Connecticut,—all but Olcott and Adams thought a dissolution of the Union inevitable. Among the Federalist members of the House, Roger Griswold of Connecticut was the most active; he too was convinced that New England must protect herself. Samuel Hunt of New Hampshire and Calvin Goddard of Connecticut held the same opinion. Indeed Pickering declared that he did not know of "one reflecting Nov-Anglian" who held any other.

In the month of January, 1804, despair turned into conspiracy. Pickering, Tracy, Griswold, Plumer and perhaps others of the New England delegation, agreed to organize a movement in their States for a dissolution of the Union. They wrote to their most influential constituents and sketched a plan of action. In a letter to George Cabot,[43] Pickering recounted the impending dangers:—

[42] John Quincy Adams: HA's grandfather.
[43] George Cabot: formerly U. S. Senator from Massachusetts.

"By the Philadelphia papers I see that the Supreme Court judges of Pennsylvania are to be hurled from their seats, on the pretense that in punishing one Thomas Passmore for a contempt they acted illegally and tyrannically. I presume that Shippen, Yates, and Smith are to be removed by the Governor, on the representation of the Legislature. And when such grounds are taken in the National and State legislatures to destroy the rights of the judges, whose rights can be safe? Why destroy *them,* unless as a prelude to the destruction of every influential Federalist and of every man of considerable property who is not of the reigning sect? New judges, of characters and tempers suited to the object, will be the selected ministers of vengeance."

A separation, Pickering inferred, had become necessary; but how was it to be effected?

"If Federalism is crumbling away in New England, there is no time to be lost, lest it should be overwhelmed and become unable to attempt its own relief; its last refuge is New England, and immediate exertion perhaps its only hope. It must begin in Massachusetts. The proposition would be welcomed in Connecticut; and could we doubt of New Hampshire? But New York must be associated; and how is her concurrence to be obtained? She must be made the center of the confederacy. Vermont and New Jersey would follow of course, and Rhode Island of necessity. Who can be consulted, and who will take the lead? The legislatures of Massachusetts and Connecticut meet in May, and of New Hampshire in the same month, or June. The subject has engaged the contemplation of many. The Connecticut gentlemen have seriously meditated upon it. . . . Tracy has written to several of his most distinguished friends in Connecticut, and may soon receive their answers. R. Griswold, examining the finances, has found that the States above mentioned, to be embraced by the Northern confederacy, now pay as much or more of the public revenues as would discharge their share of the public debts due those States and abroad, leaving out the millions given for Louisiana."

Roger Griswold wrote a few weeks afterwards to Oliver Wolcott in similar terms:—

"The project which we had formed was to induce, if possible, the legislatures of the three New England States who remain Federal to commence measures which should call for a reunion of the Northern States. The extent of those measures, and the rapidity with which they shall be followed up, must be governed by circumstances. The magnitude and jealousy of Massachusetts would render it necessary that the operation should be commenced there. If any hope can be created that

New York will ultimately support the plan, it may perhaps be supported."

The first action, he said, must come from the Legislature of Massachusetts, which was not yet elected, but would meet early in June. Connecticut and New Hampshire were to follow; and to Pickering's sanguine mind the Northern Confederacy seemed already established. "The people of the East," he said, "cannot reconcile their habits, views, and interests with those of the South and West. The latter are beginning to rule with a rod of iron."

Pickering knew that the Federalist majority in Massachusetts was none too great. The election in May, four months later, showed a Federalist vote of 30,000 against a Republican minority of 24,000, while in the Legislature Harrison Gray Otis was chosen Speaker by 129 votes to 103. Pickering knew also that his colleague, Senator Adams, was watching his movements with increasing ill-will, which Pickering lost no chance to exasperate. Nothing could be more certain that at the first suggestion of disunion Senator Adams and the moderate Federalists would attack the Essex Junto[44] with the bitterness of long suppressed hatred; and if they could not command fourteen votes in the Legislature and three thousand in the State, a great change must have occurred since the year before, when they elected Adams to the Senate for the long term over Pickering's head. Pickering concealed his doings from his colleague; but Tracy was not so cautious; and the two senators from Massachusetts drew farther and farther apart, in spite of the impeachments, which tended to force them together.

The Essex Junto, which sent Pickering to Washington, and to which he appealed for support, read his letter with evident astonishment. George Cabot, Chief Justice Parsons, Fisher Ames, and Stephen Higginson, who were the leaders consulted, agreed that the scheme was impracticable; and Cabot, as gently as possible, put their common decision into words.

"All the evils you describe," he said, "and many more, are to be apprehended; but I greatly fear that a separation would be no remedy, because the source of them is in the political theories of our country and in ourselves. A separation at some period not very remote may probably take place—the first impression of it is even now favorably received by many, but I cannot flatter myself with the expectation of

[44] Essex Junto: a group of extreme Massachusetts Federalists; habitat, Essex County.

essential good to proceed from it while we retain the maxims and principles which all experience, and I may add reason too, pronounce to be impracticable and absurd. Even in New England, where there is among the body of the people more wisdom and virtue than in any other part of the United States, we are full of errors which no reasoning could eradicate if there were a Lycurgus in every village. We are democratic altogether; and I hold democracy in its natural operation to be the government of the worst.

"There is no energy in the Federal party, and there could be none manifest without great hazard of losing the State government. Some of our best men in high places are kept in office because they forbear to exert any influence, and not because they possess right principles. They are permitted to have power if they will not use it. . . . I incline to the opinion that the essential alterations which may in future be made to amend our form of government will be the consequences only of great suffering or the immediate effects of violence. If we should be made to feel a very great calamity from the abuse of power of the National Administration, we might do almost anything; but it would be idle to talk to the deaf, to warn the people of distant evils. By this time you will suppose that I am willing to do nothing but submit to fate. I would not be so understood. I am convinced we cannot do what is wished; but we can do much, if we work with Nature (or the course of things), and not against her. A separation is now impracticable, because we do not feel the necessity or the utility of it. The same separation then will be unavoidable when our loyalty to the Union is generally perceived to be the instrument of debasement and impoverishment. If it is prematurely attempted, those few only will promote it who discern what is hidden from the multitude."

Cabot's letter, more clearly than any writing of Alexander Hamilton, expressed the philosophy and marked the tactics of their school. Neither Cabot nor Hamilton was a lively writer, and the dust which has gathered deep on their doctrines dulls whatever brilliancy they once possessed; but this letter showed why Cabot was considered the wisest head of his party, to whose rebuke even Hamilton was forced to bow. For patient and willing students who have groped in search of the idea which, used by Hamilton and Jefferson, caused bitter feeling and roused deeper terrors than civil war itself, Cabot's long and perhaps pedantic letter on the policy of disunion was full of meaning. "We shall go the way of all governments wholly popular,—from bad to worse,—until the evils no longer tolerable, shall generate their own remedies." Democracy must end in a crisis, experience and reason pronounced it impracticable and absurd, Nature would in due time vindicate her own laws; and when the inevitable chaos should come, then conservative statesmanship could set society on a sound footing by limiting the suffrage to those citizens who might hold in their own right $2,000 value in land. Meanwhile disunion would be useless, and the attempt to bring it about would break up the Federalist party. "A war with Great Britain manifestly provoked by our rulers" was the only chance which Cabot foresaw of bringing the people of New England to a dissolution of the Union. . . . (II, viii, 160-66)

The only result of the Pennsylvania Schism[45] was to check the aggressive energy of the democratic movement by alarming a few of the older leaders and causing them to halt. From the day of Jefferson's inauguration this tendency toward reaction had begun, and it developed in party schisms which could not fail to hurry the process. The symptom, however unpleasant to old political leaders such as Jefferson, McKean, and Dallas, who liked the quiet enjoyment of power, was healthy for society at large; but no one could fail to be struck by the contrast which in this respect was offered by the two great sections of the country. While the mobile, many-sided, restless democracy of New England, New York, and Pennsylvania exhibited its faults, and succeeded, with much personal abuse, in thrusting out the elements foreign to its character which retarded its movement, the society of the southern States was classically calm. Not a breath disturbed the quiet which brooded over the tobacco and cotton fields between the Potomac and Florida. A Presidential election was taking place, but the South saw only one candidate. The State legislatures quietly chose electors to vote for Jefferson and Clinton.[46] From the St. Mary's to the Potomac and the Ohio, every electoral voice was given to Jefferson. With some surprise the public learned that Maryland gave two of eleven votes to C. C. Pinckney, who received also the three votes of Delaware. This little State even went back on its path, repudiated Caesar A. Rodney, and returned to its favorite Bayard, who was sent by a handsome majority to his old seat in the House of Representatives. Broken for an instant only by this slight check, the tide of democratic triumph swept over the States of Pennsylvania, New Jersey, and New York, and burst upon Connecticut as though Jefferson's

[45] Pennsylvania Schism: William Duane of the *Aurora* and Michael Leib, then a Representative in Congress, led a revolt against Thomas McKean and other Administration leaders in 1804.
[46] Jefferson and George Clinton were opposed by C. C. Pinckney of South Carolina and Rufus King of New York.

hope of dragging even that State from its moorings were at length to be realized. With difficulty the Connecticut hierarchy held its own; and with despair after the torrent passed by, it looked about and found itself alone. Even Massachusetts cast 29,310 votes for Jefferson, against 25,777 for Pinckney.

Rarely was a Presidential election better calculated to turn the head of a President, and never was a President elected who felt more keenly the pleasure of his personal triumph. At the close of four years of administration, all Jefferson's hopes were fulfilled. He had annihilated opposition. The slanders of the Federalist press helped to show that he was the idol of four-fifths of the nation. He received one hundred and sixty-two of one hundred and seventy-six electoral votes, while in 1801 he had but seventy-three in one hundred and thirty-eight; and in the Ninth Congress, which was to meet in December, 1805, barely seven out of thirty-four senators, and twenty-five out of one hundred and forty-one representatives, would oppose his will. He described his triumph, in language studiously modest, in a letter to Volney:—[47]

"The two parties which prevailed with so much violence when you were here are almost wholly melted into one. At the late Presidential election I have received one hundred and sixty-two votes against fourteen only. Connecticut is still Federalist by a small majority, and Delaware on a poise, as she has been since 1775, and will be till Anglomany with her yields to Americanism. Connecticut will be with us in a short time. Though the people in mass have joined us, their leaders had committed themselves too far to retract. Pride keeps them hostile; they brood over their angry passions, and give them vent in the newspapers which they maintain. They still make as much noise as if they were the whole nation."

Such success might have turned the head of any philosopher that ever sat on a throne. Easily elated, unwilling to forebode trouble, devoid of humor, and unable to see himself in any but the heroic light, President Jefferson basked in the sunshine of popularity and power as though it were no passing warmth such as had led scores of kings into disaster, but shone by virtue of some democratic law which rested on truth that could never change. The White House was filled with an atmosphere of adulation. Flattery, gross as any that man could ask, was poured into the President's ear, but was as nothing compared with the more subtle flattery of the popular vote.

[47] Comte de Volney: French *savant*.

No friend stopped him to ask how such a miraculous success had been brought about. Four years had not passed since Jefferson and his party had clamored against attempts to give energy to government; and no one could ever forget that they claimed and received power from the people in order to defend States' rights, restrict Executive influence, and correct strained constructions of the Construction. Who upheld States' rights in 1804, and complained of Executive influence and strained constructions? Certainly not Jefferson or his friends, but the monarchical Federalists, who were fit inmates for an asylum. Whenever Jefferson had occasion to discuss the aims and opinions of the two parties, he did not allude to the principles set forth in 1798; not a word was said of "strict construction." The only theories opposed to his own which he could see in the political horizon were those of a few hundred conservatives of the colonial epoch.

> "What, in fact," he wrote, "is the difference of principle between the two parties here? The one desires to preserve an entire independence of the executive and legislative branches on each other and the dependence of both on the same source,—the free election of the people. The other party wishes to lessen the dependence of the Executive and of one branch of the legislature on the people, some by making them hold for life, some hereditary, and some even for giving the Executive an influence by patronage or corruption over the remaining popular branch, so as to reduce the elective franchise to its minimum."

After nearly four years of Executive authority more complete than had ever before been known in American history, Jefferson could see in himself and in his principles only a negation of Executive influence. What had become of the old radical division of parties,—the line between men who wished the national government to exercise inherent powers of sovereignty and those who held to a strict observance of powers expressly delegated by the people of the States?

Jefferson said with truth that the two old parties were almost wholly melted into one; but in this fusion his own party had shown even more willingness than its opponents to mix its principles in a useful, but not noble, amalgam. His own protests in regard to the Louisiana purchase and the branch bank at New Orleans were recorded. With such evidence on their side, the moderate Federalist who in the election of 1804 gave to Jefferson the nineteen electoral votes of Massachusetts and the seven of New Hampshire, could claim that they had altered no opinion they ever held; that the government had suffered no change in principle from what it had been under President Washington; that not a Federalist measure, not even the Alien and Sedition laws, had been expressly repudiated; that the national debt was larger than it had ever been before, the navy maintained and energetically employed, the national bank preserved and its operations extended; that the powers of the national government had been increased to a point that made blank paper of the Constitution as heretofore interpreted by Jefferson, while the national territory, vastly more than doubled in extent, was despotically enlarged and still more despotically ruled by the President and Congress, in the teeth of every political profession the Republican party had ever made. Had this been the work of Federalists, it would have been claimed as a splendid triumph of Federalist principles; and the good sense of New England was never better shown than when Massachusetts and New Hampshire flung aside their prejudices and told Jefferson that they accepted his inaugural pledge to be a Federalist as they were Republicans. . . . (II, ix, 200-205)

The impeachment of Judge Chase was a cold and colorless performance beside the melodramatic splendor of Hasting's trial;[48] but in the infinite possibilities of American democracy, the questions to be decided in the Senate chamber had a weight for future ages beyond any that were then settled in the House of Lords. Whether Judge Chase should be removed from the bench was a trifling matter; whether Chief Justice Marshall and the Supreme Court should hold their power and principles against this combination of States' rights conservatives and Pennsylvania democrats was a subject for grave reflection. Men who did not see that the tide of political innovation had long since turned and that the French revolution was no longer raging, were consumed with anxiety for the fate of Chase, and not wholly without reason; for had Marshall been a man of less calm and certain judgment, a single mistake by him might easily have prostrated the judiciary at the feet of partisans. . . . (II, x, 226-27)

The failure of Chase's impeachment was a blow to the Republican party from which it never wholly recovered. Chief Justice Mar-

[48] Samuel Chase: Federalist, Associate Justice of the U. S. Supreme Court, impeached for extreme political bias, and acquitted March 1, 1805. The Senate Chamber was draped in scarlet as if to mimic the famous trial of Warren Hastings, first Governor General of India, which lasted from 1788 to 1795.

shall at length was safe; he might henceforward at his leisure fix the principles of Constitutional law. Jefferson resigned himself for the moment to Randolph's overthrow; but the momentary consolations passed away, and a lifelong disappointment remained. Fifteen years later his regret was strongly expressed:—

"The Judiciary of the United States," mourned the old ex-President, "is the subtle corps of sappers and miners constantly working underground to undermine the foundations of our confederated fabric. They are construing our Constitution from a co-ordination of a general and special government to a general and supreme one alone. . . . Having found from experience that impeachment is an impracticable thing, a mere scarecrow, they consider themselves secure for life; they skulk from responsibility; . . . an opinion is huddled up in conclave, perhaps by a majority of one, delivered as if unanimous, and with the silent acquiescence of lazy or timid associates, by a crafty chief judge who sophisticates the law to his mind by the turn of his own reasoning."

The acquittal of Chase proved that impeachment was a scarecrow; but its effect on impeachment as a principle of law was less evident. No point was decided. The theory of Giles, Randolph, and Rodney was still intact, for it was not avowedly applied to the case. The theory of Judge Chase's counsel—that an impeachable offence must be also indictable, or even a violation of some known statute of the United States—was overthrown neither by the argument nor by the judgment. So far as Constitutional law was concerned, President Jefferson himself might still be impeached, according to the dictum of Madison, for the arbitrary removal of a useful tidewaiter, and Chief Justice Marshall might be driven from the bench, as Giles wished, for declaring the Constitution to be above the authority of a statute; but although the acquittal of Chase decided no point of law except his innocence of high crimes or misdemeanors, as charged in the indictment, it proved impeachment to be "an impracticable thing" for partisan purposes, and it decided the permanence of those lines of Constitutional development which were a reflection of the common law. Henceforward the legal profession had its own way in expounding the principles and expanding the powers of the central government through the Judiciary. . . . (II, x, 243-44)

6.

Neutral Rights and Nationality

For eighteen years after 1783 William Pitt guided England through peace and war with authority almost as absolute as that of Don Carlos IV or Napoleon himself. From him and from his country President Jefferson had much to fear and nothing to gain beyond a continuance of the good relations which President Washington, with extreme difficulty, had succeeded in establishing between the two peoples. So far as England was concerned, this understanding had been the work of Pitt and Lord Grenville, who rather imposed it on their party than accepted it as the result of any public will. The extreme perils in which England then stood inspired caution; and of this caution the treaty of 1794 was one happy result. So long as the British government remained in a cautious spirit, America was safe; but should Pitt or his successors throw off the self-imposed restraints on England's power, America could at the utmost, even by a successful war, gain nothing materially better than a return to the arrangements of 1794.

The War of Independence, which ended in the definitive treaty of 1783, naturally left the English people in a state of irritation and disgust toward America; and the long interregnum of the Confederation, from 1783 to 1789, allowed this disgust to ripen into contempt. When at length the Constitution of 1789 restored order in the American chaos, England felt little faith in the success of the experiment. She waited for time to throw light on her interests.

This delay was natural; for American independence had shattered into fragments the commercial system of Great Britain, and powerful interests were combined to resist further concession. Before 1776 the colonies of England stretched from the St. Lawrence to the Mississippi, and across the Gulf of Mexico to the coast of South

America, mutually supporting and strengthening each other. Jamaica and the other British islands of the West Indies drew their most necessary supplies from the Delaware and the Hudson. Boston and New York were in some respects more important to them than London itself. The timber, livestock, and provisions which came from the neighboring continent were essential to the existence of the West Indian planters and Negroes. When war cut off these supplies, famine and pestilence followed. After the peace of 1783 even the most conservative English statesmen were obliged to admit that the strictness of their old colonial system could not be maintained, and that the United States, though independent, must be admitted to some of the privileges of a British colony. The government unwillingly conceded what could not be refused, and the West Indian colonists compelled Parliament to relax the colonial system so far as to allow a restricted intercourse between their islands and the ports of the United States.—The relaxation was not a favor to the United States,—it was a condition of existence to the West Indies; not a boon, but a right which the colonists claimed and an Act of Parliament defined. . . . (II, xiv, 316-18)

Even when the qualified right of trade was conceded, the colonists were not satisfied; and the concession itself laid the foundation of more serious changes. From the moment that American produce was admitted to be a necessity for the colonists, it was clear that the Americans must be allowed a voice in the British system. Discussion whether the Americans had or had not a right to the colonial trade was already a long step toward revolution. One British minister after another resented the idea that the Americans had any rights in the matter; yet when they came to practical arrangements the British statesmen were obliged to concede that they were mistaken. From the necessity of the case, the Americans had rights which never could be successfully denied. Parliament struggled to prevent the rebel Americans from sharing in the advantages of the colonial system from which they had rebelled; but unreasonable as it was that the United States should be rewarded for rebellion by retaining the privileges of subjects, this was the inevitable result. Geography and Nature were stronger than Parliament and the British navy. . . . (II, xiv, 319-20)

In peace . . . the chief diplomatic difficulties between European governments and the United States had their source in the American attempt to obtain legal recognition of trade which America wished to maintain with the colonies; but in war the situation changed, and more serious disputes occurred. Then the French and Spanish West Indian ports were necessarily thrown open to neutral commerce, because their own ships were driven from the ocean by the superiority of the British navy. Besides the standing controversy about the admission of American produce to British islands, the British government found itself harassed by doubts to what extent it might safely admit the Americans into the French or Spanish West Indies, and allow them to carry French property, as though their flag were competent to protect whatever was under it. Granting that an article like French sugar might be carried in a neutral vessel, there were still other articles, called contraband, which ought not to be made objects of neutral commerce; and England was obliged to define the nature of contraband. She was also forced to make free use of the right of blockade. These delicate questions were embittered by another and more serious quarrel. The European belligerents claimed the right to the military service of their subjects, and there was no doubt that their right was perfect. In pursuance of the claim they insisted upon taking their seamen from American merchant vessels wherever met on the high seas. So far as France was concerned, the annoyance was slight; but the identity of race made the practice extremely troublesome as concerned England.

At the outbreak of the French Wars, November 6, 1793, the British government issued instructions directing all British armed vessels to seize every neutral ship they should meet, loaded with the produce of a French colony or carrying supplies for its use. These orders were kept secret for several weeks, until the whole American commerce with the Antilles, and all American ships found on the ocean, laden in whole or in part with articles of French colonial produce or for French colonial use, were surprised and swept into British harbors, where they were condemned by British admiralty courts, on the ground known as the "Rule of the War of 1756,"— that because trade between the French colonies and the United States was illegal in peace, it was illegal in war. From the point of view in which European powers regarded their colonies, much could be said in support of this rule. A colony was almost as much the property of its home government as a dockyard or a military station. France and Spain could hardly complain if England chose to treat the commerce of such government stations as contraband; but a rule which might perhaps be applied by European governments to each other worked with great injustice when applied to the United

States, who had no colonies, and made no attempt to build up a navy or support an army by such means. Taken in its broadest sense, the European colonial system might be defined by the description which the best of British commentators gave to that of England,—a "policy pursued for rendering the foreign trade of the whole world subservient to the increase of her shipping and navigation." American Independence was a protest against this practice; and the first great task of the United States was to overthrow and destroy the principle, in order to substitute freedom of trade. America naturally objected to becoming a martyr to the rules of a system which she was trying to revolutionize.

When these British instructions of November 26, 1793, became known in the United States, the Government of President Washington imposed an embargo, threatened retaliation, and sent Chief Justice Jay to London as a last chance of maintaining peace. On arriving there, Jay found that Pitt had already voluntarily retreated from his ground, and that new Orders, dated January 8, 1794, had been issued, exempting from seizure American vessels engaged in the direct trade from the United States to the French West Indies. In the end, the British government paid the value of the confiscated vessels. The trade from the United States to Europe was not interfered with; and thus American ships were allowed to carry French colonial produce through an American port to France, while Russian or Danish ships were forbidden by England to carry such produce to Europe at all, although their flags and harbors were as neutral as those of the United States. America became suddenly a much favored nation, and the enemies of England attributed this unexpected kindness to fear. In truth it was due to a natural mistake. The British Treasury calculated that the expense and trouble of carrying sugar and coffee from Martinique or St. Domingo to Boston, of landing it, paying duties, re-embarking it, receiving the drawback, and then carrying it to Bordeaux or Brest, would be such as to give ample advantages to English vessels which could transship more conveniently at London. The mistake soon became apparent. The Americans quickly proved that they could under these restrictions carry West Indian produce to Europe not only more cheaply than British ships could do it, but almost as quickly; while it was a positive advantage on the return voyage to make double freight by stopping at an American port. The consequence of this discovery was seen in the sudden increase of American shipping, and was largely due to the aid of British seamen, who found in the new service better pay, food, and treatment than in their own, and comparative safety from the press-gang and the lash. At the close of the century the British flag seemed in danger of complete exclusion from the harbors of the United States. In 1790 more than 550 British ships, with a capacity of more than 115,000 tons, had entered inward and outward, representing about half that number of actual vessels; in 1799 the custom house returns showed not 100 entries, and in 1800 about 140, representing a capacity of 40,000 tons. In the three years 1790-1792, the returns showed an average of some 280 outward and inward entries of American ships with a capacity of 54,000 tons; in 1800 the entries were 1,057, with a capacity of 236,000 tons. The Americans were not only beginning to engross the direct trade between their own ports and Europe, but were also rapidly obtaining the indirect carrying-trade between the West Indies and the European continent, and even between one European country and another. The British government began to feel seriously uneasy. At a frightful cost the people of England were striving to crush the navies and commerce of France and Spain, only to build up the power of a dangerous rival beyond the ocean. . . . (II, xiv, 321-25)

Whatever happened to the merchant service, the British navy could not be allowed to suffer. England knew no conscription for her armies, because for centuries she had felt no need of general military service; but at any moment she might compel her subjects to bear arms, if circumstances required it. Her necessities were greater on the ocean. There, from time immemorial, a barbarous sort of conscription, known as impressment, had been the ordinary means of supplying the royal navy in emergencies; and every seafaring man was liable to be dragged at any moment from his beer cellar or coasting vessel to man the guns of a frigate on its way to a three years' cruise in the West Indies or the Mediterranean. Mere engagement in a foreign merchant service did not release the British sailor from his duty. When the captain of a British frigate overhauled an American merchant vessel for enemy's property or contraband of war, he sent an officer on board who mustered the crew, and took out any seamen whom he believed to be British. The measure, as the British navy regarded it, was one of self-protection. If the American government could not or would not discourage desertion, the naval commander would recover his men in the only way he could. Thus a circle of grievances was established on each side. Pitt's concessions to the United States irritated the British navy and merchant marine, while they gave great profits to Ameri-

can shipping; the growth of American shipping stimulated desertions from the British service to the extent of injuring its efficiency;
and these desertions in their turn led to a rigorous exercise of the
right of impressment. To find some point at which this vicious circle
could be broken was a matter of serious consequence to both countries, but most so to the one which avowed that it did not mean to
protect its interests by force. . . . (II, xiv, 335-36)

Setting the matter of impressment aside, the relations between
England and America had never been better than when the new
President took office March 4, 1801. The British government seemed
earnest in conciliation, and lost no opportunity of showing its good
will. Under the Sixth Article of Jay's treaty, a commission had been
appointed to settle longstanding debts due to British subjects, but
held in abeyance by State legislation in contravention of the treaty
of 1783. After long delays the commission met at Philadelphia and
set to work, but had made little progress when the two American
commissioners, with the President's approval, in the teeth of the
treaty which created the Board, refused to accept its decisions, and
seceded. This violent measure was not taken by the Administration
without uneasiness, for England might reasonably have resented it;
but after some further delay the British government consented to
negotiate again, and at last accepted a round sum of three million
dollars in full discharge of the British claim. This was a case in
which England was the aggrieved party; she behaved equally well
in other cases where the United States were aggrieved. Rufus King
complained that her admiralty courts in the West Indies and at
Halifax were a scandal; in deference to his remonstrances these
courts were thoroughly reformed by Act of Parliament. The vice-
admiralty court at Nassau condemned the American brigantine
"Leopard," engaged in carrying Malaga wine from the United States
to the Spanish West Indies. The American minister complained of
the decision, and within three days the King's Advocate reported
in his favor. The report was itself founded on Sir William Scott's
favorable decision in the case of the "Polly." Soon afterward the
American minister complained that Captain Pellew, of the "Cleo-
patra," and Admiral Parker had not effectually restrained their subordinates on the American station; both officers were promptly recalled. Although the Ministry had not yet consented to make any
arrangement on the practice of impressment, Rufus King felt much
hope that they might consent even to this reform; meanwhile Lord

Grenville checked the practice, and professed a strong wish to find
some expedient that should take its place.

There was no reason to doubt the sincerity of the British Foreign
Office in wishing friendship. Its policy was well expressed in a
despatch written from Philadelphia by Robert Liston, the British
minister, shortly before he left the United States to return home:—

"The advantages to be ultimately reaped from a perseverance in the
line of conduct which Great Britain has adopted for the last four years
appear to my mind to be infallible and of infinite magnitude; the
profitable consequences of a state of hostility, small and uncertain. I
have been pleasing my imagination with looking forward to the distant
spectacle of all the northern continent of America covered with
friendly though not subject States, consuming our manufactures, speaking our language, proud of their parent State, attached to her prosperity. War must bring with it extensive damage to our navigation,
the probable loss of Canada, and the *world* behind it, the propagation
of enmity and prejudices which it may be impossible to eradicate.
The system of the American government does not strike me, with the
near view I have of it, as being in so perilous a situation as is imagined
in Europe. I am willing to avoid political prophecies, but I confess I
think it will get on well enough if the country remains in peace;
and if they go to war, the fabric may acquire strength. God forbid
that it should be to our detriment, and to the triumph of our enemies!"
. . . (II, xiv, 339-41)

The Louisiana question being settled, the field was clear for the
United States to take high ground in behalf of neutral rights; and
inevitably the first step must be taken against England. No one
denied that thus far the administration of Addington[49] had behaved
well toward the United States. Rufus King brought to America at
the same time with news of the Louisiana treaty, or had sent shortly
before, two conventions by which long-standing differences were
settled. One of these conventions disposed of the old subject of
British debts—the British government accepting a round sum of
£600,000 on behalf of the creditors. The other created two com-
missions for running the boundary line between Maine and Nova
Scotia, and between the Lake of the Woods and the Mississippi
River. King went so far as to express the opinion that had he not
been on the eve of his departure, he might have succeeded in mak-

[49] Henry Addington, later first Viscount Sidmouth: Tory Prime Minister,
1801-1804.

ing some arrangement about impressments; and he assured Gallatin that the actual Administration in England was the most favorable that had existed or could exist for the interests of the United States; its only misfortune was its weakness. The conduct of the British government in regard to Louisiana proved the truth of King's assertion. Not only did it offer no opposition to the sale, but it lent every possible assistance to the transfer; and under its eye, with its consent, Alexander Baring[50] made the financial arrangements which were to furnish Bonaparte with ten million American dollars to pay the preliminary expenses of an invasion of England.

Nevertheless, if the United States government intended to take a high tone in regard to neutral rights, it must do so from the beginning of the war. Aware that success in regard to England, as in regard to Spain, depended on asserting at the outset, and maintaining with obstinacy, the principles intended to be established, the President and Secretary Madison lost no time in causing their attitude to be clearly understood. An opportunity of asserting this authoritative tone was given by the appearance of a new British minister at Washington; and thus it happened that at the time when the Secretary of State was preparing for his collision with the Marquis of Casa Yrujo and the Spanish empire, he took on his hands the more serious task of curbing the pretensions of Anthony Merry and the King of England. . . . (II, xv, 357-59)

On the occasion of Merry's[51] reception, the President's chief offence in etiquette consisted in the slippers without heels. No law of the United States or treaty stipulation forbade Jefferson to receive Merry in heelless slippers, or for that matter in bare feet, if he thought proper to do so. Yet Virginia gentlemen did not intentionally mortify their guests; and perhaps Madison would have done better to relieve the President of such a suspicion by notifying Merry beforehand that he would not be expected to wear full dress. In that case the British minister might have complimented Jefferson by himself appearing in slippers without heels.

A card of invitation was next sent, asking Mr. and Mrs. Merry to dine at the White House, December 2. Such an invitation was in

---

[50] Alexander Baring: partner in the London Banking house of Baring Brothers.
[51] Anthony Merry: British Minister, sent to Washington in 1803 as a friendly gesture.

diplomatic usage equivalent to a command, and Merry at once accepted it. The new minister was then told that he must call on the heads of departments. He remonstrated, saying that Liston, his predecessor, had been required to make the first visit only to the Secretary of State; but he was told, in effect, that what had been done under the last Administration was no rule for the present one. Merry acquiesced, and made his calls. These pin thrusts irritated him; but he was more seriously inconvenienced by the sudden withdrawal of diplomatic privileges by the Senate, although Vice-President Burr took occasion to explain that the Senate's action was quite unconnected with the President's "canons of etiquette," and was in truth due to some indiscretion of Yrujo in the House of Representatives.

Meanwhile the President took an unusual step. When two countries were at war, neutral governments commonly refrained from inviting the representative of one belligerent to meet the representative of the other, unless on formal occasions where the entire diplomatic body was invited, or in crowds where contact was not necessary. Still more rarely were such incongruous guests invited to an entertainment supposed to be given in honor of either individual. No one knew this rule better than Jefferson, who had been himself four years in diplomatic service at Paris, besides being three years Secretary of State to President Washington at Philadelphia. He knew that the last person whom Merry would care to meet was Pichon,[52] the French *chargé;* yet he not only invited Pichon, but pressed him to attend. The Frenchman, aware that Merry was to be mortified by the etiquette of the dinner, and watching with delight the process by which Jefferson, day after day, took a higher tone toward England, wrote an account of the affair to Talleyrand. He said:—

"I was invited to this dinner. I had learned from the President what was the matter (*ce qui en était*), when I went to tell him that I was going for some days to Baltimore, where I was called by the affairs of the frigate "La Poursuivante." The President was so obliging as to urge my return in order to be present with Mme. Pichon at the dinner (*Le Président eut l'honnêteté de me presser de revenir pour être au diner*). I came back here, although business required a longer stay at Baltimore. Apart from the reason of respect due to the President, I had that of witnessing what might happen (*j'avais celle de connaître ce qui se passerait*)."

[52] Louis André Pichon: French *chargé d'affaires* until 1804.

Pichon accordingly hurried back from Baltimore, especially at the President's request, in order to have the pleasure of seeing Jefferson humiliate his own guest in his own house.

Pichon was gratified by the result. At four o'clock on the afternoon of December 2, 1803, this curious party assembled at the White House,—Mr. and Mrs. Merry, the Marquis Yrujo and his American wife, M. Pichon and his American wife, Mr. and Mrs. Madison, and some other persons whose names were not mentioned. When dinner was announced, the President offered his hand to Mrs. Madison and took her to table, placing her on his right. Mme. Yrujo took her seat on his left.

"Mrs. Merry was placed by Mr. Madison below the Spanish minister, who sat next to Mrs. Madison. With respect to me," continued the British minister in his account of the affair, "I was proceeding to place myself, though without invitation, next to the wife of the Spanish minister, when a member of the House of Representatives passed quickly by me and took the seat, without Mr. Jefferson's using any means to prevent it, or taking any care that I might be otherwise placed. . . .

"I will beg leave to intrude a moment longer on your Lordship's time," continued Merry's report, "by adding to this narrative that among the persons (none of those who were of this country were the principal officers of the government except Mr. Madison) whom the President selected for a dinner which was understood to be given to me, was M. Pichon the French *chargé d'affaires*. I use the word *selected*, because it could not be considered as a diplomatic dinner, since he omitted to invite to it the Danish *chargé d'affaires*, who, with the Spanish minister, form the whole body."

Merry's report was brief; but Yrujo, who also made an official report to his Government, after mentioning the neglect shown to Merry before dinner, added a remark that explained the situation more exactly:—

"I observed immediately the impression that such a preceeding of the President must have on Mr. and Mrs. Merry; and their resentment could not but be increased at seeing the manifest, and in my opinion studied, preference given by the President throughout to me and my wife over him and Mrs. Merry."

There the matter might have rested, had not Madison carried the new "canons" beyond the point of endurance. December 6, four days after the dinner at the White House, the British minister was to dine with the Secretary of State. Pichon and Yrujo were again present, and all the Cabinet with their wives. Yrujo's report described the scene that followed.

> "I should observe," said he, "that until then my wife and I had enjoyed in the houses of Cabinet ministers the precedence of which we had been deprived in the President's house; but on this day the Secretary of State too altered his custom, without informing us beforehand of his resolution, and took to table the wife of the Secretary of the Treasury. This unexpected conduct produced at first some confusion, during which the wife of the British minister was left without any one giving her his hand, until her husband advanced, with visible indignation, and himself took her to table."

Even Pichon, though pleased to see the British minister humbled, felt his diplomatic pride a little scandalized at this proceeding. He admitted that it was an innovation, and added,—

> "There is no doubt that Mr. Madison in this instance wished to establish in his house the same formality as at the President's, in order to make Mr. Merry feel more keenly the scandal he had made; but this incident increased it."

The scandal which Merry had made consisted in saying that he believed his treatment at the White House was a premeditated insult against his country. Madison's course took away any remaining doubt on the subject in his mind. Merry became bitter. He wrote home informally:—

> "On this occasion, also, the *pas* and the preference in every respect was taken by, and given to, the wives of the Secretaries of the Departments (a set of beings as little without the manners as without the appearance of gentlewomen), the foreign ministers and their wives being left to take care of themselves. In short the latter are now placed here in a situation so degrading to the countries they represent, and so personally disagreeable to themselves, as to have become almost intolerable. The case yesterday was so marked and so irritating that I determined to hand Mrs. Merry myself to the table, and to place ourselves wherever we might conveniently find seats."

Merry then received an official explanation that Jefferson invariably gave precedence to the wives of the Cabinet ministers, and that he made no exceptions in favor of foreigners in his rule of *pêle-*

mêle. Merry notified Lord Hawkesbury[53] to that effect. He did not fail to point out the signs which indicated to him that these proceedings were but part of a general plan intended to press on the British government. . . . (II, xvi, 367-72)

[53] Robert Bankes Jenkinson, Lord Hawkesbury: Tory Foreign Secretary, later (as second Earl of Liverpool) Prime Minister.

II.

Pacific Nationalism:
"...an experiment which could
succeed only in a world
of their own"—1805-1809

1.

Prologue

A second time President Jefferson appeared at the Capitol, escorted with due formalities by a procession of militiamen and other citizens; and once more he delivered an inaugural address, "in so low a voice that not half of it was heard by any part of the crowded auditory." The second Inaugural roused neither the bitterness nor the applause which greeted the first, although in part it was intended as a cry of triumph over the principles and vanishing power of New England.

Among Jefferson's manuscripts he preserved a curious memorandum explaining the ideas of this address. As the first Inaugural declared the principles which were to guide the government in Republican hands, the second should report the success of these principles, and recall the results already reached. The task deserved all the eloquence and loftiness of thought that philosophy could command; for Jefferson had made a democratic polity victorious at home and respectable in the world's eyes, and the privilege of hearing him reaffirm his doctrines and pronounce their success was one that could never be renewed. The Moses of democracy, he had the glory of leading his followers into their promised and conquered Canaan.

Jefferson began by renewing the professions of his foreign policy—

"With nations, as with individuals, our interests, soundly calculated, will ever be found inseparable from our moral duties; and history bears witness to the fact that a just nation is taken on its word, when recourse is had to armaments and wars to bridle others."

The sentiments were excellent; but many of Jefferson's followers must have asked themselves in what history they could find the fact, which the President asserted, that a just nation was taken on its word; and they must have been still more perplexed to name the nation, just or unjust, which was taken on its word by any other in the actual condition of the world. Without dwelling on this topic, which had already become one of interest in the councils of his Cabinet, Jefferson, passing to practical questions involved in redemption of debt, advanced a new idea.

"Redemption once effected," he said, "the revenue thereby liberated may, by a just repartition among the States and a corresponding amendment of the Constitution, be applied, *in time of peace*, to rivers, canals, roads, arts, manufactures, education, and other great objects within each State. *In time of war,*—if injustice, by ourselves or others, must sometimes produce war,—increased as the same revenue will be increased by population and consumption, and aided by other resources reserved for that crisis, it may meet within the year all the expenses of the year without encroaching on the rights of future generations by burdening them with the debts of the past. War will then be but a suspension of useful works, and a return to a state of peace a return to the progress of improvement."

Ten years earlier, in the mouth of President Washington, this sentiment would have been generally denounced as proof of monarchical designs. That Jefferson was willing not only to assume powers for the central government, but also to part from his States' rights associates and to gratify the Northern democrats by many concessions of principle, his first Administration had already proved; but John Randolph might wonder to see him stride so fast and far toward what had been ever denounced as Roman imperialism and corruption; to hear him advise a change of the Constitution in order to create an annual fund for public works, for the arts, for education, and even for such manufactures as the people might want—a fund which was to be distributed to the States, thus putting in the hands of the central government an instrument of corruption, and making the States stipendiaries of Congress. Every principle of the Republican party, past or to come, was put to nought by a policy which contradicted the famous sentiment of Jefferson's first annual message: "Sound principles will not justify our taxing industry of our fellow citizens to accumulate treasure for wars to happen we know not when, and which might not perhaps happen but from the temptations offered by that treasure." Yet pregnant as this new principle might be in connection with the Constitution and the Union, its bearing on foreign affairs was more startling.

Jefferson, the apostle of peace, asked for a war fund which should
enable his government to wage indefinite hostilities without borrowing money!

Quitting this dangerous ground, the President spoke of the Louisiana purchase. Then followed a paragraph upon religion. Next he
came to the subject of the Indians, and chose this unusual medium
for enforcing favorite philosophical doctrines. The memorandum
written to explain his address declared the reasons that led him
to use the mask of Indian philanthropy to disguise an attack upon
conservatism.

"Every respecter of science," said this memorandum, "every friend
to political reformation, must have observed with indignation the
hue-and-cry raised against philosophy and the rights of man; and it
really seems as if they would be overborne, and barbarism, bigotry,
and despotism would recover the ground they have lost by the advance of the public understanding. I have thought the occasion
justified some discountenance of these antisocial doctrines, some testimony against them; but not to commit myself in direct warfare on
them, I have thought it best to say what is directly applied to the
Indians only, but admits by inference a more general extension."

In truth, under the lead of Napoleon and Pitt, Europe seemed
bent on turning back the march of time and renewing the bigotry
and despotism of the Middle Ages; but this occasion hardly dignified Jefferson's method of bearing testimony against the danger,
by not committing himself to direct warfare upon it, but by applying to Indians the homily which by inference included the churches
of New England.

"The aboriginal inhabitants of these countries," said the President
to his great audience, "I have regarded with the commiseration their
history inspires. Endowed with the faculties and the rights of men,
breathing an ardent love of liberty and independence, and occupying
a country which left them no desire but to be undisturbed, the stream
of overflowing population from other regions directed itself on these
shores."

If the Boston newspapers were not weary of ridiculing Jefferson's
rhetoric, this sentence was fitted to rouse their jaded amusement;
but in a few moments they had reason to feel other emotions. He
said that he had done what humanity required, and had tried to
teach the Indians agriculture and other industries in order to pre-

pare them for new conditions of life,—a claim not only true, but also honorable to him. Unfortunately these attempts met with obstacles from the Indians themselves:—

> "They are combated by the habits of their bodies, prejudice of their minds, ignorance, pride, and the influence of interested and crafty individuals among them, who feel themselves something in the present order of things, and fear to become nothing in any other. These persons inculcate a sanctimonious reverence for the customs of their ancestors; that whatsoever they did must be done through all time; that reason is a false guide, and to advance under its counsel, in their physical, moral, or political condition, is perilous innovation; that their duty is to remain as their Creator made them, ignorance being safety, and knowledge full of danger. In short, my friends, among them is seen the action and counteraction of good sense and bigotry; they too have their antiphilosophers, who find an interest in keeping things in their present state, who dread reformation, and exert all their faculties to maintain the ascendency of habit over the duty of improving our reason and obeying its mandates."

Gallatin remonstrated in vain against this allusion to New England habits; the President could not resist the temptation to strike once more his old enemies. Gallatin, whose sense of humor was keener than that of Jefferson, must have been amused by the travesty of New England under the war-paint and blankets of the Choctaws and Kickapoos; but Jefferson was never more serious than in believing that the people of Massachusetts and Connecticut were held in darkness by a few interested "medicine men," and that he could, without committing himself in direct warfare, insult the clergy, lawyers, and keen-witted squirarchy of New England, thus held up "by inference" to the world as the equivalent to so many savages.

The rest of the Inaugural was chiefly devoted to the press and its licentiousness. Jefferson expressed himself strongly in regard to the slanders he had received, and even hinted that he would be glad to see the State laws of libel applied to punish the offenders; but he pointed out that slander had no political success, and that it might safely be disregarded as a political weapon. He urged "doubting brethren" to give up their fears and prejudices, and to join with the mass of their fellow citizens. "In the mean time let us cherish them with patient affection; let us do them justice, and more than justice, in all competitions of interest." Finally, as though to silence the New England pulpit, he closed with a few words which the clergy might perhaps think misplaced in the mouth of so earnest a deist,— an invocation of "that Being in whose hands we are, who led our forefathers, as Israel of old," to the "country flowing with all the necessaries and comforts of life, . . . and to whose goodness I ask you to join with me in supplications."

The Second Inaugural strode far beyond the first in the path of democracy, away from the landmarks of Virginia republicanism, betraying what Jefferson's friends and enemies alike thought a craving for popularity. If this instinct sometimes led him to forget principles he had once asserted, and which he would some day again declare vital, the quality was so amiable as to cover many shortcomings; but its influence on national growth could not be disputed. Jefferson cherished but one last desire,—to reach the end of his next term without disaster. He frankly expressed this feeling in a letter written to General Heath[1] soon after the autumn election of 1804, which gave him the electoral vote of Massachusetts:—

"I sincerely join you," said he, "in congratulations on the return of Massachusetts into the fold of the Union. This is truly the case wherein we may say, 'This our brother was dead, and is alive again; and was lost, and is found.' It is but too true that our Union could not be pronounced entirely sound while so respectable a member as Massachusetts was under morbid affection. All will now come to rights. . . . The new century opened itself by committing us on a boisterous ocean; but all is now subsiding; peace is smoothing our path at home and abroad; and if we are not wanting in the practice of justice and moderation, our tranquillity and prosperity may be preserved until increasing numbers shall leave us nothing to fear from abroad. With England we are in cordial friendship; with France in the most perfect understanding; with Spain we shall always be bickering, but never at war till we seek it. Other nations view our course with respect and friendly anxiety. Should we be able to preserve this state of public happiness, and to see our citizens, whom we found so divided, rally to their genuine principles, I shall hope yet to enjoy the comfort of that general good will which has been so unfeelingly wrested from me, and to sing at the close of my term that *Nunc dimittis, Domine,* with a satisfaction leaving nothing to desire but the last great audit."

He could not forgive the New England clergy their want of feeling in wresting from him ever so small a share of the general good will, and he looked forward with impatience to the moment when he should enjoy universal applause and respect. In December, 1804,

[1] General William Heath: of Massachusetts, Revolutionary soldier.

when this letter was written, he felt confident that his splendid triumph would last unchecked to the end of his public career; but the prize of general good will, which seemed then almost won, continually eluded his grasp. . . . (III, i, 1-9)

So it happened that Jefferson gave up his Virginia dogmas, and adopted Gallatin's ideas. They were both jealous of the army and navy; but they were willing to spend money with comparative liberality on internal improvements; and the wisdom of this course was evident. Even in a military point of view, roads and canals were more necessary than forts or ships.

The first evidence of change was the proposed fund for internal improvements and war purposes described in the second Inaugural Address. The suggestion was intended to prepare the public for a relaxation of Gallatin's economy. Although the entire debt could not be paid before 1817, only ten and a half millions of bonds remained to be immediately dealt with. By the year 1809 these ten and a half millions would be discharged; and thereafter Gallatin might reduce his annual payments of principal and interest from $8,000,000 to $4,500,000, freeing an annual sum of $3,500,000 for use in other directions. During the next three years Gallatin was anxious to maintain his old system, and especially to preserve peace with foreign nations; but after the year 1808 he promised to relax his severity, and to provide three or four millions for purposes of internal improvement and defence. The rapid increase of revenue helped to create confidence in this calculation, and to hasten decision as to the use of the promised surplus. The President had already decided to convert it into a permanent reserve fund. He looked forward to the moment when, as he expressed it, he could "begin upon canals, roads, colleges, etc." He no longer talked of "a wise and frugal government which shall restrain men from injuring one another, which shall leave them otherwise free to regulate their own pursuits of industry and improvement, and shall not take from the mouth of labor the bread it has earned"; he rather proposed to devote a third of the national revenues to improvements and to regulation of industries.

This theory of statesmanship was broader than that which he had proclaimed four years earlier. Jefferson proved the liberality and elevation of his mind; and if he did this at some cost to his consistency, he did only what all men had done whose minds kept pace with the movement of their time. So far as he could see, at the threshold of his second term, he had every reason to hope that it would be more successful than his first. He promised to annihilate opposition, and no serious obstacle seemed in his path. No doubt his concessions to the spirit of nationality, in winning support from moderate Federalists and self-interested democrats, alienated a few State-rights Republicans, and might arouse uneasiness among old friends; but to this Jefferson resigned himself. He parted company with the "mere metaphysical subtleties" of John Randolph. Except in his aversion to military measures and to formal etiquette, he stood nearly where President Washington had stood ten years before.

The New England hierarchy might grumble, but at heart Massachusetts was already converted. Only with the utmost difficulty, and at the cost of avoiding every aggressive movement, could the Federalists keep control of their State governments. John Randolph flattered himself that if Jefferson's personal authority were removed from the scale, Virginia would again incline to her old principles; but he was mistaken. So long as Virginia held power, she was certain to use it. At no time since the Declaration of Independence had the prospects of nationality seemed so promising as in the spring of 1805. With the stride of the last four years as a standard for the future, no man could measure the possible effects of the coming four years in extending the powers of the government and developing the prosperity of the nation. Gallatin already meditated schemes of internal improvements, which included four great thoroughfares across the Alleghanies, while Fulton was nearly ready with the steamboat. The Floridas could not escape the government's grasp. Even New England must at last yield her prejudices to the spirit of democratic nationality.

No one could wonder if Jefferson's head was somewhat turned by the splendors of such a promise. Sanguine by nature, he felt that every day made more secure the grandeur of his destiny. He could scarcely be blamed for putting a high estimate on the value of his services, for in all modesty he might reasonably ask what name recorded in history would stand higher than his own for qualities of the noblest order in statesmanship. Had he not been first to conceive and to put in practice the theories of future democracy? Had he not succeeded in the experiment? Had he not doubled the national domain? Was not his government a model of republican virtues? With what offence against the highest canons of personal merit could he be charged? What ruler of ancient or modern times,

what Trajan or Antonine, what Edward or Louis, was more un-
selfish or was truer to the interests intrusted to his care? Who had
proposed to himself a loftier ideal? Among all the kings and statesmen who swayed the power of empire, where could one be found
who had looked so far into the future, and had so boldly grappled
with its hopes? . . . (III, i, 18-21)

2.

Florida: A Missed Opportunity

During the administrations of Jefferson and Madison, the national government was in the main controlled by ideas and interests peculiar to the region south of the Potomac, and only to be understood from a Southern standpoint. Especially its foreign relations were guided by motives in which the Northern people felt little sympathy. The people of the Northern States were thinking or doing in certain directions, and their indifference was particularly marked in regard to Florida. Among the varied forms of Southern ambition, none was so constant in influence as the wish to acquire the Floridas, which at moments decided the action of the government in matters of the utmost interest; yet the Northern public, though complaining of southern favoritism, neither understood nor cared to study the subject, but turned impatiently away whenever the Floridas were discussed, as though this were a local detail which in no way concerned the North. If Florida failed to interest the North, it exercised the more control over the South, and over a government southern in character and purpose. Neither the politics of the Union nor the development of events could be understood without treating Florida as a subject of the first importance. During the summer and autumn of 1805,—a period which John Randolph justly regarded as the turning point of Republican administration,— Florida actually engrossed the attention of government. . . . (III, ii, 22-23)

The Eighth Congress had hardly expired, March 3, 1805, amid the confusion and ill-temper which followed the failure of impeachment, when President Jefferson and Secretary Madison began to hear the first mutterings of European disaster. Talleyrand's letter to Armstrong, December 21, 1804, arrived with its blunt announcement that Napoleon meant to oppose every step of Monroe's negotiation at Madrid, and with its declaration that West Florida had not been included in the retrocession of Louisiana to France, but had been refused to France by King Charles. Jefferson was then at Monticello, and thither the documents from Paris followed him. He wrote to Madison that Monroe's case was desperate.

"I consider," said the President, "that we may anticipate the effect of his mission. On its failure as to the main object, I wish he may settle the right of navigating the Mobile, as everything else may await further peaceable proceedings; but even then we shall have a difficult question to decide,—to wit, whether we will let the present crisis in Europe pass away without a settlement."

This letter showed that as early as the month of March, 1805, the President foresaw Monroe's disasters, and began to speculate upon the next step to be taken. The attempt to obtain Florida through Spanish fears had failed; but his first impression was that everything might go on as before, if the Spaniards would consent to a free navigation of the Mobile. Madison was still more vague; his first impulse was to retrace his steps. On March 27, he wrote to the President a singular letter of contradictions.

"I cannot entirely despair," said he, March 27, "that Spain, notwithstanding the support given by France to her claim to West Florida, may yield to our proposed arrangement, partly from its intrinsic value to her, partly from an apprehension of the interference of Great Britain; and that this latter consideration may, as soon as France despairs of her pecuniary object, transfer her weight into our scale. If she [France] should persist in disavowing her right to sell West Florida to the United States, and above all can prove it to have been the mutual understanding with Spain that West Florida was no part of Louisiana, it will place our claim on very different ground,— such probably as would not be approved by the world, and such certainly as would not with that approbation be maintained by force. If our right be good against Spain at all, it must be supported by those rigid maxims of technical law which have little weight in national questions generally, and none at all when opposed to the principles of universal equity. The world would decide that France having sold us the territory of a third party, which she had no right to sell, that party having even remonstrated against the whole transaction, the right of the United States was limited to a demand on France to procure and convey the territory, or to remit *pro tanto* the price, or to dissolve the bargain altogether."

For eighteen months every French and Spanish agent in Washington, Paris, and Madrid had assured Madison, in language varying between remonstrance and insult, that Spain had not ceded West Florida to France; the records of the State Department proved that France had asked for West Florida and had been refused; Jefferson had not ventured to record a claim to West Florida when he received possession of Louisiana, and had been obliged to explain, in language which Gallatin and Randolph though unsatisfactory, the words of the Mobile Act.[2] In spite of this, Madison committed himself and government to the claim that West Florida was a part of Louisiana; he pressed that claim, not against France, but against Spain; he brought Monroe to a rupture with the Spanish government on that issue. . . . (III, iii, 54-56)

Meanwhile the European packets brought news that put a different face on the problem. Sir William Scott's decision in the case of the "Essex" [3] arrived; seizures of American ships by England began; Pitt's great coalition with Russia and Austria against Napoleon took the field, and August 27 Napoleon broke up the camp at Boulogne and began his long-intended movement across the Rhine. Upon Madison's mind this European convulsion acted as an additional reason for doing nothing:—

"Considering the probability of an extension of the war against France, and the influence that may have on her temper toward the United States, the uncertainty of effecting with England such a shape for an arrangement as alone would be admissible, and the possible effects elsewhere of abortive overtures to her, I think it very questionable whether a little delay may not be expedient, especially as in the mean time the English pulse will be somewhat felt by the discussions now on foot by Mr. Monroe."

. . . (III, iii, 73-74)

[2] Mobile Act, February 24, 1804: it extended the revenue laws to all territory ceded by France and, by implication, to Spanish-held territory in West Florida.

[3] Essex Decision: Sir William Scott (later Lord Stowell), judge of the high court of admiralty, declared (July 23, 1805) that American ships, carrying French colonial goods, were liable to seizure unless the shipper could prove that the voyage was to terminate in an American port. *I.e.*, the "broken voyage"—payment of American customs duties and reshipment to a French port—was now declared illegal.

Jefferson himself was weary of indecision. He had rested his wish
for an English alliance on the belief that Napoleon meant to make
peace in Europe in order to attack America; and this idea, never
very reasonable, could have no weight after Napoleon had plunged
into a general European war. No sooner did he receive Madison's
letter of October 16, than he again changed his plan.

"The probability of an extensive war on the continent of Europe,
strengthening every day for some time past, is now almost certain,"
he wrote October 23 to Madison. "This gives us our great desideratum,
time. In truth it places us quite at our ease. We are certain of one
year of campaigning at least, and one other year of negotiation for
their peace arrangements. Should we be now forced into war, it is
become much more questionable than it was whether we should not
pursue it unembarrassed by any alliance, and free to retire from it
whenever we can obtain our separate terms. It gives us time, too, to
make another effort for peaceable settlement. Where should this be
done? Not at Madrid, certainly. At Paris! through Armstrong, or Armstrong and Monroe as negotiators, France as the mediator, the price
of the Floridas as the means. We need not care who gets that, and an
enlargement of the sum we had thought of may be the bait to France,
while the Guadalupe as the western boundary may be the soother of
Spain; providing for our spoliated citizens in some effectual way. We
may announce to France that determined not to ask justice of Spain
again, yet desirous of making one other effort to preserve peace, we
are willing to see whether her interposition can obtain it on terms
which we think just; that no delay, however, can be admitted; and
that in the mean time should Spain attempt to change the *status
quo*, we shall repel force by force, without undertaking other active
hostilities till we see what may be the issue of her interference."

. . . (III, iii, 75-76)

President Jefferson's decision, in October, 1805, to retrace his steps
and reverse a policy which had been publicly and repeatedly proclaimed, was the turning point of his second Administration. No
one can say what might have happened if in August, 1805, Jefferson
had ordered his troops to cross the Sabine and occupy Texas to
the Rio Bravo, as Armstrong[4] and Monroe advised. Such an act
would probably have been supported, as the purchase of Louisiana
had been approved, by the whole country, without regard to Constitutional theories; and indeed if Jefferson succeeded to the rights of
Napoleon in Louisiana, such a step required no defence. Spain

[4] John Armstrong: of New York, succeeded R. R. Livingston, his brother-in-
law, as Minister to France in 1804.

might then have declared war; but had Godoy taken this extreme measure, he could have had no other motive than to embarrass Napoleon by dragging France into a war with the United States, and had this policy succeeded, President Jefferson's difficulties would have vanished in an instant. He might then have seized Florida; his controversies with England about neutral trade, blockade, and impressment would have fallen to the ground, and had war with France continued two years, until Spain threw off the yoke of Napoleon and once more raised in Europe the standard of popular liberty, Jefferson might perhaps have effected some agreement with the Spanish patriots and would then have stood at the head of the coming popular movement throughout the world,—the movement which he and his party were destined to resist. Godoy, Napoleon, Pitt, Monroe, Armstrong, John Randolph, and even the New England Federalists seemed combined to drag or drive him into this path. Its advantages were so plain, even at that early moment, as to overmaster for a whole summer his instinctive repugnance to acts of force.

After long hesitation, Jefferson shrank from the step, and fell back upon his old policy of conquering by peace. . . . (III, iv, 80-81)

3.

Inertia and Uneasiness

How long a government could maintain its authority by mere momentum of inert mass had become a serious question to Jefferson and his successor. . . . (III, viii, 196)

In domestic matters no serious division of opinion existed. The American people went to their daily tasks without much competition or mental effort and had no more wish to wrangle about problems of the future than to turn back on their path and face Old-World issues. Every day a million men went to their work, every evening they came home with some work accomplished; but the result was matter for a census rather than for history. The acres brought into cultivation, the cattle bred, the houses built, proved no doubt that human beings, like ants and bees, could indefinitely multiply their numbers, and could lay up stores of food; but these statistics offered no evidence that the human being, any more than the ant and bee, was conscious of a higher destiny, or was even mechanically developing into a more efficient animal. As far as politics proved anything, the evidence seemed to show that the American tended already to become narrow in his views and timid in his methods. The great issues of 1776 and 1787 had dwindled into disputes whether robbery and violence should be punished by refusing to buy millinery and hardware from the robbers, and whether an unsuccessful attempt to purloin foreign territory should be redeemed by bribing a more powerful nation to purloin it at second hand. The great issues of democracy and republicanism were still alive, but their very success removed these subjects for the moment from the field of politics. That a democracy could for so long a time maintain itself above Old World miseries was a triumph; but thus far the democracy had been favored by constant good fortune, and even in these five years conservatives thought they felt a steady decline of moral tone. What would happen when society should be put to some violent test?

In politics nothing that proved progress could be seen. In other directions little positive result had been reached.

Far in the wilderness a few men, in the pay of the United States government, were toiling for the advancement of knowledge. In the summer of 1805 General Wilkinson ordered Lieutenant Pike, a young officer in the first infantry, to take a sergeant, a corporal, and seventeen privates, and ascertain the true sources of the Mississippi. For scientific purposes such a party of explorers could do little of permanent value, but as a military reconnoissance it might have uses. Lieutenant Pike worked his way up the stream from St. Louis. October 16, 1805, he reached a point two hundred and thirty-three miles above the Falls of St. Anthony, and there stopped to establish a winter station. December 10 he started again with a part of his men and went northward with sleds until, January 8, 1806, he reached a British trading station on Sandy Lake, from which he struggled to Leech Lake, where another British establishment existed. His visit was rather an act of formal authority than a voyage of exploration; but he notified both the British and the Indian occupants of the territory that they were under the rule of the United States government. After accomplishing this object he began his return march February 18, and reached St. Louis April 30, 1806, having shown such energy and perseverance in this winter journey as few men could have surpassed.

General Wilkinson was so well pleased with the success of the expedition that he immediately ordered Pike upon another. This time the headwaters of the Arkansas and Red rivers were to be explored as far as the Spanish settlements of New Mexico. July 15, 1806, with about the same number of men as before, Pike left St. Louis, and September 1 reached the Osage towns on the Missouri River. Striking across the prairie, he marched through a country filled with jealous Pawnee Indians, till he reached the Arkansas River, and ascending its branches, left a permanent monument to his visit by giving his name to Pike's Peak in Colorado. Turning toward the southwest, he entangled himself in the mountains; and after suffering terribly in snow and ice, at last, Feb. 26, 1807, was stopped by the Spanish authorities at Santa Fe, who sent him to Chihuahua, and thence allowed him to return through Texas to the United States.

Both these expeditions were subordinate to the larger exploration of Lewis and Clark, which President Jefferson himself organized, and in which he took deep interest. After passing the winter at the Mandan village, as has been already told, Lewis with thirty-two men set out April 7 in boats and canoes for the headwaters of the Missouri. The journey proved to be full of labor, but remarkably free from danger; the worst perils encountered were from rattle-snakes and bears. The murderous Sioux were not seen; and when, August 11, Lewis reached the end of river nagivation, and found himself at the base of the mountains that divided the waters of the Missouri from those of the Columbia, his greatest anxiety was to meet the Indians who occupied the line of passage. His troubles rose from the poverty, rather than from the hostility, of these tribes. They supplied him with horses and with such provisions as they had, and he made his way peacefully down the western slope until he could again take canoes. November 7 the explorers reached the mouth of the Columbia River, and saw at last the ocean which bounded American ambition. There they were forced to pass the winter in extreme discomfort, among thievish and flea-bitten In-dians, until March 26, 1807, they could retrace their steps.

Creditable as these expeditions were to American energy and enterprise, they added little to the stock of science or wealth. Many years must elapse before the vast region west of the Mississippi could be brought within reach of civilization. The crossing of the continent was a great feat, but nothing more. The French ex-plorers had performed feats almost as remarkable long before; but, in 1805, the country they explored was still a wilderness. Great gains to civilization could be made only on the Atlantic coast under the protection of civilized life. For many years to come progress must still center in the old thirteen States of the Union. The expeditions of Lewis and Pike returned no immediate profits; but in the city of New York men were actively engaged in doing what Lewis could not do,—bringing the headwaters of the western rivers within reach of private enterprise and industry. While Lewis slowly toiled up the Missouri River, thinking himself fortunate if he gained twenty miles a day against the stream, the engine which Robert Fulton had ordered from the works of Watt and Bolton in England had been made, and Fulton returned to New York to superintend its use. With the money of Chancellor Livingston he began to construct the hull of his new steamboat and adjust it to the engine.

The greatest steps in progress were often unconsciously taken, and Fulton's steamboat was an example of this rule. Neither in private talk nor in the newspapers did his coming experiment rouse much notice. To the public, Fulton's idea, though visionary, was not new. Indeed Fulton stood in imminent danger of being forestalled by rivals. In 1804 Oliver Evans experimented with a stern-wheel steamboat on the Delaware River, while at the same time John C. Stevens was experimenting with a screw-propeller on the Hudson. Nothing practical had as yet come from these attempts. The public seemed to regard them as matters which did not concern it, and the few thousand dollars needed to pay for a proper engine and hull could with difficulty be wrung from capitalists, who were derided for their folly. Fulton worked with better support than his predecessors had enjoyed, but with little encouragement or show of interest from the press or the public.

So far as concerned activity of mind, politics still engrossed public attention. The summer of 1806, quiet and prosperous as it seemed, betrayed uneasiness,—a mysterious political activity, connected with no legitimate purpose of party. Except in Connecticut and Massachusetts, the Federalists, as an organized body, could hardly be said to exist. Democrats, Republicans, and Federalists were divided for the moment rather by social distinctions than by principle; but the division was not the less real. Every year added strength to the national instinct; but every year brought also a nearer certainty that the denationalizing forces, whether in New England under Timothy Pickering, or in Virginia under John Randolph, or in Louisiana under some adventurer, would make an effort to break the chain that hampered local interests and fettered private ambition. Under a Virginia President and a slave-owning majority of Congress, the old antinational instinct of Virginia was paralyzed, and the dangers to rise from it were postponed; but the freer play was given to the passions of Boston and New Orleans,—to the respectable seditiousness of Timothy Pickering and the veneered profligacy of Aaron Burr. The time had come when Burr was to bring his conspiracy to the test of action, and to try the strength of a true democracy. During the autumn of 1806 Burr's projects and movements roused a sudden panic, less surprising than the tolerance with which his conspiracy had been so long treated by the President and the press. . . . (III, ix, 212-18)

When Burr ceased to be Vice-President of the United States, March 4, 1805, he had already made himself intimate with every element of conspiracy that could be drawn within his reach. The list of his connections might have startled Jefferson, if the President's easy optimism had not been proof to fears. In London, Burr's friend Colonel Williamson confided his plans to Pitt and Lord Melville. At Washington the British minister, Merry, wrote to Lord Mulgrave in support of Williamson's negotiation. The creole deputies from New Orleans were Burr's friends, and Derbigny was acquainted with "certain projects" he entertained. General Wilkinson, governor of the Louisiana Territory, whose headquarters were at St. Louis, closely attached to Burr almost from childhood, stood ready for any scheme that promised to gratify inordinate ambition. James Brown, Secretary of the Territory, was Burr's creature. Judge Prevost, of the Superior Court at New Orleans, was Burr's stepson. Jonathan Dayton, whose term as senator ended the same day with Burr's vice-presidency, shared and perhaps suggested the "projects." John Smith, the senator from Ohio, was under the influence of Burr and Dayton. John Adair of Kentucky was in Wilkinson's confidence. The Swartwouts in New York, with the "little band" who made Burr their idol, stood ready to follow him wherever he might lead. In South Carolina Joseph Allston, the husband of Theodosia Burr, might be induced to aid his father-in-law; and Allston was supposed to be the richest planter in the South, worth a million of dollars in slaves and plantations. The task of uniting these influences and at a given moment raising the standard of a new empire in the Mississippi Valley seemed to an intriguer of Burr's metal not only feasible, but certain of success. . . . (III, x, 219-20)

Burr's expedition met with an inglorious and somewhat ridiculous end before it came within sight of Wilkinson or his command. After leaving Fort Massac, the little flotilla entered the Mississippi, and in a few days reached Chickasaw Bluffs, where a small military post of nineteen men was stationed, commanded by a second lieutenant of artillery, who had received no more instructions than had been received by Captain Bissell. So far from stopping the flotilla, Lieutenant Jackson was nearly persuaded to join it, and actually accepted money from Burr to raise a company in his service. January 6, leaving Chickasaw Bluffs, the flotilla again descended the river until, January 10, it reached the mouth of Bayou Pierre, about thirty miles above Natchez. There Burr went ashore, and at the house of a certain Judge Bruin he saw a newspaper containing the letter which he had himself written in cipher to Wilkinson July 29, and which Wilkinson had published December 26.

From the moment Burr saw himself denounced by Wilkinson, his only hope was to escape. The President's proclamation[5] had reached the Mississippi Territory; Cowles Meade, the acting-governor, had called out the militia. If Burr went on he would fall into the hands of Wilkinson, who had every motive to order him to be court martialled and shot; if he stayed where he was, Cowles Meade would arrest and send him to Washington. Moving his flotilla across the river, Burr gave way to despair. Some ideas of resistance were entertained by Blennerhassett[6] and the other leaders of the party; but they were surprised to find their "emperor" glad to abdicate and submit. January 17 Burr met Acting-Governor Cowles Meade and surrendered at discretion. His conversation at that moment was such that Meade thought him insane. January 21 he caused his cases of muskets, which had been at first secreted in the brush, to be sunk in the river. After his surrender he was taken to Washington, the capital of the Territory, about seven miles from Natchez. A grand jury was summoned, and the attorney general, Poindexter, attempted to obtain an indictment. The grand jury not only threw out the bill, but presented the seizure of Burr and his accomplices as a grievance. The very militia who stopped him were half inclined to join his expedition. Except for a score of United States officials, civil and military, he might have reached New Orleans without a check.

Fortunately neither the civil nor the military authorities of the national government were disposed to be made a jest. The grand jury could grant but a respite, and Burr had still to decide between evils. If he fell into Wilkinson's hands he risked a fate of which he openly expressed fear. During the delay his men on the flotilla had become disorganized and insubordinate; his drafts on New York had been returned protested; he knew that the military authorities at Fort Adams were determined to do what the civil authorities had failed in doing; and his courage failed him when he realized that he must either be delivered to President Jefferson, whom he had defied, or to General Wilkinson, whom he had tried to deceive.

February 1, 1807, after sending to his friends on the flotilla a note to assure them of his immediate return, Burr turned his back on them, and left them to the ruin for which he alone was responsible. Disguised in the coarse suit of a Mississippi boatman, with a soiled

[5] Jefferson's Proclamation, denouncing the expedition, was issued November 27, 1806.

[6] Harman Blennerhassett: United Irish Exile, owner of Blennerhassett's island on the Ohio below Parkersburg in western Virginia.

white felt hat, he disappeared into the woods, and for nearly a
month was lost from sight. Toward the end of February he was
recognized in a cabin near the Spanish frontier, about fifty miles
above Mobile; and his presence was announced to Lieutenant
Gaines, commanding at Fort Stoddert, near by. Gaines arrested
him. After about three weeks of confinement at Fort Stoddert he
was sent to Richmond in Virginia. In passing through the town of
Chester, in South Carolina, he flung himself from his horse and
cried for a rescue; but the officer commanding the escort seized
him, threw him back like a child into the saddle, and marched on.
Like many another man in American history, Burr felt at last the
physical strength of the patient and long-suffering government
which he had so persistently insulted, outraged, and betrayed.

Not until the end of March, 1807, did Burr reach Richmond;
and in the meanwhile a whole session of Congress had passed,
revolution after revolution had taken place in Europe, and a new
series of political trials had begun for President Jefferson's troubled
Administration. The conspiracy of Burr was a mere episode, which
had little direct connection with foreign or domestic politics, and
no active popular support in any quarter. The affairs of the country
at large felt hardly a perceptible tremor in the midst of the excitement which convulsed New Orleans; and the general public obstinately refused to care what Burr was doing, or to believe that he was
so insane as to expect a dissolution of the Union. . . . (III, xiv,
325-28)

Jefferson's effort to suppress the scandal of Burr's disunion scheme
had its source in motives both pure and generous. Distressed by
the factiousness of the last session, he could feel no wish more
ardent than to restore harmony to his party. The struggle for the
succession threatened to tear from his brows the hard-won laurels
which were his only pleasure, and the reward for infinite labors
and mortifications. So far as he could, he stifled discussion in regard
to the coming change.

"The question," he wrote to Leiper of Pennsylvania, "cannot be
touched without endangering the harmony of the present session of
Congress, and disturbing the tranquillity of the nation itself prematurely and injuriously. . . . The present session is important as having new and great questions to decide, in the decision of which no
schismatic views should take any part."

In this spirit the President shaped his acts. Reunion in a common policy, a controlling impulse, was the motive of his gentleness toward Randolph[7] and the Virginia schismatics, as it was that of his blindness to the doings of Burr.

The Annual Message of December, 1806, was intended to unite the party on a new plane of action, and to prepare the way for Madison's gentle rule. Foreign affairs were to be allowed to drop from sight; France, England, and Spain were to be forgotten; Florida was to be ignored; political energy was to be concentrated upon the harvesting of fruits already ripe. For six years, carrying out the policy of discharging public debt, Gallatin had pursued his economies, in the opinion of many good men pressing them so far as to paralyze Government. The time had come when he could do no more. Twenty-four millions of debt had been paid. Of the remainder about ten millions only could be dealt with; and arrangements were made for discharging these ten millions before Jefferson's term should end. Meanwhile the revenue was growing; the surplus must be disposed of, and the period of pinching economies might cease. Henceforward, Republicans, Democrats, and Federalists might agree on some common system of expenditure.

"The question now comes forward," said the Annual Message, "to what other objects shall these surpluses be appropriated, and the whole surplus of impost, after the entire discharge of the public debt, and during those intervals when the purposes of war shall not call for them? Shall we suppress the impost, and give that advantage to foreign over domestic manufactures? On a few articles of more general and necessary use the suppression in due season will doubtless be right; but the great mass of the articles on which impost is paid are foreign luxuries, purchased by those only who are rich enough to afford themselves the use of them. Their patriotism would certainly prefer its continuance and application to the great purposes of the public education, roads, rivers, canals, and such other objects of public improvement as it may be thought proper to add to the constitutional enumeration of federal powers. By these operations new channels of communication will be opened between the States, the lines of separation will disappear, their interests will be identified, and their union cemented by new and indissoluble ties. Education is here placed among the articles of public care, not that it would be proposed to take its ordinary branches out of the hands of private enterprise, which

[7] Randolph's schismatism, leading to the formation of a dissident extremist group called the Tertium Quids, began after the failure to impeach Chase.

manages so much better all the concerns to which it is equal; but a public institution can alone supply those sciences which, though rarely called for, are yet necessary to complete the circle, all the parts of which contribute to the improvement of the country, and some of them to its preservation."

With an air of apology, as though his old opinions were no longer of practical interest, the President added that an amendment to the Constitution would be necessary in order to bring these new functions within the enumerated objects of government; but to such an amendment he saw no objection, nor did he apprehend difficulty in obtaining it. A broad system of internal improvements; a national university; "a steady, perhaps a quickened, pace in preparations for the defence of our seaport towns and waters; an early settlement of the most exposed and vulnerable parts of our country; a militia so organized that its effective portions can be called to any point in the Union, or volunteers instead of them, to serve a sufficient time,"—these were the objects to which Congress should devote its energies, in order that when the two remaining years of Jefferson's power should come to an end, the fabric of Republican government might be complete.

That Federalist and Democrat could join in accepting such a scheme of action, and could lay aside forever their old, unprofitable disputes, seemed no wild dream. The hope was strengthened by a paragraph of the Message which held out the prospect of removing another serious barrier to perfect harmony:—

. "I congratulate you, fellow citizens, on the approach of the period at which you may interpose your authority constitutionally to withdraw the citizens of the United States from all further participation in those violations of human rights which have been so long continued on the unoffending inhabitants of Africa, and which the morality, the reputation, and the best interests of our country have long been eager to proscribe."

Almost ignoring foreign politics, Jefferson recommended Congress to abolish the slave trade, begin a system of national roads and canals, found a national university, fortify the coasts, and organize the national militia; and had Congress been able or willing to follow promptly his advice, many difficulties would have been overcome before the year 1810 which seemed even twenty years later to bar the path of national progress. Congress, indeed, never succeeded in rising to the level of Jefferson's hopes and wishes; it realized but a small part of the plan which he traced, and what it did was done with little system. The slowness with which political movement lagged behind industrial and social progress could be measured by the fate of President Jefferson's scheme of 1806 for crowning the fabric of Republican government. Not by means of the government, or by virtue of wisdom in the persons trusted with the government, were Jefferson's objects destined at last to be partially attained. . . . (III, xv, 344-48)

4.

The Monroe-Pinkney Treaty

Whatever were the faults or sins of England, they were at least such as Americans could understand. Her Government was guided, as a rule, by interests which were public, permanent, and easily measured. The weight of interests which had driven Pitt into his assault on American commerce was not lessened by the death of Pitt or by the return of Lord Grenville to power. On every side Fox[8] found these interests active in opposition and earnest in pressing arguments against concession. Englishmen were used to giving and receiving hard blows. Seldom long at peace, they had won whatever was theirs by creating a national character in which personal courage was as marked a quality as selfishness; for in their situation no other than a somewhat brutal energy could have secured success. They knew what to think of war, and could measure with some approach to exactness its probable costs and returns, but they were quite unused to being conquered by peace; and they listened with as much contempt as anger to the American theory that England must surrender at discretion if Americans should refuse any longer to buy woolen shirts and tin kettles. Englishmen asked only whether America would fight, and they took some pains to make inquiries on that point; but it happened that of all the points in question this, which to Englishmen was alone decisive, could be answered in a syllable: No! America would not fight. The President, Congress, the press of both parties in the United States agreed only in this particular. . . . (III, xvii, 395-96)

[8] Charles James Fox: famous and friendly Whig, Foreign Secretary in a Tory-Whig coalition known as "The Ministry of all the Talents." He was responsible for the compromising Order-in-Council of May 16, 1806, which declared a blockade to be in existence from Brest to the Elbe, but that it would be strictly enforced only between the Seine and Ostend.

May 31, 1806, news arrived from America that Monroe's powers were superseded by the appointment of a special mission, in which he was to be associated with William Pinkney[9] of Maryland.

The blow to Monroe's pride was great, and shook his faith in the friendship of Jefferson and Madison. Three years had elapsed since he had himself been sent abroad to share Livingston's negotiations, and he had the best reason to know how easily the last comer could carry away the prizes of popularity. The nomination of a colleague warned him that he had lost influence at home, and that Jefferson, however well disposed, no longer depended on him. This was in substance the truth; but other and graver troubles were revealed in part to Monroe's eyes when William Pinkney arrived in London June 24, bringing with him the new instructions which were to become the foundation of the treaty.

These instructions began by treating the Non-importation Act[10] as at once a domestic and a foreign regulation, a pacific and a hostile act, a measure with which England had no right to be angry, and one which was calculated to anger her,—strictly amicable and at the same time sharply coercive. After this preamble, in which the threat was clearer than the explanation, followed an order precluding the possibility of successful negotiation. Monroe was to begin by imposing an ultimatum. The British government must expressly repudiate the right and forbid the practice of impressment, or not only could no treaty be made, but the Non-importation Act should be enforced. "So indispensable is some adequate provision for the case that the President makes it a necessary preliminary to any stipulation requiring a repeal of the Act shutting the market of the United States against certain British manufactures."

Besides this condition precedent, the instructions prescribed as another ultimatum the restoration of the trade with enemies' colonies on its old foundation and indemnity for the captures made under Sir William Scott's late decisions. Three ultimata, therefore, were fixed as conditions without which no treaty could receive the President's assent or procure a repeal of the Non-importation Act. . . . (III, xvii, 399-401)

No harder task could well have been imposed than was laid upon Monroe. Not even when he had been sent to Madrid in defiance of

[9] William Pinkney: a Baltimore lawyer, he had previously served eight years in London as U. S. claims commissioner.

[10] Non-Importation Act of April 18, 1806: suspended December 19, 1806, not operative until December 22, 1808, it forbade the importation of a long list of British goods.

Talleyrand and Godoy, to impose his own terms on two of the greatest powers in the world, had his chance of success been smaller than when his Government required him to obtain from England, after the battle of Trafalgar, concessions which England had steadily refused when she was supposed to be drawing almost her last gasp. For a British ministry to abandon the Rule of 1756 was to challenge opposition; to throw open the colonial trade was to invite defeat; but to surrender the so-called right of impressment was to rush upon destruction. No minister that had ever ruled over the House of Commons could at such a moment have made such a treaty without losing his place or his head.

If America wanted such concessions she must fight for them, as other nations had done ever since mankind existed. . . . (III, xvii, 403)

The negotiation began in earnest August 27, but proved to be long and arduous. The two British commissioners,[11] thought courteous and friendly, stood in constant fear of the charge that they had surrendered vital English interests under American threats. They were especially hampered by the Admiralty, the atmosphere of which, as Lord Holland complained, made those who breathed it shudder at anything like concessions to the Americans; while the Treasury, though naturally still less yielding, listened willingly to every expedient that offered hope for the revenue. September 1 began the struggle over impressments; and from the outset Monroe saw that the American claim had no chance of success, while the case of the West Indian trade was almost equally desperate. Only one serious discussion had taken place when the death of Fox, September 13, produced a new delay of several weeks; and on resuming the negotiation, Monroe and Pinkney were required to deal with a New Foreign Secretary,—Charles Grey, Lord Howick,— to be better known in English history as Earl Grey. Such a change boded no good to the Americans. All Fox's influence could not counteract the Tory instincts of Parliament; and what Fox could not do when the Whigs were strong could much less be done by Lord Howick when the Ministry was every day tottering to its fall.

November 11 the American negotiators wrote home that they had decided to disregard their instructions and to abandon impressments,—accepting, instead of a formal article on the subject, a note in which the British commissioners pledged their government to

[11] Lord Holland, Fox's nephew, and Lord Auckland, president of the Board of Trade.

exercise the strictest care not to impress American citizens, and to afford prompt redress should injury be inflicted while impressing British seamen. Having thus made up his mind to violate instructions on the chief point of negotiation, Monroe found nothing to prevent his doing so in other respects. His progress under William Pinkney's influence was rapid; his good nature, in the face of Lord Holland's difficult position, was extreme; and at the end of a few weeks, December 31, 1806, Jefferson's favorite diplomatic agent set his name to a treaty which, taking its omissions and admissions together, surpassed Jay's treaty in outraging Jefferson's prejudices and express desires.

That a people, like an individual, should for a time choose to accept a wrong, like impressment or robbery, without forcible resistance implied no necessary discredit. Every nation at one time or another had submitted to treatment it disliked and to theories of international law which it rejected. The United States might go on indefinitely protesting against belligerent aggressions while submitting to them, and no permanent evil need result. Yet a treaty was a compromise which made precedent; it recorded rules of law which could not be again discarded; and above all, it abandoned protest against wrong. This was doubtless the reason why Jefferson wished for no treaties in the actual state of the world; he was not ready to enforce his rights, and he was not willing to compromise them.

The treaty signed by Monroe and Pinkney December 1, 1806, was remarkable for combining in one instrument every quality to which Jefferson held most strenuous objections. The three ultimata were all abandoned; impressments were set aside under a diplomatic memorandum which rather recorded the right than restrained its exercise; no indemnity was obtained for the ravages made on American commerce in 1805; and in regard to the colonial trade, a compromise was invented which no self-respecting government could admit. Article XI of the treaty imposed the condition that West Indian produce, coming from French or Spanish colonies, and *bona fide* the property of United States citizens, might be exported from American ports to Europe on condition that it should have paid to the United States custom house a duty of not less than two per cent *ad valorem,* which could not be returned in drawback; while European merchandise might in the same way be re-exported from the United States to the West Indies, provided it paid not less than one per cent *ad valorem* in duties to the American Treasury. This provision was only to be compared with Article XII of Jay's treaty, in which Lord Grenville insisted and Jay agreed that the

United States should export no cotton. Even Pitt had never proposed anything so offensive as the new restriction. He had indeed required that the American merchant whose ship arrived at Baltimore or Boston with a cargo of sugar or coffee from Cuba should unload her, carry the hogsheads and cases into a warehouse, and pass them through all the forms of the American custom house; after which he must turn about and stow them again on shipboard, —an operation which was usually reckoned as equivalent, in breakage, pilfering, and wages, to a charge of about 10 per cent on the value of the cargo; but he had not ventured to levy a duty upon them to be paid to the United States government. One step more, and—as a clever London pamphleteer suggested—the British government would require the American stevedores to wear the King's livery. Had it been stipulated that the custom house payments should be taken as full proof of neutrality and complete protection from seizure, the American merchant might have found a motive for submitting to the tax; but the treaty further insisted that both goods and vessel must be in good faith American property,—a condition which left the door open as widely as ever to the arbitrary seizures of British cruisers and to the equally arbitrary decisions of admiralty courts.

> "We flatter ourselves," Monroe and Pinkney wrote to Madison, "that the sum agreed to be paid will not be felt as a heavy one by our merchants, whose patriotism will be gratified by the recollection that the duty which they pay will redound to the advantage of their country." . . . (III, xvii, 407-11)

Bad as all this was, and contrary to Madison's instructions and Jefferson's private letters, it was not yet the worst. After Monroe had violated his orders,—had abandoned the ultimata and accepted the commercial restrictions which the President disliked,—when the four commissioners were about to sign the treaty, Monroe and Pinkney were startled to hear that the two Englishmen meant to append an explanatory note to their signatures. News of the Berlin Decree[12] had reached England, and its gravity was at once recognized. The British negotiators formally notified Monroe and Pinkney that unless the American government, before ratification, should give security that it would not recognize the decree, his Majesty George

---

[12] The Berlin Decree of November 21, 1806, declared, inter alia, that no ship coming directly from England or her colonies could be received in any port of France or her subject countries. Ships that violated this decree could be confiscated.

III would not consider himself bound by the signatures of his commissioners. Signature under such a condition seemed rather the act of a suppliant people than of one which had not yet so much as bought the sword it should have used. Nevertheless Monroe signed. (III, xvii, 412-13)

March 3, 1807, the last day of the session, a rumor reached the Capitol that a messenger had arrived at the British legation with a copy of the treaty negotiated by Pinkney and Monroe. The news was true. No sooner did Erskine[13] receive the treaty than he hurried with it to Madison, "in hopes that he would be induced to persuade the President either to detain the Senate, which he has the power by the Constitution to do, or to give them notice that he should convene them again." Unlike Merry, Erskine was anxious for a reconciliation between England and America; he tried honestly and overzealously to bring the two governments into accord, but he found Madison not nearly so earnest as himself:

> The first question he asked was, what had been determined on the point of impressment of seamen, claimed as British, out of American ships; and when I informed him that I had not perceived anything that directly referred to that question in any of the Articles of the copy of the treaty which I had received, he expressed the greatest astonishment and disappointment. . . . The note which was delivered in to the American commissioners, previous to the signature of the treaty, by Lords Holland and Auckland, relative to Bonaparte's decree of November 21, particularly attracted his attention; and he observed that the note itself would have prevented, he was convinced, the ratification of the treaty, even if all the Articles of it had been satisfactory, and all the points settled upon the terms that had been required by their commissioners.

At ten o'clock the same night the two Houses of Congress, when ready to adjourn, sent a joint committee to wait upon the President, who was unwell, and unable to go as usual to the Capitol. Dr. Mitchill, the senator from New York, a member of this committee, asked the President whether there would be a call of the Senate to consider the treaty. "Certainly not," replied Jefferson; and he added that "the only way he could account for our ministers having signed such a treaty under such circumstances was by supposing that in the first panic of the French imperial decree they had supposed a war to be inevitable, and that America must make common cause

[13] David Montagu Erskine: British Minister until 1809.

with England. He should, however, continue amicable relations with England, and continue the suspension of the Non-importation Act."

The senators received this rebuff with ill-concealed annoyance. Jefferson's act in refusing to consult them about a matter so important as a British treaty—and one which from the first had been their own rather than the President's scheme—was another instance of the boldness which sometimes contradicted the theory that Jefferson was a timid man. . . . (III, xviii, 429-31)

5.

Jefferson v. Marshall: The Trial of Aaron Burr

March 30, 1807, in a room at the Eagle Tavern in Richmond, Aaron Burr was brought before Chief-Justice Marshall for examination and commitment.[14] Although Burr had been but a few days in the town, he was already treated by many persons as though he had conferred honor upon his country. Throughout the United States the Federalists, who formed almost the whole of fashionable society, affected to disbelieve in the conspiracy and ridiculed Jefferson's sudden fears. The Democrats had never been able to persuade themselves that the Union was really in danger, or that Burr's projects, whatever they were, had a chance of success; and in truth Burr's conspiracy, like that of Pickering and Griswold, had no deep roots in society, but was mostly confined to a circle of well-born, well-bred, and well-educated individuals, whose want of moral sense was one more proof that the moral instinct had little to do with social distinctions. In the case of Burr, Jefferson himself had persistently ignored danger; and no one denied that if danger ever existed, it had passed. Burr was fighting for his life against the power of an encroaching government; and human nature was too simply organized to think of abstract justice or remote principles when watching the weak fight for life against the strong. Even the Democrats were more curious to see Burr than to hang him; and had he gone to the gallows, he would have gone as a hero, like Captain Macheath amidst the admiring crowds of London.

Between Captain Macheath and Colonel Burr was more than one point of resemblance, and the "Beggar's Opera" could have been

[14] Counsel for Burr were Luther Martin, Edmund Randolph, John Wickham, Benjamin Botts, and John Baker. Counsel for the prosecution were George Hay, United States District Attorney; William Wirt; and Alexander MacRae.

easily paralleled within the prison at Richmond; but no part of
Burr's career was more humorous than the gravity with which he
took an injured tone, and maintained with success that Jefferson,
being a trivial person, had been deceived by the stories of Eaton
and Wilkinson, until, under the influence of causeless alarm, he
had permitted a wanton violation of right. From the first step toward commitment, March 30, Burr and his counsel never ceased
their effort to convict Jefferson; until the acquittal of Burr began
to seem a matter of secondary importance compared with the
President's discomfiture.

Over this tournament the chief justice presided as arbiter. Blennerhassett's island, where the overt act of treason was charged to
have taken place, lay within the chief-justice's circuit. . . . (III,
xix, 441-42)

So long as the President dealt only with grand jurors and indict-
ments, he could hardly fail to succeed; but the case was different
when he dealt directly with Chief-Justice Marshall and with the
stubborn words of the Constitution, that "no person shall be convicted of treason unless on the testimony of two witnesses to the
same overt act, or on confession in open court." The district attorney was ready with a mass of evidence, but the chief-justice alone
could say whether a syllable of this evidence should be admitted;
and hitherto the chief-justice had by no means shown a bias toward
the government. Hay was convinced that Marshall meant to protect Burr, and he wrote to the President on the subject:—

"The bias of Judge Marshall is as obvious as if it was stamped upon
his forehead. I may do him injustice, but I do not believe that I am,
when I say that he is endeavoring to work himself up to a state of
f[irmness?] which will enable [him] to aid Burr throughout the trial
without appearing to be conscious of doing wrong. He seems to think
that his reputation is irretrievably gone, and that he has now nothing
to lose by doing as he pleases. His concern for Mr. Burr is wonderful.
He told me many years ago, when Burr was rising in the estimation
of the Republican party, that he was as profligate in principle as he
was desperate in fortune. I remember his words; they astonished me.
Yet when the grand jury brought in their bill, the chief-justice gazed
at him for a long time, without appearing conscious that he was doing
so, with an expression of sympathy and sorrow as strong as the human
countenance can exhibit without palpable emotion."

August 3, the court opened its session and the trial began. Not
until August 17 was the jury impanelled. . . . (III, xix, 461-62)

For a few days the trial went on undisturbed, while the government put . . . a number of other witnesses on the stand to prove an overt act of treason at Blennerhassett's island; but nothing short of Blennerhassett's own confession could place the matter in a clear light, and Burr's chief fear was evidently that Blennerhassett should turn State's evidence. To prevent this, Allston was persuaded to pay the more pressing demands against Blennerhassett, and Burr exerted himself to conciliate him. On the other hand, Jefferson seemed to hope that he could be won over. Duane, of the "Aurora," visited him in prison August 23, and offered to serve as an intermediary with the government. Had matters gone as the President hoped, something might have come of this manoeuvre; but before further pressure could be employed, the chief-justice struck the prosecution dead.

August 19 Burr's counsel suddenly moved to arrest the evidence. The government, they said, had gone through all its testimony relating to the overt act charged in the indictment; it admitted that Burr was hundreds of miles distant from the scene; and as the district attorney was about to introduce collateral testimony of acts done beyond the jurisdiction of the court, it became the duty of the defence to object.

For ten days this vital point was argued. All the counsel on either side exerted themselves to the utmost. Wickham's opening speech on the nature of treason was declared by as good a judge as Littleton Tazewell to be "the greatest forensic effort of the American bar." Luther Martin spoke fourteen hours, beginning with an almost passionate allusion to his idol Theodosia. William Wirt exhausted his powers of argument and oratory, and in the course of his address made the rhetorical display which became familiar to every American, and which introduced a sort of appeal to Blennerhassett to turn against the more guilty crew who were trying to sacrifice him to save themselves:—

"Who is Blennerhassett? A native of Ireland, a man of letters, who fled from the storms of his own country to find quiet in ours."

George Hay was neither so efficient nor so dexterous as Wirt, and either intentionally or by awkwardness succeeded in giving the impression of threatening the court:

Mr. Bott [sic] says that we are now advocating opinions which on Fries' trial we condemned. . . . I beg leave to assure the gentleman

that the censure which the judge drew on himself was not on account
of his opinions, however incorrect they might be, but for his arbitrary
and irregular conduct at the trial, which was one of the principal causes
for which he was afterward impeached. He attempted to wrest the
decision from the jury, and prejudge the case before hearing all the
evidence in it,—the identical thing which this court is now called on
by these gentlemen to do.

That Hay, knowing well Jefferson's thoughts and the magic that
hung about the word "impeachment," should have used these words
inadvertently seemed hardly credible. If he did so, his clumsiness
was as offensive as the threat could have been, for the idea of impeachment was in the air of the court house. Burr's counsel at once
retaliated. "It was very kind of the gentleman to remind the court
of the danger of a decision of the motion in favor of the prisoner."
Hay protested that he had spoken innocently, and the chief-justice
said that the allusion had not been taken as personal; but the unpleasant impression remained. "The gentleman plainly insinuated
the possibility of danger to the court," persisted the defence; and
Luther Martin added,—

"I do not know whether it were intended by this observation that
your honors should be apprehensive of an impeachment in case you
should decide against the wishes of the government. I will not presume
that it was used with that view, but it is susceptible of being so misunderstood, however innocently or inadvertently it may have been
made."

August 31 the chief justice read his decision. Much the longest
of Marshall's judicial opinions; elaborately argued, with many cita-
tions, and with less simple adherence to one leading thought than
was usual in his logic,—this paper seemed, in the imagination of
Marshall's enemies, to betray a painful effort to reconcile his dictum
in Bollman's case[15] with the exclusion of further evidence in the
case of Burr. To laymen, who knew only the uncertainties of law;
who thought that the assemblage on Blennerhassett's island was
such an overt act as might, without violent impropriety, be held by
a jury to be an act of levying war; and who conceived that Burr,
although absent from the spot, was as principal present in a legal
sense such as would excuse a jury in finding him guilty—an uneasy

[15] On February 21, 1807, Marshall ruled, in the case of Justus Bollman, that
mere remoteness from the scene of a treasonable conspiracy did not in itself
constitute innocence.

doubt could not fail to suggest itself that the chief-justice, with an equal effort of ingenuity, might have produced equal conviction in a directly opposite result. On the other hand, the intent of the Constitution was clear. The men who framed that instrument remembered the crimes that had been perpetrated under the pretence of justice; for the most part they had been traitors themselves, and having risked their necks under the law they feared despotism and arbitrary power more than they feared treason. No one could doubt that their sympathies, at least in 1788, when the Constitution was framed, would have been on the side of Marshall's decision. If Jefferson, since 1788, had changed his point of view, the chief-justice was not under obligations to imitate him.

"If it be said that the advising or procurement of treason is a secret transaction which can scarcely ever be proved in the manner required by this opinion, the answer which will readily suggest itself is that the difficulty of proving a fact will not justify conviction without proof."

At the close of his decision the chief justice, with simple dignity which still compels respectful admiration, took up the gauntlet which the district attorney had flung at his feet. As though turning from the crowd in the court room to look for a moment directly into the eyes of the President, the threatened chief justice uttered a few words that were at once answer and defiance:—

"Much has been said in the course of the argument on points on which the Court feels no inclination to comment particularly, but which may perhaps not improperly receive some notice.

"That this Court dares not usurp power is most true; that this Court dares not shrink from its duty is not less true. No man is desirous of placing himself in a disagreeable situation; no man is desirous of becoming the peculiar subject of calumny; no man, might he let the bitter cup pass from him without self-reproach, would drain it to the bottom; but if he has no choice in the case—if there is no alternative presented to him but a dereliction of duty or the opprobrium of those who are denominated the world—he merits the contempt as well as the indignation of his country who can hesitate which to embrace. . . .

"No testimony relative to the conduct or declarations of the prisoner elsewhere and subsequent to the transactions on Blennerhassett's island can be admitted; because such testimony, being in its nature merely corroborative, and incompetent to prove the overt act in itself, is irrelevan until there be proof of the overt act by two witnesses."

On the following day, September 1, District Attorney Hay abandoned the case, and the jury entered a verdict of "Not Guilty." Hay instantly reported to Monticello the result of his efforts, and added criticisms upon Marshall:—

"Wirt, who has hitherto advocated the *integrity* of the chief justice, now abandons him. This last opinion has opened his eyes, and he speaks in the strongest terms of reprobation."

September 4, Jefferson replied in the tone which always accompanied his vexation:—

"Yours of the 1st came to hand yesterday. The event has been what was evidently intended from the beginning of the trial; that is to say, not only to clear Burr, but to prevent the evidence from ever going before the world. But this latter case must not take place. It is now, therefore, more than ever indispensable that not a single witness be paid or permitted to depart until his testimony has been committed to writing. . . . These whole proceedings will be laid before Congress, that they may decide whether the defect has been in the evidence of guilt, or in the law, or in the application of the law, and that they may provide the proper remedy for the past and the future."

Accordingly, although the trial for treason was at an end, the district attorney pressed the indictment for misdemeanor; and until October 19 the chief-justice was occupied in hearing testimony intended for use not against Burr, but against himself. Then at last the conspirators were suffered to go their way, subject to legal proceedings in Ohio which the government had no idea of prosecuting, while the President, mortified and angry, prepared to pursue Marshall instead of Burr. The Federalists, who always overrated the strength of party passions, trembled again for the Judiciary; but in truth nothing was to be feared. The days of Jefferson's power and glory had passed forever, while those of Marshall had barely begun. . . . (III, xix, 464-71)

6.

No More Neutrals

For the first time in their history the people of the United States learned, in June, 1807,[16] the feeling of a true national emotion. Hitherto every public passion had been more or less partial and one-sided; even the death of Washington had been ostentatiously mourned in the interests and to the profit of party: but the outrage committed on the "Chesapeake" stung through hidebound prejudices, and made democrat and aristocrat writhe alike. The brand seethed and hissed like the glowing olive-stake of Ulysses in the Cyclops' eye, until the whole American people, like Cyclops, roared with pain and stood frantic on the shore, hurling abuse at their enemy, who taunted them from his safe ships. . . . (IV, ii, 27)

Jefferson followed without protest the impulse toward war; but his leading thought was to avoid it. Peace was still his passion, and his scheme of peaceful coercion had not yet been tried. Even while the nation was aflame with warlike enthusiasm, his own mind always reverted to another thought. The tone of the proclamation showed it; his unwillingness to call Congress proved it; his letter dwelt upon it.

"We have acted on these principles," he wrote in regard to England,—"(1) to give that Government an opportunity to disavow and

[16] On June 22, 1807, the U. S. frigate *Chesapeake* (Commodore Barron) was hailed by the British frigate *Leopard* off Norfolk Roads. The *Leopard's* commander demanded the surrender of four members of her crew, alleged to be British deserters. When Commodore Barron refused permission to search his ship, which was not cleared for action, the *Leopard* opened fire, killing 3 men, wounding 18, and forcing Barron to strike his flag. To this grave outrage, which infuriated the nation, Jefferson replied with a Proclamation, July 2, denying British warships access to U. S. ports or territorial waters.

make reparation; (2) to give ourselves time to get in the vessels, property, and seamen now spread over the ocean; (3) to do no act which might compromit Congress in their choice between war, non-intercourse, or any other measure."

To Vice-President Clinton he wrote, that since the power of declaring war was with the Legislature, the Executive should do nothing necessarily committing them to decide for war in preference to non-intercourse, "which will be preferred by a great many." Every letter written by the President during the crisis contained some allusion to non-intercourse, which he still called the "peace-able means of repressing injustice, by making it the interest of the aggressor to do what is just, and abstain from future wrong." As the war fever grew stronger he talked more boldly about hostilities, and became silent about non-intercourse; but the delay in calling Congress was certain to work as he wished, and to prevent a com-mittal to the policy of war. . . . (IV, ii, 33-35)

A single blow, however violent, could not weld a nation. Every one saw that the very violence of temper which made the month of July, 1807, a moment without a parallel in American history since the battle of Lexington, would be followed by a long reaction of doubt and discord. If the President, the Secretary of State, and great numbers of their stanchest friends hesitated to fight when a foreign nation, after robbing their commerce, fired into their ships of war, and slaughtered or carried off their fellow citizens—if they preferred "peaceable means of repressing injustice" at the moment when every nerve would naturally have been strung to recklessness with the impulse to strike back—it was in the highest degree un-likely that they would be more earnest for war when time had deadened the sense of wrong. Neither England, France, nor Spain could fail to see that the moment when aggression ceased to be safe had not yet arrived. . . . (IV, ii, 38)

The new Ministry which succeeded "All the Talents" and took seat in Parliament April 8, 1807, represented everything in English society that was most impervious to reason. In its origin a creature of royal bigotry trembling on the verge of insanity, before it had been a few short weeks in office every liberal or tolerant Englishman was shocked to find that this band of Tories, whose prejudices were such as modern society could scarcely understand, and who had been forced into office by the personal will of an almost imbecile King, did in reality represent a great reaction of the English people against tolerant principles, and reflected the true sense of the nation as it had never been reflected by Grenville or Fox. . . . (IV, iii, 55)

From its nominal head, this Ministry was called the Portland administration; but its leader was Spencer Perceval, the Chancellor of the Exchequer, and its mouthpiece was George Canning, the Foreign Secretary. These two commoners—men of no special family connection, of no estates, and little so-called "stake in the country" —guided the aristocratic and conservative society of England, and exaggerated its tendencies. In modern days little is remembered of Spencer Perceval except that he became at last one of the long list of victims to lunatic assassins; but for a whole generation no English Liberal mentioned the name of the murdered prime minister without recalling the portrait drawn by Sydney Smith in the wittiest and keenest of his writings, in which Perceval was figured as living at Hampstead upon stewed meats and claret, and walking to church every Sunday before eleven young gentlemen of his own begetting, with their faces washed and their hair pleasingly combed. . . . (IV, iii, 55-56)

That Timothy Pickering and Roger Griswold should join hands with Aaron Burr was less wonderful that that Spencer Perceval and his friend James Stephen,[17] the author of "War in Disguise," should adopt the violence of Napoleon as the measure of their own morals, and avow that they meant to respect no other standard. With the same voice Spencer Perceval expressed fear lest calling Parliament on a Monday should lead members into Sunday travel, and justified the bombardment of Copenhagen[18] and the robbery of American commerce. . . . (IV, iii, 56-57)

Canning had several qualities in common with Bonaparte, and one of them was the habit of classifying under the head of fools persons whose opinions he did not fancy,—from the man who believed in a republic to the man who liked dry champagne. In his mouth such persons were either fools or liars; and Americans, with few exceptions, came under one or the other of these heads. After

---

[17] James Stephen: Tory M.P. author of *War in Disguise,* a pamphlet denouncing neutral evasions of British commercial regulations.

[18] In September 1807, George Canning ordered the seizure of the Danish fleet and the bombardment of Copenhagen: the purpose of this feral exploit was to preserve Danish neutrality.

the 18th Brumaire the world contained but one leader of a mob faction, brawling for liberty; but he was President of the United States. No miraculous sagacity was needed to foretell what treatment he was likely to receive at the hands of two men like Canning and Bonaparte, should the empire of the world ever be divided between them. To throw lasting ridicule upon all systems of democratic equality was Canning's most passionate wish, and his success was marvellous. . . . (IV, iii, 60)

Except a few Whig noblemen, a number of Yorkshire and Lancashire manufacturers and a great mass of the laboring people, or American merchants like the Barings, and one or two Scotch Liberals who wrote in the "Edinburgh Review," the English public had but one voice against Americans. Young Henry Brougham,[19] not yet thirty years old, whose restless mind persistently asked questions which parsons and squires thought absurd or impious, speculated much upon the causes of this prejudice. Was it because the New York dinners were less elegant than those of London, or because the Yankees talked with an accent, or because their manners were vulgar? No doubt a prejudice might seize on any justification, however small; but a prejudice so general and so deep became respectable, and needed a correct explanation. The British nation was sometimes slow-witted, and often narrow-minded, but was not insane.

For a thousand years every step in the progress of England had been gained by sheer force of hand and will. In the struggle for existence the English people, favored by situation, had grown into a new human type,—which might be brutal, but was not weak; which had little regard for theory, but an immense and just respect for facts. America considered herself to be a serious fact, and expected England to take her at her own estimate of her own value; but this was more than could reasonably be asked. England required America to prove by acts what virtue existed in her conduct or character which should exempt her from the common lot of humanity, or should entitle her to escape the tests of manhood—the trials, miseries, and martyrdoms through which the character of mankind had thus far in human history taken, for good or bad, its vigorous development. England had never learned to strike soft in battle. She expected her antagonists to fight; and if they would not fight, she took them to be cowardly or mean. Jefferson and his government

[19] Henry Peter Brougham: counsel for Liverpool merchants, 1808-1810, Whig M.P., 1810-1812, later Lord Chancellor.

had shown over and over again that no provocation would make them fight; and from the moment that this attitude was understood, America became fair prey. Jefferson had chosen his own methods of attack and defence; but he could not require England or France to respect them before they had been tried.

Contempt for America was founded on belief in American coward-ice; but beneath the disdain lurked an uneasy doubt which gave to contempt the virulence of fear. The English nation, and especially the aristocracy, believed that America was biding her time; that she expected to become a giant; and that if she succeeded, she would use her strength as every other giant in the world's history had done before her. The navy foresaw a day when American fleets might cover the ocean. The merchant dreaded competition with Yankee shrewdness, for he well knew the antiquated processes, the time-honored percentages, the gross absurdities of English trade, the abuses of the custom house, the clumsiness and extravagance of government. The shipowners had even more cause for alarm. Al-ready the American ship was far in advance of the British model —a swifter and more economical sailer, more heavily sparred and more daringly handled. In peace competition had become difficult, until the British shipowner cried for war; yet he already felt, with-out acknowledging it even to himself, that in war he was likely to enjoy little profit or pleasure on the day when the long, low, black hull of the Yankee privateer, with her tapering, bending spars, her long-range gun, and her sharp-faced captain, should ap-pear on the western horizon, and suddenly, at sight of the heavy lumbering British merchantman, should fling out her white wings of canvas and fly down on her prey. . . . (IV, iii, 73-75)

The Orders in Council of November 11, 1807,[20] gave an impulse so energetic to the history of the United States, they worked so effectually to drive America into a new path, and to break the power and blot out the memory of Virginia and Massachusetts principles—that every detail of their history was important. English-men were little likely to dwell on acts of which even at the time England was at heart ashamed, and which she afterward remem-bered with astonishment. To Americans alone the statesmanship

[20] The Orders in Council of November 11, 1807, ostensibly a retaliation upon the Berlin Decree, actually forbade any commerce with European ports *except* in vessels that had passed through a British port, paid customs duties, and obtained British licenses. By thus forcing goods through their own blockade, the British aimed, not at retaliation, but at commercial monopoly.

of Spencer Perceval and George Canning was a matter of so much interest as to deserve study. . . . (IV, iv, 79)

Many members of the British government and nearly the whole British navy were growing rich on the plunder of American commerce. From King George downward, mighty influences were involved in maintaining a system which corrupted law officers, judges, admirals, and even the King himself. Spencer Perceval's proposed Order in Council extended these abuses over whatever branches of commerce had hitherto been exempt; turned a new torrent of corruption into the government; and polluted the sources of British honor. In the light of Lord Bathurst's protest, and his significant avowal that the object of the proposed order, though general in form, was in fact nothing but the colonial trade carried on through America, Canning might well wish to *publish* nothing that would draw attention to what he called the "commercial" side of the affair. Jefferson's measures of peaceful coercion bore unexpected results, reacting upon foreign nations by stimulating every mean and sordid motive. No possible war could have so degraded England.

As the Cabinet came closer to the point, the political, or retaliatory, object of the new order disappeared, and its commercial character was exclusively set forth. In a letter written about November 30, by Spencer Perceval to Charles Abbot, Speaker of the House of Commons, not a word was said of retaliation, or of any political motive in this process of "recasting the law of trade and navigation, as far as belligerent principles are concerned, for the whole world."

"The short principle is," said Perceval, "that trade in British produce and manufactures, and trade either from a British port or with a British destination, is to be protected as much as possible. For this purpose all the countries where French influence prevails to exclude the British flag shall have no trade but to or from this country, or from its allies. All other countries, the few that remain strictly neutral (with the exception of the colonial trade, which backward and forward direct they may carry on), cannot trade but through this being done as an ally with any of the countries connected with France. If therefore we can accomplish our purpose, it will come to this—that either those countries will have no trade, or they must be content to accept it through us. This is a formidable and tremendous state of the world; but all the part of it which is particularly harassing to English interests was existing through the new severity with which Bonaparte's decrees of exclusion against our trade were called into action. Our proceeding does not aggravate our distress from it. If he can keep out our trade he will; and he would do so if he could, independent of our orders. Our orders only add this circumstance: they say to the enemy, 'if you will not have *our* trade, as far as we can help it you shall have *none;* and as to so much of any trade as you can carry on yourselves, or others carry on with you through us, if you admit it you shall pay for it. The only trade, cheap and untaxed, which you shall have shall be either direct from us, in our own produce and manufactures, or from our allies, whose increased prosperity will be an advantage to us.' "

These private expressions implied that retaliation upon France for her offence against international law was a pretence on the part of Perceval and Canning, under the cover of which they intended to force British commerce upon France contrary to French wishes. The act of Napoleon in excluding British produce from French dominions violated no rule of international law, and warranted no retaliation except an exclusion of French produce from British dominions. The rejoinder, "If you will not have *our* trade you shall have *none*," was not good law, if law could be disputed when affirmed by men like Lord Eldon and Lord Stowell, echoed by courts, parliaments, and press—not only in private, but in public; not only in 1807, but for long years afterward; and not only at moments, but without interruption. . . . (IV, iv, 97-99)

The exceptions, the qualifications, and the verbiage of the British Orders need no notice. The ablest British merchants gave up in despair the attempt to understand them; and as one order followed rapidly upon another, explaining, correcting, and developing Perceval's not too lucid style, the angry Liberals declared their belief that he intended no man to understand them without paying two guineas for a legal opinion, with the benefit of a chance to get a directly contrary opinion for the sum of two guineas more. Besides the express provisions contained in the Order of November 11, it was understood that American commerce with the enemies of England must not only pass through British ports with British license, but that colonial produce would be made to pay a tax to the British Treasury to enhance its price, while cotton would not be allowed to enter France. . . . (IV, iv, 103)

Spencer Perceval's Orders in Council had appeared in the "London Gazette" of November 14, and had followed the Emperor to Italy. Some weeks afterward war was declared between England and Russia. No neutral remained except Sweden, which was to be crushed by Russia, and the United States of America, which Napoleon meant to take in hand. December 17, from the royal palace at Milan, in retaliation for the Orders in Council, and without waiting to consult President Jefferson, Napoleon issued a new proclamation, compared with which the Berlin Decree of the year before was a model of legality.

> "Considering," began the preamble, "that by these acts the English government has denationalized the ships of all the nations of Europe; that it is in the power of no government to compound its own independence and its rights,—all the sovereigns in Europe being jointly interested in the sovereignty and independence of their flag; that if by an inexcusable weakness, which would be an ineffaceable stain in the eyes of posterity, we should allow such a tyranny to pass into a principle and to become consecrated by usage, the English would take advantage of it to establish it as a right, as they have profited by the tolerance of governments to establish the infamous principle that the flag does not cover the goods, and to give to their right of blockade an arbitrary extension, contrary to the sovereignty of all States,"—

Considering all these matters, so important to States like Denmark, Portugal, and Spain, whose flags had ceased to exist, and of whose honor and interests this mighty conqueror made himself champion, Napoleon decreed that every ship which should have been searched by an English vessel, or should have paid any duty to the British government, or should come from or be destined for any port in British possession in any part of the world, should be good prize; and that this rule should continue in force until England should have "returned to the principles of international law, which are also those of justice and honor." . . . (IV, v, 125-27)

The attack on the "Chesapeake," the trial of Aaron Burr, and the news from Copenhagen, Holland, and London made the summer and autumn of 1807 anxious and restless; but another event, under the eyes of the American people, made up a thousand fold, had they but known it, for all the losses or risks incurred through Burr, Bonaparte, or Canning. That the destinies of America must be decided in America was a maxim of true Democrats, but one which they showed little energy in reducing to practice. A few whose names could be mentioned in one or two lines—men like Chancellor Livingston, Dr. Mitchill, Joel Barlow,[21]—hailed the 17th of August, 1807, as the beginning of a new era in America—

[21] Joel **Barlow**: Connecticut entrepreneur and poet.

a date which separated the colonial from the independent stage of growth; for on that day, at one o'clock in the afternoon, the steamboat "Clermont," with Robert Fulton in command, started on her first voyage. A crowd of bystanders, partly sceptical, partly hostile, stood about and watched the clumsy craft slowly forge its way at the rate of four miles an hour up the river; but Fulton's success left room for little doubt or dispute, except in minds impervious to proof. The problem of steam navigation, so far as it applied to rivers and harbors was settled, and for the first time America could consider herself mistress of her vast resources. Compared with such a step in her progress, the mediaeval barbarisms of Napoleon and Spencer Perceval signified little more to her than the doings of Achilles and Agamemnon. Few moments in her history were more dramatic than the weeks of 1807 which saw the shattered "Chesapeake" creep back to her anchorage at Hampton Roads, and the "Clermont" push laboriously up the waters of the Hudson; but the intellectual effort of bringing these two events together, and of settling the political and economical problems of America at once, passed the genius of the people. Government took no notice of Fulton's achievement, and the public for some years continued, as a rule, to travel in sailing packets and on flatboats. The reign of politics showed no sign of ending. Fulton's steamer went its way, waiting until men's time should become so valuable as to be worth saving.

The unfailing mark of a primitive society was to regard war as the most natural pursuit of man; and history with reason began as a record of war, because, in fact, all other human occupations were secondary to this. The chief sign that Americans had other qualities than the races from which they sprang, was shown by their dislike for war as a profession, and their obstinate attempts to invent other methods for obtaining their ends; but in the actual state of mankind, safety and civilization could still be secured only through the power of self-defence. Desperate physical courage was the common quality on which all great races had founded their greatness; and the people of the United States, in discarding military qualities, without devoting themselves to science, were trying an experiment which could succeed only in a world of their own.

In charging America with having lost her national character, Napoleon said no more than the truth. . . . (IV, vi, 134-36)

Every subordinate officer of the British government thought himself at liberty to trample on American rights; and while the English

navy controlled the coast, and the English army from Canada gave
orders to the northwestern Indians, the British minister at Washington encouraged and concealed the conspiracy of Burr.

The evil had reached a point where some corrective must be
found; but four years of submission had broken the national spirit.
In 1805 the people were almost ready for war with England on the
question of the indirect, or carrying, trade of the French and Spanish West Indies. After submitting on that point, in July, 1807, they
were again ready to fight for the immunity of their frigates from
impressment; but by the close of the year their courage had once
more fallen, and they hoped to escape the necessity of fighting under
any circumstances whatever, anxiously looking for some expedient,
or compromise, which would reconcile a policy of resistance with a
policy of peace. This expedient Jefferson and Madison had for
fifteen years been ready to offer them.

So confident was Jefferson in his theory of peaceable coercion that
he would hardly have thought his administrative career complete,
had he quitted office without being allowed to prove the value of
his plan. The fascination which it exercised over his mind was quite
as much due to temperament as to logic; for if reason told him that
Europe could be starved into concession, temperament added another motive still more alluring. If Europe persisted in her conduct
America would be safe, and all the happier for cutting off connection with countries where violence and profligacy ruled supreme.
The idea of ceasing intercourse with obnoxious nations reflected
his own personality in the mirror of statesmanship. . . . (IV, vi,
137-38)

For more than six years he had conducted government on the
theory of peaceable coercion, and his own friends required that the
experiment should be tried. He was more than willing, he was
anxious, to gratify them; and he believed himself to have solved
the difficult problem of stopping his enemy, while running away
from him, without loss of dignity and without the appearance of
flight.

General Turreau,[22] after hoping for a time that the government
would accept the necessity of war with England, became more and
more bitter as he watched the decline of the war spirit; and September 4, barely two months after the assault on the "Chesapeake,"

[22] Louis Marie Turreau: ex-Jacobin, General, and now French Minister to
the U. S.

and long before the disavowal of Berkeley was known, he wrote to Talleyrand a diatribe against the Americans:—

"If the sentiments of fear and of servile deference for England with which the inhabitants of the American Union are penetrated, were not as well known as their indifference for everything which bears the name of French, what has passed since the attack on the frigate "Chesapeake" would prove to the most vulgar observer not only that the Anglo-Americans have remained in reality dependent on Great Britain, but even that this state of subjection conforms with their affections as well as with their habits. He will also be convinced that France has, and will ever have, nothing to hope from the dispositions of a people that conceives no idea of glory, of grandeur, of justice; that shows itself the constant enemy of liberal principles; and that is disposed to suffer every kind of humiliation, provided it can satisfy both its sordid avarice and its projects of usurpation over the Floridas."

Scandalized at the rapid evaporation of American courage, Turreau could explain it only as due to the natural defects of "a motley people, that will never have true patriotism, because it has no object of common interest"; a nation which looked on the most shameless outrages of its own virtue as only "unfortunate events." Yet one point remained which, although to every American it seemed most natural, was incomprehensible to the Frenchman, whose anger with America was due not so much to the dependence of the United States on England, as to their independence of France.

"What will doubtless astonish those who know the Americans but imperfectly, and what has surprised me myself,—me, who have a very bad opinion of this people, and who believe it just—is the aversion (éloignement),—and I soften the word,—which it has preserved for the French at the very moment when everything should recall a glorious and useful memory. It is hardly to be believed, yet is the exact truth, that in perhaps five hundred banquets produced by the anniversary of July 4, and among ten thousand toasts, but one has been offered in favor of France; and even this was given at an obscure meeting, and was evidently dictated by Duane."

Even the Administration press, Turreau complained, had thought proper to repudiate the idea of a French alliance. From his complaints the truth could be easily understood. In spite of reason, and in defiance of every ordinary rule of politics, France possessed in America no friend, or influence. The conclusion to be drawn was inevitable. If the United States would not accept the only alliance which could answer their purpose, England had nothing to fear. "In this state of affairs and condition of minds, it appears to me difficult to believe that Congress will take measures vigorous enough to revenge the insult offered to the Union, and to prevent the renewal of outrages."

This conclusion was reached by Turreau September 4, while as early as September 1 the same opinion was expressed by Erskine, the British minister:

> "From all the consideration which I have been able to give to the present state of things in this country, I am confirmed most strongly in the opinion which I have ventured to express in my former despatches, that, although I fear it might be possible for this government to lead the people into a war with Great Britain on the point of searching her national armed ships, yet I do not believe that there are any other grounds which would be powerful enough to urge them to so dangerous a measure to the political existence perhaps, but certainly to the general prosperity of this country."

No two men in America were better informed or more directly interested than Turreau and Erskine, and they agreed in regarding America as passive in the hands of England. . . . (IV, vi, 140-43)

7.

Embargo

In the country and in Congress, not only was Jefferson supreme, but his enemies were prostrate. Federalism in New England, for the first time, lay helpless under his feet; Burr and the "little band" in New York were crushed; the creoles in New Orleans, and the Western revolutionists, with Wilkinson at their head, were cowering before the outburst of patriotism which struck their projects dead. The hand of government rested heavily on them, and threatened nobler prey. Even Chief-Justice Marshall felt himself marked for punishment; while Monroe and Randolph were already under ban of the republic. These were triumphs which outweighed foreign disasters, and warranted Jefferson in self-confidence; but they were chiefly due to the undisputed success of his financial management. Jefferson and Madison, Dearborn and Robert Smith, might do what they would, so long as they left Gallatin free to control the results of their experiments; for Gallatin redeemed the mistakes of his party. Madison's foreign policy had brought only trouble to the government; Dearborn's army had shown itself to be more dangerous to the Union than to its enemies; Smith's gunboats were a laughing-stock; but Gallatin never failed to cover every weak spot in the Administration, and in October, 1807, the Treasury was profuse of prosperity. Congress might abolish the salt tax and Mediterranean Fund alike, and still the customs would yield fourteen millions a year; while the sales of public lands exceeded 284,000 acres and brought another half million into the Treasury. December 31, after providing for all the payments of public debt, Gallatin had a balance of $7,600,000 on hand. During the Presidency of Jefferson, $25,500,000 had been paid to redeem the principal of the public debt, and only the restraints imposed by the law prevented more rapid redemption. Even in case of war, Gallatin offered to sustain it for a year without borrowing money or increasing taxes.

There was the secret of Jefferson's strength, of his vast popularity, and of the fate which, without direct act of his, never had failed to overwhelm his enemies. The American people pardoned everything except an empty Treasury. No foreign insults troubled them long, and no domestic incompetence roused their disgust; but they were sensitive to any taxation which they directly felt. Gallatin atoned for starving the government by making it rich; and if obliged to endure disgrace and robbery abroad, he gave the President popularity at home. Conscious of this reserved strength, the President cared the less for foreign aggressions. His was, according to theory, the strongest government on earth; and at worst he had but to withdraw from intercourse with foreign nations in order to become impregnable to assault. He had no misgivings as to the result. . . . (IV, vi, 147-49)

December 14, against strong remonstrances from the merchants, the Non-importation Act of April 18, 1806, went into effect. The exact amount of British trade affected by that measure was not known. All articles of leather, silk, hemp, glass, silver, paper, woollen hosiery, ready-made clothing, millinery, malt liquors, pictures, prints, playing cards, and so forth, if of English manufacture, were henceforward prohibited; and any person who had them in his possession incurred forfeiture and fine. The measure was in its nature coercive. The debates in Congress showed that no other object than that of coercion was in the mind of the American government; the history of the Republican party and the consistent language of Jefferson, Madison, and the Virginian school proclaimed that the policy of prohibition was their substitute for war. England was to be punished, by an annual fine of several million dollars, for interference with American trade to the continent of Europe.

Two days after this law went into effect Madison received from the British government a document which threw the Non-importation Act into the background, and made necessary some measure more energetic. The King's proclamation of October 17, requiring all British naval officers to exercise the right of impressment to its full extent over neutral merchant vessels, was printed in the "National Intelligencer" of December 17; and if Sir William Scott's decision in the case of the "Essex" required the Non-importation Act as its counterpoise, the Impressment Proclamation could be fairly balanced only by a total cessation of relations.

In rapid succession the ships which sailed a month before from Europe arrived in American harbors, after unusually quick voyages. Monroe, in the "Augustus," reached Norfolk December 13; the "Edward" arrived at Boston December 12; the "Brutus" got in at New York December 14, preceded December 12 by the "Revenge." All these ships brought news to the same effect. Armstrong's despatches by the "Revenge" announced Napoleon's enforcement of the Berlin Decree. London newspapers of November 12 agreed in predicting some immediate and sweeping attack by the British government upon American commerce; and from Pinkney and Monroe came the official papers which put an end to all hope of a commercial treaty with England. Private letters bore out the worst public rumors. Among other persons who were best informed as to the intentions of the British government was Senator Pickering of Massachusetts, whose nephew Samuel Williams had been removed by Jefferson from the London consulate, and remained in that city as an American merchant, in connection with his brother Timothy Williams of Boston. December 12, Timothy Williams in Boston wrote to his uncle Senator Pickering at Washington,—

> "My brother writes me on the 9th of November "that he was informed the Government would in a few days declare Cuba, Martinique, and Guadeloupe in a state of blockade, and restrict still more the trade of neutrals with the Continent." The British no doubt had or would issue an Order above referred to, to counteract our friend Bonaparte's decree of November 21, 1806. I cannot however think the intercourse with the Continent will be entirely cut off. The influence of the West Indian planters will procure the blockading of the enemy's islands, no doubt. What has not this country lost by the miserable policy of the Administration! Your prudence will know to whom you can or cannot communicate any of the above paragraphs."

"With much solicitude respecting the present state of things," Timothy Williams concluded this letter of warning; and his anxiety was shared by every one who read the newspapers which proclaimed the danger of war. At Washington the alarming news arrived December 17, at the heels of the Impressment Proclamation. The President instantly called his Cabinet together. Under less serious circumstances in 1794, Congress had imposed an embargo for thirty days, forbidding clearances to all foreign-bound vessels while the question of war or peace was deciding. By common consent an embargo was the proper measure to be taken in the face of an expected attack on commerce. On reading the news from France and

England, every one assumed that an embargo would be imposed until the exact nature of the French and British aggressions should be learned; but safe precedent required that the law should restrict its own operation within some reasonable limit of time. An embargo for thirty or sixty days, or even for three months, might be required before reaching some decision as to peace or war.

On a loose sheet of letter paper, which happened to bear the address of General Mason, the President wrote a hasty draft of an embargo message to Congress. After referring to Armstrong's despatch announcing the Emperor's decision to enforce the Berlin Decree, Jefferson's draft noticed the threatened orders of England:—

"The British regulations had before reduced us to a direct voyage to a single port of their enemies, and it is now believed they will interdict all commerce whatever with them. A proclamation, too, of that Government (not officially, indeed, communicated to us, yet so given out to the public as to become a rule of action with them) seems to have shut the door on all negotiation with us, except as to the single aggression on the "Chesapeake." The sum of these mutual enterprises on our national rights is that France and her allies, reserving for future consideration the prohibiting our carrying anything to the British territories, have virtually done it by restraining our bringing a return cargo from them; and Great Britain, after prohibiting a great proportion of our commerce with France and her allies, is now believed to have prohibited the whole. The whole world is thus laid under interdict by these two nations, and our vessels, their cargoes, and crews are to be taken by the one or the other for whatever place they may be destined out of our own limits. If, therefore, on leaving our harbors we are certainly to lose them, is it not better, as to vessels, cargoes, and seamen, to keep them at home? This is submitted to the wisdom of Congress, who alone are competent to provide a remedy."

Unfortunately, no official document could be produced in proof of the expected British interdict, and mere newspaper paragraphs could not be used for the purpose. To avoid this difficulty Madison wrote, in pencil, another draft which omitted all direct mention of the expected British order. He proposed to send Congress the official letter in which the Grand Judge Regnier announced that the Berlin Decree would be enforced, and with this letter a copy of the British Impressment Proclamation as printed in the "National Intelligencer." On these two documents he founded his draft of a Message:—

"The communications now made showing the great and increasing danger with which our merchandise, our vessels, and our seamen are threatened on the high seas and elsewhere by the belligerent Powers of Europe, and it being of the greatest importance to keep in safety these essential resources, I deem it my duty to recommend the subject to the consideration of Congress, who will doubtless perceive all the advantages which may be expected from an immediate inhibition of the departure of our vessels from the ports of the United States."

The Cabinet, every member being present, unanimously concurred in the recommendation to Congress; but at least one member would have preferred that the embargo should be limited in time. The Cabinet meeting was held in the afternoon or evening of December 17, and early the next morning Gallatin wrote to the President suggesting a slight change in the proposed measure, and adding a serious warning which Jefferson would have done well to regard:—

"I also think," said Gallatin, "that an embargo for a limited time will at this moment be preferable in itself and less objectionable in Congress. In every point of view—privations, sufferings, revenue, effect on the enemy, politics at home, etc.—I prefer war to a permanent embargo. Governmental prohibitions do always more mischief than had been calculated; and it is not without much hesitation that a statesman should hazard to regulate the concerns of individuals, as if he could do it better than themselves. The measure being of a doubtful policy, and hastily adopted on the first view of our foreign intelligence, I think that we had better recommend it with modifications, and at first for such a limited time as will afford us all time for reconsideration, and if we think proper, for an alteration in our course without appearing to retract. As to the hope that it may have an effect on the negotiation with Mr. Rose,[23] or induce England to treat us better, I think it entirely groundless."

To this remarkable letter the President immediately replied by summoning the Cabinet together at ten o'clock in the morning. No record of the consultation was preserved; but when the Senate met at noon the Message was read by the Vice-president as it had been shaped by Madison. The suggestion of Gallatin as to a limit of time had not been adopted.

[23] George Rose: special British envoy to settle the *Chesapeake* dispute.

The Senate instantly referred the Message to a committee of five, with General Smith and J. Q. Adams at its head:—

"We immediately went into the committee room," recorded Senator Adams in his Diary—"and after some discussion, in which I suggested very strong doubts as to the propriety of the measure upon the papers sent with the President's message, I finally acquiesced in it as a compliance with the special call for it in the Message. I inquired whether there were other reasons for it besides the diplomatic papers sent with the Message, as *they* appeared to me utterly inadequate to warrant such a measure. Smith, the chairman, said that the President wanted it to aid him in the negotiation with England upon which Mr. Rose is coming out, and that perhaps it might enable us to get rid of the Non-importation Act. I yielded. But I believe there are yet other reasons, which Smith did not tell. There was no other opposition in committee."

Senator Adams was right in believing that other reasons existed; but although the "National Intelligencer" of the same morning had published the warnings of British newspapers—doubtless in order to affect the action of Congress—no one of the Republican senators seemed to rely on the expected British order as the cause of the embargo. In foreign affairs Jefferson maintained the reserve of a European monarch. He alone knew what had been done or was doing, and on him rested the whole responsibility of action. The deference paid by the Senate to the Executive in matters of foreign policy seemed patriotic, but it proved fatal to one senator at least, whose colleague had grievances to revenge. When the committee, after a short deliberation, reported an Embargo Bill, and some of the senators appealed for delay, Adams, who was chafing under the delays which had already lowered the self-respect of Government and people, broke into a strenuous appeal for energy. "The President has recommended the measure on his high responsibility. I would not consider, I would not deliberate; I would act!" The words were spoken in secret session, but Senator Pickering noted them for future use. Among the antipathies and humors of New England politics none was more characteristic than this personal antagonism, beginning a new conspiracy which was to shake the Union to its foundations.

The Senate agreed with the committee that if an embargo was to be laid it should be laid promptly; and the bill, probably drawn by the President, passed through its three stages on the same day, by a vote of twenty-two to six. At the second reading it was strongly opposed by Hillhouse, Pickering, and Sumter of South Carolina; while William H. Crawford, the new senator from Georgia, asked only time for consideration. Within four or five hours after hearing the Message read, the Senate sent its Embargo Act to the House.

Meanwhile the House also had received the President's Message, and had, like the Senate, gone at once into secret session. No sooner was the Message read than John Randolph and Jacob Crowninshield [24] sprang at the same moment to their feet. The Speaker recognized Randolph, who instantly offered a Resolution, "that an embargo be laid on all shipping, the property of citizens of the United States, now in port, or which shall hereafter arrive." After some time passed in discussion, on receiving the Senate bill the House laid Randolph's Resolution aside, and in secret session began a long and warm debate, which continued all day, and was not concluded on Saturday, December 19, when the House adjourned over Sunday.

The loss of this debate was unfortunate; for no private citizen ever knew the reasons which Congress considered sufficient to warrant a strain of the Constitution so violent as a permanent embargo implied. The debate was certainly dramatic: it was not only the first great political crisis witnessed in the new scenery of the Representatives' Chamber, but it also brought John Randolph forward in an attitude which astonished even those who had witnessed the Virginian's growing eccentricity. On Friday Randolph "scrambled" with Crowninshield for the floor, eager to force on the House a policy of embargo which he had again and again recommended as the only proper measure of national defence. On Saturday he rose again, but only to denounce his own measure as one that crouched to the insolent mandates of Napoleon, and led to immediate war with England. The cry of French influence, raised by him and by the Federalist members, began on that day, and echoed in louder and louder tones for years.

On Monday, December 21, the debate closed and the House consumed the day in voting. Amendment after amendment was rejected. Most significant of all these votes was the list of yeas and nays on the question of limiting the embargo to the term of two months. Forty-six members voted in the affirmative; eighty-two in the negative. The New England and Pennsylvania Democrats obeyed the wishes of Jefferson, and riveted a permanent embargo on the people, without public discussion of the principle or explanation of the effect which was expected from a measure more trying than war

[24] Jacob Crowninshield: Representative from Massachusetts.

itself to patriotism. The bill then passed by a vote of eighty-two to forty-four.

So small a part was played in this debate by the expected Order in Council that members afterward disputed whether the subject was mentioned at all. Probably the Administration preferred silence in public, either for fear of prejudicing the expected negotiation with Rose, or of weakening the effect of arguments which without the order were sufficiently strong; but in private no such reticence was shown. The British minister on Monday, before the bill had become law, notified Canning not only that an embargo was about to be laid, but of the cause which produced the measure:—

"It has been confidentially communicated to me that an embargo on all the shipping in the United States has been proposed in Congress, and although it is strongly resisted, it is expected that it will be carried, on the ground of expecting that a proclamation by his Majesty will be issued declaring France and her dependencies in a state of blockade. I hasten to send you this letter for fear of the effect of an embargo."

The person from whom Erskine received this confidential communication was probably the Secretary of State; for two days afterward, when the British minister wrote to say that the embargo had been laid, he added:—

"I propose to send off his Majesty's packet-boat with this intelligence immediately, and avail myself of this opportunity by a private ship to inform you that the embargo is not intended, as this Government declares, as a measure of hostility against Great Britain, but only as a precaution against the risk of the capture of their ships in consequence of the decree of Bonaparte of November 21, 1806, which they have just learned is to be rigorously enforced; and also from an apprehension of a retaliatory order by Great Britain."

Thus the embargo was imposed; and of all President Jefferson's feats of political management, this was probably the most dexterous. On his mere recommendation, without warning, discussion, or publicity, and in silence as to his true reasons and motives, he succeeded in fixing upon the country, beyond recall, the experiment of peaceable coercion. His triumph was almost a marvel; but no one could fail to see its risks. A free people required to know in advance the motives which actuated government, and the intended consequences of important laws. Large masses of intelligent men were slow to forgive what they might call deception. If Jefferson's permanent embargo should fail to coerce Europe, what would the people of America think of the process by which it had been fastened upon them? What would be said and believed of the President who had challenged so vast a responsibility? . . . (IV, vii, 165-77)

8.

Failure

Reports of open defiance and insurrection on the Canada frontier reached Washington at the same time with other reports which revealed endless annoyances elsewhere. If the embargo was to coerce England or France, it must stop supplies to the West Indian colonies, and prevent the escape of cotton or corn for the artisans of Europe. The embargo aimed at driving England to desperation, but not at famishing America; yet the President found himself at a loss to do the one without doing the other. Nearly all commerce between the States was by coasting vessels. If the coasting-trade should be left undisturbed, every schooner that sailed from an American port was sure to allege that by stress of weather or by the accidents of navigation it had been obliged to stop at some part of Nova Scotia or the West Indies, and there to leave its cargo. Only the absolute prohibition of the coasting-trade could prevent these evasions; but to prohibit the coasting-trade was to sever the Union. The political tie might remain, but no other connection could survive. Without the coasting-trade New England would be deprived of bread, and her industries would perish; Charleston and New Orleans would stagnate in unapproachable solitude.

Jefferson proclaimed the existence of an insurrection on the Canadian frontier shortly before the adjournment of Congress. Immediately after the adjournment he took in hand the more serious difficulties of the coasting-trade. The experiment of peaceable coercion was at last to have full trial, and Jefferson turned to the task with energy that seemed to his friends excessive, but expressed the vital interest he felt in the success of a theory on which his credit as a statesman depended. The crisis was peculiarly his own; and he assumed the responsibility for every detail of its management.

May 6, the President wrote to Gallatin a letter containing general directions to detain in port every coasting vessel which could be regarded as suspicious. His orders were sweeping. The power of the embargo as a coercive weapon was to be learned.

"In the outset of the business of detentions," said the President, "I think it impossible to form precise rules. After a number of cases shall have arisen, they may probably be thrown into groups and subjected to rules. The great leading object of the Legislature was, and ours in execution of it ought to be, to give complete effect to the embargo laws. They have bidden agriculture, commerce, navigation to bow before that object,—to be nothing when in competition with that. Finding all their endeavors at general rules to be evaded, they finally gave us the power of detention as the panacea; and I am clear we ought to use it freely, that we may by a fair experiment know the power of this great weapon, the embargo."

. . . (IX, xi, 250-51)

Blood was soon shed, but Jefferson did not shrink. The new army was stationed along the Canada frontier. The gunboats and frigates patrolled the coast. On every side dangers and difficulties accumulated. "I did not expect a crop of so sudden and rank growth of fraud and open opposition by force could have grown up in the United States." At Newburyport an armed mob on the wharf prevented the custom-house officers from detaining a vessel about to sail. The collectors and other officers were ill-disposed, or were harassed by suits at law for illegal detentions. Rebellion and disunion stared Jefferson in the face, but only caused him to challenge an outbreak and to invite violence.

"That the Federalists may attempt insurrection is possible," he wrote to Gallatin, "and also that the governor would sink before it; but the Republican part of the State, and that portion of the Federalists who approve the embargo in their judgments, and at any rate would not court mob law, would crush it in embryo. I have some time ago written to General Dearborn to be on the alert on such an occasion, and to take direction of the public authority on the spot. Such an incident will rally the whole body of Republicans of every shade to a single point,—that of supporting the public authority."

. . . (IV, xi, 257-58)

Of all the old Republican arguments for a policy of peace, the commonest was that a standing army would be dangerous, not to foreign enemies, but to popular liberties; yet the first use of the new army and gunboats was against fellow citizens. New England was chiefly controlled by the navy; but in New York the army was needed and was employed. Open insurrection existed there. Besides forcible resistance offered to the law, no one was ignorant that the collectors shut their eyes to smuggling, and that juries, in defiance of court and President, refused to indict rioters. Governor Tompkins[25] announced that Oswego was in active insurrection, and called on the President to issue a proclamation to that effect. Jefferson replied by offering to take into the United States service the militia required to suppress the riots, and begged Governor Tompkins to lead his troops in person. "I think it so important in example to crush these audacious proceedings and to make the offenders feel the consequences of individuals daring to oppose a law by force, that no effort should be spared to compass this object. . . . (IV, xi, 259-60)

That President Jefferson should exercise "dangerous and odious" powers, carrying the extremest results; that he should depend for constitutional law on Federalist judges[26] whose doctrines he had hitherto believed fatal to liberty—these were the first fruits of the embargo. After such an experience, if he or his party again raised the cry of States' rights, or of strict construction, the public might, with some foundation of reason, set such complaints aside as factious and frivolous, and even, in any other mouth than that of John Randolph, as treasonable. . . . (IV, xi, 271)

The economical was less serious than the moral problem. The strongest objection to war was not its waste of money or even of life; for money and life in political economy were worth no more than they could be made to produce. A worse evil was the lasting harm caused by war to the morals of mankind, which no system of economy could calculate. The reign of brute force and brutal methods corrupted and debauched society, making it blind to its own vices and ambitious only for mischief. Yet even on that ground the embargo had few advantages. The peaceable coercion which Jefferson tried to substitute for war was less brutal, but hardly less mischievous, than the evil it displaced. The embargo opened the sluice

[25] Daniel D. Tompkins: Governor of New York, 1807-1816.

[26] cp. John Davis, Federalist, judge of the Federal District Court for Massachusetts, who (September 1808) declared the Embargo constitutional, invoking the "necessary and proper" clause and the power to regulate commerce. This broad construction was not at all to Jefferson's taste.

gates of social corruption. Every citizen was tempted to evade or defy the laws. At every point along the coast and frontier the civil, military, and naval services were brought in contact with corruption; while every man in private life was placed under strong motives to corrupt. Every article produced or consumed in the country became an object of speculation; every form of industry became a form of gambling. The rich could alone profit in the end; while the poor must sacrifice at any loss the little they could produce.

If war made men brutal, at least it made them strong; it called out the qualities best fitted to survive in the struggle for existence. To risk life for one's country was no mean act even when done for selfish motives; and to die that others might more happily live was the highest act of self-sacrifice to be reached by man. War, with all its horrors, could purify as well as debase; it dealt with high motives and vast interests; taught courage, discipline, and stern sense of duty. Jefferson must have asked himself in vain what lessons of heroism or duty were taught by his system of peaceable coercion, which turned every citizen into an enemy of the laws—preaching the fear of war and of self-sacrifice, making many smugglers and traitors, but not a single hero. . . . (IV, xii, 276-77)

Except in a state of society verging on primitive civilization, the stoppage of all foreign intercourse could not have been attempted by peaceable means. The attempt to deprive the laborer of sugar, salt, tea, coffee, molasses, and rum; to treble the price of every yard of coarse cottons and woolens; to reduce by one half the wages of labor, and to double its burdens—this was a trial more severe than war; and even when attempted by the whole continent of Europe, with all the resources of manufactures and wealth which the civilization of a thousand years had supplied, the experiment required the despotic power of Napoleon and the united armies of France, Austria, and Russia to carry it into effect. Even then it failed. Jefferson, Madison, and the Southern Republicans had no idea of the economical difficulties their system created, and were surprised to find American society so complex even in their own southern States that the failure of two successive crops to find a sale threatened beggary to every rich planter from the Delaware to the Sabine. During the first few months, while ships continued to arrive from abroad and old stores were consumed at home, the full pressure of the embargo was not felt; but as the summer of 1808 passed, the outcry became violent. In the southern States, almost by common consent debts remained unpaid, and few men ventured to oppose a political system which was peculiarly a southern invention; but in the northern States, where the bankrupt laws were enforced and the habits of business were comparatively strict, the cost of the embargo was soon shown in the form of political revolution.[27] . . . (IV, xii, 282-83)

The Republican party by a supreme effort kept itself in office; but no one could fail to see that if nine months of embargo had so shattered Jefferson's power, another such year would shake the Union itself. The cost of this "engine for national purposes" exceeded all calculation. Financially, it emptied the Treasury, bankrupted the mercantile and agricultural class, and ground the poor beyond endurance. Constitutionally, it overrode every specified limit on arbitrary power and made Congress despotic, while it left no bounds to the authority which might be vested by Congress in the President. Morally, it sapped the nation's vital force, lowering its courage, paralyzing its energy, corrupting its principles, and arraying all the active elements of society in factious opposition to government or in secret paths of treason. Politically, it cost Jefferson the fruits of eight years painful labor for popularity, and brought the Union to the edge of a precipice.

Finally, frightful as the cost of this engine was, as a means of coercion the embargo evidently failed. The President complained of evasion, and declared that if the measure were faithfully executed it would produce the desired effect; but the people knew better. In truth, the law was faithfully executed. The price lists of Liverpool and London, the published returns from Jamaica and Havana, proved that American produce was no longer to be bought abroad. On the continent of Europe commerce had ceased before the embargo was laid, and its coercive effects were far exceeded by Napoleon's own restrictions; yet not a sign came from Europe to show that Napoleon meant to give way. From England came an answer to the embargo, but not such as promised its success. On all sides evidence accumulated that the embargo, as an engine of coercion, needed a long period of time to produce a decided effect. The law of physics could easily be applied to politics; force could be converted only into its equivalent force. If the embargo—an exertion of force less violent than war—was to do the work of war, it must extend over a longer time the development of an equivalent energy.

[27] *E.g.* In the spring election of 1808 Massachusetts relapsed into Federalism and Federalists made large gains in New York: while in the fall of 1808 all New England, except Vermont, repudiated Madison for President.

Wars lasted for many years, and the embargo must be calculated to last much longer than any war; but meanwhile the morals, courage, and political liberties of the American people, must be perverted or destroyed; agriculture and shipping must perish; the Union itself could not be preserved.

Under the shock of these discoveries Jefferson's vast popularity vanished, and the labored fabric of his reputation fell in sudden and general ruin. America began slowly to struggle, under the consciousness of pain, toward a conviction that she must bear the common burdens of humanity, and fight with the weapons of other races in the same bloody arena; that she could not much longer delude herself with hopes of evading laws of Nature and instincts of life; and that her new statesmanship which made peace a passion could lead to no better result than had been reached by the barbarous system which made war a duty. . . . (IV, xii, 287-89)

While the people of the United States waited to see the effect of the embargo on Europe, Europe watched with breathless interest the death throes of Spain.

The Emperor Napoleon, in December, 1807, hurried in triumphal progress from one ancient city to another, through his Italian kingdom, while his armies steadily crossed the Pyrenees, and spread over every road between Bayonne and Lisbon. From Madrid, Godoy saw that the end was near. Until that moment he had counted with certainty on the devotion of the Spanish people to their old King. In the last months of 1807 he learned that even Spanish loyalty could not survive the miseries of such a reign. Conspiracy appeared in the Escorial itself. Ferdinand, Prince of the Asturias, only son of Don Carlos IV, was discovered in a plot for dethroning his father by aid of Napoleon. Ferdinand was but twenty-three years old; yet even in the flower of youth he showed no social quality. Dull, obstinate, sullen, just shrewd enough to be suspicious, and with just enough passion to make him vindictive, Ferdinand was destined to become the last and worst of the Spanish Bourbon kings; yet in the year 1807 he had a strong bond of sympathy with the people, for he hated and feared his father and mother and the Prince of Peace. Public patience, exhausted by endless disaster, and outraged by the King's incompetence, the Queen's supposed amours, and Godoy's parade of royal rank and power, vanished at the news that Ferdinand shared in the popular disgust; and the Prince of Peace suddenly woke to find the old King already dethroned in his subjects' love, while the Prince of the Asturias, who was fitted only for confinement in an asylum, had become the popular ideal of virtue and reform. . . . (IV, xiii, 290-91)

The gradual breaking up of the old European system of politics was marked by an anniversary among each of the Western nations. The English race dated from July 4, 1776, the beginning of a new era; the French celebrated July 14, 1789, the capture of the Bastille, as decisive of their destinies. For a time, Bonaparte's *coup d'état* of the 18th Brumaire in 1799 forced both France and England back on their steps; but the dethronement of Charles IV began the process of a new direction. The Second of May,—or as the Spaniards called it, the Dos de Maio,—swept the vast Spanish empire into the vortex of dissolution. Each of the other anniversaries,—that of July 4, 1776, and of July 14, 1789,—had been followed by a long and bloody convulsion which ravaged large portions of the world; and the extent and violence of the convulsion which was to ravage the Spanish empire could be measured only by the vastness of Spanish dominion. So strangely had political forces been entangled by Napoleon's hand, that the explosion at Madrid roused the most incongruous interests into active sympathy and strange companionship. The Spaniards themselves, the least progressive people in Europe, became by necessity democratic; not only the people, but even the governments of Austria and Germany felt the movement, and yielded to it; the Tories of England joined with the Whigs and Democrats in cheering a revolution which could not but shake the foundations of Tory principles; confusion became chaos, and while all Europe, except France, joined hands in active or passive support of Spanish freedom, America, the stronghold of free government, drew back and threw her weight on the opposite side. The workings of human development were never more strikingly shown than in the helplessness with which the strongest political and social forces in the world followed or resisted at haphazard the necessities of a movement which they could not control or comprehend. Spain, France, Germany, England, were swept into a vast and bloody torrent which dragged America, from Montreal to Valparaiso, slowly into its movement; while the familiar figures of famous men,— Napoleon, Alexander, Canning, Godoy, Jefferson, Madison, Talleyrand; emperors, generals, presidents, conspirators, patriots, tyrants, and martyrs by the thousand,—were borne away by the stream, struggling, gesticulating, praying, murdering, robbing; each blind to everything but a selfish interest, and all helping more or less unconsciously to reach the new level which society was obliged to

seek. Half a century of disorder failed to settle the problems raised
by the Dos de Maio; but from the first even a child could see that
in the ruin of a world like the empire of Spain, the only nation
certain to find a splendid and inexhaustible booty was the Republic
of the United States. To President Jefferson the Spanish revolution
opened an endless vista of democratic ambition. . . . (IV, xiii,
300-302)

Yet at first the Dos de Maio seemed only to rivet Napoleon's
power, and to strengthen the reaction begun on the 18th Brumaire.
The Emperor expected local resistance, and was ready to suppress
it. He had dealt effectually with such popular outbreaks in France,
Italy, and Germany; he had been overcome in St. Domingo not by
the people, but, as he believed, by the climate. If the Germans and
Italians could be made obedient to his orders, the Spaniards could
certainly offer no serious resistance. During the two or three months
that followed the dethronement of the Bourbons, Napoleon stood
at the summit of his hopes. If the letters he wrote were not extant
to prove the plans he had in mind, common sense would refuse to
believe that schemes so insubstantial could have found lodgment in
his brain. The English navy and English commerce were to be
driven from the Mediterranean Sea, the Indian Ocean, and American waters, until the ruin of England should be accomplished, and
the empire of the world should be secured. Order rapidly followed
order for reconstructing the navies of France, Spain and Portugal.
Great expeditions were to occupy Ceuta, Egypt, Syria, Buenos Ayres,
the Isle de France, and the East Indies.

"The concurrence of these operations," he wrote May 13, "will
throw London into a panic. A single one of them, that of India, will
do horrible damage there. England will then have no means of annoying us or of disturbing America. I am resolved on this expedition."

For this purpose the Emperor required not only the submission
of Spain, but also the support of Spanish America and of the United
States. He acted as though he were already master of all these countries, which were not yet within his reach. Continuing to treat the
United States as a dependent government, he issued April 17 a new
order directing the seizure of all American vessels which should
enter the ports of France, Italy, and the Hanse towns. This measure,
which became famous as the Bayonne Decree, surpassed the Decrees

of Berlin and Milan in violence, and was gravely justified by Napoleon on the ground that, since the embargo, no vessel of the United States could navigate the seas without violating the law of its own government, and furnishing a presumption that it did so with false papers, on British account or in British connection. "This is very ingenious," wrote Armstrong in reporting the fact. Yet it was hardly more arbitrary or unreasonable than the British "Rule of 1756," which declared that a neutral should practice no trade with a belligerent which it had not practiced with the same nation during peace. . . . (IV, xiii, 302-303)

Fortunately for Jefferson . . . Joseph Bonaparte, entering his new kingdom, found himself a king without subjects. Arriving July 20 at Madrid, Joseph heard nothing but news of rebellion and disaster. On that day some twenty thousand French troops under General Dupont, advancing on Seville and Cadiz, were surrounded in the Sierra Morena, and laid down their arms to a patriot Spanish force. A few days afterward the French fleet at Cadiz surrendered. A patriot Junta assumed the government of Spain. Quick escape from Madrid became Joseph's most pressing necessity if he were to save his life. During one July week he reigned over his gloomy capital, and fled, July 29, with all the French forces still uncaptured, to the provinces beyond the Ebro.

This disaster was quickly followed by another. Junot and his army, far beyond support at Lisbon, suddenly learned that a British force under Arthur Wellesley had landed, August 1, about one hundred miles to the north of Lisbon, and was marching on that city. Junot had no choice but to fight, and August 21 he lost the battle of Vimiero. August 30, at Cintra, he consented to evacuate Portugal, on condition that he and his twenty-two thousand men should be conveyed by sea to France.

Never before in Napoleon's career had he received two simultaneous shocks so violent. The whole of Spain and Portugal, from Lisbon to Saragossa, by a spasmodic effort freed itself from Bonaparte or Bourbon; but this was nothing,—a single campaign would recover the peninsula. The real blow was in the loss of Cadiz and Lisbon, of the fleets and workshops that were to restore French power on the ocean. Most fatal stroke of all, the Spanish colonies were thenceforward beyond reach, and the dream of universal empire was already dissolved into ocean mist. Napoleon had found the limits of his range, and saw the power of England rise, more defiant than ever, over the ruin and desolation of Spain. . . . (IV, xiii, 315-16)

The exact cost of the embargo to England could not be known. The total value of British exports to America was supposed to be nearly $50,000,000; but the Americans regularly re-exported to the West Indies merchandise to the value of 10 or 15 millions. The embargo threw this part of the trade back into British hands. The true consumption of the United States hardly exceeded $35,000,000, and was partially compensated to England by the gain of freights, the recovery of seamen, and by smuggling consequent on the embargo. Napoleon's decrees must in any case have greatly reduced the purchasing power of America, and had in fact already done so. Perhaps $25,000,000 might be a reasonable estimate for the value of the remaining trade which the embargo stopped; and if the British manufacturers made a profit of 20 per cent on this trade, their loss in profits did not exceed $5,000,000 for the year,—a sum not immediately vital to English interests at a time when the annual expenditure reached $350,000,000, and when, as in 1807, the value of British exports was reckoned at nearly $200,000,000. Indeed, according to the returns, the exports of 1808 exceeded those of 1807 by about two millions.

Doubtless the embargo caused suffering. The West Indian Negroes and the artisans of Staffordshire, Lancashire, and Yorkshire were reduced to the verge of famine; but the shipowners rejoiced, and the country gentlemen and farmers were enriched. So ill balanced had the British people become in the excitement of their wars and industries that not only Cobbett but even a man so intelligent as William Spence undertook to prove that foreign commerce was not a source of wealth to England, but that her prosperity and power were derived from her own resources, and would survive the annihilation of her foreign trade. James Mill replied at great length to the eccentricities of Spence and Cobbett, which the common sense of England would in ordinary times have noticed only with a laugh.

The population of England was about ten millions. Perhaps two millions were engaged in manufactures. The embargo by raising the price of grain affected them all, but it bore directly on about one tenth of them. The average sum expended on account of the poor was £4,268,000 in 1803 and 1804; it was £5,923,000 in 1811; and in 1813, 1814, and 1815, when the restrictive system had produced its full effect, the poor-rates average £6,130,000. The increase was probably due to the disturbance of trade and was accompanied by a state of society bordering upon chronic disorder.

Probably at least five thousand families of workingmen were reduced to pauperism by the embargo and the decrees of Napoleon; but these sufferers, who possessed not a vote among them and had been in no way party to the acts of either government, were the only real friends whom Jefferson could hope to find among the people of England; and his embargo ground them in the dust in order to fatten the squires and shipowners who had devised the Orders in Council. If the English laborers rioted, they were shot; if the West Indian slaves could not be fed, they died. The embargo served only to lower the wages and the moral standards of the laboring classes throughout the British Empire, and to prove their helplessness. . . . (IV, xiv, 328-30)

. . . Madison and Gallatin decided to retain the embargo until June, 1809, but to call the new Congress together May 22, and then to declare war, unless Erskine could make concessions. President Jefferson was chiefly interested in maintaining the embargo until after March 4, and the despotism he had so long maintained over Congress seemed still to exasperate his enemies. By common consent, attack upon the embargo was regarded as attack upon the President; and the northern Democrats had so far lost respect for their old leader as to betray almost a passion for telling him unpleasant truths. . . .(IV, xix, 432)

Josiah Quincy,[28] who watched every symptom of democratic disaster, wrote as early as February 2: "There is dreadful distraction in the enemy's camp on the subject of removing the embargo. Jefferson and his friends are obstinate. Bacon[29] and the northern Democrats are equally determined that it shall be raised in March." The next day Quincy added: "Jefferson is a host; and if the wand of the magician is not broken, he will yet defeat the attempt.

The contest had become personal; to break the "wand of the magician" was as much the object of Democrats as of Federalists, and neither Madison nor Gallatin could restore discipline. February 4 the Secretary of the Treasury wrote; "As far as my information goes, everything grows more quiet in Massachusetts and Maine. All would be well if our friends remained firm here."

[28] Josiah Quincy: Federalist Representative from Massachusetts.
[29] Ezekiel Bacon: Republican Representative from Massachusetts.

The attempt to hold the friends of the Administration firm brought only greater disaster. The vote in committee refusing to recommend reprisals took place February 7; and the next day Quincy wrote again: "Great caucusing is the order of the day and the night here. The Administration is determined to rally its friends, and postpone the removal of the embargo till May. But I think they cannot succeed. Bacon, I am told, stands firm and obstinate against all their solicitations and even almost denunciations. However, they had another caucus last night. The event is unknown. Jefferson has prevailed." . . . (IV, xix, 440)

President Jefferson, though his name was still a terror to his enemies, accepted whatever decision his Cabinet advised. Till the day of his death he never forgot the violence of these last weeks of his administration, or the outcry of the New England towns. "How powerfully did we feel the energy of this organization in the case of the embargo," he wrote long years afterward. "I felt the foundations of the government shaken under my feet by the New England townships." He showed the same lack of interest in February which had marked his conduct in November; not even the certainty of his own overthrow called out the familiar phrases of vexation. February 7 he wrote his son-in-law, Thomas Mann Randolph,—

"I thought Congress had taken their ground firmly for continuing the embargo till June, and then war. But a sudden and unaccountable revolution of opinion took place last week, chiefly among the New England and New York members, and in a kind of panic they voted the 4th of March for removing the embargo, and by such a majority as gave all reason to believe they would not agree either to war or non-intercourse. This, too, was after we had become satisfied that the Essex Junto had found their expectation desperate, of inducing the people there either to separation or forcible opposition. The majority of Congress, however, has now rallied to the removing of the embargo on the 4th March, non-intercourse with France and Great Britain, trade everywhere else, and continuing war preparations. The further details are not yet settled, but I believe it is perfectly certain that the embargo will be taken off the 4th of March."
. . . (IV, xix, 441-42)

The Republican caucus, February 7, decided in favor of returning to Jefferson's pacific non-intercourse,—the system which had been, by common consent, thrown aside as insufficient even before the embargo. February 10 Erskine gave an account of the new measure, and of its probable effect on American politics:—

"It is true that a non-intercourse law may be considered by the
Eastern States very objectionable; but as it would be rather a nominal
prohibition than a rigorous enforcement, a resistance to it would be
less likely to be made, and of less importance if it should take place.
The ultimate consequences of such differences and jealousies arising
between the Southern and Eastern States would inevitably tend to
a dissolution of the Union, which has been for some time talked of,
and has of late, as I have heard, been seriously contemplated by
many of the leading people of the Eastern division."

The Non-Intercourse Bill, which Erskine described February 10
as likely to be no more than a nominal prohibition of commerce,
was reported February 11 to the House from the Committee of
Foreign Relations. The bill excluded all public and private vessels
of France and England from American waters; forbade under severe
penalties the importation of British and French goods; repealed the
embargo laws, "except so far as they relate to Great Britain or
France or their colonies or dependencies, or places in the actual possession of either"; and gave the President authority to reopen by
proclamation the trade with France or England in case either of
these countries should cease to violate neutral rights. That the
proposed non-intercourse was in truth submission to the Orders in
Council, no one denied.

"I conceive that great advantages may be reaped from it by England," wrote Erskine, "as she has the command of the seas, and can
procure through neutrals any of the produce of this country, besides
the immense quantity which will be brought direct to Great Britain
under various pretences, whereas France will obtain but little, at a
great expense and risk."

Such a non-intercourse merely sanctioned smuggling, and was
intended for no other purpose. Gallatin in his disgust flung open
the doors to illicit commerce. When Erskine went to him to ask
what was meant by "France, England, and their dependencies,"
Gallatin replied that only places in actual possession of France and
England were intended; that it was impossible to say what nations
had decrees in force infringing neutral rights, but that even Holland would be considered an independent country.

"The intention of this indefinite description," continued Erskine,
"is undoubtedly to leave open as many places for their commerce as
they can, consistently with keeping up an appearance of resistance

to the belligerent restrictions; but it is thoroughly understood that the whole measure is a mere subterfuge to extricate themselves from the embarrassments of the embargo system, and is never intended to be enforced."

When this bill came before the House, another long debate arose. Hardly a trace of national pride remained. No one approved the bill, but no one struggled longer against submission. . . . (IV, xix, 444-46)

Non-intercourse must ruin the South, in order to offer an immense bribe to the shipping and manufactures of New England as an inducement for New England to remain in the Union. The manufacturing interests never ventured to ask such an extravagant protection as was thrust upon them in 1809 by the fears of the agricultural States; the greed of corporate capital never suggested the monopoly created for eastern ships and factories by a measure which shut from America all ships and manufactures but theirs. Even if partially enforced, such legislation was ruinous to agriculture.

Entreaty and argument were thrown away. The House lost discipline, self-respect, and party character. No one felt responsible for any result, no majority approved any suggestion. As the last days of the session drew near, the machinery of legislation broke down, and Congress became helpless. So strange and humiliating a spectacle had not before been seen. The nation seemed sinking into the weakness of dissolution. . . . (IV, xix, 449-50)

February 27, the Non-Intercourse Bill in its most unresisting shape received the approval of the House. Not a speaker defended it; at the last moment the charge was freely made that the bill had not a single friend. The members who voted for it declared in doing so that the measure was a weak and wretched expedient, that they detested it, and took it merely as a choice of evils; but eighty-one members voted in its favor, and only forty in the negative. More extraordinary still, this non-intercourse, which bound the South to the feet of New England, was supported by forty-one southern members, while but twelve New England representatives recorded their names in its favor. . . . (IV, xix, 451)

. . . Nathaniel Macon, February 28, wrote to his friend Nicholson,—

"Otis, the Secretary of the Senate, has this moment informed the House of Representatives that the Senate has agreed to the amendments made by the House to the Bill to repeal the embargo.

The Lord, the mighty Lord, must come to our assistance, or I fear weare undone as a nation!"

... (IV, xix, 453)

The repeal of the embargo, which received the President's signature March 1, closed the long reign of President Jefferson; and with but one exception the remark of John Randolph was destined to remain true, that "never has there been any Administration which went out of office and left the nation in a state so deplorable and calamitous." That the blame for this failure rested wholly upon Jefferson might be doubted; but no one felt more keenly than he the disappointment under which his old hopes and ambitions were crushed.

Loss of popularity was his bitterest trial. He who longed like a sensitive child for sympathy and love left office as strongly and almost as generally disliked as the least popular President who preceded or followed him. He had undertaken to create a government which should interfere in no way with private action, and he had created one which interfered directly in the concerns of every private citizen in the land. He had come into power as the champion of States' rights, and had driven States to the verge of armed resistance. He had begun by claiming credit for stern economy, and ended by exceeding the expenditure of his predecessors. He had invented a policy of peace, and his invention resulted in the necessity of fighting at once the two greatest Powers in the world.

The feelings of the New England Democrats have been described in their own words. Angry as Ezekiel Bacon and Joseph Story[30] were, their bitterness against Jefferson was hardly so great as that of Clintonians in New York; but the same irritation extended even into the compact democracy of Pennsylvania. In the preceding summer, before the Presidential election, A. J. Dallas said to Gallatin: "I verily believe one year more of writing, speaking, and appointing would render Mr. Jefferson a more odious President, even to the Democrats, than John Adams." So far as could be judged from the conduct of the party, the prophecy became truth. The southern Republicans, always loyal to a southern President, would not openly turn against their old leader, but the northern Democrats made no disguise of their aversion.

[30] Joseph Story: Republican Representative from Massachusetts.

Not even in 1798 had factiousness been so violent as in the last month of President Jefferson's power; in 1800 the country in comparison had been contented. February 23, 1809, nearly three weeks after the disastrous overthrow of the embargo in Congress, the Connecticut legislature met in special session to "interpose" between the people and the national government. In a Report echoing the words of Governor Trumbull's speech, the House instantly approved his refusal to aid in carrying out the "unconstitutional and despotic" Enforcement Act, and pledged itself to join the legislature of Massachusetts in the measures proposed "to give to the commercial States their fair and just consideration in the Union." . . .(IV, xx, 454-56)

Of all Jefferson's hopes, perhaps the warmest had been that of overthrowing the power of his New England enemies—those whom he had once called the monarchical Federalists—the clergy and the Essex Junto. Instead of overthrowing them he had given them, for the first time in their lives, unlimited power for mischief; he had overthrown only the moderate Federalists, who when forced to choose between treason and embargo submitted to the embargo and hated its author. The Essex Junto became supreme in New England; and behind it stood the power of Great Britain, ready to interpose, if necessary, for its defence.

Jefferson submitted in silence, and even with an air of approval, to the abrupt abandonment of his favorite measure. He admitted that the embargo had failed; he even exaggerated its evils, and described it as more costly than war. His language implied that the failure of peaceable coercion was no longer a matter of doubt in his mind.

"The belligerent edicts," he wrote to Armstrong, "rendered our embargo necessary to call home our ships, our seamen, and property. We expected some effect, too, from the coercion of interest. Some it has had, but much less on account of evasions and domestic opposition to it. After fifteen months' continuance, it is now discontinued because, losing fifty million dollars of exports annually by it, it costs more than war, which might be carried on for a third of that, besides what might be got by reprisal."

To Dupont de Nemours, Jefferson wrote in the same strain. He signed without the betrayal of a protest the bill repealing the embargo, and talked of war as a necessary evil. Not until more than a year afterward did he admit the bitterness of his disappointment and mortification; but July 16, 1810, he wrote to his old Secretary

of War a letter which expressed, in his familiar note of irritability,
the feelings he had pent up:—

"The Federalists during their short-lived ascendency have nevertheless, by forcing us from the embargo, inflicted a wound on our interests which can never be cured, and on our affections which will
require time to cicatrize. I ascribe all this to one pseudo-Republican,
—Story. He came on in place of Crowninshield, I believe, and stayed
only a few days,—long enough, however, to get complete hold of
Bacon, who, giving in to his representations, became panic-struck,
and communicated the panic to his colleagues, and they to a majority of the sound members of Congress. They believed in the
alternative of repeal or civil war, and produced the fatal measure of
repeal. . . . I have ever been anxious to avoid a war with England
unless forced by a situation more losing than war itself; but I did
believe we could coerce her to justice by peaceable means; and the
embargo, evaded as it was, proved it would have coerced her had it
been honestly executed. The proof she exhibited on that occasion
that she can exercise such an influence in this country as to control
the will of its government and three fourths of its people is to me
the most mortifying circumstance which has occurred since the establishment of our government."

In truth, the disaster was appalling; and Jefferson described it in
moderate terms by admitting that the policy of peaceable coercion
brought upon him mortification such as no other President ever
suffered. So complete was his overthrow that his popular influence
declined even in the South. Twenty years elapsed before his political authority recovered power over the northern people; for not
until the embargo and its memories faded from men's minds did
the mighty shadow of Jefferson's Revolutionary name efface the
ruin of his Presidency. Yet he clung with more and more tenacity
to the faith that his theory of peaceable coercion was sound; and
when within a few months of his death he alluded for the last time
to the embargo, he spoke of it as "a measure which, persevered in
a little longer, we had subsequent and satisfactory assurance would
have effected its object completely."

A discomfiture so conspicuous could not fail to bring in its train
a swarm of petty humiliations which for the moment were more
painful than the great misfortune. Jefferson had hoped to make his
country forever pure and free; to abolish war, with its train of debt,
extravagance, corruption, and tyranny; to build up a government
devoted only to useful and moral objects; to bring upon earth a new

era of peace and goodwill among men. Throughout the twistings and windings of his course as President he clung to this main idea; or if he seemed for a moment to forget it, he never failed to return and to persist with almost heroic obstinacy in enforcing its lessons. By repealing the embargo, Congress avowedly and even maliciously rejected and trampled upon the only part of Jefferson's statesmanship which claimed originality, or which in his own opinion entitled him to rank as a philosophic legislator. The mortification he felt was natural and extreme, but such as every great statesman might expect, and such as most of them experienced. The supreme bitterness of the moment lay rather in the sudden loss of respect and consideration which at all times marked the decline of power, but became most painful when the surrender of office followed a political defeat at the hands of supposed friends. . . . (IV, xx, 461-65)

Under the weight of these troubles, public and private, Jefferson's longing to escape became intense; and his letters repeated, in accents more and more earnest, the single wish that filled his mind.

"I shall within a few days," he wrote February 25, "divest myself of the anxieties and the labors with which I have been oppressed, and retire with inexpressible delight to my family, my friends, my farms, and books. There I may indulge at length in that tranquillity and those pursuits from which I have been divorced by the character of the times in which I have lived, and which have forced me into the line of political life under a sense of duty and against a great and constant aversion to it."

March 2, he wrote to Dupont de Nemours, in stronger terms of weariness and disgust: "Never did a prisoner released from his chains feel such relief as I shall on shaking off the shackles of power. Nature intended me for the tranquil pursuits of science by rendering them my supreme delight." March 4 he rode once more on horseback to the Capitol, and stood by the side of Madison while John Marshall administered the oath of office. The weight of administration was at last removed, but the longing for home became only the greater. March 5 he wrote to Armstrong: "Within two or three days I retire from scenes of difficulty, anxiety, and of contending passions, to the elysium of domestic affections and the irresponsible direction of my own affairs." A week afterward Jefferson quitted Washington forever. On horseback, over roads impassable to wheels, through snow and storm, he hurried back to Monticello to recover in the quiet of home the peace of mind he had lost in the disappointments of his statesmanship. He arrived at Monticello March 15, and never again passed beyond the bounds of a few adjacent counties.

With a sigh of relief which seemed as sincere and deep as his own, the Northern people saw him turn his back on the White House and disappear from the arena in which he had for sixteen years challenged every comer. In the northern States few regrets were wasted upon his departure, for every mind was intent on profiting by the overthrow of his system; but Virginia was still loyal to him, and the citizens of his own county of Albemarle welcomed with an affectionate address his final return. His reply, dignified and full of grateful feeling, seemed intended as an answer to the attacks of partisan grossness and a challenge to the judgment of mankind:—

"The anxieties you express to administer to my happiness do of themselves confer that happiness; and the measure will be complete if my endeavors to fulfil my duties in the several public stations to which I have been called have obtained for me the approbation of my country. The part which I have acted on the theatre of public life has been before them, and to their sentence I submit it; but the testimony of my native county, of the individuals who have known me in private life, to my conduct in its various duties and relations is the more grateful as proceeding from eye-witnesses and observers, from triers of the vicinage. Of you, then, my neighbors, I may ask in the face of the world, 'Whose ox have I taken or whom have I defrauded? Whom have I oppressed, or of whose hand have I received a bribe to blind mine eyes therewith?' On your verdict I rest with conscious security."

. . . (IV, xx, 471-74)

History of the United States

*During the Administrations of
Jefferson and Madison*

II. MADISON

CONTENTS

VOLUME II

III.

End of "The Long Decline"—
1809-1811

1.

Erskine and Jackson:
The End of Accommodation

The "National Intelligencer," which called public attention only to such points of interest as the Government wished to accent, noticed that President Madison was "dressed in a full suit of cloth of American manufacture" when he appeared at noon, March 4, 1809, under escort of the "troops of cavalry of the city and Georgetown," amid a crowd of ten thousand people, to take the oath of office at the Capitol. The suit of American clothes told more of Madison's tendencies than was to be learned from the language of the Inaugural Address, which he delivered in a tone of voice so low as not to be heard by the large audience gathered in the new and imposing Representatives' Hall. Indeed, the Address suggested a doubt whether the new President wished to be understood. The conventionality of his thought nowhere betrayed itself more plainly than in this speech on the greatest occasion of Madison's life, when he was required to explain the means by which he should retrieve the failures of Jefferson.

"It is a precious reflection," said Madison to his anxious audience, "that the transition from this prosperous condition of our country to the scene which has for some time been distressing us, is not chargeable on any unwarrantable views, nor as I trust on any voluntary errors, in the public councils. Indulging no passions which trespass on the rights or the repose of other nations, it has been the true glory of the United States to cultivate peace by observing justice, and to entitle themselves to the respect of the nations at war by fulfilling their neutral obligations with the most scrupulous impartiality. If there be candor in the world, the truth of these assertions will not be questioned; posterity at least will do justice to them."

3

Since none of Madison's enemies, either abroad or at home, intended to show him candor, his only hope was in posterity; yet the judgment of posterity depended chiefly on the course which the new President might take to remedy the misfortunes of his predecessor. The nation expected from him some impulse toward the end he had in mind; foreign nations were also waiting to learn whether they should have to reckon with a new force in politics; but Madison seemed to show his contentment with the policy hitherto pursued, rather than his wish to change it.

"This unexceptionable course," he continued, "could not avail against the injustice and violence of the belligerent Powers. In their rage against each other, or impelled by more direct motives, principles of retaliation have been introduced equally contrary to universal reason and acknowledged law. How long their arbitrary edicts will be continued, in spite of the demonstrations that not even a pretext for them has been given by the United States, and of the fair and liberal attempt to induce a revocation of them, cannot be anticipated. Assuring myself that under every vicissitude the determined spirit and united councils of the nation will be safeguards to its honor and essential interests, I repair to the post assigned me, with no other discouragement than what springs from my own inadequacy to its high duties."

Neither the actual world nor posterity could find much in these expressions on which to approve or condemn the policy of Madison, for no policy could be deduced from them. The same iteration of commonplaces marked the list of general principles which filled the next paragraph of the Address. Balancing every suggestion of energy by a corresponding limitation of scope, Madison showed only a wish to remain within the limits defined by his predecessor. "To cherish peace and friendly intercourse with all nations having corresponding dispositions" seemed to imply possible recourse to war with other nations; but "to prefer in all cases amicable discussion and reasonable accommodation of differences to a decision of them by an appeal to arms" seemed to exclude the use of force. "To promote by authorized means improvements friendly to agriculture, to manufactures, and to external as well as internal commerce" was a phrase so cautiously framed that no one could attack it. "To support the Constitution, which is the cement of the Union, as well in its limitations as in its authorities," seemed a duty so guarded as to need no further antithesis; yet Madison did not omit the usual obligation "to respect the rights and authorities reserved to the

States and to the people, as equally incorporated with, and essential to, the success of the general system." No one could object to the phrases with which the Address defined Executive duties; but no one could point out a syllable implying that Madison would bend his energies with sterner purpose to maintain the nation's rights.

At the close of the speech Chief Justice Marshall administered the oath; the new President then passed the militia in review, and in the evening Madison and Jefferson attended an inauguration ball, where "the crowd was excessive, the heat oppressive, and the entertainment bad." With this complaint, so familiar on the occasion, the day ended, and President Madison's troubles began. . . . (V, i, 1-4)

The year 1809 began with a . . . new spirit of accommodation in British councils. The causes which produced it were notorious. From the moment Europe closed her ports, in the autumn of 1807, articles commonly supplied from the Continent rose to speculative prices, and after the American embargo the same effect followed with American produce. Flax, linseed, tallow, timber, Spanish wool, silk, hemp, American cotton doubled or trebled in price in the English markets during the years 1807 and 1808. Colonial produce declined in the same proportion. Quantities of sugar and coffee overfilled the warehouses of London, while the same articles could not be bought at Amsterdam and Antwerp at prices three, four, and five times those asked on the Royal Exchange. Under the Orders in Council, the whole produce of the West Indies, shut from Europe by Napoleon and from the United States by the embargo, was brought to England, until mere plethora stopped accumulation.

Debarred from their natural outlets, English merchandise and manufactures were forced into every other market which seemed to offer a hope of sale or barter. When Portugal fell into Napoleon's hands, and the royal family took refuge in Brazil under British protection, English merchants glutted Brazil with their goods, until the beach at Rio Janeiro was covered with property, which perished for want of buyers and warehouses. The Spanish trade, thrown open soon afterward, resulted in similar losses. In the effort to relieve the plethora at home, England gorged the few small channels of commerce that remained in her control.

These efforts coincided with a drain of specie on government account to support the Spanish patriots. The British armies sent to Spain required large sums in coin for their supplies, and the Spaniards required every kind of assistance. The process of paying money on every hand and receiving nothing but worthless produce could not long continue without turning the exchanges against London; yet a sudden call for specie threatened to shake the foundations of society. Never was credit so rotten. Speculation was rampant, and inflation accompanied it. None of the familiar signs of financial disaster were absent. Visionary joint-stock enterprises flourished. Discounts at long date, or without regard to proper security, could be obtained with ease from the private banks and bankers who were competing for business; and although the Bank of England followed its usual course, neither contracting nor expanding its loans and issues, suddenly, at the close of 1808, gold coin rose at a leap from a nominal rate of 103 to the alarming premium of 113. The exchanges had turned, and the inevitable crash was near. . . . (V, iii, 46-47)

. . . The irritation of Canning's tone showed him to be ill at ease—he felt the ground slipping under his feet. The public had become weary of him and his colleagues. The commercial system they had invented seemed to create the evils it was made to counteract. The press began to complain. As early as January 13 the "Times" showed signs of deserting the orders, which it declared to be no "acts of retaliation," but "measures of counter-action," complicated by transit duties doubtful either in expediency or justice. "If America will withdraw her Embargo and Non-importation Acts as far as they relate to England, provided we rescind the Orders in Council, we cannot consider this as a disgraceful concession on our part." After the debate of March 6, the "Times" renewed its complaints. Every day increased the difficulties of ministers, until mere change became relief.

At length, April 26, the reality of the weakness of Perceval and Canning became clear. On that day a new Order in Council appeared, which roused great interest because it seemed to abandon the whole ground taken in the Orders of November, 1807, and to return within the admitted principles of international law. The machinery of the old orders was apparently discarded; the machinery of blockade was restored in its place. The Order of April 26, 1809, declared that the old orders were revoked and annulled except so far as their objects were to be attained by a general blockade of all ports and places under the government of France. The blockade thus declared was to extend northward as far as Ems, and was to include on the south the ports of northern Italy. Of course the new blockade was not even claimed to be effective. No squadrons were to enforce its provisions by their actual presence before the blockaded ports. In that respect the Order of April 26, 1809, was as illegal as that of November 11, 1807; but the new arrangement opened to neutral commerce all ports not actually ports of France, even though the British flag should be excluded from them,—retaliating upon France only the injury which the French decrees attempted to inflict on England.

Pinkney was greatly pleased and wrote to Madison in excellent spirits that the change gave all the immediate benefits which could have arisen from the arrangement proposed by him in the previous August, except the right to demand from France the recall of her edicts. "Our triumph is already considered as a signal one by everybody. The pretexts with which ministers would conceal their motives for a relinquishment of all which they prized in their system are seen through, and it is universally viewed as a concession to America. Our honor is now safe; and by management we may probably gain everything we have in view." Canning said to Pinkney: "If these alterations did not do all that was expected, they at least narrowed extremely the field of discussion, and gave great facilities and encouragement to reviving cordiality." Government took pains to impress the idea that it had done much, and wished to do more for conciliation; yet the doubt remained whether Government was acting in good faith. Pinkney overestimated its concessions. If the British navy was to blockade Holland, France, and northern Italy only in order that British commerce might be forced, through the blockade and license system, into the place of neutral commerce, the new system was only the old one in disguise. Under a blockade, in good faith, licenses seemed to have no place. In that case, the Order in Council on April 26 might lead to a real settlement; but how was it possible that Perceval, George Rose, and James Stephen should have given up what they believed to be the only hope for England's safety? . . . (V, iii, 62-65)

Going at once to Secretary Robert Smith,[1] Erskine began on the "Chesapeake" affair, and quickly disposed of it. The President abandoned the American demand for a court-martial on Admiral Berkeley, finding that it would not be entertained. Erskine then wrote a letter offering the stipulated redress for the "Chesapeake"

---

[1] Robert Smith had been nominated Secretary of State because of an intrigue in the Senate, headed by Samuel Smith and Michael Leib, against Albert Gallatin, whom Madison favored for the post. Smith's incompetence was such that Madison wrote all his important papers for him.

outrage, and Madison wrote a letter accepting it, which Robert Smith signed, and dated April 17.

Two points in Madison's "Chesapeake" letter attracted notice. Erskine began his official note by alluding to the Non-intercourse Act of March 1, as having placed Great Britain on an equal footing with the other belligerents, and warranting acknowledgment on that account. The idea was far-fetched, and Madison's reply was ambiguous:—

"As it appears at the same time, that in making this offer his Britannic Majesty derives a motive from the equality now existing in the relations of the United States with the two belligerent Powers, the President owes it to the occasion and to himself to let it be understood that this equality is a result incident to a state of things growing out of distinct considerations."

If Madison knew precisely what "distinct considerations" had led Congress and the country to that state of things to which the Non-intercourse Act was incident, he knew more than was known to Congress; but even though he owed this statement to himself, so important an official note might have expressed his ideas more exactly. "A result incident to a state of things growing out of distinct considerations" was something unusual, and to say the least wanting in clearness, but seemed not intended to gratify Canning.

The second point challenged sharper criticism.

"With this explanation, as requisite as it is frank," Smith's note continued, "I am authorized to inform you that the President accepts the note delivered by you in the name and by the order of his Britannic Majesty, and will consider the same with the engagement therein, when fulfilled, as a satisfaction for the insult and injury of which he has complained. But I have it in express charge from the President to state that while he forbears to insist on the further punishment of the offending officer, he is not the less sensible of the justice and utility of such an example, nor the less persuaded that it would best comport with what is due from his Britannic Majesty to his own honor."

According to Robert Smith's subsequent account, the last sentence was added by Madison in opposition to his secretary's wishes. One of Madison's peculiarities showed itself in these words, which endangered the success of all his efforts. If he wished a reconciliation,

they were worse than useless; but if he wished a quarrel, he chose
the right means. The President of the United States was charged
with the duty of asserting in its full extent what was due to his own
honor as representative of the Union; but he was not required,
either by the laws of his country or by the custom of nations, to
define the conduct which in his opinion best comported with what
was due from his Britannic Majesty to the honor of England. That
Erskine should have consented to receive such a note was matter
for wonder, knowing as he did that Kings of England had never
smiled on servants who allowed their sovereign's honor to be questioned; and the public surprise was not lessened by his excuse.

"It appeared to me," he said, "that if any indecorum could justly
be attributed to the expressions in the official notes of this Government, the censure due would fall upon them; and that the public
opinion would condemn their bad taste or want of propriety in coldly
and ungraciously giving up what they considered as a right, but
which they were not in a condition to enforce."

Under the impression that no "intention whatever existed in the
mind of the President of the United States to convey a disrespectful
meaning toward his Majesty by these expressions," Erskine accepted
them in silence, and Madison himself never understood that he had
given cause of offence.

Having thus disposed of the "Chesapeake" grievance, Erskine
took up the Orders in Council. His instructions were emphatic, and
he was in effect ordered to communicate these instructions *in
extenso* to the President, for in such cases permission was equivalent
to order. He disobeyed; in official sense he did not communicate his
instructions at all. "I considered that it would be in vain," he
afterward said. This was his first exercise of discretion; and his
second was more serious. After reading Canning's repeated and
positive orders to require from the American government "a distinct and official recognition" of three conditions, he decided to
treat these orders as irrelevant. He knew that the President had no
Constitutional power to bind Congress, even if Madison himself
would patiently bear a single reading of three such impossible
requirements, and that under these circumstances the negotiation
had better never begin than end abruptly in anger. Erskine would
have done better not to begin it; but he thought otherwise. Under
more favorable circumstances, Monroe and Pinkney had made the
same experiment in 1806.

Canning offered to withdraw the Orders in Council, on three conditions precedent:

(1) That all interdicts on commerce should be revoked by the United States so far as they affected England, while they were still to be enforced against France. When Erskine submitted this condition to Robert Smith, he was assured that the President would comply with it, and that Congress would certainly assert the national rights against France, but that the President had no power to pledge the government by a formal act. Erskine decided to consider Canning's condition fulfilled if the President, under the eleventh section of the Non-intercourse Act, should issue a proclamation renewing trade with Great Britain, while retaining the prohibition against France. This settlement had the disadvantage of giving no guarantee to England, while it left open the trade with Holland, which was certainly a dependency of France.

(2) Canning further required that the United States should formally renounce the pretension to a colonial trade in war which was not permitted in time of peace. To this condition, which Erskine seems to have stated as applying only to the direct carrying-trade to Europe, Robert Smith replied that it could not be recognized except in a formal treaty; but that it was practically unimportant, because this commerce, as well as every other with France or her dependencies, was prohibited by Act of Congress. Erskine accepted this reasoning, and left the abstract right untouched.

(3) Canning lastly demanded that the United States should recognize the right of Great Britain to capture such American vessels as should be found attempting to trade with any of the Powers acting under the French Decrees. To this suggestion Secretary Smith replied that the President could not so far degrade the national authority as to authorize Great Britain to execute American laws; but that the point seemed to him immaterial, since no citizen could present to the United States government a claim founded on a violation of its own laws. Erskine once more acquiesced, although the trade with Holland was not a violation of law, and would probably give rise to the very claims which Canning meant to preclude.

Having thus disposed of the three conditions which were to be distinctly and officially recognized, Erskine exchanged notes with Robert Smith, bearing date April 18 and 19, 1809, chiefly admirable for their brevity, since they touched no principle. In his note of April 18, Erskine said that the favorable change produced by anticipation of the Non-intercourse Act had encouraged his Government to send out a new envoy with full powers; and that meanwhile his Majesty would recall his Orders in Council if the President would issue a Proclamation renewing intercourse with Great Britain. Secretary Smith replied on the same day that the President would not fail in doing so. April 19, Erskine in a few lines announced himself "authorized to declare that his Majesty's Orders in Council of January and November, 1807, will have been withdrawn as respects the United States on the 10th of June next." Secretary Smith answered that the President would immediately issue his Proclamation. Two days afterward the four notes and the Proclamation itself were published in the "National Intelligencer."

The United States heard with delight that friendship with England had been restored. Amid an outburst of joy commerce resumed its old paths, and without waiting for June 10, hurried ships and merchandise to British ports. No complaints were heard; not a voice was raised about impressments; no regret was expressed that war with France must follow reconciliation with England; no one found fault with Madison for following in 1809 the policy which had raised almost a revolution against President Washington only fourteen years before. Yet Madison strained the law, besides showing headlong haste, in acting upon Erskine's promises without waiting for their ratification, and without even asking to see the British negotiator's special powers of instructions. The haste was no accident or oversight. When Turreau remonstrated with Gallatin against such precipitate conduct contrary to diplomatic usage, Gallatin answered,

"The offers could not be refused."
"But you have only promises," urged Turreau: "and already twelve hundred vessels, twelve thousand sailors, and two hundred million [francs] of property have left your ports. May not the English take all this to serve as a guarantee for other conditions which their interest might care to impose?"
"We would like it!" replied the Secretary of the Treasury. "Perhaps our people may need such a lesson to cure them of British influence and the mania of British commerce."

Impatient at the conduct of Congress and the people, Madison was glad to create a new situation, and preferred even hostilities to the Orders in Council. Erskine's conduct was unusual, yet Great Britain had shown no such regard for Madison's feelings that Madison should hesitate before the eccentricities of British diplomacy. Perplexed to account for Canning's sudden change, the President and his friends quieted their uneasiness by attributing their triumph to their own statesmanship. . . . (V, iv, 67-75)

Although no one ventured to avow suspicion that Canning would refuse to ratify Erskine's act, news continued to arrive from England which seemed hard to reconcile with any immediate thought, in the British ministry, of giving up their restrictive system. June 10, the day when amid universal delight the new arrangement went into effect, the public pleasure was not a little disturbed by the arrival of news that on April 26 the British government had issued a very important Order in Council, revoking the order of November 11, 1807, and establishing in its place a general blockade of Holland, France, and Italy. This step, though evidently a considerable concession,—which would have produced its intended effect in checking hostile feeling if Erskine had not intervened,—roused anxiety because of its remote resemblance to Erskine's arrangement, which it seemed to adopt by means that the United States could not admit as legal or consistent with the terms of Erskine's letters.

"The new Orders," wrote Madison to Jefferson, . . . "present a curious feature in the conduct of the British Cabinet. It is explained by some at the expense of its sincerity. It is more probably ascribed, I think, to an awkwardness in getting out of an awkward situation, and to the policy of withholding as long as possible from France the motive of its example to have advances on her part toward adjustment with us. The crooked proceeding seems to be operating as a check to the extravagance of credit given to Great Britain for the late arrangement with us, and so far may be salutary."

Such reasoning was soon felt to be insufficient. The more the new order was studied, the less its motive was understood. How could Canning in January have authorized Erskine to withdraw the orders in 1807 without reserve, when in April, without waiting to hear from Erskine, he himself withdrew those orders only to impose another that had every mark of permanence? How could Erskine, April 18, have been authorized to throw open the ports of Holland, when his Government, April 26, was engaged in imposing a new blockade upon them? So rapidly did the uneasiness of Congress increase that Erskine was obliged to interpose. June 15, he wrote an official note to the Secretary of State, which the President sent the same day to Congress.

"I have the honor," said Erskine, "to enclose a copy of an Order of his Majesty in Council issued on the 26th of April last. In consequence of official communications sent to me from his Majesty's government since the adoption of that measure, I am enabled to assure you that it has no connection whatever with the overtures which I have been authorized to make to the government of the United States; and that I am persuaded that the terms of the agreement so happily concluded by the recent negotiation will be strictly fulfilled on the part of his Majesty."

The expressions of this letter, if carefully read, still left cause for doubt; and Madison saw it, although he clung to what he thought he had gained. . . . (V, iv, 81-83)

So completely was discipline restored, that June 27 he ventured to send the name of J. Q. Adams a second time to the Senate as minister to Russia; and nineteen Republicans confirmed the nomination, while but one adhered to the opinion that the mission was unnecessary. The power of England over America was never more strikingly shown than by the sudden calm which fell on the country, in full prospect of war with France, at a word from a British minister. As Canning frowned or smiled, faction rose to frenzy or lay down to slumber throughout the United States. No sooner did the news of Erskine's arrangement reach Quebec May 1, than Sir James Craig[2] recalled his secret agent, John Henry, from Boston, where he still lingered. "I am cruelly out of spirits," wrote Secretary Ryland to Henry, "at the idea of Old England truckling to such a debased and accursed government as that of the United States"; but since this was the case, Henry's services could no longer be useful. He returned to Montreal early in June.

June 28 Congress adjourned, leaving the Executive, for the first time in many years, almost without care, until the fourth Monday in November. . . . (V, iv, 86)

The news of Erskine's disavowal reached America so slowly that merchants enjoyed three months of unrestricted trade, and shipped to England or elsewhere the accumulations of nearly two years' produce. From April 21 till July 21 this process of depletion continued without an anxiety; and when July 21 news arrived that the arrangement had been repudiated, merchants still had time

[2] Sir James Craig: Governor-General of Canada, 1807-1811.

to hurry their last cargoes to sea before the government could again interpose.

The first effect of Canning's disavowal seemed bewilderment. No one in the United States, whether enemy or friend of England, could for a time understand why Canning had taken so perplexing a course. Very few of England's friends could believe that her conduct rested on the motives she avowed; they sought for some noble, or at least some respectable, object behind her acts. For several months the Federalist newspapers were at a loss for words, and groped in the dark for an English hand to help them; while the Republican press broke into anger, which expressed the common popular feeling. "The late conduct of the British ministry," said the "National Intelligencer" of July 26, "has capped the climax of atrocity toward this country." Every hope of reconciliation or even of peace with England seemed almost extinguished; yet the country was still far from a rupture. Not until popular feeling could express itself in a new election would the national will be felt; and the next election was still more than a year away, while the Congress to be then chosen would meet only in December, 1811. Until then war was improbable, perhaps impossible, except by the act of England. . . . (V, vi, 109-10)

The President heard the news with as much perplexity as anger, and even tried to persuade himself that Canning would be less severe than he threatened. Madison still clung to hope when he first replied to Gallatin's summons:—

"The conduct of the British government in protesting the arrangement of its minister surprises one in spite of all their examples of folly. If it be not their plan, now that they have filled their magazines with our supplies and ascertained our want of firmness in withholding them, to adopt openly a system of monopoly and piracy, it may be hoped that they will not persist in the scandalous course in which they have set out. Supposing Erskine to have misunderstood or overstrained his instructions, can the difference between our trading directly and indirectly with Holland account for the violent remedy applied to the case? Is it not more probable that they have yielded to the clamors of the London smugglers in sugar and coffee, whose numbers and impudence are displayed in the scandalous and successful demand from their government that it should strangle the lawful trade of a friendly nation lest it should interfere with their avowed purpose of carrying on a smuggling trade with their enemies? Such an outrage on all decency was never before heard of even on the shores of Africa."

Madison exaggerated. The outrage on decency committed by the British government in May, 1809, was on the whole not so great as that of Sir William Scott's decision in the case of the "Essex" in July, 1805; or that of the blockade of New York and the killing of Pierce in April, 1806; or that of Lord Howick's Order in Council of January, 1807, when the signatures to Monroe's treaty were hardly dry; or that of Spencer Perceval's Orders in November, 1807, and the speeches made in their defence; or the mission of George Henry Rose in the winter of 1807-1808; or Erskine's letter of February 23, or Canning's letters of September 23, 1808,—for all these left the United States in a worse position than that created by the disavowal of Erskine. Indeed, except for the disgrace of submitting to acts of illegal force, the United States stood in a comparatively easy attitude after the orders of April 26, 1809, so long as Napoleon himself enforced within his empire a more rigid exclusion of neutral commerce than any that could be effected by a British blockade.

"Still, I cannot but hope," continued Madison, "on the supposition that there be no predetermined hostility against our commerce and navigation, that things may take another turn under the influence of the obvious and striking considerations which advise it."

The hope vanished when Erskine's instructions became known, and was succeeded by consternation when the public read the reports made by Erskine and Canning of the language used by Madison, Gallatin, and Pinkney. For the first time in this contest, Englishmen and Americans could no longer understand each other's meaning. Erskine had so confused every detail with his own ideas, and Canning's course on one side the Atlantic seemed so little to accord with his tactics on the other, that neither party could longer believe in the other's good faith. Americans were convinced that Canning had offered terms which he intended them to refuse. Englishmen were sure that Madison had precipitated a settlement which he knew could not be carried out. . . . (V, vi, 111-13)

The month passed only too soon for Jackson's[3] comfort, and October 1, punctual to his word, the President arrived. The next day Erskine had his farewell audience, and October 3 Jackson was officially received. Merry's experience had not been without advantage to both sides; and Jackson, who seemed to feel more contempt

[3] Francis James Jackson: British Minister to Washington, succeeding Erskine.

for his own predecessors—Merry and Erskine—than for his American antagonists, accepted everything in good part.

"Madison, the President, is a plain and rather mean-looking little man, of great simplicity of manners, and an inveterate enemy to form and ceremony; so much so that I was officially informed that my introduction to him was to be considered as nothing more than the reception of one gentleman by another, and that no particular dress was to be worn on the occasion,—all which I was very willing to acquiesce in. Accordingly I went in an afternoon frock, and found the President in similar attire. Smith, the Secretary of State, who had walked from his office to join me, had on a pair of dusty boots, and his round hat in his hand. When he had introduced us he retired, and the President then asked me to take a chair. While we were talking, a Negro servant brought in some glasses of punch and a seedcake. The former, as I had been in conference the whole morning, served very agreeably to wet, or whet, my whistle, and still more strongly to contrast this audience with others I had had with most of the sovereigns of Europe."

Perhaps this passing allusion to previous acquaintance with "most of the sovereigns of Europe" threw a light, somewhat too searching, into the recesses of Jackson's character. The weakness was pardonable, and not specially unsuited to success in his career, but showed itself in private as a form of self-deception which promised ill for his coming struggle. Madison's civility quite misled him.

"I do not know," he wrote October 24, "that I had ever more civility and attention shown me than at a dinner at the President's yesterday, where I was treated with a distinction not lately accorded to a British minister in this country. A foolish question of precedence, which ever since Merry's time has been unsettled, and has occasioned some heart-burnings among the ladies, was also decided then by the President departing from his customary indifference to ceremony and etiquette, and taking Elizabeth in to dinner, while I conducted Mrs. Madison."

Evidently this deference pleased the British minister, who saw nothing behind it but a social triumph for himself and his wife; yet he had already been forced to protest against the ceremonial forms with which Madison studiously surrounded him, and had he read Shakespeare rather than Erskine's writings, he might have learned from Julius Caesar the general diplomatic law that "when

love begins to sicken and decay, it useth ever an enforced ceremony." A man of tact would have seen that from the moment
Madison became formal he was dangerous. The dinner of October
23 at the White House came at a moment when Jackson had been
so carefully handled and so effectually disarmed as to stand at
Madison's mercy; and although he was allowed to please himself by
taking Mrs. Madison to dinner, the "mean-looking little man" at
the head of the table, was engaged only in thinking by what stroke
the British minister's official life should be most quickly and quietly
ended. . . . (V, vi, 120-22)

The American note of October 19, far too long to quote or even
to abridge, was perhaps the best and keenest paper Madison ever
wrote. His faults of style and vagueness of thought almost wholly
disappeared in the heat of controversy; his defence was cool, his
attack keen, as though his sixty years weighed lightly the day when
he first got his young antagonist at his mercy. He dealt Jackson
a fatal blow at the outset, by reminding him that in July, 1808,
only the previous year, Canning had put an end to oral communication after two interviews with Pinkney on the subjects under negotiation. He then made three points, well stated and easily remembered: (1) That when a government refuses to fulfil a pledge, it owes
a formal and frank disclosure of its reasons. (2) That, in the actual
situation, Mr. Erskine's successor was the proper channel for that
disclosure. (3) That since Mr. Jackson disclaimed authority to make
either explanations or proposals, the President could do no more
than express his willingness to favor any honorable mode of settling
the matters in dispute. . . . (V, vi, 127)

The letter of October 19 forced Jackson one step backward, and
drove him nearly to the wall. Obliged to choose between the avowal
that he had no proposal to make, or the assertion that he had both
explanations and proposals, he yielded, somewhat surily, to the
weakness of offering explanations, such as they were, and of inviting
proposals eventually to be embodied in a convention. In a note
dated October 23 he answered the American note of October 19.
If Madison had doubted his own advantage, his doubts must have
vanished in reading Jackson's second note, which shuffled and
evaded the issues in a manner peculiar to disconcerted men; but
the most convincing proof of Jackson's weakness appeared in the
want of judgment he showed in exposing himself to attack at the
moment when he was seeking safety. He committed the blunder of

repeating the charge that Madison was responsible for Erskine's violation of instructions:—

"These instructions . . . were at the time, in substance, made known to you. . . . So far from the terms which he was actually induced to accept having been contemplated in that instruction, he himself states that they were substituted by you in lieu of those originally proposed."

Jackson's folly in thus tempting his fate was the more flagrant because his private letters proved that he knew something of his true position. "Madison is now as obstinate as a mule," he wrote October 26. "Until he gets [the absolute surrender of the Orders in Council] he will not even accept any satisfaction for the affair of the 'Chesapeake,' which has been now for the third time offered to him in vain"; and he added: "There is already a great and growing fermentation in the United States, which shows itself in a manner highly prejudicial to the amity and good understanding which doubtless our ministers wish to see established between the two countries."

A few days after writing this evidence of his own uneasiness, the British minister received from the Department of State a third note, dated November 1, which left no doubt that the President meant to push his antagonist to extremes. After accepting the explanations at last made in regard to the Orders in Council, and pointing out that they did not apply to the case of the "Chesapeake," Madison requested Jackson to show his full powers, as an "indispensable preliminary to further negotiation." The letter was short, and ended with a stern warning:—

"I abstain, sir, from making any particular animadversions on several irrelevant and improper allusions in your letter, not at all comporting with the professed disposition to adjust, in an amicable manner, the differences unhappily subsisting between the two countries; but it would be improper to conclude the few observations to which I purposely limit myself, without adverting to your repetition of a language implying a knowledge on the part of this Government that the instructions of your predecessor did not authorize the arrangement formed by him. After the explicit and peremptory asseveration that this Government had no such knowledge, and that with such a knowledge no such arrangement would have been entered into, the view which you have again presented of the subject makes it my duty to apprise you that such insinuations are inadmissible in the intercourse of a foreign minister with a Government that understands what it owes to itself."

This letter placed Jackson in a position which he could not defend, and from which he thought, perhaps with reason, that he could not without disgrace retreat. The insinuations he had made were but a cautious expression of the views he was expressly ordered to take. November 4 he replied, with more ability than he had hitherto shown, to the letter of November 1; but he gave himself, for a mere point of temper, into Madison's hands.

"I am concerned, sir, to be obliged, a second time, to appeal to those principles of public law, under the sanction and protection of which I was sent to this country. . . . You will find that in my correspondence with you I have carefully avoided drawing conclusions that did not necessarily follow from the premises advanced by me, and least of all should I think of uttering an insinuation where I was unable to substantiate a fact. To facts, such as I have become acquainted with them, I have scrupulously adhered; and in so doing I must continue, whenever the good faith of his majesty's government is called in question, to vindicate its honor and dignity in the manner that appears to me best calculated for that purpose."

When Jackson was sent to Copenhagen with a message whose general tenor resembled that which he brought to the United States, he was fortunate enough to be accompanied by twenty ships of the line, forty frigates, and thirty thousand regular troops. Even with this support, if court gossip could be believed, King George expressed to him surprise that he had escaped being kicked downstairs. At Washington he had no other force on his side than such as his footman or his groom could render, and the destiny that King George predicted for him could not, by any diplomatic weapons, be longer escaped. November 8, Secretary Smith sent to the Legation one more note, which closed Jackson's diplomatic career:—

"Sir, . . . Finding that in your reply of the 4th instant you have used a language which cannot be understood but as reiterating and even aggravating the same gross insinuation, it only remains, in order to preclude opportunities which are thus abused, to inform you that no further communications will be received from you. . . ."

. . . (V, vi, 129-32)

2.

The Duc De Cadore's Letter

This was the situation of the American dispute June 13, 1809, at Vienna, at the moment Canning's disavowal of Erskine became certain. Thus far Napoleon's mind had passed through two changes —the first, in consequence of the British Order in Council of April 26, which led him to decide on withdrawing the Milan Decree; the second, in consequence of Erskine's arrangement, which led him to promise America everything she asked. The news of Canning's refusal to carry out the arrangement stopped Napoleon short in his career of concession; he left the American affair untouched until after the battle of Wagram, July 6, which was followed by the submission of Austria, July 12. The battle of Wagram placed him in a position to defy resistance. Immediately afterward he sent orders to Paris to stop Hauterive's[4] negotiation. About the middle of July, Hauterive told the American minister "that a change had taken place in the views of the Emperor; and in particular that a decree prepared by his orders as a substitute for those of November, 1806, and December, 1807, and which would have been a very material step toward accommodation, had been laid aside."

In the heat and fury of the battle of Wagram this order must have been given, for it was known at Paris only one week afterward; and Armstrong reported the message, July 24, as a notice that unless America resisted the British doctrines of search and blockade she need expect no relaxation on the part of Napoleon. . . . (V, vii, 141-42)

No decision seems to have been reached until August. Then Maret, the Secretary of State in personal attendance on the Em-

---

[4] Alexandre Maurice d'Hauterive: Acting Minister for Foreign Affairs.

peror, created Duc de Bassano a few days later, enclosed to Champagny,[5] August 4, the draft of a new decree, which was never published, but furnished the clue to most of the intricate movements of Napoleon for the following year:—

"Napoleon, etc.—considering that the American Congress by its Act of March 1, 1809, has forbidden the entrance of its ports to all French vessels under penalty of confiscation of ships and cargo,—on the report of our Minister of Finance have decreed and decree what follows:—

"Art. 1. The American schooner loaded with colonial produce and entered at San Sebastian the 20th May, 1809, will be seized and confiscated.

"Art. 2. The merchandise composing the cargo of the vessel will be conveyed to Bayonne, there to be sold, and the produce of the sale paid into the *caisse de l'amortissement* (sinking fund).

"Art. 3. Every American ship which shall enter the ports of France, Spain, or Italy will be equally seized and confiscated, as long as the same measure shall continue to be executed in regard to French vessels in the harbors of the United States."

Probably the ministers united in objecting to a general confiscation founded on the phrase of a penalty which the customs laws of every country necessarily contained. Whatever the reason, this draft rested in the files of the office over which Champagny presided, and the Emperor seemed to forget it; but its advantages from his standpoint were too great to be lost, and its principle was thenceforward his guide. . . . (V, vii, 143-44)

Under such conditions commerce between the United States and France seemed impossible. One prohibition crowded upon another. First came the Berlin Decree of November 21, 1806, which turned away or confiscated every American vessel voluntarily entering a British port after that date. Second, followed the Milan Decree of November 11, 1807, which denationalized and converted into English property every American ship visited by a British cruiser or sent into a British port, or which had paid any tax to the British government. Third, the Bayonne Decree of April 5, 1808, sequestered all American vessels arriving in France subsequent to the embargo, as being presumably British property. Fourth, the American Non-intercourse Act of March 1, 1809, prohibited all

[5] Jean Baptiste de Champagny (later Duc de Cadore): Minister for Foreign Affairs in place of Talleyrand.

commerce with France or her dependencies. Fifth, the British Orders in Council of April 26, 1809, established a blockade of the whole coast of France. Sixth, the secret Decree of Vienna, of August, 1809, enforced in principle, sequestered every American vessel arriving within the Emperor's military control, in reprisal for the Non-intercourse Act which threatened French ships with confiscation. . . . (V, viii, 152-53)

The President's Annual Message, read November 29 before Congress, threw no light on the situation. . . . (V, ix, 176)

No course would have pleased Congress so much as to do nothing at all; but this wish could not be fully gratified. The Non-intercourse Act of March 1, 1809, was to expire by limitation with the actual session. As early as December 1, the House referred the matter to a committee with Macon for its head. Macon probably went to the Treasury for instructions. A plan drawn by Gallatin, and accepted without opposition by the Cabinet, was reported December 19 to the House in the form of a bill which had less the character of a Non-intercourse than of a Navigation Act; for while it closed American ports to every British or French vessel public and private, it admitted British and French merchandise when imported directly from their place of origin in vessels wholly American. The measure was as mild a protest as human skill could devise if compared with the outrages it retaliated, but it had the merit of striking at the British shipping interest which was chiefly to blame for the conduct of the British government. Under the provisions of the bill, American shipping would gain a monopoly of American trade. Not a British vessel of any kind could enter an American port. . . . (V, ix, 183-84)

January 29, by a vote of seventy-three to fifty-two, the House passed the bill. The Senate soon afterward took it up; and then, as was to be expected, the factions broke loose. February 21, at the motion of Senator Samuel Smith, by a vote of sixteen to eleven the Senate struck everything from the bill except the enacting clause and the exclusion of belligerent war vessels from United States' harbors.

An Administration measure could not without rousing angry feelings be so abruptly mutilated by a knot of Administration senators. Samuel Smith's motives, given in his own words, were entitled to proper attention; but President Madison's opinion on the subject, whether correct or mistaken, had even more effect on what was to follow. Madison believed that the rejection of the bill was an intrigue of the Smiths for selfish or personal objects. . . . (V, ix, 185-86)

Perhaps this explanation, however offensive to the Smiths, injured them less than the other suspicion which had as much vogue as the first—that their conduct toward Macon's bill was a part of their feud against Gallatin, and proved their determination to oppose everything he suggested. At the moment when Samuel Smith revolted against Macon's measure, Washington was filled with tales of quarrels in the Cabinet. In truth, these reports were greatly exaggerated. Robert Smith had not the capacity to develop or to pursue a difficult line of argument even without opposition. Against Gallatin he could not, and as Madison testified did not, open his mouth, nor did Gallatin or Madison ever complain except of Smith's silence in the Cabinet; but he talked freely in society, and every one heard of battles supposed to be raging. . . . (V, ix, 187-88)

Upon feelings so irritable and at a moment when schism was imminent, as Walter Jones[6] described, the action of Samuel Smith and Michael Leib with six or eight more Republican senators, in emasculating Macon's bill, left small chance of reconciliation. Giles, having declared himself in favor of energy, did not vote at all. The debate being for the most part not reported, the arguments of the dissenting senators have been lost. One speaker alone broke the monotony of the discussion by an address that marked the beginning of an epoch.

Henry Clay had been barely two weeks a senator, when, February 22, he rose to move that the bill as amended by Samuel Smith be recommitted; and this motion he supported by a war speech of no great length, but full of Western patriotism.

"The conquest of Canada is in your power," he said. "I trust I shall not be deemed presumptuous when I state that I verily believe that the militia of Kentucky are alone competent to place Montreal and Upper Canada at your feet. . . . The withered arm and wrinkled brow of the illustrious founders of our freedom are melancholy indications that they will shortly be removed from us. Their deeds of glory and renown will then be felt only through the cold medium of the historic page; we shall want the presence and living

[6] Walter Jones: Representative from Virginia.

example of a new race of heroes to supply their places, and to animate us to preserve inviolate what they achieved. . . . I call upon
the members of this House to maintain its character for vigor. I beseech them not to forfeit the esteem of the country. Will you set the
base example to the other House of an ignominious surrender of our
rights after they have been reproached for imbecility and you extolled for your energy! But, sir, if we could be so forgetful of ourselves, I trust we shall spare you [Vice-President George Clinton]
the disgrace of signing, with those hands so instrumental in the
Revolution, a bill abandoning some of the most precious rights which
it then secured. . . ."

Other members both of the House and of the Senate had made
war speeches, and in Clay's harangue no idea could be called original; yet apart from the energy and courage which showed a new
and needed habit of command, these sentences of Clay's maiden
speech marked the appearance of a school which was for fifty
years to express the national ideals of statesmanship, drawing elevation of character from confidence in itself, and from devotion to
ideas of nationality and union, which redeemed every mistake
committed in their names. In Clay's speech almost for the first
time the two rhetorical marks of his generation made their appearance, and during the next half century the Union and the Fathers
were rarely omitted from any popular harangue. The ideas became
in the end fetiches and phrases; but they were at least more easily
understood than the fetiches and phrases of Jeffersonian republicanism which preceded them. Federalists used the name of Washington in the same rhetorical manner, but they used it for party
purposes to rebuke Washington's successors. The Union and the
Fathers belonged to no party, and might be used with equal advantage by orators of every section. Clay enjoyed almost alone for
years the advantage of winning popularity by this simple means.
. . . (V, ix, 189-91)

Macon's bill No. 2 was the last of the annual legislative measures
taken by Congress to counteract by commercial interest the encroachments of France and Great Britain. The first was the Partial
Non-intercourse Act of April, 1806; the second was the Embargo
Act with its supplements, dating from December 22, 1807; the
third was the Total Non-intercourse Act of March 1, 1809; and the
fourth was Macon's bill No. 2. Each year produced a new experiment; but the difference could be easily remembered, for after
the climax of the embargo each successive annual enactment showed

weakening faith in the policy, until Macon's bill No. 2 marked the last stage toward the admitted failure of commercial restrictions as a substitute for war. Abandoning the pretence of direct resistance to France and England, this measure repealed the Non-intercourse Act of March 1, 1809, leaving commercial relations with all the world as free as ever before, but authorizing the President "in case either Great Britain or France shall, before the 3d day of March next, so revoke or modify her edicts as that they shall cease to violate the neutral commerce of the United States," to prohibit intercourse with the nation which had not revoked its edicts.

The objections to the bill were overpowering, for its effect was equivalent to alliance with England. Had the United States taken active part in the war against France, they could have done Napoleon no greater injury than by the passage of this Act, which invited Great Britain to control American commerce for her military purposes. On the other hand the bill conferred on the President a discretion dangerous, unconstitutional, and unnecessary,—a power once before conferred by the Non-intercourse Act of March 1, 1809, and then resulting in the mistakes of Erskine's arrangement, which seemed warning enough against repeating the same risk. . . . (V, ix, 194-95)

April 19 the bill passed the House by a vote of sixty-one to forty. The Senate referred it to a select committee with Samuel Smith at its head—a committee made for Smith to control. As before, he reported the measure with its only effective provision—the additional duty—struck out, and with the addition of a convoy clause. The Senate, by nineteen votes to eight, sustained Smith; nor did one New England senator, Federalist or Republican, vote for the protection offered by Kentucky and Virginia. The bill went to a third reading by a vote of twenty-one to seven, and April 28, having passed the Senate as Smith reported it without a division, was sent back to the House for concurrence.

Irritated though the House was by the Senate's hostility to every measure which had support from the Treasury or was calculated to give it support, the members were for the most part anxious only to see the session ended. No one cared greatly for Macon's bill No. 2 in any shape. The House refused to accept the Senate's amendments, and found itself May 1 within a few hours of adjournment, and within the same time of seeing the Non-intercourse Act expire, without having made provision for the commercial relations that were to follow. Perhaps Congress might have shown wisdom by doing nothing; but the instinct to do something was strong, and party feeling mixed with the sense of responsibility. At five o'clock in the afternoon committees of conference were appointed, and at the evening session, Samuel Smith having abandoned his convoy clause, the House gave up its extra duties and the bill came to its passage. . . . (V, ix, 197-98)

When Congress adjourned, May 2, 1810, the result attained during five months passed in continuous labor amounted to little more than the constitutional necessities of government—the appropriation bills; a loan for five million dollars; an Act for taking a census of persons; an Act appropriating sixty thousand dollars toward making the Cumberland Road; an appropriation of five thousand dollars for experiments on Fulton's torpedoes; in regard to foreign affairs, Giles's Resolution blaming the conduct of the British minister, and Macon's or Taylor's Act, which condoned that conduct. The old Non-intercourse Act of March 1, 1809, expired by limitation with the expiring Congress May 1, 1810.

"We adjourned last night," wrote Randolph to Nicholson the next day, "a little after twelve, having terminated a session of more than five months by authorizing a loan of as many millions, and—all is told. The incapacity of Government has long ceased to be a laughing matter. The Cabinet is all to pieces, and the two Houses have tumbled about their own ears."

With all Randolph's faults, he had more of the qualities, training, and insight of a statesman that were to be found elsewhere among the representatives in the Eleventh Congress; and although himself largely the cause of the chaos he described, he felt its disgraces and dangers. Society in general troubled itself little about them. The commercial class, pleased to be freed from restraints, and the agricultural class, consoled by the fair prices of their produce, thought as little as possible about their failure in government; what was called good society for the most part drew a bitter pleasure from it. Yet beneath the general physical contentment almost equally general moral disgust existed and made itself felt. President Madison, who was in the best position to gauge popular opinion, began to suspect the hardly perceptible movement of a coming tide. After the adjournment he wrote to William Pinkney at London:

"Among the inducements to the experiment of an unrestricted commerce now made were two which contributed essentially to the majority of votes in its favor—the first, a general hope, favored by daily accounts from England, that an adjustment of differences there, and thence in France, would render the measure safe and proper; second, a willingness in not a few to teach the advocates for an open trade the folly as well as degradation of their policy. . . . It will not be wonderful, therefore, if the passive spirit which marked the late session of Congress should at the next meeting be roused to the opposite point, more especially as the tone of the nation has never been so low as that of its representatives."

. . . (V, x, 209-10)

Boston newspapers of February 9, 1810, contained the report and resolutions in which the Massachusetts legislature, by a vote of 254 to 145, declared that "they can perceive no just or adequate cause" for breaking relations with the British minister, F. J. Jackson; and this challenge to their own Government, backed by Governor Gore's[7] invitation of Jackson to Boston, was intended to carry political weight, even to the extent of forcing Madison to renew commercial relations, with England. Had public opinion taken the intended course, Jackson's visit to Boston would have marked a demonstration of popular feeling against the national government; nor were the Federalists in any way parties consenting to the defeat of the scheme. The measures adopted by the Massachusetts legislature in February came before the people at the State election early in April, only six weeks after the General Court and Governor Gore had condemned Madison. More than ninety thousand votes were cast, and the Republican party, by a majority of about two thousand, not only turned Governor Gore out of office, but also chose a General Court with a Republican majority of twenty. At the same time similar changes of public opinion restored New Hampshire to Republican control, and strengthened the Republicans in New York and the Middle States. Not a doubt could exist that the country sustained Madison, and that Jackson was not only an object of decided unpopularity in America, but was far from being favored in England. . . . (V, x, 214-15)

For three weeks Napoleon made no decision on the subject of the American Act; then, after settling the annexation of Holland, he wrote to Cadore[8] July 3:

[7] Christopher Gore: Governor of Massachusetts.
[8] Duc de Cadore: see Champagny, n. 5, *supra.*

"After having much reflected on the affairs of America, I have thought
that to repeal my Decrees of Berlin and Milan would have no effect;
that it would be better for you to take a note to Mr. Armstrong by
which you should let him know that you have put under my eyes
the details contained in the American newspaper; that I should have
liked to have a more official communication, but that time passes,
and that—since he assures me we may regard this as official—he can
consider that my Decrees of Berlin and Milan will have no effect,
dating from November 1; and that he is to consider them as withdrawn in consequence of such Act of the American Congress, on condition that (*à condition que*) if the British Council does not withdraw its Orders of 1807, the United States Congress shall fulfil the
engagement it has taken to re-establish its prohibitions on British
commerce. This appears to me more suitable than a decree which
would cause a shock (*qui ferait secousse*) and would not fulfil my
object. This method appears to me more conformable to my dignity
and to the seriousness of the affair."

The Emperor himself, August 2, dictated the letter—the most
important he ever sent to the United States government. During
the next three days he made numerous changes in the draft; but
at last it was signed and sent to the American Legation. Upon that
paper, long famous as Cadore's letter of August 5, 1810, turned the
course of subsequent events; but apart from its practical consequences the student of history, whether interested in the character
of Napoleon or of Madison, or in the legal aspects of war and
peace, or in the practice of governments and the capacity of different peoples for self-government, could find few examples or illus-
trations better suited to his purpose than the letter itself, the policy
it revealed, and the manner in which it was received by the United
States and Great Britain.

Cadore began by saying that he had communicated to the Emperor the newspaper containing the Act of Congress of May 1. The
Emperor could have wished that all the acts of the United States
government which concerned France had always been officially
made known to him:—

"In general, he has only had indirect knowledge of them after a
long interval of time. From this delay serious inconveniences have
resulted which would not have existed had these acts been promptly
and officially communicated.

"The Emperor applauded the general embargo laid by the United
States on all their vessels, because that measure, if it has been prejudicial to France, had in it at least nothing offensive to her honor.

It has caused her to lose her colonies of Martinique, Guadeloupe, and Cayenne; the Emperor has not complained of it. He has made this sacrifice to the principle which has determined the Americans to lay the embargo. . . . The Act of March 1 [1809] raised the embargo and substituted for it a measure the most injurious to the interests of France. This Act, of which the Emperor knew nothing until very lately, interdicted to American vessels the commerce of France at the time it authorized that to Spain, Naples, and Holland,—that is to say, to the countries under French influence,—and denounced confiscation against all French vessels which should enter the ports of America. Reprisal was a right, and commanded by the dignity of France,—a circumstance on which it was impossible to make a compromise (de transiger). The sequestration of all the American vessels in France has been the necessary consequence of the measure taken by Congress."

This preamble, interesting for the novelty of its assertions both of fact and law, led to the conclusion that the Act of May 1, 1810, was a retreat from the Act of March 1, 1809, and warranted France in accepting the offer extended by both laws to the nation which should first "cease to violate the neutral commerce of the United States."

"In this new state of things," concluded Cadore, "I am authorized to declare to you, sir, that the Decrees of Berlin and Milan are revoked, and that after November 1 they will cease to have effect,— it being understood (bien entendu) that in consequence of this declaration the English are to revoke their Orders in Council, and renounce the new principles of blockade which they have wished to establish; or that the United States, conformably to the Act you have just communicated, cause their rights to be respected by the English."

No phraseology could have more embarrassed President Madison, while, as Napoleon had remarked to Montalivet a few days before, "it is evident that we commit ourselves to nothing." So closely was the Imperial promise imitated from that given by Erskine that the President could hardly reject it, although no American merchant would have risked so much as a cargo of salt fish on a pledge of such a kind from such a man. As though to warn the Americans, Napoleon added personal assurances that gave to the whole proceeding an unpleasant air of burlesque:—

"It is with the most particular satisfaction, sir, that I make known to you this determination of the Emperor. His Majesty loves the

Americans. Their prosperity and their commerce are within the scope of his policy. The independence of America is one of the principal titles of glory to France. Since that epoch the Emperor is pleased in aggrandizing the United States; and under all circumstances that which can contribute to the independence, to the prosperity, and to the liberty of the Americans the Emperor will consider as conformable with the interests of his empire."

One might doubt whether Napoleon or Canning were the more deficient in good taste; but Americans whose nerves were irritated to fury by the irony of Canning, found these expressions of Napoleon's love rather absurd than insulting. So little had the mere fact of violence to do with the temper of politics, compared with the sentiments which surrounded it, that Napoleon could seize without notice ten million dollars' worth of American property, imprisoning the American crews of two or three hundred vessels in his dungeons, while at the same instant he told the Americans that he loved them, that their commerce was within the scope of his policy, and as a climax avowed a scheme to mislead the United States government, hardly troubling himself to use forms likely to conceal his object; yet the vast majority of Americans never greatly resented acts which seemed to them like the exploits of an Italian brigand on the stage. Beyond doubt, Napoleon regarded his professions of love and interest not as irony or extravagance, but as adapted to deceive. A few weeks earlier he sent a message to the Czar of Russia, who asked him to disavow the intention of restoring the kingdom of Poland. "If I should ever sign," replied Napoleon, "a declaration that the kingdom of Poland shall never be restored, it would be for the reason that I intended to restore it,—a trap I should set for Russia"; and in signing a declaration to the President that his decrees were repealed, he set a trap for the United States, which he baited with professions of love that to a more refined taste would have seemed fatal to his object.

The mixture of feline qualities,—energy, astuteness, secrecy, and rapidity,—combined with ignorance of other natures than his own, was shown in the act with which he concluded his arrangements of August 5, 1810. About a fortnight before, by a secret decree dated July 22, 1810, he had ordered the proceeds of the American cargoes seized at Antwerp and in Dutch and Spanish ports, valued by him at six million dollars, to be turned into the Treasury as a part of his customs revenue devoted to the service of 1809-10. In French ports he held still some fifty ships in sequestration. Cadore's letter

of August 5 mentioned these ships as sequestered,—a phrase implying that they would be held subject to future negotiation and decision, liable to be returned to their owners; yet on the same day
Napoleon signed another secret decree which condemned without
hearing or judgment all the ships and cargoes declared to be still
in sequestration by the letter that could hardly have yet been sent
from Cadore's office. Every vessel which had arrived in French ports
between May 20, 1809, and May 1, 1810, suffered confiscation by this
decree, which further ordered that the American crews should be
released from the dungeons where they were held as prisoners of
war, and that from August 5 to November 1, 1810, American ships
should be allowed to enter French ports, but should not discharge
their cargoes without a license.

The Decree of August 5 was never made public. Armstrong indeed employed the last hours of his stay in Paris in asking whether
the French government meant to admit further negotiation about
these seizures, and Cadore replied that the law of reprisals was
final; but when Albert Gallatin, as minister at Paris some ten
years afterward, happened to obtain a copy of the document, he
expressed his anger at its secrecy in language such as he used in
regard to no other transaction of his public life. "No one can suppose," he wrote, "that if it had been communicated or published
at the same time, the United States would with respect to the promised revocation of the Berlin and Milan Decrees have taken that
ground which ultimately led to the war with Great Britain. It is
indeed unnecessary to comment on such a glaring act of combined
injustice, bad faith, and meanness as the enacting and concealment
of that decree exhibits." These epithets would not have disturbed
Napoleon. Politics were to him a campaign, and if his opponents
had not the sense to divine his movements and motives, the disgrace
and disaster were none of his. . . . (V, xii, 252-59)

The summer of 1810 was quiet and hopeful in America. For the
first time since December, 1807, trade was free. Although little
immigration occurred, the census showed an increase in population
of nearly 37 per cent in ten years—from 5,300,000 to 7,240,000, of
which less than one hundred thousand was due to the purchase of
Louisiana. Virginia and Massachusetts still fairly held their own,
and New York strode in advance of Pennsylvania, while the West
gained little relative weight. Ohio had not yet a quarter of a million
people, Indiana only twenty-four thousand, and Illinois but twelve
thousand, while Michigan contained less than five thousand. The

third census showed no decided change in the balance of power from any point of view bounded by the usual horizon of human life. Perhaps the growth of New York city and Philadelphia pointed to a movement among the American people which might prove more revolutionary than any mere agricultural movement westward. Each of these cities contained a population of ninety-six thousand, while Baltimore rose to forty-six thousand, and Boston to thirty-two thousand. The tendency toward city life, if not yet unduly great, was worth noticing, especially because it was confined to the seaboard States of the North.

The reason of this tendency could in part be seen in the Treasury reports on American shipping, which reached in 1810 a registered tonnage of 1,424,000—a point not again passed until 1826. The registered foreign tonnage sprang to 984,000—a point not again reached in nearly forty years. New vessels were built to the amount of 127,000 tons in the year 1810. The value of all the merchandise exported in the year ending Sept. 30, 1810, amounted to nearly $67,000,000, and of this sum about $42,000,000 represented articles of domestic production. Except in the year before the embargo this export of domestic produce had never been much exceeded. The imports, as measured by the revenue, were on the same scale. The net customs-revenue which reached $16,500,000 in 1807, after falling in 1808 and 1809 to about $7,000,000, rose again to $12,750,-000 in 1810. The profits of the export and import business fell chiefly to Boston, New York, Philadelphia, and Baltimore, where the shipping belonged; and these cities could not fail to attract labor as well as capital beyond the degree that a conservative republican of the Revolutionary time would have thought safe.

More than half of these commercial exchanges were with England or her dependencies. Great Britain and her American colonies, Portugal and Spain in her military protection, and British India consumed at least one half of the exports; while of the net revenue collected on imports, Gallatin estimated $6,500,000 as derived from articles imported from Great Britain and the British dependencies, all other sources supplying hardly $6,000,000. The nature of these imports could be only roughly given. In general, sugar, molasses, coffee, wines, silk, and tea were not British; but manufactures of cotton, linen, leather, paper, glass, earthenware, iron, and other metals came chiefly from Great Britain. To the United States this British trade brought most of the articles necessary to daily comfort in every part of the domestic economy. The relief of recovering a full and cheap supply exceeded the satisfaction of handsome profits on the renewed trade. Experience of the hourly annoyance, expense, and physical exposure caused by deprivation of what society considered necessities rendered any return to the restrictive system in the highest degree unwise, especially after the eastern people acquired conviction that the system had proved a failure.

Thus the summer passed with much of the old contentment that marked the first Administration of Jefferson. Having lost sight of national dignity, the commercial class was contented under the protection of England; and American ships in the Baltic, in Portugal, and in the West Indies never hesitated to ask and were rarely refused the assistance of the British navy. From time to time a few impressments were reported; but impressment had never been the chief subject of complaint, and after the withdrawal of the frigates blockading New York, little was heard of British violence. On the other hand, Napoleon's outrages roused great clamor in commercial society, and his needless harshness to every victim, from the Pope to the American sailors whom he shut up as prisoners of war, went far to palliate British offences in the eyes of American merchants.

News of Napoleon's seizures at San Sebastian arrived before the adjournment of Congress May 1; and as fresh outrages were reported from every quarter by every new arrival, and as Cadore's letters became public, even Madison broke into reproaches. May 25 he wrote to Jefferson: "The late confiscations by Bonaparte comprise robbery, theft, and breach of trust, and exceed in turpitude any of his enormities not wasting human blood." These words seemed to show intense feeling, but Madison's temper indulged in outbursts of irritability without effect on his action; in reality, his mind was bent beyond chance of change on the old idea of his Revolutionary education,—that the United States must not regard France, but must resist Great Britain by commercial restrictions. "This scene on the Continent," he continued to Jefferson, "and the effect of English monopoly on the value of our produce are breaking the charm attached to what is called free trade, foolishly by some and wickedly by others." He reverted to his life-long theory of commercial regulations. . . . (V, xiv, 289-93)

Cadore's letter of August 5 announcing that the French Decrees were withdrawn, on the understanding that the United States should by November 1 enforce their rights against England, reached Washington September 25, but not in official form. Nothing is known of the impression it produced on the Cabinet; nothing remains of any discussions that ensued. If Gallatin was consulted, he left no trace of his opinion. Hamilton and Eustis had little weight in deciding foreign questions. Robert Smith within a year afterward publicly attacked the President for the course pursued, and gave the impression that it was taken on Madison's sole judgment. The President's only authority to act at all without consulting Congress depended on the words of the law of May 1: "In case either Great Britain or France shall, before the third day of March next, so revoke or modify her edicts as that they shall cease to violate the neutral commerce of the United States, which fact the President of the United States shall proclaim by proclamation," the non-intercourse of March 1, 1809, should at the end of three months revive against the nation which had not revoked its edicts. Under this authority, President Madison was required by Cadore's letter to proclaim that France had revoked or modified her edicts so that they ceased to violate the neutral commerce of the United States.

Madison was doubtless a man of veracity; but how was it possible that any man of veracity could proclaim that France had revoked or modified her edicts so that they ceased to violate the neutral commerce of the United States when he had every reason to think that at least the Bayonne Decree, barely six months old, would not be revoked, and when within a few weeks he had officially declared that the revocation of the Bayonne Decree was "an indispensable evidence of the just purpose of France" preliminary to a non-intercourse with England? If the President in June and July thought that provision indispensable to the true intent of the law which he aided in framing, he would assume something more than royal dispensing power by setting the indispensable provision aside in November.

This objection was light in comparison with others. The law required the President to proclaim a fact—that France had revoked or modified her decrees so that they ceased to violate the commerce of America. Of this fact Cadore's letter was the only proof; but evidently Cadore's letter pledged the Emperor to nothing. "I am authorized to declare to you," wrote Cadore, "that the Decrees of Berlin and Milan are revoked, and that after November 1 they will cease to have effect, on the understanding that in consequence of this declaration . . . the United States, conformably to the Act you have just communicated, shall cause their rights to be respected by the English." Napoleon not only reserved to himself the right of judging whether the measures to be taken by the United States should "cause their rights to be respected," but in doing so he reversed the process prescribed by the Act, and required the President to enforce his rights before the Emperor should withdraw his decrees. . . . (V, xiv, 296-98)

Having decided to accept Cadore's letter as proof that an actual repeal of the French Decrees, within the meaning of the Act of Congress, had taken place November 1, the President issued, November 2, his proclamation declaring that "it has been officially made known to this Government that the said edicts of France have been so revoked as that they ceased, on the said first day of the present month, to violate the neutral commerce of the United States"; and simultaneously Gallatin issued a circular to the collectors of customs, announcing that commercial intercourse with Great Britain would cease February 2, 1811.

By this means Madison succeeded in reverting to his methods of peaceful coercion. As concerned England, he could be blamed only on the ground that his methods were admittedly inadequate, as Gallatin, only a year before, had officially complained. Toward England the United States had stood for five years in a position which warranted them in adopting any measure of reprisal. The people of America alone had a right to object that when Madison began his attack on England by proclaiming the French Decrees to be revoked, he made himself a party to Napoleon's fraud, and could scarcely blame the Federalists for replying that neither in honor nor in patriotism were they bound to abet him in such a scheme. . . . (V, xiv, 303-304)

President Madison's Annual Message, December 5, called attention to such business as he wished to present. Naturally, the revocation of the French Decrees took the first place. The President assumed that the revocation was complete, and that his proclamation was issued in regular course, "as prescribed by law," the President having no discretion; but he admitted disappointment that the sequestered property had not been restored. "It was particularly anticipated that as a further evidence of just disposition toward them, restoration would have been immediately made of the property of our citizens, seized under a misapplication of the principle of reprisals, combined with a misconstruction of a law of the United States. This expectation has not been fulfilled." England had not yet relinquished her illegitimate blockades, and she avowed that

the blockade of May, 1806, was comprehended in the subsequent
Orders in Council; the withdrawal of that blockade had therefore
been required by the President as one of the conditions of renewing intercourse with Great Britain. . . . (V, xiv, 317-18)

3.

The 11th Congress: " . . . The Last Stage of Imbecility": March 3, 1811

Congress . . . turned to the charter of the United States Bank. Long hesitation had ended by creating difficulties. Local interests hostile to the Bank sprang into existence. In many States private banks were applying for charters, and preparing to issue notes in the hope of seizing their share of the profits of the United States Bank. The influence of these new corporations was great. They induced one State legislature after another to instruct their senators on the subject. That Massachusetts, Pennsylvania, and Maryland should wish to appropriate the profits of the National Bank was not surprising, but that Virginia and Kentucky should make themselves instruments of the capitalist States showed little knowledge of their true interests. As the crisis came near, the struggle became hotter, until it rivalled the embargo excitement, and every hour of delay increased the vehemence of opposition to the charter.

The Bank was vulnerable on more than one side. Largely owned in England, it roused jealousy as a foreign influence. Congress could hardly blame this ownership, since Congress itself, in 1802, aided President Jefferson in selling to the Barings, at a premium of 45 per cent, the 2,220 Bank shares still belonging to the government. The operation brought to the Treasury not only a profit of $400,000 in premiums, but also about $1,300,000 of British capital to be used for American purposes. Fully two thirds of the Bank stock, amounting to $10,000,000, were owned in England; all the 5,000 shares originally subscribed by the United States government had been sold to England; and as the Bank was a mere creature of the United States government, these $7,000,000 of British capital were equivalent to a score of British frigates or regiments lent to the

United States to use against England in war. By returning them, the United States seriously weakened themselves and strengthened their enemy.

Unfortunately this interest was national. Local interests felt that Englishmen received profits which should belong to Americans; and capitalists in general were not inclined to lower their profits by inviting foreign capital into the country unless they shared its returns. The second misfortune of the Bank was that of being a Federalist creation, chiefly used for the benefit of Federalists, who owned most of the active capital in the country. The third objection went deeper. The Bank was the last vestige of strong government created by the Federalists,—a possible engine of despotism; and no one could deny that if decentralization was wise, the Bank should be suppressed. Finally, the Bank was a bulwark to Gallatin; its destruction would weaken Madison and drive Gallatin from office.

Doubtless the objections to the Bank were so strong as some day to become fatal. In a society and government so little developed as those of America, a National Bank was out of keeping with other institutions. Even in England and France these banks exercised more influence over the Treasury than was proper; and in America, if once the Bank should unite in political sympathy with the Government, it might do no little harm. The necessity for such an institution was merely one of the moment, but in the period of national history between 1790 and 1860, the year 1811 was perhaps the only moment when destruction of the Bank threatened national ruin. . . . (V, xv, 327-30)

When the Senate, February 20, divided on the motion to strike out the enacting clause, seventeen senators voted for the Bank and seventeen voted against it. Nine northern senators voted in its favor, including seven of the ten from New England, and nine on the opposite side. Eight southern senators voted one way, and eight the other. Of the twenty-seven Republican senators, seventeen voted against the Bank, and ten in its favor; while the three senators who were supposed to be in personal opposition to the President— Giles, Samuel Smith, and Michael Leib—all voted in opposition. The force of personal feeling was credited with still another vote; for when the result was announced, the Vice-President, George Clinton, whose attitude was notorious, made a short address to the effect that "the power to create corporations is not expressly granted; it is a high attribute of sovereignty, and in its nature not accessorial or derivative by implication, but primary and independent." On this ground he threw his casting vote against the bill.

So perished the first Bank of the United States; and with its destruction the Federalist crisis, so long threatened, began at last to throw its shadow over the government. . . . (V, xv, 336-37)

The Tenth Congress had increased the military establishment, until in 1808 the appropriations exceeded $4,700,000. The Eleventh Congress reduced them in 1809-1810 to about $3,100,000; in 1811 Congress appropriated barely $3,000,000. The naval appropriations in 1809 reached nearly $3,000,000; in 1810 they were reduced to about $1,600,000; in 1811 Congress appropriated $1,870,000. Even in a time of profound peace, when no thought of war disturbed the world, such armaments would have been hardly sufficient for purposes of police on the coasts and in the territories.

A short debate took place at the last moment of the session, on a bill authorizing the President to accept a corps of fifty thousand volunteers. The measure had been reported by Crawford of Georgia in the Senate, from a committee appointed to consider the occupation of West Florida. March 1 the Senate passed the bill without a division, for it implied neither a new principle nor any necessary expense; while the President, without such authority, would find himself helpless to deal with any trouble that might arise from the affairs of Florida. When the bill reached the House, John Dawson of Virginia urged its adoption; "it was incumbent on them," he said, "to do something to provide for defence." Matthew Lyon[9] said he had frequently voted for such bills when there was no prospect of war; "and now, when we were going to war [with Spain], and giving the provocation ourselves, he was of opinion it ought to be passed." The House, without a division, indefinitely postponed the bill; and thus refusing to do more business of any kind, toward midnight of Sunday, March 3, the Eleventh Congress expired, leaving behind it, in the minds of many serious citizens, the repute of having brought Government to the last stage of imbecility before dissolution. . . . (V, xvi, 357-58)

The government of the United States reached, March 4, 1811, the lowest point of its long decline. (V, xvii, 359)

[9] Matthew Lyon: Representative from Kentucky.

IV.

Toward a Moving Equilibrium:
The War of 1812 and Its Consequences

1.

Portents of a New Energy:
". . . The War Fever of 1811"

When November arrived, the day on which Napoleon's Decrees stood revoked according to the Duc de Cadore, Pinkney acted in London on his own responsibility, as Madison acted at Washington, and sent to Lord Wellesley[1] a note, dated November 3, asking for an immediate repeal of the British Orders in Council, on the ground that Napoleon's revocation had taken effect. "That it has taken effect cannot be doubted," he said; but he offered no evidence to support his assertion. He also assumed that England was bound to withdraw Fox's blockade to the French coast from Brest to the Elbe, as well as Spencer Perceval's subsequent measures which were called into existence by Napoleon's Continental system, and were to cease with it. . . . (VI, i, 3-4)

The withdrawal of the Orders in Council . . . was required on the ground that England had pledged her faith to withdraw them whenever France revoked her decrees. France had revoked her decrees, and England could not honorably refuse to withdraw the orders.

"As to the Orders in Council which professed to be a reluctant departure from all ordinary rules, and to be justified only as a system of retaliation for a pre-existing measure of France, their foundation, such as it was, is gone the moment that measure is no longer in operation. But the Berlin Decree is repealed, and even the Milan

[1] Richard Colley Wellesley, Marquis Wellesley: Foreign Secretary succeeding George Canning.

43

Decree, the successor of your Orders in Council, is repealed also. Why is it, then, that your orders have outlived those edicts?"

In both instances the American position lost character by connection with Napoleon's acts. Pinkney repudiated such a connection in the first case, and his argument would have been stronger could he have repudiated it in the second. Unable or unwilling to do this, he had no resource but to lose his temper, which he did with proper self-control. . . . (VI, i, 11)

Pinkney . . . consulted his instructions. These were dated November 15, 1810, and ordered Pinkney, in case no successor to F. J. Jackson should then have been appointed, to take leave of absence, entrusting the legation to a *chargé d'affaires;* but this positive order was practically revoked in the concluding sentence: "Considering the season at which this instruction may have its effect, and the possibility of a satisfactory change in the posture of our relations with Great Britain, the time of your return to the United States is left to your discretion and convenience."

These instructions did not warrant Pinkney in demanding leave of absence on any other ground than that of failure to appoint a minister at Washington. They did not warrant him in returning to America at all if he saw the possibility of such an appointment. Pinkney was obliged to put a free construction on the President's language. Abandoning the ground that his departure was a necessary result of the absence of a British minister at Washington, he asked Lord Wellesley, in an official note, dated February 17, what Mr. Foster[2] was to do when he arrived there? "I presume that for the restoration of harmony between the two countries, the Orders in Council will be relinquished without delay; that the blockade of 1806 will be annulled; that the case of the 'Chesapeake' will be arranged in the manner heretofore intended; and in general that all such just and reasonable acts will be done as are necessary to make us friends." So important a letter was probably never written by any other American diplomatist without instructions from his Government—for it was in effect an ultimatum, preliminary to the rupture of relations and ultimate war. . . . (VI, i, 16-18)

In order to leave no doubt of his meaning, Pinkney instantly claimed his audience of leave for February 28, declining, in the

[2] Augustus John Foster: British Minister to the United States, succeeding Jackson.

meantime, to attend the diplomatic levee which by postponement took place only February 26. His conduct was noticed and understood, as he meant it should be; and as his audience still remains the only occasion when an American minister at London has broken relations in a hostile manner, with resulting war, it has an interest peculiar to itself. Several accounts were preserved of what passed at the interview. Pinkney's official report recorded the words used by him:—

> "I stated to the Prince Regent the grounds upon which it had become my duty to take my leave and to commit the business of the legation to a *chargé d'affaires;* and I concluded by expressing my regret that my humble efforts in the execution of the instructions of my Government to set to rights the embarrassed and disjointed relations of the two countries had wholly failed; and that I saw no reason to expect that the great work of their reconciliation was likely to be accomplished through any other agency."

According to Pinkney, and according to the official report of Lord Wellesley, the Prince Regent replied in terms of the utmost amity toward the United States. Another account of the interview gave the impression that the Prince Regent had not shown himself so gracious toward the departing minister as the official reports implied. . . . (VI, i, 18-19)

So closed Pinkney's residence in London. He had passed there nearly five years of such violent national hostility as no other American minister ever faced during an equal length of time, or defied at last with equal sternness; but his extraordinary abilities and character made him greatly respected and admired while he stayed, and silenced remonstrance when he left. For many years afterward, his successors were mortified by comparisons between his table oratory and theirs. As a writer he was not less distinguished. Canning's impenetrable self-confidence met in him powers that did not yield, even in self-confidence, to his own; and Lord Wellesley's oriental dignity was not a little ruffled by Pinkney's handling. As occasion required, he was patient under irritation that seemed intolerable, as aggressive as Canning himself, or as stately and urbane as Wellesley; and even when he lost his temper, he did so in cold blood, because he saw no other way to break through the obstacles put in his path. America never sent an abler representative to the Court of London. . . . (VI, i, 20-21)

Although no one doubted that the year 1812 was to witness a new convulsion of society, if signs of panic occurred they were less marked in crowded countries where vast interests were at stake, than in remote regions which might have been thought as safe from Napoleon's wars as from those of Genghis Khan. As in the year 1754 a petty fight between two French and English scouting parties on the banks of the Youghiogheny River, far in the American wilderness, began a war that changed the balance of the world, so in 1811 an encounter in the Indian country, on the banks of the Wabash, began a fresh convulsion which ended only with the fall of Napoleon. The battle of Tippecanoe was a premature outbreak of the great wars of 1812.

Governor William Henry Harrison, of the Indiana Territory, often said he could tell by the conduct of his Indians, as by a thermometer, the chances of war and peace for the United States as estimated in the Cabinet at London. The remark was curious, but not surprising. Uneasiness would naturally be greatest where least control and most irritation existed. Such a region was the Northwestern Territory. Even the spot where violence would break out might be predicted as somewhere on the waterline of the Maumee and the Wabash, between Detroit at one extremity and Vincennes at the other. If a guess had been ventured that the most probable point would be found on that line, about half way between Lake Erie and the Ohio River, the map would have shown that Tippecanoe Creek, where it flowed into the Wabash, corresponded with the rough suggestion.

The Indiana Territory was created in 1800; and the former delegate of the whole Northwestern Territory, William Henry Harrison, was then appointed governor of the new division. Until the year 1809, Illinois formed part of the Indiana Territory; but its single settlement at Kaskaskia was remote. The Indiana settlement consisted mainly of two tracts,—one on the Ohio, opposite Louisville in Kentucky, at the falls, consisting of about one hundred and fifty thousand acres, called Clark's Grant; the other, at Vincennes on the Wabash, where the French had held a post, without a definite grant of lands, under an old Indian treaty, and where the Americans took whatever rights the French enjoyed. One hundred miles of wilderness separated these two tracts. In 1800, their population numbered about twenty-five hundred persons; in 1810, nearly twenty-five thousand.

Northward and westward, from the bounds of these districts the Indian country stretched to the Lakes and the Mississippi, unbroken except by military posts at Fort Wayne and Fort Dearborn, or Chicago, and a considerable settlement of white people in the neighborhood of the fortress at Detroit. Some five thousand Indian warriors held this vast region, and were abundantly able to expel every white man from Indiana if their organization had been as strong as their numbers. The whites were equally eager to expel the Indians, and showed the wish openly.

Governor Harrison was the highest authority on matters connected with the northwestern Indians. During eight years of Harrison's government Jefferson guided the Indian policy; and as long as Jefferson insisted on the philanthropic principles which were his pride, Harrison, whose genius lay in ready adaptation, took his tone from the President, and wrote in a different spirit from that which he would have taken had he represented an aggressive chief. His account of Indian affairs offered an illustration of the law accepted by all historians in theory, but adopted by none in practice; which former ages called "fate," and metaphysicians called "necessity," but which modern science has refined into the "survival of the fittest." No acid ever worked more mechanically on a vegetable fiber than the white man acted on the Indian. As the line of American settlements approached, the nearest Indian tribes withered away.

Harrison reported conscientiously the incurable evils which attended the contact of the two hostile forms of society. The first, but not the most serious, was that the white man, though not allowed to settle beyond the Indian border, could not be prevented from trespassing far and wide on Indian territory in search of game. The practice of hunting on Indian lands, in violation of law and existing treaties, had grown into a monstrous abuse. The Kentucky settlers crossed the Ohio River every autumn to kill deer, bear, and buffalo for their skins, which they had no more right to take than they had to cross the Alleghanies, and shoot or trap the cows and sheep in the farmyards of Bucks County. Many parts of the Northwestern Territory which as late as 1795 abounded in game, ten years afterward contained not game enough to support the small Indian parties passing through them, and had become worthless for Indian purposes except as a barrier to further encroachment.

The tribes that owned these lands were forced either to remove elsewhere, or to sell their old hunting grounds to the government for supplies or for an annuity. The tribes that sold, remaining near the settlements to enjoy their annuity, were more to be pitied than those that removed, which were destined to destruction by war. Harrison reported that contact with white settlements never failed to ruin them. "I can tell at once," he wrote in 1801, "upon looking at an Indian whom I may chance to meet, whether he belongs to a neighboring or to a more distant tribe. The latter is generally well clothed, healthy, and vigorous; the former half-naked, filthy, and enfeebled by intoxication, and many of them without arms excepting a knife, which they carry for the most villanous purposes." Harrison estimated the number of Indian warriors then in the whole valley of the Wabash as not exceeding six hundred; the sale of whiskey was unlawful, yet they were supposed to consume six thousand gallons of whiskey a year, and their drunkenness so often ended in murder that among three of the tribes scarcely a chief survived.

"I have had much difficulty," wrote Harrison in the same letter from Vincennes, "with the small tribes in this immediate neighborhood; namely the Piankeshaws, the Weas, and the Eel River Miamis. These three tribes form a body of the most depraved wretches on earth. They are daily in this town in considerable numbers, and are frequently intoxicated to the number of thirty or forty at once, when they commit the greatest disorders, drawing their knives, and stabbing every one they meet with; breaking open the houses of the citizens, killing their cattle and hogs, and breaking down their fences. But in all their frolics they generally suffer the most themselves. They kill each other without mercy. Some years ago as many as four were found dead in a morning; and although those murders were actually committed in the streets of the town, yet no attempt to punish them has ever been made."

The Piankeshaws were reduced to twenty-five or thirty warriors; the Weas and Eel River Indians were mere remnants. The more powerful tribes at a distance saw with growing alarm the steady destruction of the border warriors; and the intelligent Indians everywhere forbade the introduction of whiskey, and tried to create a central authority to control the degraded tribes.

A third evil was much noticed by Harrison. By treaty, if an Indian killed a white man the tribe was bound to surrender the murderer for trial by American law; while if a white man killed an Indian, the murderer was also to be tried by a white jury. The Indians surrendered their murderers, and white juries at Vincennes hung them without scruple; but no jury in the territory ever convicted a white man of murdering an Indian. Harrison complained to the President of the wanton and atrocious murders committed by white men on Indians, and the impossibility of punishing them in a society where witnesses would not appear, criminals broke jail, and juries refused to convict. Throughout the territory the people avowed the opinion that a white man ought not in justice to suffer for killing an Indian; and many of them, like the uncle of Abraham Lincoln, thought it a virtuous act to shoot an Indian at sight. Harrison could combat this code of popular law only by proclamations offering rewards for the arrest of murderers, who were never punished when arrested. In 1801 the Delawares alone complained of six unatoned murders committed on their tribe since the Treaty of Greenville, and every year increased the score.

> "All these injuries," reported Harrison in 1801, "the Indians have hitherto borne with astonishing patience; but though they discover no disposition to make war on the United States at present, I am confident that most of the tribes would eagerly seize any favorable opportunity for that purpose; and should the United States be at war with any of the European nations who are known to the Indians, there would probably be a combination of more than nine tenths of the Northern tribes against us, unless some means are used to conciliate them. . . ."

So warmly were the French remembered by the Indians, that if Napoleon had carried out his Louisiana scheme of 1802 he could have counted on the active support of nearly every Indian tribe on the Mississippi and the Lakes; from Pensacola to Detroit his orders would have been obeyed. Toward England the Indians felt no such sentimental attachment; but interest took the place of sentiment. Their natural line of trade was with the Lakes, and their relations with the British trading post at Malden, opposite Detroit, became more and more close with every new quarrel between Washington and London.

President Jefferson earnestly urged the Indians to become industrious cultivators of the soil; but even for that reform one condition was indispensable. The Indians must be protected from contact with the whites; and during the change in their mode of life, they must not be drugged, murdered, or defrauded. Trespasses on Indian land and purchases of tribal territory must for a time cease, until the Indian tribes should all be induced to adopt a new system. Even then the reform would be difficult, for Indian warriors thought death less irksome than daily labor; and men who did not fear death were not easily driven to toil.

There President Jefferson's philanthropy stopped. His greed for land equaled that of any settler on the border, and his humanity to the Indian suffered the suspicion of having among its motives the purpose of gaining the Indian lands for the whites. Jefferson's policy in practice offered a reward for Indian extinction, since he not only claimed the territory of every extinct tribe on the doctrine of paramount sovereignty, but deliberately ordered his Indian agents to tempt the tribal chiefs into debt in order to oblige them to sell the tribal lands, which did not belong to them, but to their tribes:—

> "To promote this disposition to exchange lands which they have to spare and we want, for necessaries which we have to spare and they want, we shall push our trading houses, and be glad to see the good and influential individuals among them in debt; because we observe that when these debts get beyond what the individuals can pay, they become willing to lop them off by a cession of lands."

No one would have felt more astonishment than Jefferson had some friend told him that this policy, which he believed to be virtuous, was a conspiracy to induce trustees to betray their trusts; and that in morals it was as improper as though it were not virtuously intended. Shocked as he would have been at such a method of obtaining the neighboring estate of any Virginia family, he not only suggested but vigorously carried out the system toward the Indians.

In 1804 and 1805, Governor Harrison made treaties with the Miamis, Eel Rivers, Weas, Piankeshaws, and Delawares—chiefly the tribes he called "a body of the most depraved wretches upon earth," —by which he obtained the strip of country, fifty miles wide, between the Ohio and the White rivers, thus carrying the boundary back toward the Wabash. The treaty excited deep feeling among the better Indians throughout the territory, who held long debates on their means of preventing its execution. (VI, iv, 67-75)

The treaties of 1804-1805, which threatened the Indians with immediate loss of their hunting grounds in the Wabash valley, caused a fermentation peculiarly alarming because altogether new. Early in 1806 Harrison learned that a Shawanee Indian, claiming to be a prophet, had gathered a number of warriors about him at Greenville, in Ohio, and was preaching doctrines that threatened trouble. Harrison attributed the mischief to the Prophet; but he learned in time that the Prophet's brother Tecumseh—or more properly Tecumthe—gave the movement its chief strength.

Indians and whites soon recognized Tecumthe as a phenomenon. His father was a Shawanee warrior, in no way distinguished; his mother, a Creek or Cherokee Indian, captured and adopted by the Shawanee—and of these parents three children at one birth were born about the year 1780, a few miles from Springfield, Ohio. The third brother lived and died obscure; Tecumthe and the Prophet became famous, although they were not chiefs of their tribe, and had no authority of office or birth. Such of the chiefs as were in the pay or under the power of the United States government were jealous of their influence, and had every reason for wishing to suppress the leaders of a movement avowedly designed to overthrow the system of tribal independence. From the first, Tecumthe aimed at limiting the authority of the tribes and their chiefs in order to build up an Indian confederacy, embracing not the chiefs but the warriors of all the tribes, who should act as an Indian Congress and assume joint ownership of Indian lands.

This scheme was hostile to the plans though not to the professions of President Jefferson. Its object was to prevent the piecemeal sale of Indian lands of petty tribal chiefs, under pressure of government agents. No one could honestly deny that the object was lawful and even regular; for in the Treaty of Greenville in 1795, which was the only decisive authority or precedent, the United States had admitted and acted on the principle for which Tecumthe contended —of accepting its cessions of land, not from single tribes, but from the whole body of northwestern Indians, without entering on the subject of local ownership. Governor Harrison and President Jefferson were of course aware of the precedent, and decided to disregard it in order to act on the rule better suited to their purposes; but their decision was in no way binding on Tecumthe or the tribes who were parties to the treaty of Greenville.

During the year 1807 Tecumthe's influence was increased by the "Chesapeake" excitement, which caused the Governor-general of Canada to intrigue among the Indians for aid in case of war. Probably their increase of influence led the Prophet and his brother, in May or June, 1808, to establish themselves on Tippecanoe Creek, the central point of Indian strategy and politics. Vincennes lay one hundred and fifty miles below, barely four-and-twenty hours down the stream of the Wabash; Fort Dearborn, or Chicago, was a hundred miles to the northwest; Fort Wayne the same distance to the northeast; and excepting a short portage, the Tippecanoe Indians could paddle their canoes to Malden and Detroit in one direction, or to any part of the waters of the Ohio and Mississippi in the other. At the mouth of Tippecanoe Creek the reformers laid out a village that realized Jefferson's wish, for the Indians there drank

no whiskey, and avowed themselves to be tillers of the soil. . . .
(VI, iv, 77-80)

Nothing could be more embarrassing to Jefferson than to see
the Indians follow his advice; for however well-disposed he might
be, he could not want the Indians to become civilized, educated,
or competent to protect themselves,—yet he was powerless to protect
them. The Prophet asked that the sale of liquor should be stopped;
but the President could no more prevent white settlers from selling
liquor to the Indians than he could prevent the Wabash from flowing. The tribes asked that white men who murdered Indians should
be punished; but the President could no more execute such male-
factors than he could execute the smugglers who defied his embargo.
The Indians had rights recognized by law, by treaty, and by custom,
on which their existence depended; but these rights required force
to maintain them, and on the Wabash President Jefferson had less
police power than the Prophet himself controlled.

Wide separation could alone protect the Indians from the whites,
and Tecumthe's scheme depended for its only chance of success on
holding the white settlements at a distance. . . . (VI, iv, 81-82)

Aware of the danger, Harrison decided to challenge it. The people of his Territory wanted the lands of the Wabash, even at the
risk of war. The settlement at Tippecanoe was supposed to contain
no more than eighty or a hundred warriors, with four of five times
that number within a radius of fifty miles. No immediate outbreak
was to be feared; and Harrison, "conceiving that a favorable opportunity then offered" for carrying the boundary from the White River
to the Wabash, asked authority to make a new purchase. Secretary
Eustis,[3] July 15, 1809, wrote him a cautious letter, giving the required permission, but insisting that, "to prevent any future dis-
satisfaction, the chiefs of all the nations who had or pretended right
to these lands" were to be present as consenting parties to the treaty.
On this authority Harrison once more summoned together "the
most depraved wretches upon earth,"—Miamis, Eel Rivers, Delawares, Pottawatomies, and Kickapoos,—and obtained from them,
September 30, 1809, several enormous cessions of territory which
cut into the heart of the Indian country for nearly a hundred miles
up both banks of the Wabash valley. These transfers included
about three million acres.

[3] William Eustis: a well-known Massachusetts physician, now Secretary of War.

Harrison knew that this transaction would carry despair to the heart of every Indian in his Territory. . . . (VI, iv, 82-83)

The Secretary of War had already ordered the Fourth Regiment of U. S. Infantry, under Colonel Boyd, with a company of riflemen —making in the whole a force of five hundred regular troops—to descend the Ohio from Pittsburg as rapidly as possible, and place themselves under Harrison's orders; but Eustis added instructions not easily followed or understood. July 17 he wrote to Harrison,—

"In case circumstances shall occur which may render it necessary or expedient to attack the Prophet and his followers, the force should be such as to insure the most complete success. This force will consist of the militia and regular troops. . . . If the Prophet should commence or seriously threaten hostilities, he ought to be attacked."

Under these instructions, Harrison was warranted in doing what he pleased. Not even Tecumthe denied the seriousness of his hostile threats, and Harrison had every reason to begin the war at once, if war must be; but although Eustis spoke his own mind clearly, he failed to reckon upon the President, and this neglect was the cause of another letter to Harrison, written three days later:—

"Since my letter of the 17th instant, I have been particularly instructed by the President to communicate to your Excellency his earnest desire that peace may, if possible, be preserved with the Indians, and that to this end every proper means may be adopted. . . . Circumstances conspire at this particular juncture to render it peculiarly desirable that hostilities of any kind or to any degree, not indispensably required, should be avoided. The force under Colonel Boyd has been ordered to descend the Ohio, . . . and although the force is at the disposal of your Excellency, I am instructed to inform you that the President indulges the hope and expectation that your exertions and measures with the Indians will be such as may render their march to the Indian Territory unnecessary, and that they may remain liable to another disposition."

Without paying attention to the President's wishes emphatically expressed in these orders of July 20, Harrison passed the next month in raising forces for an expedition to satisfy the wishes of the western people. No doubt was felt on the Ohio that Harrison meant to attack the Indians at Tippecanoe. . . . (VI, v, 92-94)

The night was dark, with light rain at intervals; the troops slept on their arms, and their rest was disturbed by no sound. Many accounts have been given of what passed in the Prophet's town, but none of them deserve attention. During the night neither Harrison nor his sentinels heard or saw anything that roused their suspicions. Harrison, in a brief report of the next day, said that the first alarm was given at half-past four o'clock in the morning. His full report of November 18 corrected the time to a few minutes before four. Still another account, on the day after the battle, named five o'clock as the moment. Harrison himself was about to leave his tent, before calling the men to parade, when a sentinel at the farthest angle of the camp above the creek fired a shot. In an instant the Indian yell was raised, and before the soldiers at that end of the camp could leave their tents, the Indians had pierced the line, and were shooting the men by the light of the campfires. Within a few moments, firing began along the whole line, until the camp, except for a space next the creek, was encircled by it. Fortunately for Harrison, the attacking party at the broken angle had not strength to follow up its advantage, and the American line was soon reformed in the rear. Harrison rode to the point, and at the northeast angle met Daveiss and his dismounted dragoons. Daveiss reported that the Indians, under cover of the trees, were annoying the troops severely, and asked leave to dislodge them. The order was given; and Daveiss, followed by only a few men, rushed forward among the trees, where he soon fell, mortally wounded. The troops, after forming, held their position without further disaster till daybreak, when they advanced and drove the Indians into the swamp. With this success the battle ended, having lasted two hours.

For the moment the army was saved, but only at great cost. Daveiss, who held an anomalous position almost as prominent as that of Harrison himself, died in the afternoon. Captain Baen, acting major of the Fourth Regiment, two lieutenants, and an ensign of the same regiment, were killed or wounded; two lieutenant colonels, four captains, and several lieutenants of the Indiana militia were on the same list, and the general's aid-de-camp was killed. One hundred and fifty-four privates were returned among the casualties, fifty-two of whom were killed or mortally wounded. The total loss was one hundred and eighty-eight, of whom sixty-one were killed or mortally wounded. The bodies of thirty-eight Indians were found on the field. . . . (VI, v, 102-04)

The battle of Tippecanoe at once became a point of pride throughout the Western country, and Harrison received the official applause and thanks of Kentucky, Indiana, and Illinois; but Harrison's account of his victory was not received without criticism, and the battle was fought again in the press and in private. The Fourth Regiment more than hinted that had it not been for their steadiness the whole party would have been massacred. At Vincennes, Harrison was severely attacked. In Kentucky criticism was open, for the family and friends of Joseph Daveiss were old Federalists, who had no interest in the military triumphs of a Republican official. Humphrey Marshall, Daveiss's brother-in-law, published a sharp review of Harrison's report, and hinted plainly that Daveiss had fallen a victim to the General's blunders. With characteristic vigor of language, Marshall called Harrison "a little, selfish, intriguing busybody," and charged him with having made the war without just cause, for personal objects. These attacks caused the western Republicans to sustain with the more ardor their faith in Harrison's military genius, and their enthusiasm for the victory of Tippecanoe; but President Madison and Secretary Eustis guarded themselves with some care from expressing an opinion on the subject.

Whatever his critics might say, Harrison gained his object, and established himself in the West as the necessary leader of any future campaign. That result, as far as it was good, seemed to be the only advantage gained at Tippecanoe. Harrison believed that the battle had broken the Prophet's influence, and saved the frontier from further alarm; he thought that in the event of a British war, the Indians would remain neutral having "witnessed the inefficacy of British assistance"; he expected the tribes to seek peace as a consequence of what he considered the severest defeat they had ever received since their acquaintance with the white people; and the expectation was general that they would deliver the Prophet and Tecumthe into the hands of the American government. For a time these impressions seemed reasonable. The Prophet lost influence, and the peace was not further disturbed; but presently the Western people learned that the Prophet had returned to Tippecanoe, and that all things had resumed their old aspect, except that no one could foresee when the Indians would choose to retaliate for Harrison's invasion. . . . (VI, v, 106-108)

The Indian hesitation was probably due to doubt whether war would take place between the United States and England. The whole influence of the British agents was exerted to unite the Indians and to arm them, but to prevent a premature outbreak. The British Indian agent at Amherstburg sent Tecumthe a message blaming the attack on Harrison. Tecumthe replied:—

"You tell us to retreat or turn to one side should the Big Knives come against us. Had I been at home in the late unfortunate affair I should have done so; but those I left at home were (I cannot call them men) a poor set of people, and their scuffle with the Big Knives I compared to a struggle between little children who only scratch each other's faces. The Kickapoos, Winnebagoes have since been at Post Vincennes and settled the matter amicably."

The situation was well understood. "If we have a British war, we shall have an Indian war," wrote the commandant from Fort Wayne. "From the best information I can get, I have every reason to believe we shall have an Indian war this spring, whether we have a British war or not." . . . (VI, v, 109)

This was the situation on the Wabash in May and June, 1812. Not only was Tecumthe unwilling to strike the first blow, but he would not even retaliate Harrison's invasion and seizure of the disputed territory. He waited for Congress to act, but every one knew that whenever Congress should declare war against England, war must also be waged with the Indians; and no one could doubt that after provoking the Indian war, Americans ought to be prepared to wage it with effect, and without complaint of its horrors. . . . (VI, v, 112)

The war fever of 1811 swept far and wide over the country, but even at its height seemed somewhat intermittent and imaginary. A passion that needed to be nursed for five years before it acquired strength to break into act, could not seem genuine to men who did not share it. A nation which had submitted to robbery and violence in 1805, in 1807, in 1809, could not readily lash itself into rage in 1811 when it had no new grievance to allege; nor could the public feel earnest in maintaining national honor, for every one admitted that the nation had sacrificed its honor, and must fight to regain it. Yet what honor was to be hoped from a war which required continued submission to one robber as the price of resistance to another? President Madison submitted to Napoleon in order to resist England; the New England Federalists preferred submitting to England in order to resist Napoleon; but not one American expected the United States to uphold their national rights against the world.

Politicians of the old school looked coldly on the war spirit. Nations like individuals, when driven to choose between desperate courses, might at times be compelled to take the chances of destruction, often destroying themselves, or suffering irreparable harm. Yet the opponents of war could argue that Americans were not placed between desperate alternatives. They had persevered hitherto, in spite of their leaders, in the policy of peace; had suffered much injury and acute mortification, but had won Louisiana and West Florida, had given democracy all it asked, and had remained in reasonable harmony with the liberal movement of the world. They were reaping the fruit of their patient and obstinate husbandry; for Russia and Sweden were about to fight their battles without reward. Napoleon offered them favors more or less real, and even England could not long resist the pressure of her interests. Jefferson's policy had wrought all the evil it could cause,—perhaps it had cost the highest price the nation could pay; but after the nation had suffered the evil and paid the price, it had a right to the profit. With more force than in 1798, the old Republicans pleaded that if they should throw aside their principles and plunge into hostilities with England, they would not only sacrifice the results of six years' humiliation, but would throw the United States athwart the liberal movement of Europe, destroy the hopes of pure government at home, and with more eagerness than they had shown for the past ten years in stripping government of its power, must devote themselves to the task of rebuilding a sovereignty as terrible in peace as in war. . . . (VI, vi, 113-14)

2.

The 12th Congress Declares War

Both Foster and Serurier[4] felt that the people were further advanced than the Government in hostility to England, and that this was especially true in the matter of impressments; but no one, even at the White House, knew certainly what to expect from the new Congress assembling at Washington November 4, 1811. That this body differed greatly from any previous Congress was clear, if only because it contained some seventy new members; but another difference, less easily measured, was more serious. The active leaders were young men. Henry Clay of Kentucky, William Lowndes, John Caldwell Calhoun, David R. Williams, Langdon Cheves of South Carolina, Felix Grundy of Tennessee, Peter Buell Porter of New York, Richard Mentor Johnson of Kentucky, had none of them reached their fortieth year; while Madison and his Cabinet belonged to a different generation. None of the new leaders could remember the colonial epoch, or had taken a share in public life except under the Constitution of 1798, or had been old enough to feel and understand the lessons taught by opposition to the Federalist rule. They knew the Federalists only as a faction, more or less given to treasonable talk, controlling some thirty or forty votes in the House, and proclaiming with tedious iteration opinions no one cared to hear. The young war Republicans, as they were called, felt only contempt for such a party; while, as their acts showed, they were filled with no respect for the technicalities of their Executive head, and regarded Gallatin with distrust. Of statesmanship, in the old sense, they took little thought. Bent on war with England, they were willing to face debt and probable bankruptcy on the chance of creating

[4] Jean Serurier: French Minister to the United States, succeeding Turreau.

a nation, of conquering Canada, and carrying the American flag to Mobile and Key West.

After ten years devoted to weakening national energies, such freshness of youth and recklessness of fear had wonderful popular charm. The reaction from Jefferson's system threatened to be more violent than its adoption. Experience seemed to show that a period of about twelve years measured the beat of the pendulum. After the Declaration of Independence, twelve years had been needed to create an efficient Constitution; another twelve years of energy brought a reaction against the government then created; a third period of twelve years was ending in a sweep toward still greater energy; and already a child could calculate the result of a few more such returns. . . . (VI, vi, 122-23)

Castlereagh's[5] long note of April 10, communicated by Foster to the American government, contained a paragraph defining the British doctrine of retaliation:—

"What Great Britain always avowed was her readiness to rescind her orders as soon as France rescinded, absolutely and unconditionally, her decrees. She never engaged to repeal those orders as affecting America alone, leaving them in force against other States, upon condition that France would except, singly and especially, America from the operation of her decrees. She could not do so without the grossest injustice to her allies, as well as all other neutral nations; much less could she do so upon the supposition that the special exception in favor of America was to be expressly granted by France, as it has been hitherto tacitly accepted by America, upon conditions utterly subversive of the most important and indisputable maritime rights of the British empire."

Long afterward Madison objected to the common accounts of the war, that they brought too little into view "the more immediate impulse to it" given by this formal notice communicated to him officially by Foster, which left no choice between war and degradation. He regarded this notice as making further discussion impossible. His idea was perhaps too strongly asserted, for Foster offered, under other instructions, a new and important concession,—that England should give up altogether her system of licensing trade with the Continent, and in its place should enforce a rigorous blockade; but Madison and Monroe declined listening to any offer that did not admit in principle the right of the United States to trade

[5] Robert Stewart, Viscount Castlereagh: Foreign Secretary, 1812-1822.

with every European country. Thus at the last moment the dispute seemed to narrow itself to the single point of belligerent right to blockade a coast.

Acting at once on the theory that Castlereagh's instructions of April 10 gave the last formal notice intended by the British government, President Madison prepared a Message recommending an immediate declaration of war. This Message was sent to Congress June 1; the two Houses instantly went into secret session, and the Message was read. No one could dispute the force of Madison's long recital of British outrages. For five years, the task of finding excuses for peace had been more difficult than that of proving a *casus belli;* but some interest still attached to the arrangement and relative weight of the many American complaints.

Madison, inverting the order of complaints previously alleged, began by charging that British cruisers had been "in the continued practice of violating the American flag on the great highway of nations, and of seizing and carrying off persons sailing under it." The charge was amply proved, was not denied, and warranted war; but this was the first time that the Government had alleged impressment as its chief grievance, or had announced, either to England or to America, the intention to fight for redress—and England might fairly complain that she had received no notice of intended war on such ground. The second complaint alleged that British cruisers also violated the peace of the coasts, and harassed entering and departing commerce. This charge was equally true and equally warranted war, but it was open to the same comment as that made upon the first. The third grievance on which the President had hitherto founded his coercive measures consisted in "pretended blockades, without the presence of an adequate force and sometimes without the practicability of applying one," by means of which American commerce had been plundered on every sea—a practice which had come to its highest possible development in the fourth grievance, the sweeping system of blockades known as the Orders in Council. These four main heads of complaint covered numbers of irritating consequences, but no other separate charge was alleged, beyond an insinuation that the hostile spirit of the Indians was connected with their neighborhood to Canada.

On the four great grievances thus defined every American could in theory agree; but these admitted wrongs had hitherto been endured as a matter of expediency, rather than resort to war; and the opposition still stood on the ground that had been so obstinately held by Jefferson,—that war, however just, was inexpedient. If union in the war policy was to be hoped, the President must rather prove its expediency than its justice. Even from his own point of view, two doubts of expediency required fresh attention. For the first time, England showed distinct signs of giving away; while on the other hand France showed only the monomania of insisting on her decrees, even to the point of conquering Russia. In the face of two such movements, the expediency of war with England became more than ever doubtful; and if the President wished for harmony, he must remove these doubts. This he did not attempt, further than by alluding to the sense of Castlereagh's late despatch, as yet not in his possession. What was still more remarkable, he said nothing in regard to the contract with France, which since November, 1809, he had made the ground for every measure of compulsion against England. Indeed, not only was the contract ignored, but if any meaning could be placed on his allusions to France, the theory of contract seemed at last to be formally abandoned.

"Having presented this view of the relations of the United States with Great Britain, and of the solemn alternative growing out of them, I proceed to remark that the communications last made to Congress on the subject of our relations with France will have shown that since the revocation of her decrees, as they violated the neutral rights of the United States, her government has authorized illegal captures by its privateers and public ships; and that other outrages have been practised on our vessels and our citizens. It will have been seen, also, that no indemnity had been provided, or satisfactorily pledged, for the extensive spoliations committed under the violent and retrospective orders of the French government against the property of our citizens, seized within the jurisdiction of France. I abstain at this time from recommending to the consideration of Congress definite measures with respect to that nation."

The war of 1812 was chiefly remarkable for the vehemence with which, from beginning to end, it was resisted and thwarted by a very large number of citizens who were commonly considered, and who considered themselves, by no means the least respectable, intelligent, or patriotic part of the nation. That the war was as just and necessary as any war ever waged, seemed so evident to Americans of another generation that only with an effort could modern readers grasp the reasons for the bitter opposition of large and respectable communities which left the government bankrupt, and nearly severed the union; but if students of national history can bear with patience the labor of retaining in mind the threads of negotiation which President Madison so thoroughly tangled before breaking, they can partially enter into the feelings of citizens who held themselves aloof from Madison's war. In June, 1812, the reasons for declaring war on Great Britain, though strong enough, were weaker than they had been in June, 1808, or in January, 1809. In the interval the British government had laid aside the arrogant and defiant tones of Canning's diplomacy; had greatly modified the Orders in Council; had offered further modifications; and had atoned for the "Chesapeake" outrage. In 1807 England would have welcomed a war with the United States; in 1812 she wanted peace, and yielded much to secure it. In 1808 America was almost unanimous, her government still efficient, well supplied with money, and little likely to suffer from war; in 1812 the people were greatly divided, the government had been weakened, and the Treasury was empty. Even Gallatin, who in 1809 had been the most decided for war, was believed in 1812 to wish and to think that it might be avoided. Probably four fifths of the American people held the same opinion. Not merely had the situation in every other respect changed for the worse, but the moral convictions of the country were outraged by the assertion of a contract with Napoleon—in which no one believed—as the reason for forcing religious and peaceful citizens into what they regarded as the service of France.

The war Message of June 1 rather strengthened than removed grounds of opposition. The President alleged but one reason for thinking war expedient at that moment rather than at another; but when in after years he insisted that Castlereagh's instructions were the immediate cause which precluded further negotiation, he admitted his own mistake and presumed that had Congress known what was then passing in England the declaration of war would have been suspended and negotiations renewed. Such a succession of mistakes, admitted one after another almost as soon as they were made, might well give to Madison's conduct the air so often attributed to it, of systematic favor to Napoleon and equally systematic hostility to England.

The House went at once into secret session; the Message was referred to the Committee of Foreign Relations; and two days afterward, June 3, Calhoun brought in a report recommending an immediate appeal to arms. . . . (VI, xi, 220-26)

Proverbially wars are popular at their beginning; commonly, in representative government, they are declared by aid of some part of the opposition. In the case of the War of 1812 the party in power, instead of gaining strength by the declaration, lost about one fourth of its votes, and the opposition actually gained nearly one fifth of the Administration's strength. In the Senate the loss was still greater. There too the President's Message was debated in secret, but the proceedings were very deliberate. A select committee, with Senator Anderson of Tennessee at its head, took charge of the Message, and consumed a week in studying it. June 8 the committee reported the House bill with amendments. June 11 the Senate, by a vote of seventeen to thirteen, returned the bill to the committee for further amendment. June 12 the committee reported the amendments as instructed. The Senate discussed them, was equally divided, and accordingly threw out its own amendments. June 15 the Senate voted the third reading of the House bill by a vote of nineteen to thirteen. June 16, after a strong speech for delay from Senator James A. Bayard, the Senate again adjourned without action; and only June 18, after two weeks of secret discussion, did the bill pass. Nineteen senators voted in its favor; thirteen in opposition. Samuel Smith, Giles, and Leib, the three Republican senators most openly hostile to Madison, voted with the majority. Except Pennsylvania, the entire representation of no northern State declared itself for the war; except Kentucky, every State south of the Potomac and the Ohio voted for the declaration. Not only was the war to be a party measure, but it was also sectional; while the Republican majority, formerly so large, was reduced to dependence on the factious support of Smith, Giles, and Leib.

The bill with its amendments was at once returned to the House and passed. Without a moment's delay the President signed it, and the same day, June 18, 1812, the war began. . . . (VI, xi, 228-29)

From the pacific theories of 1801 to the military methods of 1812 was a vast stride. When Congress rose, July 6, 1812, the whole national frontier and coast from Prairie du Chien to Eastport, from Eastport to St. Mary's, from St. Mary's to New Orleans—three thousand miles, incapable of defence—was open to the attacks of powerful enemies; while the Government at Washington had taken measures for the military occupation of the vast foreign territories northward of the Lakes and southward to the Gulf of Mexico. . . . (VI, xi, 243-44)

3.

Parliament Repeals the Orders in Council

While Napoleon . . . tried the temper of America, the Government of England slowly and with infinite reluctance yielded to American demands. Not for the first time experience showed that any English minister whose policy rested on jealousy of America must sooner or later come to ruin and disgrace. . . . (VI, xiii, 267)

Many reasons combined to show that concessions were inevitable. The sweeping ruin that overwhelmed British commerce and industry in 1810 sank deep among the laboring classes in 1811. The seasons doubled the distress. The winter had been intense, the summer was unfavorable; wheat rose in the autumn to one hundred and forty-five shillings, or about thirty-six dollars the quarter, and as the winter of 1811 began, disorders broke out in the manufacturing districts. The inland counties reached a state of actual insurrection which no exercise of force seemed to repress. The American non-importation aggravated the trouble, and worked unceasingly to shake the authority of Spencer Perceval, already one of the most unpopular ministers England had ever seen.

Popular distress alone could hardly have effected a change in Perceval's system; so great a result was not to be produced by means hitherto so little regarded. The moment marked an era in English history, for the new class of laborers, the mill-operatives and other manufacturing workmen, took for the first time an active share in shaping legislation. In their hostility to Perceval's policy they were backed by their employers; but the united efforts of employers and workmen were not yet equal to controlling the Government, even though they were aided by the American non-importation. They worried Perceval, but did not break him down. At the close of 1811 he showed still no signs of yielding; but news then arrived that the

64

American Congress had met, and that the President's Message, the debates in the House, the tone of the press, and the feelings of the American people announced war. This was a new force with which Perceval could not deal.

No man of common sense could charge England with want of courage, for if ever a nation had fought its way, England had a right to claim whatever credit such a career bestowed; but England lived in war, she knew its exact cost, and at that moment she could not afford it. The most bigoted Tory could see that if Napoleon succeeded in his coming attack on Russia, as he had hitherto succeeded in every war he had undertaken in Europe even when circumstances were less favorable, he would need only the aid of America to ruin beyond redemption the trade and finances of Great Britain. Little as Englishmen believed in the military capacity of the United States, they needed too much the markets and products of America to challenge war. . . . (VI, xiii, 268-69)

Had the United States at that moment been so fortunate as to enjoy the services of Pinkney in London, or of any man whose position and abilities raised him above the confusion of party politics, he might have convinced them that war was unnecessary. The mere threat was sufficient. Sidmouth's[6] entrance into the Cabinet showed the change of current, and once Perceval began to give way, he could not stop. Unfortunately the United States had no longer a minister in England. In July, 1811, the President ordered Jonathan Russell[7] to London to act as *chargé* until a minister should be appointed, which he added would be done as soon as Congress met; but he changed his mind and appointed no minister, while Jonathan Russell, seeing that Perceval commanded a majority and was determined to maintain his system, reported the situation as hopeless.

Brougham, without taking the precaution of giving Russell the daily information he so much needed, devoted all his energies to pressing the popular movement against the Orders in Council. Petition after petition was hurried to Parliament, and almost every petition caused a new debate. George Rose, who possessed an unhappy bluntness, in conversation with a Birmingham committee said that the two countries were like two men with their heads in buckets of water, whose struggle was which of the two could hold out longest before suffocation. The phrase was seized as a catchword, and helped

[6] Henry Addington, Viscount Sidmouth: former Tory Prime Minister.
[7] Jonathan Russell: of Rhode Island, now *chargé d'affaires* in London.

agitation. April 28 Lord Stanley, in the House, renewed the motion for a committee on the petitions against the orders. Perceval had been asked whether he would consent to the committee, and had refused; but on consulting his followers he found such symptoms of disaffection as obliged him to yield rather than face defeat. George Rose then announced, greatly against his will, that as a matter of respect to the petitioners he would no longer oppose their request; Castlereagh and Perceval, cautioning the House that nothing need be expected from the investigation, followed Rose; while Stephen, after denouncing as a foul libel the charge that the orders had been invented to extend the commerce of Great Britain, also yielded to the committee "as a negative good, and to prevent misconstruction."

Stimulated by the threatening news from America, Brougham pressed with his utmost energy the victory he had won. The committee immediately began its examination of witnesses, who appeared from every quarter to prove that the Orders in Council and the subsequent non-importation had ruined large branches of British trade, and had lopped away a market that consumed British products to the value of more than ten million pounds sterling a year. Perceval and Stephen did their best to stem the tide, but were slowly overborne, and seemed soon to struggle only for delay.

Then followed a melodramatic change. May 11, as the prime minister entered the House to attend the investigation, persons about the door heard the report of a pistol, and saw Spencer Perceval fall forward shot through the heart. By the hand of a lunatic moved only by imaginary personal motives, this minister, who seemed in no way a tragical figure, became the victim of a tragedy without example in modern English history; but although England had never been in a situation more desperate, the true importance of Spencer Perceval was far from great, and when he vanished in the flash of a pistol from the stage where he seemed to fill the most considerable part, he stood already on the verge of overthrow. His death relieved England of a burden. Brougham would not allow his inquiry to be suspended, and the premier's assassination rather concealed than revealed the defeat his system must have suffered.

During the negotiations which followed, in the midst of difficulties in forming a new Ministry, Castlereagh received from Jonathan Russell Napoleon's clandestine Decree of Repeal.[8] Brougham

---

[8] In September, 1811, the Duc de Bassano, now Foreign Minister, had showed the new American Minister, Joel Barlow, a "Decree of St. Cloud," supposedly signed by Napoleon on April 28, 1811, but never published. This Decree declared the Berlin and Milan Decrees repealed as of November 1, 1810.

asked, May 22, what construction was to be put by ministers on this paper. Castlereagh replied that the decree was a trick disgraceful to any civilized government, and contained nothing to satisfy the conditions required by England. Apart from the subordinate detail that his view of the decree was correct, his remarks meant nothing. The alarm caused by news that Congress had imposed an embargo as the last step before war, the annoyance created by John Henry's revelations and Castlereagh's lame defence, the weight of evidence pressing on Parliament against the Orders in Council, the absence of a strong or permanent Ministry—these influences, gaining from day to day, forced the conviction that a change of system must take place. June 8 Lord Liverpool announced that he had formed an Administration, and would deal in due course with the Orders in Council. June 16 Brougham made his motion for a repeal of the orders. When he began his speech he did not know what part the new Ministry would take, but while he unfolded his long and luminous argument he noticed that James Stephen failed to appear in the House. This absence could mean only that Stephen had been deserted by ministers; and doubt ceased when Brougham and Baring ended, for then Lord Castlereagh—after Perceval's death the leader of the House—rose and awkwardly announced that the Government, though till within three or four days unable to deliberate on the subject, had decided to suspend immediately the Orders in Council.

Thus ended the long struggle waged for five years by the United States against the most illiberal Government known in England within modern times. . . . (VI, xiii, 282-86)

4.

Reductio ad Absurdum: A Jeffersonian General

For civil affairs Americans were more or less trained; but they had ignored war, and had shown no capacity in their treatment of military matters. Their little army was not well organized or equipped; its civil administration was more imperfect than its military, and its military condition could hardly have been worse. The ten old regiments, with half-filled ranks, were scattered over an enormous country on garrison service, from which they could not be safely withdrawn; they had no experience, and no organization for a campaign, while thirteen new regiments not yet raised were expected to conquer Canada.

If the army in rank and file was insufficient, its commanding officers supplied none of its wants. The senior major-general appointed by President Madison in February, 1812, was Henry Dearborn, who had retired in 1809 from President Jefferson's Cabinet into the Custom House of Boston. Born in 1751, Dearborn at the time of his nomination as major-general was in his sixty-second year, and had never held a higher grade in the army than that of deputy quartermaster-general in 1781, and colonel of a New Hampshire regiment after active service in the Revolutionary War had ended.

The other major-general appointed at the same time was Thomas Pinckney, of South Carolina, who received command of the Southern Department. Pinckney was a year older than Dearborn; his military service was chiefly confined to the guerilla campaigns of Marion and Sumter, and to staff duty as aid to General Gates in the Southern campaign of 1780; he had been minister in England and Envoy Extraordinary to Spain, where he negotiated the excellent treaty known by his name; he had been also a Federalist

68

member of Congress in the stormy sessions from 1797 to 1801—but none of these services, distinguished as they were, seemed to explain his appointment as major-general. Macon, whose opinions commonly reflected those of the southern people, was astonished at the choice.

"The nomination of Thomas Pinckney for major-general," he wrote, "is cause of grief to all men who wish proper men appointed; not that he is a Federal or that he is not a gentleman, but because he is thought not to possess the talents necessary to his station. I imagine his nomination must have been produced through the means of P. Hamilton, who is about as fit for his place as the Indian Prophet would be for Emperor of Europe. I never was more at a loss to account for any proceeding than the nomination of Pinckney to be major-general."

Even the private report that Pinckney had become a Republican did not reconcile Macon, whose belief that the "fighting secretaries" would not do for real war became stronger than ever, although he admitted that some of the military appointments were supposed to be tolerably good.

Of the brigadier-generals the senior was James Wilkinson, born in 1757, and fifty-five years old in 1812. Wilkinson had recently been tried by court-martial on a variety of charges, beginning with that of having been a pensioner of Spain and engaged in treasonable conspiracy; then of being an accomplice of Aaron Burr; and finally, insubordination, neglect of duty, wastefulness, and corruption. The court acquitted him, and February 14 President Madison approved the decision, but added an irritating reprimand. Yet in spite of acquittal Wilkinson stood in the worst possible odor, and returned what he considered his wrongs by bitter and contemptuous hatred for the President and the Secretary of War.

The next brigadier was Wade Hampton, of South Carolina, who entered the service in 1808, and was commissioned as brigadier in 1809. Born in 1754, he was fifty-seven years old, and though understood to be a good officer, he had as yet enjoyed no opportunity of distinguishing himself. Next in order came Joseph Bloomfield of New Jersey, nominated as brigadier-general of the regular army March 27, 1812; on the same day James Winchester, of Tennessee, was named fourth brigadier; and April 8 William Hull, of Massachusetts, was appointed fifth in rank. Bloomfield, a major in the Revolutionary War, had been for the last ten years Governor of New Jersey. Winchester, another old Revolutionary officer, originally from Maryland, though mild, generous, and rich, was not the best choice that might have been made from Tennessee. William Hull, civil Governor of Michigan since 1805, was a third of the same class. All were sixty years of age or thereabout, and none belonged to the regular service. Excepting Hull, none seems ever before to have commanded a regiment in face of an enemy.

Of the inferior appointments, almost as numerous as the enlistments, little could be said. Among the officers of the regiment of Light Artillery raised in 1808, after the "Chesapeake" alarm, was a young captain named Winfield Scott, born near Petersburg, Virginia, in 1786, and in the prime of his energies when at the age of twenty-six he saw the chance of distinction before him. In after life Scott described the condition of the service as he found it in 1808.

"The army of that day," he said, "including its general staff, the three old and the nine new regiments, presented no pleasing aspect. The old officers had very generally sunk into either sloth, ignorance, or habits of intemperate drinking. . . . Many of the appointments were positively bad, and a majority of the remainder indifferent. Party spirit of that day knew no bounds, and of course was blind to policy. Federalists were almost entirely excluded from selection, though great numbers were eager for the field, and in New England and some other States there were but very few educated Republicans; hence the selections from those communities consisted mostly of coarse and ignorant men. In the other States, where there was no lack of educated men in the dominant party, the appointments consisted generally of swaggerers, dependants, decayed gentlemen, and others, 'fit for nothing else,' which always turned out utterly unfit for any military purpose whatever."

This account of the army of 1808 applied equally, said Scott, to the appointments of 1812. Perhaps the country would have fared as well without a regular army, by depending wholly on volunteers, and allowing the States to choose general officers. In such a case Andrew Jackson would have taken the place of James Winchester, and William Hull would never have received an appointment from Massachusetts.

No one in the government gave much thought to the military dangers created by the war, yet these dangers seemed evident enough to warrant keen anxiety. The seashore was nowhere capable of defence; the Lakes were unguarded; the Indians of the Northwestern Territory were already in arms, and known to be waiting only a word from the Canadian governor-general; while the whole country beyond the Wabash and Maumee rivers stood nearly defenceless. At Detroit one hundred and twenty soldiers garrisoned the old British fort; eighty-five men on the Maumee held Fort Wayne; some fifty men guarded the new stockade called Fort Harrison, lately built on the Wabash; and fifty-three men, beyond possibility of rescue, were stationed at Fort Dearborn, or Chicago; finally, eighty-eight men occupied the Island of Michillimackinaw in the straits between Lake Huron and Lake Michigan. These were all the military defences of a vast territory, which once lost would need another war to regain; and these petty garrisons, with the settlers about them, were certain, in the event of an ordinary mischance, to be scalped as well as captured. The situation was little better in the South and Southwest, where the Indians needed only the support of a British army at New Orleans or Mobile to expel every American garrison from the territory.

No serious preparations for war had yet been made when the war began. In January, Congress voted ten new regiments of infantry, two of artillery, and one of light dragoons; the recruiting began in March, and in June the Secretary of War reported to Congress that although no returns had been received from any of the recruiting offices, yet considering the circumstances "the success which has attended this service will be found to have equaled any reasonable expectations." Eustis was in no way responsible for the failure of the service, and had no need to volunteer an opinion as to the reasonable expectations that Congress might entertain. Every one knew that the enlistments fell far below expectation; but not the enlistments alone showed torpor. In February, Congress authorized the President to accept fifty thousand volunteers for one year's service. In June, the number of volunteers who had offered themselves was even smaller than that of regular recruits. In April, Congress authorized the President to call out one hundred thousand State militia. In June, no one knew whether all the States would regard the call, and still less whether the militia would serve beyond the frontier. One week after declaring war, Congress fixed the war establishment at twenty-five regiments of infantry, four of artillery, two of dragoons, and one of riflemen,—making, with the engineers and artificers, an army of thirty-six thousand seven hundred; yet the actual force under arms did not exceed 10,000 of whom four thousand were new recruits. Toward no part of the service did the people show a sympathetic spirit before the war was declared; and even where the war was most popular, as in Kentucky and Tennessee, men showed themselves determined to fight in their own way or not at all. . . . (VI, xiv, 289-95)

Although the loss of Detroit caused the greatest loss of territory that ever before or since befell the United States, the public at large understood little of the causes that made it inevitable, and saw in it only an accidental consequence of Hull's cowardice. Against this victim, who had no friend in the world, every voice was raised. He was a coward, an imbecile, but above all unquestionably a traitor, who had, probably for British gold, delivered an army and a province, without military excuse, into the enemy's hands. If any man in the United States was more responsible than Hull for the result of the campaign it was Ex-President Jefferson, whose system had shut military efficiency from the scope of American government; but to Jefferson, Hull and his surrender were not the natural products of a system, but objects of hatred and examples of perfidy that had only one parallel. "The treachery of Hull, like that of Arnold, cannot be a matter of blame to our government," he wrote on learning the story of Lewis Cass and the Ohio militia officers, who told with the usual bitterness of betrayed men what they knew of the causes that had brought their betrayal to pass. "The detestable treason of Hull," as Jefferson persisted in calling it, was the more exasperating to him because, even as late as August 4, he had written with entire confidence to the same correspondent that "the acquisition of Canada this year, as far as the neighborhood of Quebec, will be a mere matter of marching, and will give us experience for the attack of Halifax the next, and the final expulsion of England from the American continent." . . . (VI, xvi, 336-37)

Hitherto the military movements against Canada had been directed by Eastern men. Alexander Smyth belonged to a different class. Born in Ireland in 1765, his fortunes led him to Virginia, where he became a respectable member of the Southwestern bar and served in the State legislature. Appointed in 1808 by President Jefferson colonel of the new rifle regiment, in 1812 he became inspector-general, with the rank of brigadier. By his own request he received command of the brigade ordered to Niagara, and his succession to Van Rensselaer followed of course. Dearborn, knowing little of Smyth, was glad to intrust the army to a regular officer in whom he felt confidence; yet an Irish temperament with a Virginian education promised the possibility of a campaign which if not more disastrous than that led by William Hull of Massachu-

setts, or by Stephen Van Rensselaer of New York, might be equally
eccentric.

October 24 Smyth took command at Buffalo, and three weeks
later the public read in the newspapers an address issued by him to
the "Men of New York," written in a style hitherto unusual in
American warfare.

"For many years," Smyth announced to the Men of New York,
"you have seen your country oppressed with numerous wrongs. Your
government, although above all others devoted to peace, has been
forced to draw the sword, and rely for redress of injuries on the valor
of the American people. That valor has been conspicuous. But the
nation has been unfortunate in the selection of some of those who
have directed it. One army has been disgracefully surrendered and
lost. Another has been sacrificed by a precipitate attempt to pass it
over at the strongest point of the enemy's lines with most incompetent means. The cause of these miscarriages is apparent. The commanders were popular men, 'destitute alike of theory and experience'
in the art of war."

Unmilitary as such remarks were, the address continued in a tone
more and more surprising, until at last it became burlesque.

"In a few days the troops under my command will plant the American standard in Canada. They are men accustomed to obedience,
silence, and steadiness. They will conquer, or they will die.

"Will you stand with your arms folded and look on this interesting
struggle? Are you not related to the men who fought at Bennington
and Saratoga? Has the race degenerated? Or have you, under the
baneful influence of contending factions, forgot your country? Must
I turn from you and ask the men of the Six Nations to support the
government of the United States? Shall I imitate of officers of the
British King, and suffer our ungathered laurels to be tarnished by
ruthless deeds? Shame, where is thy blush! No!"

The respectable people of the neighborhood were not wholly
discouraged by this call or by a second proclamation, November
17, as little military as the first; or even by an address of Peter B.
Porter offering to lead his neighbors into Canada under the command of the "able and experienced officer" who within a few days
could and would "occupy all the British fortresses on the Niagara
River." A certain number of volunteers offered themselves for the
service, although not only the attack but also its details were an-

nounced in advance. The British responded by bombarding Black
Rock and Fort Niagara; and although their cannon did little harm,
they were more effective than the proclamations of the American
generals.

November 25 General Smyth issued orders for the invasion,
which were also unusual in their character, and prescribed even
the gestures and attitudes of the attacking force: "At twenty yards
distance the soldiers will be ordered to trail arms, advance with
shouts, fire at five paces distance, and charge bayonets. The soldiers
will be *silent* above all things." In obedience to these orders, everything was prepared, November 27, for the crossing, and once more
orders were issued in an inspiring tone:

> "Friends of your country! ye who have 'the will to do, the heart to
> dare!' the moment ye have wished for has arrived! Think on your
> country's honors torn! her rights trampled on! her sons enslaved! her
> infants perishing by the hatchet! Be strong! be brave! and let the
> ruffian power of the British King cease on this continent!"

Two detachments were to cross the river from Black Rock before
dawn, November 28, to surprise and disable the enemy's batteries
and to destroy a bridge five miles below; after this should be done
the army was to cross. The British were supposed to have not more
than a thousand men within twenty miles to resist the attack of
three thousand men from Buffalo. Apparently Smyth's calculations
were correct. His two detachments crossed the river at three o'clock
on the morning of November 28 and gallantly, though with severe
loss, captured and disabled the guns and tore up a part of the
bridge without destroying it. At sunrise the army began to embark
at the navy yard, but the embarkation continued so slowly that
toward afternoon, when all the boats were occupied, only twelve
hundred men, with artillery, were on board. "The troops thus
embarked," reported Smyth, "moved up the stream to Black Rock
without sustaining loss from the enemy's fire. It was now afternoon,
and they were ordered to disembark and dine."

This was all. No more volunteers appeared, and no other regulars fit for service remained. Smyth would not cross without three
thousand men, and doubtless was right in his caution; but he
showed want of courage not so much in this failure to redeem his
pledges, as in his subsequent attempt to throw responsibility on
subordinates, and on Dearborn who had requested him to consult
some of his officers occasionally, and be prepared if possible to

cross into Canada with three thousand men at once. Smyth consulted his officers at the moment when consultation was fatal.

"Recollecting your instructions to cross with three thousand men at *once,* and to consult some of my principal officers in 'all important movements,' I called for the field officers of the regulars and twelve-months volunteers embarked."

The council of war decided not to risk the crossing. Winder, who was considered the best of Smyth's colonels, had opposed the scheme from the first, and reported the other officers as strongly against it. Smyth was aware of their opinions, and his appeal to them could have no object but to shift responsibility. After receiving their decision, Smyth sent a demand for the surrender of Fort Erie, "to spare the effusion of blood," and then ordered his troops to their quarters. The army obeyed with great discontent, but fifteen hundred men still mustered in the boats, when two days afterward Smyth issued another order to embark. Once more Smyth called a council of war, and once more decided to abandon the invasion. With less than three thousand men in the boats at once, the General would not stir.

Upon this, General Smyth's army dissolved. "A scene of confusion ensued which it is difficult to describe," wrote Peter B. Porter soon afterward—"about four thousand men without order or restraint discharging their muskets in every direction." They showed a preference for General Smyth's tent as their target, which caused the General to shift his quarters repeatedly. A few days afterward Peter B. Porter published a letter to a Buffalo newspaper, attributing the late disgrace "to the cowardice of General Smyth." The General sent a challenge to his subordinate officer, and exchanged shots with him. Smyth next requested permission to visit his family, which Dearborn hastened to grant; and three months afterward, as General Smyth did not request an inquiry into the causes of his failure, the President without express authority of law dropped his name from the army roll. . . . (VI, xvi, 353-58)

5.

Energy at Sea, Apathy on Land

Culpable as was the helplessness of the War Department in 1812, the public neither understood nor knew how to enforce responsibility for disasters which would have gone far to cost a European war minister his life, as they might have cost his nation its existence. By fortune still kinder, the Navy Department escaped penalty of any sort for faults nearly as serious as those committed by its rival. The navy consisted, besides gunboats, of three heavy frigates rated as carrying forty-four guns; three lighter frigates rated at thirty-eight guns; one of thirty-two, and one of twenty-eight; besides two ships of eighteen guns, two brigs of sixteen, and four brigs of fourteen and twelve—in all sixteen seagoing vessels, twelve of which were probably equal to any vessels afloat of the same class. The eight frigates were all built by Federalist Congresses before President Jefferson's time; the smaller craft, except one, were built under the influence of the war with Tripoli. The Administration which declared war against England did nothing to increase the force. Few of the ships were in first-rate condition. The officers complained that the practice of laying up the frigates in port hastened their decay, and declared that hardly a frigate in the service was as sound as she should be. For this negligence Congress was alone responsible. . . . (VI, xvii, 362-63)

The American navy seemed ready to outstrip the army in the race for disaster. The "Constitution," the best frigate in the United States service, sailed into the midst of Broke's five ships. Captain Isaac Hull, in command of the "Constitution," had been detained at Annapolis shipping a new crew, until July 5, the day when Broke's squadron left Halifax; then the ship got under way and

stood down Chesapeake Bay on her voyage to New York. The wind
was ahead and very light. Not till July 10 did the ship anchor off
Cape Henry lighthouse, and not till sunrise of July 12 did she
stand to the eastward and northward. Light head winds and a
strong current delayed her progress till July 17, when at two o'clock
in the afternoon, off Barnegat on the New Jersey coast, the lookout
at the masthead discovered four sails to the northward, and two
hours later a fifth sail to the northeast. Hull took them for Rodger's
squadron. The wind was light, and Hull being to windward determined to speak the nearest vessel, the last to come in sight. The
afternoon passed without bringing the ships together, and at ten
in the evening, finding that the nearest ship could not answer the
night signal, Hull decided to lose no time in escaping.

Then followed one of the most exciting and sustained chases
recorded in naval history. At daybreak the next morning one British frigate was astern within five or six miles, two more were to
leeward, and the rest of the fleet some ten miles astern, all making
chase. Hull put out his boats to tow the "Constitution"; Broke summoned the boats of his squadron to tow the "Shannon." Hull then
bent all his spare rope to the cables, dropped a small anchor half
a mile ahead, in twenty-six fathom water, and warped his ship
along. Broke quickly imitated the device, and slowly gained on the
chase. The "Guerrière" crept so near Hull's lee-beam as to open
fire, but her shot fell short. Fortunately the wind, though slight,
favored Hull. All night the British and American crews toiled on,
and when morning came the "Belvidera," proving to be the best
sailer, got in advance of her consorts, working two kedge anchors,
until at two o'clock in the afternoon she tried in her turn to reach
the "Constitution" with her bow guns, but in vain. Hull expected
capture, but the "Belvidera" could not approach nearer without
bringing her boats under the "Constitution's" stern guns; and the
wearied crews toiled on, towing and kedging, the ships barely out
of gunshot, till another morning came. The breeze, though still
light, then allowed Hull to take in his boats, the "Belvidera" being
two and a half miles in his wake, the "Shannon" three and a half
miles on his lee, and the three other frigates well to leeward. The
wind freshened, and the "Constitution" drew ahead, until toward
seven o'clock in the evening of July 19 a heavy rain-squall struck
the ship, and by taking skilful advantage of it Hull left the "Belvidera" and "Shannon" far astern; yet until eight o'clock the next
morning they were still in sight keeping up the chase.

Perhaps nothing during the war tested American seamanship

more thoroughly than these three days of combined skill and endurance in the face of an irresistible enemy. The result showed
that Hull and the "Constitution" had nothing to fear in these
respects. There remained the question whether the superiority extended to his guns; and such was the contempt of British naval
officers for American ships, that with this experience before their
eyes they still believed one of their 38-gun frigates to be more
than a match for an American forty-four, although the American, besides the heavier armament, had proved his capacity to
out-sail and out-manoeuvre the Englishman. Both parties became
more eager than ever for the test. For once, even the Federalists of
New England felt their blood stir; for their own President and
their own votes had called these frigates into existence, and a victory won by the "Constitution," which had been built by their
hands, was in their eyes a greater victory over their political opponents than over the British. With no half-hearted spirit, the seagoing Bostonians showered well-weighed praises on Hull when his
ship entered Boston harbor, July 26, after its narrow escape; and
when he sailed again, New England waited with keen interest to
learn his fate.

Hull could not expect to keep command of the "Constitution."
Bainbridge was much his senior, and had the right to a preference
in active service. Bainbridge then held and was ordered to retain
command of the "Constellation," fitting out at the Washington
Navy Yard; but Secretary Hamilton, July 28, ordered him to take
command also of the "Constitution" on her arrival in port. Doubtless Hull expected this change, and probably the expectation induced him to risk a dangerous experiment; for without bringing
his ship to the Charlestown Navy Yard, but remaining in the outer
harbor, after obtaining such supplies as he needed, August 2, he
set sail without orders, and stood to the eastward. Having reached
Cape Race without meeting an enemy he turned southward, until
on the night of August 18 he spoke a privateer, which told him of
a British frigate near at hand. Following the privateersman's directions the "Constitution" the next day, August 19, at two o'clock in
the afternoon, latitude 41° 42', longitude 55° 48', sighted the
"Guerrière."

The meeting was welcome on both sides. Only three days before,
Captain Dacres had entered on the log of a merchantman a challenge to any American frigate to meet him off Sandy Hook. Not
only had the "Guerrière" for a long time been extremely offensive
to every seafaring American, but the mistake which caused the

"Little Belt" to suffer so seriously for the misfortune of being taken for the "Guerrière" had caused a corresponding feeling of anger in the officers of the British frigate. The meeting of August 19 had the character of a preconcerted duel.

The wind was blowing fresh from the northwest, with the sea running high. Dacres backed his maintopsail and waited. Hull shortened sail and ran down before the wind. For about an hour the two ships wore and wore again, trying to get advantage of position; until at last, a few minutes before six o'clock, they came together side by side, within pistol shot, the wind almost astern, and running before it they pounded each other with all their strength. As rapidly as the guns could be worked, the "Constitution" poured in broadside after broadside, double-shotted with round and grape, —and without exaggeration, the echo of these guns startled the world. "In less than thirty minutes from the time we got alongside of the enemy," reported Hull, "she was left without a spar standing, and the hull cut to pieces in such a manner as to make it difficult to keep her above water."

That Dacres should have been defeated was not surprising; that he should have expected to win was an example of British arrogance that explained and excused the war. The length of the "Constitution" was 173 feet; that of the "Guerrière" was 156 feet; the extreme breadth of the "Constitution" was 44 feet; that of the "Guerrière" was 40 feet, or within a few inches in both cases. The "Constitution" carried thirty-two long 24-pounders, the "Guerrière" thirty long 18-pounders and two long 12-pounders; the "Constitution" carried twenty 32-pound carronades, the "Guerrière" sixteen. In every respect the "Constitution" was the better ship; her crew was more numerous in proportion of ten to six. Dacres knew this very nearly as well as it was known to Hull, yet he sought a duel. What he did not know was that in a still greater proportion the American officers and crew were better and more intelligent seamen than the British, and that their passionate wish to repay old scores gave them extraordinary energy. So much greater was the moral superiority than the physical, that while the "Guerrière's" force counted as seven against ten, her losses counted as though her force were only two against ten.

Dacres' error cost him dear, for among the "Guerrière's" crew of two hundred and seventy-two, seventy-nine were killed or wounded; and the ship was injured beyond saving before Dacres realized his mistake, although he needed only thirty minutes of close fighting for the purpose. He never fully understood the causes of his defeat, and never excused it by pleading, as he might have done, the great superiority of his enemy.

Hull took his prisoners on board the "Constitution," and after blowing up the "Guerrière" sailed for Boston, where he arrived on the morning of August 30. The Sunday silence of the Puritan city broke into excitement as the news passed through the quiet streets that the "Constitution" was below, in the outer harbor, with Dacres and his crew prisoners on board. No experience of history ever went to the heart of New England more directly than this victory, so peculiarly its own; but the delight was not confined to New England, and extreme though it seemed it was still not extravagant, for however small the affair might appear on the general scale of the world's battles, it raised the United States in one half hour to the rank of a first-class Power in the world. . . . (VI, xvii, 369-75)

During the six months the war had lasted the little United States navy captured three British frigates, besides the 20-gun "Alert" and the 18-gun "Frolic"; privateers by scores had ravaged British commerce, while the immense British force on the ocean had succeeded only in capturing the little "Nautilus," the 12-gun brig "Vixen," and the "Wasp." The commerce of America had indeed suffered almost total destruction; but the dispute was to be decided not so much by the loss which England could inflict upon America, as by that which America could inflict upon England. . . . (VI, xvii, 386-87)

In such a war the people of the United States had only themselves to fear; but their dangers were all the more formidable. Had the war deeply disturbed the conditions of society, or brought general and immediate distress, government and Union might easily have fallen to pieces; but in the midst of military disaster and in plain sight of the Government's incompetence, the general public neither felt nor had reason to fear much change in the routine of life. Commerce had long accustomed itself to embargoes, confiscations, and blockades, and ample supplies of foreign goods continued to arrive. The people made no serious exertions; among a population exceeding seven millions, not ten thousand men entered the military service. The militia, liable to calls to the limit of one hundred thousand, served for the most part only a few weeks in the autumn, went home in whole regiments when they pleased, and in the East refused to go out at all. The scarcity of men was so great that even among the seagoing class, for whose rights the war was waged, only with the utmost difficulty and long delays, in spite of bounties and glory, could sailors be found to man half-a-dozen frigates for a three-months cruise, although the number of privateers was never great.

The nation as a whole saw nothing of actual warfare. While scarcely a city in Europe had escaped capture, and hardly a province of that continent was so remote as not to be familiar with invading armies or to have suffered in proportion to its resources, no American city saw or greatly feared an enemy. The rich farms of New York, New Jersey, Pennsylvania, and Virginia produced their usual harvests, and except on exposed parts of the coast the farmers never feared that their crops might be wasted by manoeuvring armies, or their cattle, pigs, and poultry be disturbed by marauders. The country was vast, and quiet reigned throughout the whole United States. Except at the little point of Niagara, occupied by a few hundred scattered farmers, and on the extreme outskirts of Ohio and Indiana, the occupations and industries of life followed in the main their daily course.

The country refused to take the war seriously. A rich nation with seven million inhabitants should have easily put one hundred thousand men into the field, and should have found no difficulty in supporting them; but no inducement that the Government dared offer prevailed upon the people to risk life and property on a sufficient scale in 1812. The ranks of the army were to be filled in one of two ways,—either by enlistment in the regular service for five years, with pay at five dollars a month, sixteen dollars bounty, and on discharge three months pay and one hundred and sixty acres of land; or by volunteer organizations to the limit of fifty thousand men in all, officered under State laws, to serve for one year, with the pay of regular troops but without bounty, clothed, and in case of cavalry corps mounted, at their own expense. In a society where the day laborers' wages were nowhere less than nine dollars a month, these inducements were not enough to supply the place of enthusiasm. The patriotic citizen who wished to serve his country without too much sacrifice, chose a third course,—he volunteered under the Act of Congress which authorized the President to call one hundred thousand State militia into service for six months; and upon this State militia Dearborn, Hull, Van Rensselaer, and Smyth were obliged chiefly to depend. . . . (VI, xviii, 388-90)

Except beyond the mountains the war party was everywhere a social minority, and perhaps such strength as Madison retained in the East consisted partly in the popular impression that he was not a favorite with the authors of the war. . . . (VI, xviii, 409)

In the midst of confusion the election took place. Few moments in the national history were less cheerful. In the Northwest the force organized to recapture Detroit, commanded by General Harrison, was still at Franklinton in the center of Ohio, unable to advance and preparing to disband. At Niagara, Van Rensselaer had failed, and Smyth was in command. At sea, the "Guerrière" and the "Frolic" had been captured, but Decatur's victory over the "Macedonian" was still unknown. Napoleon, though supposed to be dictating peace at Moscow, was actually in full retreat. Every hope of the war party had already proved mistaken. Canada was not in their hands; no army had been enlisted; the people were less united than ever; taxation and debt could no longer be avoided; and military disgrace had been incurred beyond the predictions of John Randolph and Josiah Quincy. All this took place before the country had seen five hundred enemies except its own Indians on its soil, and when it had no reason to fear immediate attack.

Once more the steadiness of Pennsylvania saved the Administration from its worst perils. The election took place, and the electoral votes of New England, except Vermont, were duly thrown for De Witt Clinton, while under the management of Martin Van Buren the Republicans of the New York legislature chose Clinton electors by Federalist aid. New Jersey and Delaware also voted for Clinton. Maryland gave five of her electoral votes to Clinton, six to Madison, and elected a legislature strongly Federalist. A change of twenty electoral votes would have turned the scale. In 1808, under all the disadvantages of the embargo, Madison received one hundred and twenty-two votes in an Electoral College of one hundred and seventy-five; but in 1812 he obtained only one hundred and twenty-eight votes in an Electoral College of two hundred and seventeen, although the three new votes of Louisiana increased his proportion. In Massachusetts the Federalists surprised even themselves by their immense majority of twenty-four thousand, and the peace party swept the Congressional districts throughout New England and New York, doubling Federalist strength in the Thirteenth Congress.

If John Taylor of Caroline was to be believed, the support given by Virginia to the Administration was hardly more flattering than the sweeping condemnation of the North and East. The County of Caroline, south of the Rappahannock on the road to Richmond, was distinguished by no peculiarities from the other seaboard counties in the Southern States, and Colonel Taylor himself did not openly oppose the war; but he saw no enthusiasm for it among his neighbors. November 8 he wrote to Monroe,—

"I think I expressed my opinion to you during the last Congress that the people were not for the war in these parts, though they were attached to Mr. Monroe and Mr. Madison. In that opinion I am confirmed by the apathy in choosing electors. Those respectable and popular men, Colonel James Taylor and Dr. Bankhead, could not, I am told, get more than about one hundred and thirty out of about seven hundred freeholders to attend and vote for Mr. Madison. Among these were the most prominent minority-men."

This apathy extended through the three great States of Pennsylvania, Virginia, and North Carolina. Only along the Indian frontier, west of the Alleghany Mountains, could enthusiasm be said to exist, and even there took rather the form of hostilities against the Indians than against the British. . . . (VI, xix, 412-14)

President Madison's Annual Message of November 4, 1812, was an interesting paper. Gliding gently over the disasters of the Northern campaign; dilating on British iniquity in using Indians for allies; commenting on the conduct of Massachusetts and Connecticut with disfavor, because it led to the result that the United States were "not one nation for the purpose most of all requiring it"; praising Rodgers and Hull for the results of their skill and bravery —the Message next touched upon the diplomatic outlook and the future objects of the war in a paragraph which needed and received much study:—

"Anxious to abridge the evils from which a state of war cannot be exempt, I lost no time, after it was declared, in conveying to the British government the terms on which its progress might be arrested without awaiting the delays of a formal and final pacification; and our *chargé d'affaires* at London was at the same time authorized to agree to an armistice founded upon them. These terms required that the Orders in Council should be repealed as they affected the United States, without a revival of blockades violating acknowledged rule; and that there should be an immediate discharge of American seamen from British ships, and a stop to impressment from American ships, with an understanding that an exclusion of the seamen of each nation from the ships of the other should be stipulated; and that the armistice should be improved into a definite and comprehensive adjustment of depending controversies. Although a repeal of the orders susceptible of explanations meeting the views of this Government had taken place before this pacific advance was communicated to that of Great Britain, the advance [made by us] was declined [by the British government] from an avowed repugnance to a suspension of the practice of impressments during the armistice, and without any intimation that the arrangement proposed with respect to seamen would be accepted. Whether the subsequent communications from this Government, affording an occasion for reconsidering the subject on the part of Great Britain, will be viewed in a more favorable light remains to be known. It would be unwise to relax our measures in any result on a presumption of such a result."

Not without difficulty could one understand from this statement precisely what prevented the restoration of peace. England had never refused to discharge American seamen on sufficient evidence of wrongful impressment. According to the Message, the President asked only "an immediate discharge of American seamen from British ships, and a stop to impressment from American ships." The demand of this point seemed to imply that England had made or would probably make satisfactory concessions on all others. The Message therefore narrowed the cause of war to the requirement of a formal suspension of impressments from American ships, though not of American citizens on shore, pending negotiations, and to be made permanent by treaty. The demand was proper, and its only fault was to fall short of full satisfaction; but considered in its effect upon the politics of the moment the attitude was new, unsupported by a precedent, unwarranted by any previous decision or declaration of President or Congress, and open to the Federalist charge that Madison sought only an excuse for continuing to stake the national existence on the chance of success in his alliance with Bonaparte. The rest of the Message helped to strengthen the impression that a policy of permanent war was to be fixed upon the country; for it recommended higher pay for recruits and volunteers, an increase in the number of general officers, a reorganization of the general staff of the army, and an increase of the navy. The impression was not weakened by the President's silence in regard to the financial wants of the government, which left to the Secretary of the Treasury the unpleasant duty of announcing that the enormous sum of twenty million dollars must be borrowed for the coming year. Every one knew that such a demand was equivalent to admitting the prospect of immediate bankruptcy.

"I think a loan to that amount to be altogether unattainable," Gallatin told Madison in private. "From banks we can expect little or nothing, as they have already lent nearly to the full extent of their faculties. All that I could obtain this year from individual subscriptions does not exceed three million two hundred thousand dollars."

The President refrained from presenting this demand to Congress, and not until after the election was the financial situation made known; but then Gallatin's report, sent to the House December 5, estimated the military expenses at seventeen millions, the naval at nearly five millions, and the civil at fifteen hundred thousand dollars, besides interest on the public debt to the amount of three million three hundred thousand, and reimbursements of loans, treasury notes, etc., reaching five million two hundred thousand more,—in all, thirty-one million nine hundred and twenty-five thousand dollars. This estimate omitted every expenditure not already authorized by law, such as the proposed increase of army and navy.

To meet these obligations, amounting probably to thirty-three million dollars, Gallatin counted on a revenue of eleven million five hundred thousand dollars from imports, and half a million from the sale of lands—making twelve millions in all; leaving a sum of at least twenty millions to be borrowed, with an increase of debt to the amount of fifteen millions.

The state of war brought the advantage of compelling the Legislature to act or perish; and although Congress had seldom if ever been so unanimously dissatisfied, it was never so docile. For the first time Madison could recommend a measure with some certainty that Congress would listen, and with some confidence that it would act. Faction began to find its limits, and an Executive order had no longer to excuse itself; while Congress on its side, with shut eyes, broke through the barriers hitherto set to its powers, and roamed almost at will beyond the limits which the Republican party assigned to the Constitution. . . . (VI, xix, 430-34)

The theory that the American was a degenerate Englishman,— a theory chiefly due to American teachings,—lay at the bottom of British politics. Even the late British minister at Washington, Foster, a man of average intelligence, thought it manifest good taste and good sense to say of the Americans in his speech of February 18, 1813, in Parliament, that "generally speaking, they were not a people we should be proud to acknowledge as our relations." Decatur and Hull were engaged in a social rather than in a political contest, and were aware that the serious work on their hands had little to do with England's power, but much to do with her manners. The mortification of England at the capture of her frigates was the measure of her previous arrogance.

The process of acquiring knowledge in such light as was furnished by the cannon of Hull, Decatur, and Bainbridge could not be rendered easy or rapid. News of the American victories dropped in at intervals, as though American captains intentionally prolonged the enjoyment of their certain success, in order to keep England in constant ill temper. News of the "Java" arrived about the middle of March, and once more the press broke into a chorus of complaints. The "Times" renewed its outcry; the "Courier" abused the "Times" for its "tone of whining lamentation, of affected sensibility, and puerile grief," but admitted that the behavior of the American frigates seemed extraordinary; while the "Pilot," the chief naval authority, lamented in set periods the incomprehensible event:—

"The public will learn, with sentiments which we shall not presume to anticipate, that a third British frigate has struck to an American. This is an occurrence that calls for serious reflection,—this, and the fact stated in our paper of yesterday, that Loyd's list contains notices of upwards of five hundred British vessels captured in seven months by the Americans. Five hundred merchantmen and three frigates! Can these statements be true; and can the English people hear them unmoved? Any one who had predicted such a result of an American war this time last year would have been treated as a madman or a traitor. He would have been told, if his opponents had condescended to argue with him, that long ere seven months had elapsed the American flag would be swept from the seas, the contemptible navy of the United States annihilated, and their maritime arsenals rendered a heap of ruins. Yet down to this moment not a single American frigate has struck her flag. They insult and laugh at our want of enterprise and vigor. They leave their ports when they please, and return to them when it suits their convenience; they traverse the Atlantic; they beset the West India Islands; they advance to the very chops of the Channel; they parade along the coasts of South America; nothing chases, nothing intercepts, nothing engages them but to yield them triumph."

The immediate moral drawn from these complaints was the necessity of punishing the United States; but no one could longer deny that the necessary punishment was likely to prove tedious and costly. . . . (VII, i, 15-17)

A long war, with no prospect of success, lay before the United States. New York harbor, the Delaware River, and Chesapeake Bay were already so nearly closed to commerce as to foreshadow complete stoppage; and if Boston was still open, its privileges must soon cease unless Great Britain deliberately intended to regard New England as neutral. All this, though alarming enough, might be met with courage; but against the pronounced disaffection of Massachusetts and Connecticut no defence existed; and whenever those States should pass from stolid inertia into the stage of active resistance to the war, the situation would become hopeless. Under such circumstances England would have a strong motive for refusing peace on any terms.

The shadow of these fears lay over the Inaugural Address which the President pronounced March 4, 1813, after taking for a second time the oath of office at the Capitol. His speech contained only the defence of a war that needed no defence, and complaints against England which were drowned in the tumult of war, the loudest complaint that man could make. Every tone showed that Madison felt doubtful of support, and that in proving the war to be just he betrayed consciousness that it was not energetic. Perhaps the most characteristic sentence in the Address was that in which he congratulated the country "with a proud satisfaction," that in carrying on the war, "no principle of justice or honor, no usage of civilized nations, no precept of courtesy or humanity, have been infringed; the war has been waged on our part with scrupulous regard to all these relations, and in a spirit of liberality which was never surpassed." Madison's phrases were the more remarkable because at about the same time the British government announced its intention of making America feel what war meant. The courtesy and humanity of the war were to be all on the American side; while not a word in the Inaugural Address gave the pledge which could win victories,—the assurance that the President himself had energy and meant to exert it. . . . (VII, ii, 33-34)

An illustration of the dangers into which the spirit of faction at that excited moment led the factious, was furnished by the legislature of Massachusetts, which met, May 26, and after listening to a long speech from Governor Strong arraigning the national government for its injustice to England and partiality to France, referred the subject to committees which lost no time in reporting. One of these reports, presented June 4 by Josiah Quincy of the State Senate, closed with a Resolution that the Act admitting Louisiana into the

Union violated the Constitution, and that the Massachusetts senators in Congress should use their utmost endeavors to obtain its repeal. Another report, by a joint committee, contained a remonstrance addressed to Congress against the war, couched in terms of strong sectional hostility to the Southern States, and marked throughout by a covert argument for disunion. A third report, also by Josiah Quincy, on a naval victory lately won by Captain James Lawrence of the "Hornet," contained a phrase even longer remembered than Quincy's assertion that the Government could not be kicked into a war. The Government could not be kicked into the war, but Quincy was not the better pleased. He reported that in order not to give offence to many of the good people of the Commonwealth by appearing to encourage the continuance of an unjust, unnecessary, and iniquitous war, the Massachusetts senate while admiring Lawrence's virtues refrained from approving his acts:—

"And to the end that all misrepresentations on this subject may be obviated,—

Resolved, as the sense of the Senate of Massachusetts, that in a war like the present, waged without justifiable cause, and prosecuted in a manner which indicates that conquest and ambition are its real motives, it is not becoming a moral and religious people to express any approbation of military or naval exploits which are not immediately connected with the defence of our seacoast and soil."

Such tactics, whether in or out of Congress, were more dangerous to their authors than any blunders of the Administration could ever be to the party in power. If the nation should be successful in the war, it might perhaps in good nature leave unpunished the conduct of its malcontents; but if by their means the nation should be conquered or forced into a humiliating peace, the people could never forget, and never forego revenge. Mere opposition to foreign war rarely injured public men, except while the war fever lasted. Many distinguished statesmen of Europe and America had been, at one time or another, in opposition to some special war,—as was the case with Talleyrand, Charles James Fox, Lord Grey, Jefferson, and Madison; but opposition became unpardonable when it took a form which could have no apparent object except national ruin. The Federalists who held the ideas expressed by the legislature of Massachusetts could explain or defend their future course only by the conviction that the inevitable and long-expected "crisis" was at hand, which must end either in disunion or in reconstruction of the Union on new ground. As "a moral and religious people," they separated from the common stock, and thenceforward, if the Union lasted, could expect no pardon.

The extravagance of the Massachusetts Federalists was counterbalanced by the same national disasters which caused it. Nothing showed that the war was popular in any of the seaboard States; but the pressure of circumstances, little by little, obliged lukewarm and even hostile communities to support it. Virginia and the Southern States were drawn into relations toward the government which they had never intended to accept. Pennsylvania, Kentucky, and Tennessee submitted to exactions that would at any previous stage of their history have produced a revolution. Perhaps the strongest proof of change in popular prejudices was furnished by the taxes. Tax-bills which were supposed to have already overthrown one great political party,—bills which inflicted the evils so hotly and persistently denounced by Jefferson, Gallatin, and John Randolph in opposition, and which had been long delayed by fear of their popular effect,— were passed by Congress quickly, by decided votes, and with less debate than was given to the discussion whether the President had or had not told all he knew about Bassano's Decree of April 28, 1811. From the time they were approved by the President, in July and August, 1813, to the time of their appeal, neither the President nor his party was troubled by popular discontent on account of the passage of these Acts. They were accepted as a necessary part of the national system, and of a war policy.

The most curious symptom, and the one which most perplexed the Federalists, was that this popular movement of concentration acted in direct resistance to the movement of events. In every respect as the Federalists looked back at the past twelve years their prophecies had come true. The Republican party, they argued, had proved itself incompetent, and had admitted the failure of its principles; it had been forced to abandon them in practice, to replace the government where the Federalists had put it, and to adopt all the Federalists' methods; and even then the party failed. Equally imbecile in peace and war, the democratic movement had ended in such disgrace and helplessness as few governments had ever outlived, and such as no nation with a near and powerful neighbor could have survived. In 1813 the evidence of downfall had become patent. The government was ruined in credit and character; bankrupt, broken, and powerless, it continued to exist merely because of habit, and must succumb to the first shock. All this the Federalists had long foreseen. Fisher Ames in the press, scores of clergymen in the pulpit, numberless politicians in Congress, had made no other use of their leisure than to point out, step by step, every succeeding stage in the coming decline. The catastrophe was no longer far away, it was actually about them,—they touched and felt it at every moment of their lives. Society held itself together merely because it knew not what else to do.

Under circumstances following each other in necessity so stringent, no Federalist could doubt that society would pursue the predicted course; but it did not. Illogical and perverse, society persisted in extending itself in lines which ran into chaos. The threatened "crisis" had arrived, wanting no characteristic of those so long foretold; but society made no effort to save itself. A vaster ruin and still more terrible retribution lay beyond. The Federalists were greatly and naturally perplexed at discovering the silent undercurrent which tended to grow in strength precisely as it encountered most resistance from events. They tried to explain the phenomenon in their own way,—the clergy according to religious conceptions, the politicians according to their ideas of popular character. The political theory was the more plausible and less respectable. A. C. Hanson, the extreme Maryland Federalist, mobbed and nearly killed in Baltimore in June, 1812, only to be elected to Congress in November, thought that the national movement of 1813 was due to military glory. Hanson wrote to Pickering on the subject, in the autumn:—

"The war is becoming more popular every day in this State [Maryland]. Our successes, and the weak manner in which it is conducted by the enemy make it so. . . . It would seem that after a while, unless the British can gather the sense and courage to strike some severe blows, the war by its own generative powers will create the means for its support. The vanity of a people cannot bear these brilliant naval victories, and there is no passion to which the rulers of a people can address themselves with greater effect. Even in my district the active opposers of the war are falling off every day, and unless we shortly meet with some reverses, the Administration will shortly find more friends than enemies in this State by a great deal. . . . The impression is becoming universal that the enemy cannot harm us if he would. A few hard blows struck in the right place would be of great service to the country."

A people that could feel its vanity flattered by such glories as the war gave in 1813 must have felt the want of flattery to an unusual degree. The idea was extravagant. Not so much the glories as the disgraces of the war roused public sympathy; not so much the love of victory as the ignominy of defeat, and the grinding necessity of supporting government at any cost of private judgment. At such a moment any success was keenly felt, and covered every failure. The slow conviction that come what would the nation must be preserved, brought one man after another into support of the war, until the Federalists found their feet in a quicksand. The "crisis" produced the opposite effect to that which Burke's philosophy predicted. . . . (VII, iii, 64-70)

6.

Vindication of National Character

In the enthusiasm over the frigates in 1812, Congress voted that six forty-fours should be built, besides four ships-of-the-line. The Act was approved Jan. 2, 1813. Not until March 3 did Congress pass an Act for building six new sloops-of-war. The loss of two months was not the only misfortune in this legislation. Had the sloops been begun in January, they might have gone to sea by the close of the year. The six sloops were all launched within eleven months from the passage of the bill, and the first of them, the "Frolic," got to sea within that time, while none of the frigates or line-of-battle ships could get to sea within two years of the passage of the law. A more remarkable oversight was the building of only six sloops, when an equal number of forty-fours and four seventy-fours were ordered. Had Congress voted twenty-four sloops, the proportion would not have been improper; but perhaps the best policy would have been to build fifty such sloops, and to prohibit privateering. The reasons for such a course were best seen in the experiences of the privateers.

The history of the privateers was never satisfactorily written. Neither their number, their measurements, their force, their captures, nor their losses were accurately known. Little ground could be given for an opinion in regard to their economy. Only with grave doubt could any judgment be reached even in regard to their relative efficiency compared with government vessels of the same class. Yet their experience was valuable, and their services were very great. . . . (VII, xiii, 313-14)

The government sloop-of-war was not built for privateering purposes. Every government vessel was intended chiefly to fight, and required strength in every part and solidity throughout. The frame needed to be heavy to support the heavier structure; the quarters needed to be thick to protect the men at the guns from grape and musketry; the armament was as weighty as the frame would bear. So strong were the sides of American frigates that even thirty-two-pound shot fired at forty or fifty feet distance sometimes failed to penetrate, and the British complained as a grievance that the sides of an American forty-four were thicker than those of a British seventy-four. The American ship-builders spared no pains to make all their vessels in every respect—in size, strength, and speed—superior to the vessels with which they were to compete; but the government ship-carpenter had a harder task than the private ship-builder, for he was obliged to obtain greater speed at the same time that he used heavier material than the British constructors. As far as the navy carpenters succeeded in their double object, they did so by improving the model and increasing the proportions of the spars.

The privateer was built for no such object. The last purpose of a privateer was to fight at close range, and owners much preferred that their vessels, being built to make money, should not fight at all unless much money could be made. The private armed vessel was built rather to fly than to fight, and its value depended far more on its ability to escape than on its capacity to attack. If the privateer could sail close to the wind, and wear or tack in the twinkling of an eye; if she could spread an immense amount of canvas and run off as fast as a frigate before the wind; if she had sweeps to use in a calm, and one long-range gun pivoted amidships, with plenty of men in case boarding became necessary,—she was perfect. To obtain these results the builders and sailors ran excessive risks. Too lightly built and too heavily sparred, the privateer was never a comfortable or a safe vessel. Beautiful beyond anything then known in naval construction, such vessels roused boundless admiration, but defied imitators. British constructors could not build them, even when they had the models; British captains could not sail them; and when British admirals, fascinated by their beauty and tempted by the marvellous qualities of their model, ordered such a prize to be taken into the service, the first act of the carpenters in the British navy yards was to reduce to their own standard the long masts, and to strengthen the hull and sides till the vessel should be safe in a battle or a gale. Perhaps an American navy carpenter must have done the same; but though not a line in the model might be altered, she never sailed again as she sailed before. She could not bear conventional restraints.

Americans were proud of their privateers, as they well might be; for this was the first time when in competition with the world, on an element open to all, they proved their capacity to excel, and produced a creation as beautiful as it was practical. The British navy took a new tone in regard to these vessels. Deeply as the American frigates and sloops-of-war had wounded the pride of the British navy, they never had reduced that fine service to admitted inferiority. Under one pretext or another, every defeat was excused. Even the superiority of American gunnery was met by the proud explanation that the British navy, since Trafalgar, had enjoyed no opportunity to use their guns. Nothing could convince a British admiral that Americans were better fighters than Englishmen; but when he looked at the American schooner he frankly said that England could show no such models, and could not sail them if she had them. In truth, the schooner was a wonderful invention. Not her battles, but her escapes won for her the open-mouthed admiration of the British captains, who saw their prize double like a hare and slip through their fingers at the moment when capture was sure. Under any ordinary condition of wind and weather, with an open sea, the schooner, if only she could get to windward, laughed at a frigate.

As the sailing rather than the fighting qualities of the privateer were the chief object of her construction, those were the points best worth recording; but the newspapers of the time were so much absorbed in proving that Americans could fight, as to cause almost total neglect of the more important question whether Americans could sail better than their rivals. All great nations had fought, and at one time or another every great nation in Europe had been victorious over every other; but no people, in the course of a thousand years of rivalry on the ocean, had invented or had known how to sail a Yankee schooner. Whether ship, brig, schooner, or sloop, the American vessel was believed to outsail any other craft on the ocean, and the proof of this superiority was incumbent on the Americans to furnish. They neglected to do so. No clear evidence was ever recorded of the precise capacities of their favorite vessels. Neither the lines of the hull, the dimensions of the spars, the rates of sailing by the log in different weather, the points of sailing,— nothing precise was ever set down.

Of the superiority no doubts could be entertained. The best proof of the American claim was the British admission. Hardly an English writer on marine affairs—whether in newspapers, histories, or novels —failed to make some allusion to the beauty and speed of American vessels. The naval literature of Great Britain from 1812 to 1860 was full of such material. The praise of the invention was still commonly accompanied by some expression of dislike for the inventor, but even in that respect a marked change followed the experiences of 1812-1814. Among the Englishmen living on the island of Jamaica, and familiar with the course of events in the West Indies from 1806 to 1817, was one Michael Scott, born in Glasgow in 1789, and in the prime of his youth at the time of the American war. In the year 1829, at the age of forty, he began the publication in "Blackwood's Magazine" of a series of sketches which rapidly became popular as "Tom Cringle's Log." Scott was the best narrator and probably the best informed man who wrote on the West Indies at that period; and his frequent allusions to the United States and the war threw more light on the social side of history than could be obtained from all official sources ever printed.

"I don't like Americans," Scott said; "I never did and never shall like them. I have seldom met an American gentleman in the large and complete sense of the term. I have no wish to eat with them, drink with them, deal with or consort with them in any way; but let me tell the whole truth,—nor fight with them, were it not for the laurels to be acquired by overcoming an enemy so brave, determined, and alert, and every way so worthy of one's steel as they have always proved."

The Americans did not fight the War of 1812 in order to make themselves loved. According to Scott's testimony they gained the object for which they did fight. "In gunnery and small-arm practice we were as thoroughly weathered on by the Americans during the war as we overtopped them in the bulldog courage with which our boarders handled those genuine English weapons,—the cutlass and the pike." Superiority in the intellectual branches of warfare was conceded to the Americans; but even in regard to physical qualities, the British were not inclined to boast.

"In the field," said Scott, "or grappling in mortal combat on the blood-slippery quarterdeck of an enemy's vessel, a British soldier or sailor is the bravest of the brave. No soldier or sailor of any other country, saving and excepting those damned Yankees, can stand against them."

Had English society known so much of Americans in 1807, war would have been unnecessary.

Yet neither equality in physical courage nor superiority in the higher branches of gunnery and small arms was the chief success of Americans in the war. Beyond question the schooner was the most conclusive triumph. Readers of Michael Scott could not forget the best of his sketches,—the escape of the little American schooner "Wave" from two British cruisers, by running to windward under the broadside of a man-of-war. With keen appreciation Scott detailed every motion of the vessels, and dwelt with peculiar emphasis on the apparent desperation of the attempt. Again and again the thirty-two-pound shot, as he described the scene, tore through the slight vessel as the two crafts raced through the heavy seas within musket-shot of one another, until at last the firing from the corvette ceased. "The breeze had taken off, and the 'Wave,' resuming her superiority in light winds, had escaped." Yet this was not the most significant part of "Tom Cringle's" experience. The "Wave," being afterward captured at anchor, was taken into the royal service and fitted as a ship-of-war. Cringle was ordered by the vice admiral to command her, and as she came to report he took a look at her:—

"When I had last seen her she was a most beautiful little craft, both in hull and rigging, as ever delighted the eye of a sailor; but the dockyard riggers and carpenters had fairly bedeviled her, at least so far as appearances went. First they had replaced the light rail on her gunwale by heavy solid bulwarks four feet high, surmounted by hammock nettings at least another foot; so that the symmetrical little vessel that formerly floated on the foam light as a sea-gull now looked like a clumsy, dish-shaped Dutch dogger. Her long, slender wands of masts which used to swing about as if there were neither shrouds nor stays to support them were now as taut and stiff as church-steeples, with four heavy shrouds of a side, and stays and back-stays, and the Devil knows what all."

"If them heave-'emtaughts at the yard have not taken the speed out of the little beauty I am a Dutchman" was the natural comment, —as obvious as it was sound.

The reports of privateer captains to their owners were rarely published, and the logs were never printed or deposited in any public office. Occasionally, in the case of a battle or the loss of guns or spars or cargo in a close pursuit, the privateer captain described the causes of his loss in a letter which found its way into print; and from such letters some idea could be drawn of the qualities held in highest regard, both in their vessels and in themselves. The first and commonest remark was that privateers of any merit never seemed to feel anxious for their own safety so long as they could get to windward a couple of gunshots from their enemy. They would risk a broadside in the process without very great anxiety. They chiefly feared lest they might be obliged to run before the wind in heavy weather. The little craft which could turn on itself like a flash and dart away under a frigate's guns into the wind's eye long before the heavy ship could come about, had little to fear on that point of sailing; but when she was obliged to run to lee-ward, the chances were more nearly equal. Sometimes, especially in light breezes or in a stronger wind, by throwing guns and weighty articles overboard privateers could escape; but in heavy weather the ship-of-war could commonly outcarry them, and more often could drive them on a coast or into the clutches of some other man-of-war.

Of being forced to fly to leeward almost every privateer could tell interesting stories. A fair example of such tales was an adventure of Captain George Coggeshall, who afterward compiled, chiefly from newspapers, an account of the privateers, among which he preserved a few stories that would otherwise have been lost. Coggeshall commanded a two-hundred-ton schooner, the "David Porter," in which he made the run to France with a cargo and a letter of marque. The schooner was at Bordeaux in March, 1814, when Wellington's army approached. Afraid of seizure by the British if he remained at Bordeaux, Coggeshall sailed from Bordeaux for La Rochelle with a light wind from the eastward, when at daylight March 15, 1814, he found a large ship about two miles to windward. Coggeshall tried to draw his enemy down to leeward, but only lost ground until the ship was not more than two gunshots away. The schooner could then not run to windward without taking the enemy's fire within pistol shot, and dared not return to Bordeaux. Nothing remained but to run before the wind. Coggeshall got out his square sail and studding sails ready to set, and when everything was prepared he changed his course and bore off suddenly, gaining a mile in the six or eight minutes lost by the ship in spreading her studding sails. He then started his water casks, threw out ballast, and drew away from his pursuer, till in a few hours the ship became a speck on the horizon. . . . (VII, xiii, 317-25)

No one disputed that the privateers were a very important branch of the American navy; but they suffered under serious drawbacks, which left doubtful the balance of merits and defects. Perhaps their chief advantage compared with government vessels was their lightness,—a quality which no government would have carried to the same extent. The long-range pivot gun was another invention of the privateer, peculiarly successful and easily adapted for government vessels. In other respects, the same number or even half the number of sloops-of-war would have probably inflicted greater injury at less cost. The "Argus" showed how this result could have been attained. The privateer's first object was to save prizes; and in the effort to send captured vessels into port the privateer lost a large proportion by recapture. Down to the moment when Admiral Warren established his blockade of the American coast from New York southward, most of the prizes got to port. After that time the New England ports alone offered reasonable chance of safety and privateering received a check. During the war about twenty-five hundred vessels all told were captured from the British. Many were destroyed; many released as cartels; and of the remainder not less than seven hundred and fifty, probably one half the number sent to port, were recaptured by the British navy. Most of these were the prizes of privateers, and would have been destroyed had they been taken by government vessels. They were usually the most valuable prizes, so that the injury that might have been inflicted on British commerce was diminished nearly one half by the system which encouraged private war as a moneymaking speculation.

Another objection was equally serious. Like all gambling ventures, privateering was not profitable. In the list of five hundred privateers furnished by the Navy Department, three hundred were recorded as having never made a prize. Of the remainder, few made their expenses. One of the most successful cruises of the war was that of Joshua Barney on the Baltimore schooner "Rossie" at the outbreak of hostilities, when every prize reached port. Barney sent in prizes supposed to be worth fifteen hundred thousand dollars; but after paying charges and duties and selling the goods, he found that the profits were not sufficient to counterbalance the discomforts, and he refused to repeat the experiment. His experience was common. As early as November, 1812, the owners of twenty-four New York privateers sent to Congress a memorial declaring that the profits of private naval war were by no means equal to the hazards, and that the spirit of privateering stood in danger of extinction unless the government would consent in some manner to grant a bounty for the capture or destruction of the enemy's property.

If private enterprise was to fail at the critical moment, and if the government must supply the deficiency, the government would have done better to undertake the whole task. In effect, the government in the end did so. The merchants asked chiefly for a reduction of duties on prize goods. Gallatin pointed out the serious objections to such legislation, and the little probability that the measure would increase the profits of privateering or the number of privateers. The actual privateers, he said, were more than enough for the food offered by the enemy's trade, and privateering, like every other form of gambling, would always continue to attract more adventurers than it could support.

Congress for the time followed Gallatin's advice, and did nothing; but in the summer session of 1813, after Gallatin's departure for Europe, the privateer owners renewed their appeal, and the acting Secretary of the Treasury, Jones,[9] wrote to the chairman of the Naval Committee July 21, 1813,—

"The fact is that . . . privateering is nearly at an end; and from the best observation I have been enabled to make, it is more from the deficiency of remuneration in the net proceeds of their prizes than from the vigilance and success of the enemy in recapturing."

In deference to Jones's opinion, Congress passed an Act, approved August 2, 1813, reducing one third the duties on prize-goods. Another Act, approved August 3, granted a bounty of twenty-five dollars for every prisoner captured and delivered to a United States agent by a private armed vessel. A third Act, approved August 2, authorized the Secretary of the Navy to place on the pension list any privateersman who should be wounded or disabled in the line of his duty.

These complaints and palliations tended to show that the privateer cost the public more than the equivalent government vessel would have cost. If instead of five hundred privateers of all sizes and efficiency, the government had kept twenty sloops-of-war constantly at sea destroying the enemy's commerce, the result would have been about the same as far as concerned injury to the enemy, while in another respect the government would have escaped one of its chief difficulties. Nothing injured the navy so much as privateering. Seamen commonly preferred the harder but more profitable and shorter cruise in a privateer, where fighting was not expected or wished, to the strict discipline and murderous battles of government ships, where wages were low and prize-money scarce. Of all

[9] William Jones: of Philadelphia, acting Secretary of the Treasury, May 1813 to February 1814, and Secretary of the Navy, January 12, 1813 to December 2, 1814.

towns in the United States, Marblehead was probably the most devoted to the sea; but of nine hundred men from Marblehead who took part in the war, fifty-seven served as soldiers, one hundred and twenty entered the navy, while seven hundred and twenty-six went as privateersmen. Only after much delay and difficulty could the frigates obtain crews. The "Constitution" was nearly lost by this cause at the beginning of the war; and the loss of the "Chesapeake" was supposed to be chiefly due to the determination of the old crew to quit the government service for that of the privateers.

Such drawbacks raised reasonable doubts as to the balance of advantages and disadvantages offered by the privateer system. Perhaps more careful inquiry might show that, valuable as the privateers were, the government would have done better to retain all military and naval functions in its own hands, and to cover the seas with small cruisers capable of pursuing a system of thorough destruction against the shipping and colonial interests of England. . . . VII, xiii, 333-38)

Little by little the pressure of necessity compelled Congress and the country to follow Madison's lead. Whether for good or for evil, he had his way. His enemies were overcome and driven from the field; his friends were rewarded, and his advice followed. Of revolt within the party he stood no longer in fear. Already political intrigue and factiousness began to take a direction which concerned him only so far as he felt an interest in the choice of his successor. Three years more would complete Madison's public career, and in all probability if another President of the United States were ever elected, he would be one of Madison's friends; but many persons doubted whether the country would reach another Presidential election, and the jealousy which actuated New England against the South was not the only ground for that opinion. In Madison's immediate circle of friends, the jealousy between Virginia and New York threatened to tear the government in pieces. These States did not, like Massachusetts, threaten to leave the Union, but their struggles for power promised to bring government to a standstill.

The antipathy of New York for Virginia was not lessened by the success of Virginia in overthrowing Aaron Burr and DeWitt Clinton. The Republican party in New York quickly produced two new aspirants to the Presidency, whose hopes were founded on public weariness of Virginian supremacy. One of the two candidates was Governor Daniel D. Tompkins, whose services as war-governor of New York were great, and were rewarded by great popularity. Governor Tompkins was too remote from the capital to annoy Madison by direct contact with factions or activity in intrigue; but the other rival stood at the center of Executive patronage. John Armstrong[10] was a man capable of using power for personal objects, and not easily to be prevented from using it as he pleased.

Armstrong was an unusual character. The local influences which shaped Americans were illustrated by the leaders whom New York produced, and by none better than by Armstrong. Virginians could not understand, and could still less trust, such a combination of keenness and will, with absence of conventional morals as the Secretary of War displayed. The Virginians were simple in everything; even their casuistry was old-fashioned. Armstrong's mind belonged to modern New York. The Virginians were a knot of country gentlemen, inspired by faith in rural virtues, and sustained by dislike for the city tendencies of Northern society. Among themselves they were genial, reluctant to offend, and eager to remove causes of offence. The domestic history of the government at Washington repeated the Virginian traits. Jefferson and his friends passed much time in making quarrels, and more in making peace. Unlike Pennsylvania, New York, and New England, Virginia stood stoutly by her own leaders; and however harsh Virginians might be in their judgment of others, they carried delicacy to an extreme in their treatment of each other. Even John Randolph and W. B. Giles, who seemed to put themselves beyond the social pale, were treated with tenderness and regarded with admiration.

The appearance of a rough and harshly speaking friend in such a society was no slight shock, and for that reason William Henry Crawford was regarded with some alarm; but Crawford was socially one of themselves, while Armstrong belonged to a different type and class. The faculty of doing a harsh act in a harsh way, and of expressing rough opinions in a caustic tone, was not what the Virginians most disliked in Armstrong. His chief fault in their eyes, and one which they could not be blamed for resenting, was his avowed want of admiration for the Virginians themselves. Armstrong's opinion on that subject, which was but the universal opinion of New York politicians, became notorious long before he entered the Cabinet, and even then annoyed Madison. The newspapers gossiped about the mean estimate which Armstrong expressed for the capacities of the Virginia statesmen. So old and fixed was the feud, that from the first the Virginians lost no opportunity to ex-

[10] John Armstrong: became Secretary of War February 5, 1813, replacing William Eustis.

press their opinion of Armstrong, especially in the Senate, whenever he was nominated for office. Madison unwillingly selected him for the post of Secretary after Crawford refused it, but neither of the Virginia senators voted on the question of confirmation. In appointing Armstrong, Madison bestowed on him neither respect nor confidence. He afterward declared the reasons that caused him to invite a person whom he distrusted into a position of the highest importance.

"Should it be asked," wrote Madison ten years after the war, "why the individual in question was placed, and after such developments of his career continued, at the head of the War Department, the answer will readily occur to those best acquainted with the circumstances of the period. Others may be referred for an explanation to the difficulty, which had been felt in its fullest pressure, of obtaining services which would have been preferred, several eminent citizens to whom the station had been offered having successively declined it. It was not unknown at the time that objections existed to the person finally appointed, as appeared when his nomination went to the Senate, where it received the reluctant sanction of a scanty majority [eighteen to fifteen]. Nor was the President unaware or unwarned of the temper and turn of mind ascribed to him, which might be uncongenial with the official relations in which he was to stand. But these considerations were sacrificed to recommendations from esteemed friends; a belief that he possessed, with known talents, a degree of military information which might be useful; and a hope that a proper mixture of conciliating confidence and interposing control would render objectionable peculiarities less in practice than in prospect."

Possibly Armstrong took a different view of Madison's conduct, and regarded his own acceptance of the War Department in January, 1813, as proof both of courage and disinterestedness. He knew that he could expect no confidence from Virginians; but apparently he cared little for Virginian enmity, and was chiefly fretted by what he thought Virginian incompetence. No one could fail to see that he came into the Government rather as a master than a servant. According to General Wilkinson, he was quite as much feared as hated. "I am indeed shocked," wrote Wilkinson in his Memoirs, "when I take a retrospect of the evidence of the terror in which that minister kept more than one great man at Washington." Wilkinson, who hated Madison even more than he hated Armstrong, evidently believed that the President was afraid of his secretary. Madison himself explained that he thought it better to bear with

Armstrong's faults than to risk another change in the Department of War.

In that decision Madison was doubtless right. Whatever were Armstrong's faults, he was the strongest Secretary of War the government had yet seen. Hampered by an inheritance of mistakes not easily corrected, and by a chief whose methods were unmilitary in the extreme, Armstrong still introduced into the army an energy wholly new. Before he had been a year in office he swept away the old generals with whom Madison and Eustis had encumbered the service, and in their place substituted new men. While Major-Generals Dearborn, Pinckney, and Morgan Lewis were set over military districts where active service was unnecessary, and while Major General Wilkinson was summoned to the last of his many courts of inquiry, the President sent to the Senate, January 21 and February 21, the names of two new major-generals and six brigadiers of a totally different character from the earlier appointments.

The first major-general was George Izard of South Carolina, born at Paris in 1777, his father Ralph Izard being then American commissioner with Franklin and Deane. Returning to America only for a few years after the peace, George Izard at the age of fifteen was sent abroad to receive a military education in England, Germany, and France in the great school of the French Revolution. As far as education could make generals, Izard was the most promising officer in the United States service. Appointed in March, 1812, colonel of the Second Artillery, promoted to brigadier in March, 1813, he served with credit under Hampton at Chateaugay, and received his promotion over the heads of Chandler, Boyd, and one or two other brigadiers his seniors. He was intended to succeed Hampton on Lake Champlain.

The second new major-general was Jacob Brown, who after receiving the appointment of brigadier, July 19, 1813, was suddenly promoted to major-general at the same time with Izard. The selection was the more remarkable because Brown had no military education, and was taken directly from the militia. Born in Pennsylvania in 1775 of Quaker parentage, Brown began life as a schoolmaster. At the instance of the Society of Friends, he taught their public school in New York city for several years with credit. He then bought a large tract of land near Sackett's Harbor, and in 1799 undertook to found a town of Brownville. He soon became a leading citizen in that part of New York, and in 1809 was appointed to the command of a militia regiment. In 1811 he was made a brigadier of militia, and at the beginning of the war distinguished himself by activity and success at Ogdensburg. His defence of Sackett's Harbor in 1813 won him a brigade in the regular service, and his share in Wilkinson's descent of the St. Lawrence led to his further promotion.

Wilkinson, who regarded Brown as one of his enemies, declared that he knew not enough of military duty to post the guards of his camp, and that he compelled his battery to form in a hollow for the advantage of elevating the pieces to fire at the opposite heights. Winfield Scott, who was one of Brown's warmest friends, described him as full of zeal and vigor, but not a technical soldier, and but little acquainted with organization, tactics, police, and camp duties in general. The promotion of an officer so inexperienced to the most important command on the frontier, gave a measure of Armstrong's boldness and judgment.

The six new brigadiers were also well chosen. They were Alexander Macomb, T. A. Smith, Daniel Bissell, Edmund P. Gaines, Winfield Scott, and Eleazer W. Ripley, all colonels of the regular army, selected for their merits. Armstrong supplied Brown's defects of education by giving him the aid of Winfield Scott and Ripley, who were sent to organize brigades at Niagara.

The energy thus infused by Armstrong into the regular army lasted for half a century. . . . (VII, xvi, 402-409)

During the early summer the war took a different and unexpected direction, following the steps of the new Major General Brown; for wherever Brown went, fighting followed.

General Brown marched from French Mills, February 13, with two thousand men. February 28, Secretary Armstrong wrote him a letter suggesting an attack on Kingston, to be covered by a feint on Niagara. Brown, on arriving at Sackett's Harbor, consulted Chauncey,[11] and allowed himself to be dissuaded from attacking Kingston. "By some extraordinary mental process," Armstrong thought, Brown and Chauncey "arrived at the same conclusion,— that the main action, an attack on Kingston, being impracticable, the *ruse,* intended merely to mask it, might do as well." Brown immediately marched with two thousand men for Niagara.

When the secretary learned of this movement, although it was contrary to his ideas of strategy, he wrote an encouraging letter to Brown, March 20:

[11] Isaac Chauncey: Captain, U. S. Navy, commander of naval forces on Lakes Ontario and Erie.

"You have mistaken my meaning. . . . If you hazard anything by this mistake, correct it promptly by returning to your post. If on the other hand you left the Harbor with a competent force for its defence, go on and prosper. Good consequences are sometimes the result of mistakes."

The correspondence showed chiefly that neither the Secretary nor the general had a distinct idea, and that Brown's campaign, like Dearborn's the year before, received its direction from Chauncey, whose repugnance to attacking Kingston was invincible.

Brown was shown his mistake by Gaines, before reaching Buffalo March 24, and leaving his troops, he hurried back to Sackett's Harbor, "the most unhappy man alive." He resumed charge of such troops as remained at the Harbor, while Winfield Scott formed a camp of instruction at Buffalo, and, waiting for recruits who never came, personally drilled the officers of all grades. Scott's energy threw into the little army a spirit and an organization strange to the service. Three months of instruction converted the raw troops into soldiers.

Meanwhile Brown could do nothing at Sackett's Harbor. The British held control of the Lake, while Commodore Chauncey and the contractor Eckford were engaged in building a new ship which was to be ready in July. The British nearly succeeded in preventing Chauncey from appearing on the Lake during the entire season, for no sooner did Sir James Yeo[12] sail from Kingston in the spring than he attempted to destroy the American magazines. Owing to the remote situation of Sackett's Harbor in the extreme northern corner of the State, all supplies and war material were brought first from the Hudson River to Oswego by way of the Mohawk River and Oneida Lake. About twelve miles above Oswego the American magazines were established, and there the stores were kept until they could be shipped on schooners, and forwarded fifty miles along the lakeshore to Sackett's Harbor,—always a hazardous operation in the face of an enemy's fleet. The destruction of the magazines would have been fatal to Chauncey, and even the capture or destruction of the schooners with stores was no trifling addition to his difficulties.

Sir James Yeo left Kingston May 4, and appeared off Oswego the next day, bringing a large body of troops, numbering more

[12] Sir James Lucas Yeo: Commodore, Royal Navy, Commander in Chief of British naval forces on the Lakes.

than a thousand rank and file. They found only about three hundred men to oppose them, and having landed May 6, they gained possession of the fort which protected the harbor of Oswego. The Americans made a resistance which caused a loss of seventy-two men killed and wounded to the British, among the rest Captain Mulcaster of the Royal Navy, an active officer, who was dangerously wounded. The result was hardly worth the loss. Four schooners were captured or destroyed, and some twenty-four hundred barrels of flour, pork, and salt, but nothing of serious importance. Yeo made no attempt to ascend the river, and retired to Kingston after destroying whatever property he could not take away.

Although the chief American depot escaped destruction, the disgrace and discouragement remained, that after two years of war the Americans, though enjoying every advantage, were weaker than ever on Lake Ontario, and could not defend even so important a point as Oswego from the attack of barely a thousand men. Their coastwise supply of stores to Sackett's Harbor became a difficult and dangerous undertaking, to be performed mostly by night. Chauncey remained practically blockaded in Sackett's Harbor; and without his fleet in control of the Lake the army could do nothing effectual against Kingston.

In this helplessness, Armstrong was obliged to seek some other line on which the army could be employed against Upper Canada; and the idea occurred to him that although he had no fleet on Lake Ontario he had one on Lake Erie, which by a little ingenuity might enable the army to approach the heart of Upper Canada at the extreme western end of Lake Ontario. "Eight or even six thousand men," Armstrong wrote to the President, April 30, "landed in the bay between Point Abino and Fort Erie, and operating either on the line of the Niagara, or more directly if a more direct rout is found, against the British post at the head of Burlington Bay, cannot be resisted with effect without compelling the enemy so to weaken his more eastern posts as to bring them within reach of our means at Sackett's Harbor and Plattsburg."

Armstrong's suggestion was made to the President April 30. Already time was short. The allies had entered Paris March 31; the citadel of Bayonne capitulated to Wellington April 28. In a confidential despatch dated June 3, Lord Bathurst notified the governor-general of Canada that ten thousand men had been ordered to be shipped immediately for Quebec. July 5, Major General Torrens at the Horse-guards informed Prevost[13] that four brigades,—

---

[13] Sir George Prevost: Governor-General of Canada, 1811-1815, succeeding Craig.

Brisbane's, Kempt's, Power's, and Robinson's; fourteen regiments of Wellington's best troops,—had sailed from Bordeaux for Canada. Prevost could afford in July to send westward every regular soldier in Lower Canada, sure of replacing them at Montreal by the month of August.

"A discrepancy in the opinions of the Cabinet," according to Armstrong, delayed adoption of a plan till June, when a compromise scheme was accepted, but not carried out.

> "Two causes prevented its being acted upon *in extenso*," Armstrong afterward explained,—"the one, a total failure in getting together by militia calls and volunteer overtures a force deemed competent to a campaign of demonstration and manoeuvre on the peninsula; the other, an apprehension that the fleet, which had been long inactive, would not yet be found in condition to sustain projects requiring from it a vigorous co-operation with the army."

Brown might have been greatly strengthened at Niagara by drawing from Detroit the men that could be spared there; but the Cabinet obliged Armstrong to send the Detroit force—about nine hundred in number—against Mackinaw. Early in July the Mackinaw expedition, commanded by Lieutenant Colonel Croghan, started from Detroit, and August 4 it was defeated and returned. Croghan's expedition did not even arrive in time to prevent a British expedition from Mackinaw crossing Wisconsin and capturing, July 19, the distant American post at Prairie du Chien.

Armstrong did not favor Croghan's expedition, wishing to bring him and his two batteries to reinforce Brown, but yielded to the Secretary of the Navy, who wished to capture Mackinaw, and to the promises of Commodore Chauncey that on or before July 1 he would sail from Sackett's Harbor, and command the Lake. In reliance on Chauncey, the Cabinet, except Monroe, decided that Major General Brown should cross to the Canadian side, above the Falls of Niagara, and march, with Chauncey's support, to Burlington Heights and to York.

This decision was made June 7, and Armstrong wrote to Brown, June 10, describing the movement intended. The Secretary of the Navy, he said, thought Chauncey could not be ready before July 15:

> "To give, however, immediate occupation to your troops, and to prevent their blood from stagnating, why not take Fort Erie and its garrison, stated at three or four hundred men? Land between Point Abino and Erie in the night; assail the Fort by land and water;

push forward a corps to seize the bridge at Chippawa; and be governed by circumstances in either stopping there or going farther. Boats may follow and feed you. If the enemy concentrates his whole force on this line, as I think he will, it will not exceed two thousand men."

Brown had left Sackett's Harbor, and was at Buffalo when these orders reached him. He took immediate measures to carry them out. Besides his regular force, he called for volunteers to be commanded by Peter B. Porter; and he wrote to Chauncey, June 21, an irritating letter, complaining of having received not a line from him, and giving a sort of challenge to the navy to meet the army before Fort George, by July 10. The letter showed that opinion in the army ran against the navy, and particularly against Chauncey, whom Brown evidently regarded as a sort of naval Wilkinson. In truth, Brown could depend neither upon Chauncey nor upon volunteers. The whole force he could collect was hardly enough to cross the river, and little exceeded the three thousand men on whose presence at once in the boats Alexander Smyth had insisted eighteen months before, in order to capture Fort Erie.

So famous did Brown's little army become, that the details of its force and organization retained an interest equaled only by that which attached to the frigates and sloops-of-war. Although the existence of the regiments ceased with the peace, and their achievements were limited to a single campaign of three or four months, their fame would have insured them in any other service extraordinary honors and sedulous preservation of their identity. Two small brigades of regular troops, and one still smaller brigade of Pennsylvania volunteers, with a corps of artillery, composed the entire force. The first brigade was commanded by Brigadier-General Winfield Scott, and his monthly return of June 30, 1814, reported its organization and force as follows:—

Strength of the First, or Scott's, Brigade.

| | Present for Duty. | | Aggregate. |
	Non-com. Officers, rank and file.	Officers.	Present and absent.
Ninth Regiment....................	332	16	642
Eleventh Regiment.................	416	17	577
Twenty-second Regiment...........	217	12	287
Twenty-fifth Regiment.............	354	16	619
General Staff.....................		4	4
Total	1319	65	2129

The Ninth regiment came from Massachusetts, and in this campaign was usually commanded by its lieutenant-colonel, Thomas Aspinwall, or by Major Henry Leavenworth. The Eleventh was raised in Vermont, and was led by Major John McNeil. The Twenty-second was a Pennsylvania regiment, commanded by its colonel, Hugh Brady. The Twenty-fifth was enlisted in Connecticut, and identified by the name of T. S. Jesup, one of its majors. The whole brigade, officers and privates, numbered thirteen hundred and eighty-four men present for duty on the first day of July, 1814.

The Second, or Ripley's, brigade was still smaller, and became even more famous. Eleazar Wheelock Ripley was born in New Hampshire, in the year 1782. He became a resident of Portland in Maine, and was sent as a representative to the State legislature at Boston, where he was chosen speaker of the Massachusetts House of Representatives, Jan. 17, 1812, on the retirement of Joseph Story to become a Justice of the Supreme Court of the United States. A few weeks afterward, March 12, 1812, Ripley took the commission of lieutenant-colonel of the Twenty-first regiment, to be enlisted in Massachusetts. A year afterward he became colonel of the same regiment, and took part in the battle of Chrystler's Field. Secretary Armstrong made him a brigadier-general April 15, 1814, his commission bearing date about a month after that of Winfield Scott. Both the new brigadiers were sent to Niagara, where Scott formed a brigade from regiments trained by himself; and Ripley was given a brigade composed of his old regiment, the Twenty-first, with detachments from the Seventeenth and Nineteenth and Twenty-third. The strength of the brigade, July 1, 1814, was reported in the monthly return as follows:

Strength of the Second, or Ripley's, Brigade.

	Present for Duty.		Aggregate.
	Non-com. Officers, rank and file.	Officers.	Present and absent.
Twenty-first Regiment............	651	25	917
Twenty-third Regiment...........	341	8	496
General staff.....................		2	2
Total......................	992	35	1415

Ripley's old regiment, the Twenty-first, was given to Colonel James Miller, who had served in the Tippecanoe campaign as major in the Fourth Infantry and had shared the misfortune of that regiment at Detroit. The other regiment composing the brigade—the Twenty-third—was raised in New York, and was usually commanded by one or another of its majors, McFarland or Brooke. Ripley's brigade numbered 1,027 men present for duty, on the first day of July.

The artillery, under the command of Major Hindman, was composed of four companies.

Strength of Hindman's Battalion of Artillery.

	Present for Duty.	Aggregate.
Towson's Company	89	101
Biddle's Company	80	104
Ritchie's Company	96	133
Williams's Company	62	73
Total	327	413

The militia brigade was commanded by Peter B. Porter, and consisted of 600 Pennsylvania volunteer militia, with about the same number of Indians, comprising nearly the whole military strength of the Six Nations.

Strength of Major-General Brown's Army, Buffalo, July 1, 1814.

	Present for Duty.		Aggregate.
	Non-com. Officers, rank and file.	Officers.	Present and absent.
Artillery	330	15	413
Scott's Brigade	1312	65	2122
Ripley's Brigade	992	36	1415
Porter's Brigade	710	43	830
Total	3344	159	4780

Thus the whole of Brown's army consisted of half-a-dozen skeleton regiments, and including every officer, as well as all Porter's volunteers, numbered barely thirty-five hundred men present for duty. The aggregate, including sick and absent, did not reach five thousand.

The number of effectives varied slightly from week to week, as men joined or left their regiments; but the entire force never exceeded thirty-five hundred men, exclusive of Indians.

According to the weekly return of June 22, 1814, Major-General Riall, who commanded the right division of the British army, had a force of four thousand rank and file present for duty; but of this number the larger part were in garrison at York, Burlington Heights, and Fort Niagara. His headquarters were at Fort George, where he had nine hundred and twenty-seven rank and file present for duty. Opposite Fort George, in Fort Niagara on the American side, five hundred and seventy-eight rank and file were present for duty. At Queenston were two hundred and fifty-eight; at Chippawa, four hundred and twenty-eight; at Fort Erie, one hundred and forty-six. In all, on the Niagara River Riall commanded two thousand three hundred and thirty-seven rank and file present for duty. The officers, musicians, etc., numbered three hundred and thirty-two. At that time only about one hundred and seventy men were on the sick list. All told, sick and well, the regular force numbered two thousand eight hundred and forty. They belonged chiefly to the First, or Royal Scots; the Eighth, or King's; the Hundredth, the Hundred-and-third regiments, and the Artillery, with a few dragoons.

As soon as Porter's volunteers were ready, the whole American army was thrown across the river. The operation was effected early in the morning of July 3; and although the transport was altogether insufficient, the movement was accomplished without accident or delay. Scott's brigade with the artillery landed below Fort Erie; Ripley landed above; the Indians gained the rear; and the Fort, which was an open work, capitulated at five o'clock in the afternoon. One hundred and seventy prisoners, including officers of all ranks, being two companies of the Eighth and Hundredth British regiments were surrendered by the major in command.

The next British position was at Chippawa, about sixteen miles below. To Chippawa, Major-General Riall hastened from Fort George, on hearing that the American army had crossed the river above; and there, within a few hours, he collected about fifteen hundred regulars and six hundred militia and Indians, behind the Chippawa River, in a position not to be assailed in front. The American army also hastened toward Chippawa. On the morning of July 4 Scott's brigade led the way, and after an exhausting march of twelve hours, the enemy tearing up the bridges in retiring, Scott reached Chippawa plain toward sunset, and found Riall's force in a position beyond the Chippawa River. Scott could only retire a mile or two, behind the nearest water—a creek, or broad ditch, called Street's Creek,—where he went into camp. Brown and Ripley, with the second brigade and artillery, came up two or three hours later, at eleven o'clock in the night. Porter followed the next morning.

Brown, knowing his numbers to be about twice those of Riall, was anxious to attack before Riall could be reinforced; and on the morning of July 5, leaving Ripley and Porter's brigades encamped in the rear, he reconnoitred the line of the Chippawa River, and gave orders for constructing a bridge above Riall's position. The bridge was likely to be an affair of several days, and Riall showed a disposition to interfere with it. His scouts and Indians crossed and occupied the woods on the American left, driving in the pickets and annoying the reconnoitring party, and even the camp. To dislodge them, Porter's volunteers and Indians were ordered forward to clear the woods; and at about half-past four o'clock in the afternoon, Porter's advance began to drive the enemy's Indians back, pressing forward nearly to the Chippawa River. There the advancing volunteers and Indians suddenly became aware that the whole British army was in the act of crossing the Chippawa Bridge on their flank. The surprise was complete, and Porter's brigade naturally broke and fell back in confusion.

No one could have been more surprised than Brown, or more incredulous than Scott, at Riall's extraordinary movement. The idea that a British force of two thousand men at most should venture to attack more than three thousand with artillery, covered by a deep, miry creek, had not entered their minds. Riall drew up his little army in three columns on the Chippawa plain—the King's regiment four hundred and eighty strong in advance, supported by the Royal Scots five hundred strong, and the Hundredth four hundred and fifty strong, with a troop of dragoons and artillerists; in all about fifteen hundred regular troops, with two twenty-four-pound field-pieces and a five-and-a-half inch howitzer. Six hundred militia and Indians occupied the woods. The whole force advanced in order of battle toward Street's Creek.

Brown was at the front when this movement was made. Porter was routed. Ripley with the second brigade was in the rear. Scott, having rested his brigade in the morning and given them a dinner to celebrate the Fourth of July, had ordered a grand parade "to keep his men in breath," as he said; and while Riall's regular force, fifteen hundred strong, formed on the Chippawa plain a mile away, Scott's brigade—which a week before had been reported as containing thirteen hundred men present for duty, and if all its details had been called in could hardly have exceeded thirteen hundred men in the ranks on the afternoon of July 5—was forming, before crossing the little bridge over Street's Creek to parade on the plain already occupied by the British. Owing to the brushwood that lined the creek Scott could not see the plain, and received no notice of danger until he approached the bridge at the head of his brigade. At that moment General Brown in full gallop from the front rode by, calling out in passing, "You will have a battle!" Scott remarked that he did not believe he should find three hundred British to fight, and crossed the bridge.

If Riall was unwise to attack, Scott tempted destruction by leaving his secure position behind the creek; but at that moment he was in his happiest temper. He meant to show what he and his brigade could do. As his thin column crossed the bridge, the British twenty-four-pound guns opened upon it; but the American line moved on, steady as veterans, and formed in order of battle beyond. Towson's three twelve-pounders were placed in position near the river on the extreme right, and opened fire on the heavier British battery opposite. The infantry deployed in three battalions,—the right, under Major Leavenworth of the Ninth; the center, under Major McNeil of the Eleventh; the left, under Major Jesup of the Twenty-fifth. Throwing the flanks obliquely forward, and extending Jesup's battalion into the woods on the left to prevent outflanking, Scott ordered an advance; and at the same time Riall directed the Royal Scots and the Hundredth to charge. The two lines advanced, stopping alternately to fire and move forward, while Towson's guns, having blown up a British caisson, were turned on the British column. The converging American fire made havoc in the British ranks, and when the two lines came within some sixty or seventy paces of each other in the centre, the flanks were actually in contact. Then the whole British line broke and crumbled away. Ripley's brigade, arriving soon afterward, found no enemy on the plain. The battle had lasted less than an hour.

Riall's report made no concealment of his defeat.

"I placed two light twenty-four-pounders and a five-and-a-half inch howitzer," he said, "against the right of the enemy's position, and formed the Royal Scots and Hundredth regiment with the intention of making a movement upon his left, which deployed with the greatest regularity and opened a very heavy fire. I immediately moved up the King's regiment to the right, while the Royal Scots and Hundredth regiments were directed to charge the enemy in front, for which they advanced with the greatest gallantry under a most destructive fire. I am sorry to say, however, in this attempt they suffered so severely that I was obliged to withdraw them, finding their further efforts against the superior numbers of the enemy would be unavailing."

For completeness, Scott's victory at Chippawa could be compared with that of Isaac Hull over the "Guerrière"; but in one respect Scott surpassed Hull. The "Constitution" was a much heavier ship than its enemy; but Scott's brigade was weaker, both in men and guns, than Riall's force. Even in regulars, man against man, Scott was certainly outnumbered. His brigade could not have contained, with artillerists, more than thirteen hundred men present on the field, while Riall officially reported his regulars at fifteen hundred, and his irregular corps at six hundred. Scott's flank was exposed and turned by the rout of Porter. He fought with a creek in his rear, where retreat was destruction. He had three twelve-pound field-pieces, one of which was soon dismounted, against two twenty-four-pounders and a five-and-a-half howitzer. He crossed the bridge and deployed under the enemy's fire. Yet the relative losses showed that he was the superior of his enemy in every respect, and in none more than in the efficiency of his guns.

Riall reported a total loss in killed, wounded, and missing of five hundred and fifteen men, not including Indians. Scott and Porter reported a total loss of two hundred and ninety-seven, not including Indians. Riall's regular regiments and artillery lost one hundred and thirty-seven killed, and three hundred and five wounded. Scott's brigade reported forty-eight killed and two hundred and twenty-seven wounded. The number of Riall's killed was nearly three times the number of Scott's killed, and proved that the battle was decided by the superior accuracy or rapidity of the musketry and artillery fire, other military qualities being assumed to be equal.

The battle of Chippawa was the only occasion during the war when equal bodies of regular troops met face to face, in extended lines on an open plain in broad daylight, without advantage of position; and never again after that combat was an army of American regulars beaten by British troops. Small as the affair was, and unimportant in military results, it gave to the United States army a character and pride it had never before possessed. . . . (VIII, ii, 27-45)

Assuming Sir George Prevost's report to have been correct, the two fleets [on Lake Champlain] compared as [shown opposite].

In this calculation the possible error consists only in one disputed eighteen-pound columbiad on the "Finch," and three disputed guns—one long and two short—on the British gunboats. In one case the British would have thrown about nineteen hundred pounds of metal—in the other, about eighteen hundred. A glance

Force of British Fleet.

Vessels.	Guns.	Long.	Short.	Long metal.	Short metal.	Weight of metal.
Confiance.........	37	31	6	744	192	936
Linnet............	16	16		192		192
Chubb............	11	1	10	6	180	186
Finch.............	10	4	6	24	108	132
Twelve Gunboats....	16	8	8	162	256	418
Total.........	90	60	30	1128	736	1864

Force of American Fleet.

Vessels.	Guns.	Long.	Short.	Long metal.	Short metal.	Weight of metal.
Saratoga..........	26	8	18	192	636	828
Eagle.............	20	8	12	144	384	528
Ticonderoga.......	17	12	5	168	146	314
Preble............	7	7		63		63
Ten Gunboats.....	16	10	6	192	108	300
Total.........	86	45	41	759	1274	2033

at the two tables shows that in one respect Downie[14] held a decisive superiority in his guns. He had no less than sixty long-range pieces, while Macdonough had but forty-five. Downie's long-range guns threw at least eleven hundred pounds of metal; Macdonough's threw but seven hundred and sixty. If Downie chose his own distance beyond range of the thirty-two pound carronades, and fought only his long guns, nothing could save Macdonough except extreme good fortune, for he had but fourteen twenty-four-pound guns against Downie's thirty-four. Firing by broadsides, Downie could throw from his single ship, the "Confiance," sixteen twenty-four-pound shot, to which Macdonough could reply only with eight, even if he used all his long guns on the same side.

The Americans had a decided advantage only in their commander. Thomas Macdonough, born in Delaware in 1783, was thirty years old when this responsibility fell upon him. He had been educated, like most of the naval heroes, in the hard service of the Tripolitan war, and had been sent to construct and command the naval force on Lake Champlain in the spring of 1813. Macdonough's superiority over ordinary commanders consisted in the intelligent forethought with which he provided for the chances of

[14] George Downie: Captain, Royal Navy, commanding British fleet on Lake Champlain.

battle. His arrangement showed that he foresaw, and as far as possible overcame in advance, every conceivable attack. He compelled the enemy to fight only as pleased himself.

Macdonough anchored his four large vessels across Plattsburg Bay, where it was a mile and a half wide, and placed his gunboats in their rear to fill the gaps. Cumberland Head on his left and front, and Crab Island on his right obliged the enemy to enter in a line so narrow that Downie would find no room to anchor on his broadside out of carronade range, but must sail into the harbor under the raking fire of the American long guns, and take a position within range of the American carronades. As the battle was to be fought at anchor, both squadrons would as a matter of course be anchored with springs on their cables; but Macdonough took the additional precaution of laying a kedge off each bow of the "Saratoga," bringing their hawsers in on the two quarters, and letting them hang in bights under water. This arrangement enabled him to wind his ship at any time without fear of having his cables cut by the enemy's shot, and to use his larboard broadside if his starboard guns should be disabled. In effect, it doubled his fighting capacity.

Sir George Prevost and the army were ready to move before Downie's fleet could be prepared. Marching directly forward with the utmost confidence, Sir George turned the advanced American position at Dead Creek Bridge and drove away the gunboats that covered it. He reached the Saranac River September 6, and saw beyond it a ridge "crowned with three strong redoubts and other field works, and blockhouses armed with heavy ordnance, with their flotilla at anchor out of gunshot from the shore." The description was not exaggerated. Izard was himself a trained engineer, and the works built by him, under the direction of Major Totten of the Engineer Corps, were believed capable of resisting for three weeks a combined attack by land and water, even if the British fleet were victorious. Three good companies of artillery manned the guns. Excellent officers of every arm were in command.

Prevost properly halted, and declined to assault without the co-operation of the fleet. He waited five days impatiently for Downie to appear. Not till seven o'clock in the morning of September 11 did the British flotilla sail round Cumberland Head. At the same time Prevost ordered his troops to cross the Saranac and storm the American works.

Downie intended, without regarding his superiority in long-range guns, to sail in and to lay the "Confiance" alongside of the "Saratoga"; but the wind was light and baffling, and his approach was so slow that he could not long bear the raking fire of the American guns. As he came within carronade range the wind baffling, he was obliged to anchor at two cables' lengths, or three hundred yards, and begin action. With the same discipline that marked the movements of the troops on shore, Downie came to, anchored, made everything secure, and then poured a full broadside into Macdonough's ship. The "Saratoga" shivered under the shock of sixteen twenty-four-pound shot and canister charges striking her hull; almost one-fifth of her crew were disabled; but she stood stoutly to her work, and the whole line was soon hotly engaged.

Americans usually had a decided advantage in their better gunnery, but three hundred yards was a long range for thirty-two-pound carronades, which at point-blank carried less than two hundred and fifty yards, and lost accuracy in proportion to elevation. Macdonough was slow to prove superiority. Early in the battle the British suffered a severe, and perhaps in the experience of this war a decisive, loss in their commander, Captain Downie, instantly killed by one of his own guns thrown off its carriage against him by a solid shot. Yet at the end of two hours' combat the British squadron was on the whole victorious, and the American on the point of capture. Of the three smaller American vessels, the "Preble" on the extreme right was driven out of the engagement, and the British gun-boats, turning the American flank, attacked the "Ticonderoga," which maintained a doubtful battle. The American left was also turned, the "Eagle" having been driven to take refuge between the "Saratoga" and "Ticonderoga," in the centre. Macdonough's ship was then exposed to the concentrated fire of the "Confiance" and "Linnet," and his battery was soon silenced. The "Saratoga" could no longer use a gun on the engaged side, and the battle was nearly lost.

Then Macdonough's forethought changed the impending defeat into victory. His fire had nearly silenced the "Confiance," and disregarding the "Linnet," he ceased attention to the battle in order to direct the operation of winding ship. Little by little hauling the ship about, he opened on the "Confiance" with one gun after another of the fresh broadside, as they bore; and the "Confiance," after trying in vain to effect the same operation, struck her colors. Then the British fleet was in the situation which Downie had anticipated for the Americans in the event of silencing the "Saratoga."

The three smaller vessels were obliged to surrender, and the gun-boats alone escaped. The battle had lasted from quarter past eight till quarter before eleven.

By land, the British attack was much less effective than by water. The troops were slow in reaching their positions, and had time to take no decisive movement. A column under Major General Robin-son[15] was ordered to move round by the right flank to a ford previously reconnoitred, some distance up the Saranac, in order to gain a position whence they could reverse the American works and carry them by assault; but Robinson's column missed its way, and before reaching the ford heard the cheers of the American troops, and halted to ascertain its cause. The remainder of the army waited for Robinson's column to assault. The casualties showed that nothing like a serious engagement took place. The entire loss of the British army from September 6 to September 14 was officially reported as only thirty-seven killed and one hundred and fifty wounded, and of this loss a large part occurred previous to the battle of September 11. The entire American loss was thirty-seven killed and sixty-two wounded.

In the naval battle, Macdonough reported fifty-two killed and fifty-eight wounded, among about eight hundred and eighty. The British reported fifty-seven killed and seventy-two wounded, in crews whose number was never precisely known, but was probably fully eight hundred. In neither case was the loss, though severe, as great relatively to the numbers as the severity of the action seemed to imply. The "Saratoga" lost twenty-eight killed in a crew of two hundred and forty. In Perry's battle on Lake Erie, the "Lawrence" lost twenty-two men killed in a crew of one hundred and thirty-one. About one man in eight was killed on Macdonough's ship; about one man in six on Perry's.

With needless precipitation, Prevost instantly retreated the next day to Champlain, sacrificing stores to a very great amount, and losing many men by desertion. The army was cruelly mortified, and Prevost lost whatever military reputation he still preserved in Canada. In England the impression of disgrace was equally strong. "It is scarcely possible to conceive the degree of mortification and disappointment," said the "Annual Register," "which the intelligence of this defeat created in Great Britain." Yeo brought official charges of misconduct against Prevost, and Prevost defended himself by unusual arguments.

[15] Frederick Philipse Robinson: British major general at the battle of Platts-burg, the land accompaniment of the battle of Lake Champlain.

"With whatever sorrow I may think of the unfortunate occurrences to which I allude," he wrote to Bathurst, three weeks later, "I consider them as light and trivial when compared to the disastrous results which, I am solemnly persuaded, would have ensued had any considerations of personal glory, or any unreflecting disregard of the safety of the province, or of the honor of the army committed to my charge, induced me to pursue those offensive operations by land, independent of the fleet, which it would appear by your Lordships' despatch were expected of me. Such operations, my Lord, have been attempted before, and on the same ground. The history of our country records their failure; and had they been undertaken again with double the force placed under my command, they would have issued in the discomfiture of his Majesty's arms, and in a defeat not more disastrous than inevitable."

The Duke of Wellington was not so severe as other critics, and hesitated to say that Prevost was wrong; "though of this I am certain, he must equally have returned . . . after the fleet was beaten; and I am inclined to think he was right. I have told the ministers repeatedly that a naval superiority on the Lakes is a *sine qua non* of success in war on the frontier of Canada, even if our object should be wholly defensive." . . . (VIII, iv, 105-13)

7.

The Paralysis of National Government

The British in their camp that evening were about eight miles from Bladensburg battlefield. Winder was about five miles distant from the same point. By a quick march at dawn he might still have arrived there, with six hours to spare for arranging his defence. He preferred to wait till he should know with certainty that the British were on their way there. On the morning of Wednesday, August 24, he wrote to Armstrong:—

"I have found it necessary to establish my headquarters here, the most advanced position convenient to the troops, and nearest information. I shall remain stationary as much as possible, that I may be the more readily found, to issue orders, and collect together the various detachments of militia, and give them as rapid a consolidation and organization as possible. . . . The news up the river is very threatening. Barney's or some other force should occupy the batteries at Greenleaf's Point and the navy yard. I should be glad of the assistance of counsel from yourself and the Government. If more convenient, I should make an exertion to go to you the first opportunity."

This singular note was carried first to the President, who, having opened and read it, immediately rode to headquarters. Monroe, Jones, and Rush[16] followed. Armstrong and Campbell [17] arrived last. Before Armstrong appeared, a scout arrived at ten o'clock with information that the British army had broken up its camp at daylight, and was probably more than half way to Bladensburg.

[16] Richard Rush: of Pennsylvania, Attorney General.
[17] George W. Campbell: of Tennessee, Secretary of the Treasury.

Winder's persistence in remaining at the navy yard was explained as due to the idea that the enemy might move toward the Potomac, seize Fort Washington or Warburton, secure the passage of his ships, and approach the city by the river. The general never explained how his presence at the navy yard was to prevent such a movement if it was made.

The whole eastern side of Washington was covered by a broad estuary called the Eastern Branch of the Potomac, bridged only at two points, and impassable, even by pontoons, without ample warning. From the Potomac River to Bladensburg, a distance of about seven miles, the city was effectually protected. Bladensburg made the point of a right angle. There the Baltimore road entered the city as by a pass; for beyond, to the west, no general would venture to enter, leaving an enemy at Bladensburg in his rear. Roads were wanting, and the country was difficult. Through Bladensburg the attacking army must come; to Bladensburg Winder must go, unless he meant to retreat to Georgetown, or to recross the Eastern Branch in the enemy's rear. Monroe notified Serurier Monday evening that the battle would be fought at Bladensburg. Secretary Jones wrote to Commodore Rodgers, Tuesday morning, that the British would probably "advance today toward Bladensburg." Every one looked instinctively to that spot, yet Winder to the last instant persisted in watching the navy-yard bridge, using the hours of Wednesday morning to post Barney's[18] sailors with twenty-four-pound guns to cover an approach where no enemy could cross.

No sooner did Winder receive intelligence at ten o'clock Wednesday morning that the British were in Bladensburg, than in the utmost haste he started for the same point, preceded by Monroe and followed by the President and the rest of the Cabinet and the troops. Barney's sailors and their guns would have been left behind to guard the navy-yard bridge had Secretary Jones not yielded to Barney's vigorous though disrespectful remonstrances, and allowed him to follow.

In a long line the various corps, with their military and civil commanders, streamed toward Bladensburg, racing with the British, ten miles away, to arrive first on the field of battle. Monroe was earliest on the ground. Between eleven and twelve o'clock he reached the spot where hills slope gently toward the Eastern Branch a mile or more in broad incline, the little straggling town of Bladensburg opposite, beyond a shallow stream, and hills and woods in the distance. Several militia corps were already camped

[18] Joshua Barney: Captain, U. S. Navy.

on the ground, which had been from the first designated as the point of concentration. A Baltimore brigade, more than two thousand strong, had arrived there thirty-six hours before. Some Maryland regiments arrived at the same time with Monroe. About three thousand men were then on the field, and their officers were endeavoring to form them in line of battle. General Stansbury of the Baltimore brigade made such an arrangement as he thought best. Monroe, who had no military rank, altered it without Stansbury's knowledge. General Winder arrived at noon, and rode about the field. At the same time the British light brigade made its appearance, and wound down the opposite road, a mile away, a long column of redcoats, six abreast, moving with the quick regularity of old soldiers, and striking directly at the American center. They reached the village on one side of the stream as Winder's troops poured down the hill on the other; and the President with two or three of his Cabinet officers, considerably in advance of all their own troops, nearly rode across the bridge into the British line, when a volunteer scout warned them of their danger.

Much the larger portion of the American force arrived on the ground when the enemy was in sight, and were hastily drawn up in line wherever they could be placed. They had no cover. Colonel Wadsworth's intrenchments were not used, except in the case of one field work which enfiladed the bridge at close range, where fieldpieces were placed. Although some seven thousand men were present, nothing deserving the name of an army existed. "A few companies only," said the Subaltern, "perhaps two or at the most three battalions, wearing the blue jacket which the Americans have borrowed from the French, presented some appearance of regular troops. The rest seemed country people, who would have been much more appropriately employed in attending to their agricultural occupations than in standing with muskets in their hands on the brow of a bare, green hill." Heterogeneous as the force was, it would have been sufficient had it enjoyed the advantage of a commander.

The British light brigade, some twelve or fifteen hundred men, under Colonel Thornton of the Eighty-fifth regiment, without waiting for the rear division, dashed across the bridge, and were met by a discharge of artillery and musketry directly in their face. Checked for an instant, they pressed on, crossed the bridge or waded the stream, and spread to the right and left, while their rockets flew into the American lines. Almost instantly a portion of the American line gave way; but the rest stood firm, and drove the British skirmishers back under a heavy fire to the cover of the bank with its trees and shrubs. Not until a fresh British regiment, moving well to the right, forded the stream and threatened to turn the American left, did the rout begin. Even then several strong corps stood steady, and in good order retired by the road that led to the Capitol; but the mass, struck by panic, streamed westward toward Georgetown and Rockville.

Meanwhile Barney's sailors, though on the run, could not reach the field in time for the attack, and halted on the hillside, about a mile from Bladensburg, at a spot just outside the District line. The rout had then begun, but Barney put his five pieces in position and waited for the enemy. The American infantry and cavalry that had not fled westward moved confusedly past the field where the sailors stood at their guns. Winder sent Barney no orders, and Barney, who was not acting under Winder, but was commander in chief of his own forces under authority of the Navy Department, had no idea of running away. Four hundred men against four thousand were odds too great even for sailors, but a battle was not wholly disgraceful that produced such a commander and such men. Barney's account of the combat was as excellent as his courage:—

"At length the enemy made his appearance on the main road in force and in front of my battery, and on seeing us made a halt. I reserved our fire. In a few minutes the enemy again advanced, when I ordered an eighteen-pounder to be fired, which completely cleared the road; shortly after, a second attempt was made by the enemy to come forward, but all were destroyed. They then crossed over into an open field, and attempted to flank our right. He was met there by three twelve-pounders, the marines under Captain Miller, and my men acting as infantry, and again was totally cut up. By this time not a vestige of the American army remained, except a body of five or six hundred posted on a height on my right, from which I expected much support from their fine situation."

Such a battle could not long continue. The British turned Barney's right; the corps on the height broke and fled, and the British, getting into the rear, fired down upon the sailors. The British themselves were most outspoken in praise of Barney's men. "Not only did they serve their guns with a quickness and precision that astonished their assailants," said the Subaltern, "but they stood till some of them were actually bayoneted with fuses in their hands; nor was it till their leader was wounded and taken, and they saw themselves deserted on all sides by the soldiers, that they left the field." Barney held his position nearly half an hour, and then, being severely wounded, ordered his officers to leave him where he lay. There he was taken by the British advance, and carried to their hospital at Bladensburg. The British officers, admiring his gallantry, treated him, he said, "with the most marked attention, respect, and politeness as if I was a brother,"—as though to show their opinion that Barney instead of Winder should have led the American army.

After the sailors retired, at about four o'clock, the British stopped two hours to rest. Their victory, easy as it seemed, was not cheaply bought. General Ross officially reported sixty-four killed and one hundred and eighty-five wounded. A loss of two hundred and fifty men among one thousand five hundred said to be engaged was not small; but Gleig, an officer of the light brigade, himself wounded, made twice, at long intervals, an assertion which he must have intended as a contradiction of the official report. "The loss on the part of the English was severe," he said, "since out of two thirds of the army which were engaged upward of five hundred men were killed and wounded." According to this assertion, Ross lost five hundred men among three thousand engaged, or one in six. Had Winder inflicted that loss while the British were still on the Patuxent, Ross would have thought long before risking more, especially as Colonel Thornton was among the severely injured. The Americans reported only twenty-six killed and fifty-one wounded.

At six o'clock, after a rest of two hours, the British troops resumed their march; but night fell before they reached the first houses of the town. As Ross[19] and Cockburn,[20] with a few officers, advanced before the troops, some men, supposed to have been Barney's sailors, fired on the party from the house formerly occupied by Gallatin, at the northeast corner of Capitol Square. Ross's horse was killed, and the general ordered the house to be burned, which was done. The army did not enter the town, but camped at eight o'clock a quarter of a mile east of the Capitol. Troops were then detailed to burn the Capitol, and as the great building burst into flames, Ross and Cockburn, with about two hundred men, marched silently in the darkness to the White House, and set fire to it. At the same time Commodore Tingey, by order

[19] Robert Ross: British major general, commander of the forces to ravage the American coast.
[20] George Cockburn: Rear Admiral, Royal Navy, head of British naval squadron in Chesapeake Bay.

of Secretary Jones, set fire to the navy yard and the vessels in the Eastern Branch. Before midnight the flames of three great conflagrations made the whole country light, and from the distant hills of Maryland and Virginia the flying President and Cabinet caught glimpses of the ruin their incompetence had caused. . . . (VIII, v, 136-45)

In the tempest of war that raged over land and ocean during the months of August and September, 1814, bystanders could not trust their own judgment of the future; yet shrewd observers, little affected either by emotion or by interest, inclined to the belief that the United States government was near exhaustion. The immediate military danger on Lake Champlain was escaped, and Baltimore was saved; but the symptoms of approaching failure in government were not to be mistaken, and the capture of Washington, which was intended to hurry the collapse, produced its intended effect.

From the first day of the war the two instruments necessary for military success were wanting to Madison,—money and men. After three campaigns, the time came when both these wants must be supplied, or the national government must devolve its duties on the States. When the President, preparing his Annual Message, asked his Cabinet officers what were the prospects of supplying money and men for another campaign, he received answers discouraging in the extreme.

First, in regard to money. In July, Secretary Campbell advertised a second loan, of only six million dollars. He obtained but two and a half millions at eighty. His acceptance of this trifling sum obliged him to give the same terms to the contractors who had taken the nine millions subscribed in the spring at eighty-eight. Barker found difficulty in making his payments, and from both loans the Treasury could expect to obtain only $10,400,000, owing to the contractors' failures. The authorized loan was twenty-five millions. The secretary could suggest no expedient, except Treasury notes, for filling the deficit.

Bad as this failure was,—though it showed Secretary Campbell's incapacity so clearly as to compel his retirement, and obliged the President to call a special session of Congress,—the Treasury might regard it as the least of its embarrassments. Commonly governments had begun their most desperate efforts only after ordinary resources failed; but the United States government in 1814 had so inextricably involved its finances that without dictatorial powers of seizing property its functions could not much longer be continued. The general bankruptcy, long foreseen, at length occurred.

The panic caused by the capture of Washington, August 24, obliged the tottering banks of Philadelphia and Baltimore to suspend specie payments. The banks of Philadelphia formally announced their suspension, August 31, by a circular explaining the causes and necessity of their decision. The banks of New York immediately followed, September 1; and thenceforward no bank between New Orleans and Albany paid its obligations except in notes. Only the banks of New England maintained specie payments, with the exception of those in least credit, which took the opportunity to pay or not pay as they pleased. The suspension was admitted to be permanent. Until the blockade should be raised and domestic produce could find a foreign market, the course of exchange was fixed, and specie payments could not be resumed. The British navy and the Boston Federalists held the country firmly bound, and peace alone could bring relief.

Suspension mattered little, and had the National Bank been in existence the failure might have been an advantage to the government; but without a central authority the currency instantly fell into confusion. No medium of exchange existed outside of New England. Boston gave the specie standard, and soon the exchanges showed wide differences. New York money stood at twenty per cent discount, Philadelphia at twenty-four per cent, Baltimore at thirty per cent. Treasury notes were sold in Boston at twenty-five per cent discount, and United States six-per-cents stood at sixty in coin. The Treasury had no means of transferring its bank deposits from one part of the country to another. Unless it paid its debts in Treasury notes, it was unable to pay them at all. No other money than the notes of suspended banks came into the Treasury. Even in New England, taxes, customs-duties, and loans were paid in Treasury notes, and rarely in local currency. Thus, while the government collected in the Middle and Southern States millions in bank notes, it was obliged to leave them in deposit at the local banks where the collection was made, while its debts in Boston and New York remained unpaid. The source of revenue was destroyed. The whole South and West, and the Middle States as far north as New York, could contribute in no considerable degree to the support of government.

The situation was unusual. The government might possess immense resources in one State and be totally bankrupt in another; it might levy taxes to the amount of the whole circulating medium, and yet have only its own notes available for payment of debt; it might borrow hundreds of millions and be none the better for the loan. All the private bank notes of Pennsylvania and the Southern country were useless in New York and New England where they must chiefly be used. An attempt to transfer such deposits in any quantity would have made them quite worthless. The Treasury already admitted bankruptcy. The interest on the national obligations could not be paid.

The President's second inquiry regarded men. The new Secretary of War, Monroe, gave him such information as the Department possessed on the numbers of the army. A comparative account showed that in June, 1813, the regular troops numbered 27,609; in December, 34,325. In January, 1814, the number was nominally 33,282; in July the aggregate was 31,503, the effectives being 27,010. Since July the recruits had declined in numbers. The three months of March, April, and May produced 6,996 recruits; the three months of July, August, and September were reported as furnishing 4,477. The general return of September 30 reported the strength of the army at 34,029 men. The government was not able to provide the money necessary to pay bounties due for the last three months' recruiting. The Secretary of War admitted the failure of the recruiting service, and attributed it to the high bounties given for substitutes in the militia detached for United States service.

The smallness of the armies in the field showed worse results than were indicated by the returns. Macomb at Plattsburg claimed to have only fifteen hundred effectives. Izard carried with him to Buffalo only four thousand men. Brown's effectives at Fort Erie numbered two thousand. Apparently these three corps included the entire force in the field on the Canada frontier, and their combined effective strength did not exceed eight thousand men. The year before, Wilkinson and Hampton commanded fully eleven thousand effectives in their movements against Montreal. Nothing showed that the victories at Niagara and Plattsburg had stimulated enlistments, or that the army could be raised above thirty thousand effectives even if the finances were in a condition to meet the expense.

Much was said of the zeal shown by the State militia in hastening to the defence of their soil, and the New England Federalists were as loud as the Kentucky and Tennessee Democrats in praise of the energy with which the militia rose to resist invasion; but in reality this symptom was the most alarming of the time. Both in the military and in the political point of view, the persistence in depending on militia threatened to ruin the national government. The military experience of 1814 satisfied the stanchest war Democrats that the militia must not be their dependence. . . . (VIII, viii, 212-17)

Massachusetts gave little aid and made a profession of her wish to give none at all; but the difficulty did not end there. Massachusetts and Virginia were States of the first class. The census of 1810 allotted to Massachusetts, including Maine, a population of about seven hundred thousand; to Virginia, a white population of five hundred and fifty-one thousand, and a colored population of four hundred and twenty-three thousand,—nine hundred and seventy-four thousand in all. In the ratio of representation Massachusetts counted for twenty, Virginia for twenty-three. The quota of Massachusetts in the direct tax was $316,000; that of Virginia was $369,-000. On the scale furnished by these data, Virginia should have contributed in support of the war about one eighth or one seventh more men and money than were required from Massachusetts. The actual result was different.

The amount of money contributed by Massachusetts could not be compared with that contributed by Virginia, partly because of the severe blockade which closed the Virginian ports. The net revenue from customs derived from Virginia in 1814 was $4,000; that from Massachusetts was $1,600,000. Unlike the customs revenue, the receipts from internal revenue were supposed to be reasonably equalized, so that each State should contribute in due proportion. According to the official return, dated Nov. 24, 1815, the total internal duties which had then been paid to the collectors for the year 1814 in Massachusetts was $198,400; in Virginia it was $193,500. The total amount then paid to the Treasury was $178,400 in Massachusetts, and $157,300 in Virginia. The direct tax was fixed by Congress and was assumed by the State in Virginia, but regularly assessed in Massachusetts. One paid $316,000; the other, $369,000. The total revenue derived from Massachusetts was therefore $2,114,400 in the year 1814; that from Virginia, $566,500. Of the loans effected in the same year, Massachusetts took a small part considering her means—hardly a million dollars. Virginia took still less,—only two hundred thousand. . . . (VIII, viii, 233-34)

The relative numbers of regular troops were also somewhat doubtful; but the paymaster of the army reported Oct. 26, 1814, that he had distributed in bounties during the year $237,400 for

Massachusetts, and $160,962 for Virginia. During the year, six regular regiments—the Ninth, Twenty-first, Thirty-third, Thirty-fourth, Fortieth, and Forty-fifth—recruited in Massachusetts. Three —the Twelfth, Twentieth, and Thirty-fifth—recruited in Virginia. Perhaps the military aid furnished by the different sections of the seaboard could be better understood by following the familiar divisions. New England furnished thirteen regiments. New York, New Jersey, and Pennsylvania furnished fifteen. The Southern States, from Delaware to South Carolina inclusive, furnished ten. Of all the States in the Union New York alone supplied more regular soldiers than Massachusetts, and Massachusetts supplied as many as were furnished by Virginia and the two Carolinas together.

Judged by these standards, either Massachusetts had done more than her share, or Virginia had done less than hers. The tests were material, and took no moral element in account; but in moral support the relative failure of Massachusetts was not beyond dispute. Public opinion in New England was almost equally divided, and the pronounced opposition to the war was much greater in the Eastern States than in the Southern; but in the serious work of fighting, New England claimed a share of credit. In the little army at Niagara New York supplied the Major-General, Virginia and Massachusetts the two brigadiers; but Winfield Scott's brigade was chiefly composed of New England men; and when, nearly half a century afterward, Scott in his old age was obliged to choose between his allegiance to his State and allegiance to the Union, the memory of the New England troops who had won for him his first renown had its influence in raising his mind above the local sympathies which controlled other Virginia officers. . . . (VIII, viii, 235-36)

These comparisons were of little weight to prove that New England was either better or worse than other parts of the Union, but they showed that the difficulties that depressed Madison's mind were not merely local. He might have disregarded the conduct of State governments of Massachusetts and Connecticut had he enjoyed the full support of his own great Republican States, Pennsylvania, Virginia, and North Carolina. Except New York, Kentucky, Tennessee, and perhaps Ohio, no State gave to the war the full and earnest co-operation it needed. Again and again, from the beginning of the troubles with England, Madison had acted on the conviction that at last the people were aroused; but in every instance he had been disappointed. After the burning of Washington, he was more than ever convinced that the moment had come when the entire people would rally in their self-respect; but he was met by the Hartford Convention and the November elections. If the people would not come to the aid of their government at such a moment, Madison felt that nothing could move them. Peace was his last hope. . . . (VIII, viii, 237-38)

The medium of depreciated and depreciating bank paper in which the taxes were to be paid, secured the States outside of New England from intolerable pressure by giving the means of indefinite depreciation; but to the government such a resource meant merely a larger variety of bank credits, which were of no certain value even in the towns where the banks existed, and were of no value at all elsewhere. The burden of taxation would be thrown chiefly on New England; and if the Hartford Convention did nothing else, it was sure to take measures for sequestering the proceeds of taxation in New England for military purposes. The hope of restoring the finances by taxation was faint. Until the currency could be established and exchanges made secure, the government was helpless.

The House having broken down November 28,[21] the Senate next took the matter in hand. Rufus King reported, December 2, a bill to incorporate a bank, which was in effect the bill recommended by Dallas.[22] After a week's consideration the Senate passed the bill, December 9, by the vote of seventeen to fourteen,—King and the Federalists, with four Republican senators, voting against it. The House referred it to the Committee of Ways and Means, which reported it, December 14, with amendments. The debate began December 23, and was cut short December 27 by C. J. Ingersoll, who by the close vote of seventy-two to seventy obliged the House to call for the previous question, and order the bill to its third reading. This energy was followed by a reaction; the bill was recommitted for amendment, again reported, and vehemently attacked.

Never had the House shown itself more feeble. The Federalists took the lead in debate; and January 2 Daniel Webster, in a speech that placed him at the head of the orators of the time, dictated the action of Congress:—

[21] The House broke down in its effort to charter a Second Bank of the United States.

[22] A. J. Dallas succeeded, October 6, 1814, the incompetent Campbell at the Treasury.

"What sort of an institution, sir, is this? It looks less like a bank than like a department of government. It will be properly the paper-money department. Its capital is government debts; the amount of issues will depend on government necessities; government in effect absolves itself from its own debts to the bank, and by way of compensation absolves the bank from its own contracts with others. This is indeed a wonderful scheme of finance. The government is to grow rich because it is to borrow without the obligation or repaying, and is to borrow of a bank which issues paper without the liability to redeem it. . . . They provide for an unlimited issue of paper in an entire exemption from payment. They found their bank in the first place on the discredit of government, and then hope to enrich government out of the insolvency of the bank."

Webster was a master of antithesis, and the proposed bank was in effect what he described; but had he been a member of the British Parliament he might have made the same objections, with little alteration, to the Bank of England. The Hartford Convention was in session while he spoke. Every word of his speech was a shock to the government and the Union, for his only suggestion was equivalent to doing nothing. He moved to instruct the committee to report a bill creating a bank with thirty millions of capital, composed one fourth of specie and three fourths of government securities; without power to suspend specie payments, and without obligation to lend three fifths of its capital to the government. To such a bank he would give his support, "not as a measure of temporary policy, or an expedient to find means of relief from the present poverty of the Treasury," but as an institution most useful in times of peace.

The House came to a vote the same day, and divided eighty-one to eighty. Then the Speaker, Langdon Cheves, rose, and after denouncing the proposed bank as "a dangerous, unexampled, and he might almost say a desperate resort," gave his casting vote against the bill.

No sooner had the House struck this blow at Dallas than it shrank back. The next day, amid complaints and objections, it reconsidered its matured decision by the sudden majority of 107 to 54. Once more the bill was recommitted, and once more reported, January 6, in the form that Webster proposed. Weary of their own instability, the majority hastened to vote. Most of the Federalists supported the bill; but Grosvenor of New York, one of the ablest, frankly said what every one felt, that the proposed institution could not be a specie bank, or get a million of its notes into circulation.

132 THE PARALYSIS OF NATIONAL GOVERNMENT

"The government relying on it would be disappointed, and ruin soon stare them in the face." With this understanding the House passed the bill, January 7, by a vote of one hundred and twenty to thirty-eight; and the Senate, after a struggle with the House, accepted it, January 20, by a vote of twenty to fourteen.

Dallas was not a man to be easily daunted even in so desperate a situation. After ten days deliberation, the President sent to Congress a veto message.

> "The most the bank could effect," said Madison, "and the most it could be expected to aim at, would be to keep the institution alive by limited and local transactions . . . until a change from war to peace should enable it, by a flow of specie into its vaults and a removal of the external demand for it, to derive its contemplated emoluments from a safe and full extension of its operations."

"I hope this will satisfy our friends," wrote Webster to his brother, "that it was not a bank likely to favor the Administration." Either with or without such a bank, the Administration was equally helpless. The veto left the Treasury, February 1, without a resource in prospect. The unsatisfied demands reached nearly twenty millions. The cash balance, chiefly in bank credits, was little more than six millions. A further deficit of forty millions remained to be provided above the estimated revenue of 1815. United States six-per-cents commanded only a nominal price, between fifty and sixty cents on the dollar, and were quoted in Boston at a discount of forty cents. Treasury notes being in demand for taxes, were worth about seventy-five cents in the dollar. Dallas had no serious hope of carrying on the government. In a letter to the Committee of Ways and Means, dated January 17, he could only propose to add six millions more to the taxes, issue fifteen millions in Treasury notes, and borrow twenty-five millions on any terms that could be obtained. In making these recommendations he avowed in grave words his want of confidence in their result:—

> "In making the present communication I feel, sir, that I have performed my duty to the Legislature and to the country; but when I perceive that more than forty millions of dollars must be raised for the service of the year 1815, by an appeal to public credit through the medium of the Treasury notes and loans, I am not without sensations of extreme solicitude."

Young George Ticknor of Boston happened to be in the gallery of the House of Representatives when Eppes read this letter, January 21, and the next day he wrote,—

"The last remarkable event in this history of this remarkable Congress is Dallas's report. You can imagine nothing like the dismay with which it has filled the Democratic party. All his former communications were but emollients and palliations compared with this final disclosure of the bankruptcy of the nation. Mr. Eppes[23] as Chancellor of the Exchequer, or Chairman of the Committee of Ways and Means, read it in his place yesterday, and when he had finished, threw it upon the table with expressive violence, and turning round to Mr. Gaston, asked him with a bitter levity between jest and earnest—

" 'Well, sir! will your party take the government if we will give it up to them?'

" 'No, sir!' said Gaston[24]; . . . 'No, sir! Not unless you will give it to us as we gave it to you!' "

. . . (VIII, ix, 257-62)

[23] John Wayles Eppes: Representative from Virginia, nephew to Thomas Jefferson.

[24] William Gaston: Federalist Representative from North Carolina.

8.

Denationalization at Hartford

The Massachusetts legislature issued, October 17, its invitation to the New England States for a conference, and on the same day the newspapers published the despatches from Ghent, to August 20, containing British conditions of peace,—which required, among greater sacrifices, a cession of Massachusetts territory, and an abandonment of fisheries and fishing rights conceded with American independence. Two counties of the State beyond the Penobscot were then in British military possession, and a third, Nantucket, was a British naval station. Yet even under these circumstances the British demands did not shock the Federalist leaders. Governor Strong, after reading the Ghent documents October 17, wrote to Pickering at Washington,—

> "If Great Britain had discovered a haughty or grasping spirit, it might naturally have excited irritation; but I am persuaded that in the present case there is not a member of Congress who, if he was a member of Parliament, would have thought that more moderate terms ought in the first instance to have been offered."

The argument seemed to prove only that members of Congress could also be haughty and grasping; but Governor Strong thought the British demands reasonable, and began at once to sound his friends in regard to the proposed concessions. The following day he wrote that the Essex people expected to lose the fisheries, but were ready to give up a portion of Maine to retain them.

Pickering wrote in reply, acquiescing in the proposed barter of territory for fisheries, and also in the more extravagant British demands for the Indians and the Lakes. "I was gratified," said

134

Pickering, "to find my own sentiments corresponding with yours." The leading Federalists united with Pickering and Strong in blaming the American negotiators[25] and the government for rejecting the British offers. The same view was taken by the chief Federalist newspaper of the State, the Boston "Centinel."

Thus in the November election, a few weeks later, two issues were impressed on the people of New England. In regard to neither issue did the Federalist leaders attempt concealment. The people were invited, as far as the press of both parties could decide the points of dispute, to express their opinion,—first, whether the British conditions of peace should have been taken into consideration; second, whether the States should be represented at the Hartford Convention. The popular response was emphatic. Everywhere in New England the Republican candidates were defeated; and the Federalists, encouraged by the result—believing the Hartford Convention to be the most popular action taken by Massachusetts since the State adopted the Federal Constitution,—prepared to support measures, looking to the restoration of peace and to the establishment of a new Federal compact comprising either the whole or a portion of the actual Union.

However varied the wishes of the majority might be, they agreed in requiring a radical change in the organic law. This intention was their chief claim to popularity. The Boston "Centinel," announcing November 9 the adhesion of Connecticut and Rhode Island to the Hartford Convention, placed over the announcement the head-line, "Second and third Pillars of a new Federal Edifice reared." During November and December, almost every day, the newspapers discussed the question what the convention should do; and the chief divergence of opinion seemed to regard rather the immediate than the ultimate resort to forcible means of stopping the war. The extremists, represented in the press by John Lowell,[26] asked for immediate action.

"Throwing off all connection with this wasteful war," wrote "A New England Man" in the "Centinel," of December 17,—"making peace with our enemy and opening once more our commerce with the world, would be a wise and manly course. The occasion demands it of us, and the people at large are ready to meet it."

Apparently Lowell was right. The people showed no sign of unwillingness to meet any decision that might be recommended by the

[25] The American negotiators at Ghent, see pp. 149-166.
[26] John Lowell: Federalist Boston lawyer.

convention. As the moment approached, the country waited with increasing anxiety for the result. The Republican press—the "National Intelligencer" as well as the Boston "Patriot"—at first ridiculed the convention, then grew irritable, and at last betrayed signs of despair. On both sides threats were openly made and openly defied; but in Massachusetts the United States government had not five hundred effective troops, and if the convention chose to recommend that the State should declare itself neutral and open its ports, no one pretended that any national power existed in Massachusetts capable of preventing the legislature from carrying the recommendation into effect if it pleased.

From immediate extravagance Massachusetts was saved by the leaders who, knowing the popular excitement, feared lest the convention should be carried too fast into disorder, and for that reason selected representatives who could be trusted to resist emotion. When George Cabot was chosen as the head of the State delegation, the character of the body was fixed. The selection of Cabot did not please the advocates of action. Pickering wrote to Lowell suggesting doubts whether Cabot was the fittest choice. Lowell replied that he shared these doubts, and that in consequence he had been led to oppose the convention altogether, because it would not withdraw the State resources from the general government. Cabot, he said, was "most reluctantly dragged in like a conscript to the duty of a delegate"; he had always been despondent as to the course of public affairs, and felt no confidence in the possibility of awakening the people to their true disease,—which was not the war or the Union, but democracy. Lowell did not know "a single bold and ardent man" among the Massachusetts or Connecticut delegates. In the "Centinel" of December 7 he described Cabot's tendencies in language evidently intended as a warning to Cabot himself:—

"There are men who know that our troubles are not the offspring of this war alone, and will not die with it. But they despair of relief, and think resistance unavailing. They consider the people in their very nature democratic, and that nothing but the severity of their sufferings has driven them from those men and that system out of which have grown all our evils; that should they be restored to that state of prosperity which they once enjoyed, the same passions and opinions would diffuse themselves through the country, and the same course of conduct be again followed out."

Cabot shocked Pickering by expressing all his favorite political views in one brief question: "Why can't you and I let the world ruin itself its own way?" Such a turn of mind was commonly the mark of a sceptical spirit, which doubted whether the world at best was worth the trouble of saving; and against this inert and indifferent view of human affairs New England offered a constant protest. Yet the Massachusetts delegation to Hartford was in sympathy with Cabot, while the Massachusetts legislature seemed to sympathize with Pickering. William Prescott, another member of the delegation, was chiefly remarkable for prudence and caution; Nathan Dane bore the same stamp; Harrison Gray Otis took character and color from his surroundings. The Connecticut delegation —James Hillhouse, Chauncey Goodrich, Roger M. Sherman, and others—were little likely to recommend "effectual measures." The convention consisted of men supposed to be inclined to resist popular pressure, and Cabot was probably serious in replying to a young friend who asked him what he was to do at Hartford: "We are going to keep you young hot-heads from getting into mischief."

In the Council Chamber of the State House at Hartford the delegates assembled, December 15, and gave instant evidence of their intention to discourage appeals to popular emotion. Their earliest steps decided their whole course. They chose George Cabot as their President, and they made their sessions secret. Under no circumstances could the convention have regarded itself as a popular body, for the delegates numbered only twenty-three persons, mostly cautious and elderly men, who detested democracy, but disliked enthusiasm almost as much. Two new members, appointed by popular meetings in New Hampshire, were next admitted; and toward the close of the sessions another member, representing the county of Windham in Vermont, was given a seat. Thus enlarged, the convention over which George Cabot presided numbered twenty-six members besides the secretary, Theodore Dwight.

Excess of caution helped to give the convention an air of conspiracy, which warned future conspirators to prefer acting, or appearing to act, in public. The secrecy of the Hartford conference was chiefly intended to secure freedom for the exchange of opinion, and also in some degree to prevent premature excitement and intrusion of popular feeling; but the secrecy created a belief that the debates would not bear publicity. Possibly much was said which verged on treasonable conspiracy; but the members were not men of a class likely to act beyond their instructions, and they adhered strictly to the practical task imposed on them. Some years afterward, Harrison Gray Otis, laboring to clear his political reputation from the stigma of membership, caused the official journal of the convention to be published; and the record, though revealing nothing of what was said, proved that nothing was formally done or proposed which contradicted the grave and restrained attitude maintained in its public expressions.

On the first day of its meeting the convention appointed a committee to consider and report upon the business to be done. Chauncey Goodrich, Otis, and three other members formed this committee, which reported the next day the points in dispute, between the States and the national government,—the militia power, conscription power, duty and means of defence, and matters of a like nature. After two days of discussion, the convention appointed another committee to frame a general project of measures, and again placed a Connecticut man—Nathaniel Smith—at its head, with Otis second. Still another committee was appointed, December 21, to prepare a report showing the reasons which guided the convention to its results; and of that committee Otis was chairman.

Clearly, Otis took the chief burden of business; and the result could scarcely fail to reflect in some degree the character of the man as well as of the body for which he was acting. Though ambitious of leading, Otis never led. John Lowell described his character, as it was understood in Boston, perhaps somewhat harshly, for Otis was no favorite with any class of men who held fixed opinions:—

"Mr. Otis is naturally timid and frequently wavering,—today bold, and tomorrow like a hare trembling at every breeze. It would seem by his language that he is prepared for the very boldest measures, but he receives anonymous letters every day or two threatening him with bodily harm. It seems the other party suspect his firmness. He is sincere in wishing thorough measures, but a thousand fears restrain him."

Otis was the probable author of the report, adopted December 24, recommending a course to the convention; and he was chairman of the larger committee to which that report was referred, and within which the final report—after a discussion lasting from December 24 to December 30—was framed. The discussions, both in committee and in convention, took much time and caused some difficulties; but nothing was ever known of the speeches made, or of the motions proposed, or of the amendments offered. All the reports were finally adopted by the convention; and all proposed business then having been finished, January 5 the convention adjourned without delay, authorizing Cabot to call another meeting at Boston if he should at any time see occasion for it.

The report, therefore, contained all the information which the convention intended to make public, and only from that document could the ultimate object of the members be inferred. It was immediately published in Connecticut, and at the meeting of the legislatures of Massachusetts and Connecticut in January it was laid before them for approval.

Considering the conservative temper of the delegates and their dislike for extreme measures, the report bore striking evidence of the popular passion which urged them forward. A few paragraphs in its first pages showed the spirit of its recommendations, and a few more showed the effect expected from them:—

"It is a truth not to be concealed that a sentiment prevails to no inconsiderable extent . . . that the time for a change is at hand. . . . This opinion may ultimately prove to be correct; but as the evidence on which it rests is not yet conclusive, . . . some general considerations are submitted in the hope of reconciling all to a course of moderation and firmness which may . . . probably avert the evil, or at least insure consolation and success in the last resort. . . . A severance of the Union by one or more States against the will of the rest, and especially in time of war, can be justified only by absolute necessity."

Having thus discouraged precipitation, and argued in favor of firm and moderate measures as a probable means of preserving the Union, the report sketched the limits of the Union that was to be preserved. In a paragraph closely following the precedent of the Virginia Resolutions of 1798, the report asserted the right and duty of a State to "interpose its authority" for the protection of its citizens from infractions of the Constitution by the general government. In the immediate crisis, this interposition should take the form of State laws to protect the militia or citizens from conscriptions and drafts; of an arrangement with the general government authorizing the States to assume their own defence, and to retain "a reasonable portion of the taxes collected within the said States" for the purpose; and of State armies to be held in readiness to serve for the defence of the New England States upon the request of the governor of the State invaded.

Such measures involved the establishment of a New England Confederation. The proposed union of the New England States for their own defence ignored any share to be taken by the general

government in the defence of the national territory, and reduced
that government to helplessness. What could be done by New
England might be done by all; and the Federalists assumed that
all would be obliged to do it.

If the general government should reject the request for the proposed arrangement, the ultimate emergency must arise; but with
the measures to be then taken the convention would not interfere.

> "It would be inexpedient for this convention to diminish the hope
> of a successful issue to such an application by recommending, upon
> supposition of a contrary event, ulterior proceedings. Nor is it indeed
> within their province. In a state of things so solemn and trying as
> may then arise, the legislatures of the States, or conventions of the
> whole people, or delegates appointed by them for the express pur-
> pose in another convention, must act as such urgent circumstances
> may then require."

Besides the measures of urgency which must be immediately accepted by the national government, the convention recommended
seven amendments to the Constitution; but on these no immediate
action was required. The single issue forced on the government by
the convention was that of surrendering to Massachusetts, Connecticut, and Rhode Island "a reasonable portion of the taxes
collected within said States," and consenting to some arrangement
"whereby the said States may, separately or in concert, be empow-
ered to assume upon themselves the defence of their territory against
the enemy." If the United States government should decline such
an arrangement, the State legislatures were to send delegates to
another convention to meet at Boston, June 15, "with such powers
and instructions as the exigency of a crisis so momentous may
require."

While the convention was preparing its report, from December 15
to January 5, the public waited with the utmost curiosity for the
result. Major Jesup, famous at Chippawa and Lundy's Lane, was
then recruiting for the Twenty-fifth United States Infantry at Hartford, and reported constantly to the President and War Department;
but he could tell nothing of the convention that was not notorious.
His letters were mere surmises or unmilitary comments on the treasonable intentions of the meeting. The Federalists knew no more
than was known to the Republicans; but while they waited, they
expressed fear only lest the convention should fall short of their
wishes.

"I care nothing more for your actings and doings," wrote Gouverneur Morris[27] to Pickering in Congress. "Your decree of conscriptions and your levy of contributions are alike indifferent to one whose eyes are fixed on a star in the East, which he believes to be the day-spring of freedom and glory. The traitors and madmen assembled at Hartford will, I believe, if not too tame and timid, be hailed hereafter as the patriots and sages of their day and generation."

As far as newspapers reflected public opinion, the people of New England held the same views as those expressed by Gouverneur Morris. The Boston "Centinel" contained, December 28, an address to the Hartford Convention announcing that the once venerable Constitution had expired: "At your hands, therefore, we demand deliverance. New England is unanimous. And we announce our irrevocable decree that the tyrannical oppression of those who at present usurp the powers of the Constitution is beyond endurance. And we will resist it." A meeting at Reading in Massachusetts, January 5, pledged itself to make no more returns for taxation and to pay no more national taxes until the State should have made its decision known.

A newspaper paragraph copied by the Federalist press advised the President to provide himself with a swifter horse than he had at Bladensburg if he meant to attempt to subjugate the Eastern States. "He must be able to escape at a greater rate than forty miles a day, or the swift vengeance of New England will overtake the wretched miscreant in his fight." Such expressions of the press on either side were of little authority, and deserved no great attention; but the language of responsibility and representative bodies could not be denied weight. Opposition to the convention seemed cowed. Apparently the State was ready for immediate action; and the convention, in recommending a delay of six months, risked general disapproval.

While the public was in this temper, the convention adjourned, and its report was given to the press. No one doubted that moderate men would approve it. The only persons whose approval was in question were "bold and ardent" partisans, like Gouverneur Morris, Pickering, and John Lowell, who wanted instant action. Chiefly for the sake of unanimity, these men gave in their adhesion. John Lowell hastened to publish his acquiescence in the convention's report. Pickering also approved it, although Pickering's approval

[27] Gouverneur Morris: of New York, Founding Father, now an extreme Federalist.

was partly founded on the belief that the Union was already dissolved, and no further effort in that direction need be made.

"If the British succeed in their expedition against New Orleans," Pickering wrote to Lowell,—"and if they have tolerable leaders I see no reason to doubt of their success,—I shall consider the Union as severed. This consequence I deem inevitable. I do not expect to see a single representative in the next Congress from the Western states."

Governor Strong and Senator Gore also approved the convention's report. On receiving it at Washington, January 14, Gore wrote to Strong: "The result of the Hartford Convention is here, and affords satisfaction to most if not to all,—to some because they see not the point nor consequence of the recommendation as relates to taxes." The point and consequence of that recommendation were clear to Gore, and he approved of both.

If any leading Federalist disapproved the convention's report, he left no record of the disapproval. In such a case, at such a moment, silence was acquiescence. As far as could be inferred from any speeches made or letters written at the time, the Federalist party was unanimous in acquiescing in the recommendations of the Hartford Convention.

In Massachusetts and Connecticut the acquiescence was express. The legislature, convened at Boston, January 18, hastened to refer the convention's report to a joint committee, which reported, January 24, Resolutions that the legislature "do highly approve" the proceedings of the convention, and that State commissioners should immediately proceed to Washington to effect the arrangement proposed. By a very large majority of three to one, the legislature adopted the Resolutions, making the acts of the convention their own. Three commissioners were quickly appointed,—Harrison Gray Otis at their head,—and in the early days of February started for Washington. . . . (VIII, xi, 287-302)

In later times the Hartford Convention was often and vigorously defended by writers whose works were friendly to the national government, and whose influence was popular. The wisdom, loyalty, and patriotism of George Cabot and his associates became the theme of authors whose authority was above dispute. Nearly always the defence rested on the argument that popular opinion went beyond the convention's report, and that the convention risked its credit by refusing to advise instant withdrawal from the Union. This view was apparently correct. The efforts of the moderate Federalists to praise the moderation of the report, and the labored protests of the extremists against the possible suspicion that they objected to its moderation, showed that the convention was then believed to have offered resistance to what Governor Smith stigmatized as "rash councils or precipitate measures." The tone of the press and the elections bore out the belief that a popular majority would have supported an abrupt and violent course.

The tone of the minority at the time showed a similar belief that Massachusetts favored disunion. During all the proceedings of the State legislatures and the convention, the loyal press and citizens never ceased to point out the dangerous, treasonable, and absurd results to be expected from the course pursued. In the Massachusetts Senate John Holmes of Maine attacked the convention and its doings in a speech that gave him wide reputation. Threats of civil war were freely uttered and defied. Among the least violent of Federalists was James Lloyd, recently United States senator from Massachusetts; and to him as a man of known patriotism John Randolph addressed a letter, December 15, 1814, remonstrating against the Hartford Convention that day to meet. Lloyd replied in a letter also published, advising Randolph and the Virginians to coerce Madison into retirement, and to place Rufus King in the Presidency as the alternative to a fatal issue. The assertion of such an alternative showed how desperate the situation was believed by the moderate Federalists to be. . . . (VIII, xi, 305-306)

In the Republican party the belief was universal that the Hartford Convention could lead only to a New England Confederation; and the belief was not confined to partisans. An anecdote that George Ticknor delighted in telling, illustrated the emotion that then agitated men far beyond the passing and fitful excitements of party politics. Ticknor, a young Federalist twenty-three years old, wished for letters of introduction to Virginia, and asked them from John Adams, then a man of eighty, whose support of the war made him an object of antipathy to the party he had led.

"When I visited him in Quincy to receive these letters," related Ticknor, "I had a remarkable interview with him, which at the time disturbed me not a little. . . . Soon after I was seated in Mr. Adams's parlor,—where was no one but himself and Mrs. Adams, who was knitting,—he began to talk of the condition of the country with great earnestness. I said not a word; Mrs. Adams was equally silent; but Mr. Adams, who was a man of strong and prompt passions,

went on more and more vehemently. He was dressed in a single-
breasted dark green coat, buttoned tightly by very large white metal
buttons over his somewhat rotund person. As he grew more and more
excited in his discourse, he impatiently endeavored to thrust his
hand into the breast of his coat. The buttons did not yield readily; at
last he *forced* his hand in saying, as he did so, in a very loud voice
and most excited manner: 'Thank God! thank God! George Cabot's
close-buttoned ambition has broke out at last: he wants to be
President of New England, sir!' "

Whether George Cabot wanted it or not, he was in danger of
becoming what John Adams predicted. He was far from being the
first man who had unwillingly allowed himself to be drawn into
a position from which escape was impossible. After going so far,
neither leaders nor people could retreat. The next and easy step
of sequestrating the direct and indirect taxes was one to which the
State stood pledged in the event of a refusal by President Madison
and Congress to surrender them. After such an act, the establishment of a New England Confederation could hardly be matter of
choice. . . . (VIII, xi, 307-308)

9.

Triumph of Democratic Nationality

When the month of February arrived, government and people were waiting with keen apprehension for some new disaster, and the least probable solution was that England knowing the situation would consent to any tolerable peace. The "Federal Republican" of January 28, commenting on the expected bank veto, summed up the consequences, not unfairly from its point of view, in few words:—

> "It is impossible, as Mr. Giles said in his luminous and eloquent argument upon the measure [of a national bank], that the government can stand these reiterated shocks. . . . The interest upon the public debt remains unpaid, and there exists not the means, without making the most ruinous sacrifices, to pay it. The government is in arrears to the army upward of nine million dollars; to the navy, about four million. . . . The condition of our finances is known to the enemy; and is it possible he will be such a fool as to give us peace, after the mortal blow we aimed at him when he knows we cannot pay the interest on the public debt, that we cannot pay our army or our navy, and when he finds us unable to defend any part of the country at which he strikes? . . ." (VIII, xi, 309-10)

Hitherto the frequent British disasters at Plattsburg, Sackett's Harbor, Fort Erie, and the Moravian towns had been attributed to their generals. Sir George Prevost, Major-Generals Drummond and Riall, and Major-General Proctor were not officers of Wellington's army. The British government, in appointing Sir Edward Pakenham to command at New Orleans, meant to send the ablest officer at their disposal. Pakenham was not only one of Wellington's best generals, but stood in the close relation of his brother-in-law,

Pakenham's sister being Wellington's wife. In every military respect Sir Edward Pakenham might consider himself the superior of Andrew Jackson. He was in the prime of life and strength, thirty-eight years of age, while Jackson, nearly ten years older, was broken in health and weak in strength. Pakenham had learned the art of war from Wellington, in the best school in Europe. He was supported by an efficient staff and a military system as perfect as experience and expenditure could make it, and he commanded as fine an army as England could produce, consisting largely of Peninsula veterans. . . . (VIII, xiii, 352-53)

The Duke of Wellington believed such a force fully competent to capture New Orleans, or to rout any American army he ever heard of; and his confidence would have been, if possible, still stronger, had he known his opponent's resources, which were no greater and not very much better than those so easily overcome by Ross at Bladensburg. The principal difference was that Jackson commanded.

Jackson's difficulties were very great, and were overcome only by the desperate energy which he infused even into the volatile creoles and sluggish Negroes. When he retired from the field of the night battle, he withdrew, as has been told, only two miles. About five miles below New Orleans he halted his troops. Between the river and the swamp, the strip of open and cultivated land was there somewhat narrower than elsewhere. A space of a thousand yards, or about three fifths of a mile, alone required a strong defence. A shallow, dry canal, or ditch, ten feet wide, crossed the plain and opened into the river on one side and the swamp on the other. All day the troops, with the Negroes of the neighborhood, worked, deepening the canal, and throwing up a parapet behind it. The two six-pound field-pieces commanded the road on the riverbank, and the "Louisiana" descended the river to a point about two miles below Jackson's line. A mile below the "Louisiana" the "Carolina" remained in her old position, opposite the British camp. By nightfall the new lines were already formidable, and afforded complete protection from musketry. For further security the parapet was continued five hundred yards, and turned well on the flank in the swamp; but this task was not undertaken until December 28. . . . (VIII, xiii, 354-55)

The Americans also prepared batteries. From the lines one thirty-two-pounder, three twenty-four-pounders, and one eighteen-pounder commanded the plain in their front. Besides these heavy guns, three twelve-pounders, three six-pounders, a six-inch howitzer or mortar, and a brass carronade, useless from its bad condition—in all, twelve or thirteen guns, capable of replying to the British batteries, were mounted along the American lines. On the west bank of the river, three quarters of a mile away, Commodore Patterson established, December 30 and 31, a battery of one twenty-four-pounder and two long twelve-pounders, which took the British batteries in flank. Thus the Americans possessed fifteen effective guns, six of which were heavy pieces of long range. They were worked partly by regular artillerists, partly by sailors, partly by New Orleans militia, and partly by the "hellish banditti" of Barataria, who to the number of twenty or thirty were received by General Jackson into the service and given the care of two twenty-four-pounders.

The number and position of the British guns were given in Lieutenant Peddie's sketch of the field. Before the reconnaisance of December 28, fieldpieces had been placed in battery on the riverside to destroy the "Carolina" and "Louisiana." Canon Gleig said that "nine field-pieces, two howitzers, and one mortar" were placed in battery on the riverside during the night of December 25. Captain Henley of the "Carolina" reported that five guns opened upon him on the morning of December 26. Captain Peddie's sketch marked seven pieces mounted in battery on the riverside, bearing on Commodore Patterson's battery opposite, besides four pieces in two batteries below. Their range was sufficient to destroy the "Carolina" and pierce the breastwork across the river, and therefore they were probably twelve- and nine-pounders.

Besides these lighter long-range guns, the British constructed three batteries in the night of December 31.

"Four eighteen-pounders," reported Major Forrest, British assistant-quartermaster general, "were placed in a battery formed of hogsheads of sugar, on the main road, to fire upon the ship if she dropped down. Preparations were also made to establish batteries,—one of six eighteen-pounders, and one of four twenty-four-pound carronades; also batteries for the field-pieces and howitzers, the latter to keep the fire of the enemy under, while the troops were to be moved forward in readiness to storm the works as soon as a practicable breach was effected."

According to Peddie's sketch the Battery No. 6, on the road or new levee, contained not four but two guns. Battery No. 5, some fifty yards from No. 6, contained six guns, as Major Forrest reported. Battery No. 4, to the left of the old levee, contained four guns, probably the carronades. Battery No. 3, to the right of the old levee, contained five guns, probably the fieldpieces and howitzers. In all, seventeen guns bore on the American lines—besides seven, in Batteries No. 7 and No. 8, bearing on Commodore Patterson's three-gun battery across the river. According to Gleig, the British had thirty guns; but in any case they used not less than twenty-four guns, throwing a heavier weight of metal than was thrown by the fifteen pieces used by the Americans. The British artillery was served by regular artillerists.

These details were particularly interesting, because the artillery battle of January 1, 1815, offered the best test furnished during the war of relative skill in the use of that arm. The attack had every advantage over the defence. The British could concentrate their fire to effect a breach for their troops to enter; the Americans were obliged to disperse their fire on eight points. The American platforms being elevated, offered a better target than was afforded by the low British batteries, and certainly were no better protected. Three of the American guns were in battery across the river, three quarters of a mile from the main British battery of six eighteen-pounders, while the "Louisiana's" carronades were beyond range, and the "Louisiana" herself was not brought into action. On the American side the battle was fought entirely by the guns in Jackson's lines and in Patterson's battery across the river,—one thirty-two-pounder, four twenty-four-pounders, one eighteen-pounder, five twelve-pounders, three six-pounders, and a howitzer,—fifteen American guns in all, matched against ten British eighteen-pounders, four twenty-four-pound carronades, and ten field-pieces and howitzers,—twenty-four guns in all. If the British field-pieces were twelve and nines, the weight of metal was at least three hundred and fifty pounds on the British side against two hundred and twenty-four pounds on the American side, besides two howitzers against one.

The main British batteries were about seven hundred yards distant from Jackson's line. Opposite to the battery of six eighteen-pounders were the American thirty-two and three twenty-four-pounders. Behind the British batteries the British army waited for the order to assault. Toward eight o'clock on the morning of January 1, 1815, the British opened a hot fire accompanied by a shower of rockets. The American guns answered, and the firing continued without intermission until toward noon, when the British fire slackened, and at one o'clock the British artillerists abandoned their batteries, leaving the guns deserted.

No other battle of the war, except that at Chrystler's Farm, left the defeated party with so little excuse for its inferiority. Commonly apologists ascribed greater force to the victor than to the vanquished, or dwelt upon some accident or oversight which affected the result. For the defeat of the British artillery, January 1, 1815, no excuse was ever suggested. The British army and navy frankly admitted that the misfortune was due to American superiority in the use of artillery. British evidence on that point was ample, for their surprise and mortification were extreme; while the Americans seemed never fully to appreciate the extraordinary character of the feat they performed. . . . (VIII, xiii, 358-63)

Immediately after the capitulation of Paris, March 31, the [British] Ministry turned its attention to the United States, and the "Courier" announced, April 15, that twenty thousand men were to go from the Garonne to America. Mr. Madison, the "Courier" added, had "made a pretty kettle of fish of it." Twenty thousand men were about two thirds of Wellington's English force, and their arrival in America would, as every Englishman believed, insure the success of the campaign. Not until these troops were embarked would the Ministry begin to negotiate; but in the middle of May the military measures were complete, and then the "Courier" began to prepare the public mind for terms of peace.[28]

These terms were the same as those announced by the "Times," except that the "Courier" did not object to treating with Madison. The United States were to be interdicted the fisheries; Spain was to be supported in recovering Louisiana; the right of impressment must be expressly conceded,—anything short of this would be unwise and a disappointment. "There are points which must be conceded by America before we can put an end to the contest." Such language offered no apparent hope of peace; yet whatever hope existed lay in Castlereagh, who inspired it. Extravagant as the demands were, they fell short of the common expectation. The "Courier" admitted the propriety of negotiation; it insisted neither on Madison's retirement nor on a division of the Union, and it

---

[28] "Terms of peace": In response to the Czar's offer to mediate (21 September 1812) Madison sent James A. Bayard, Federalist Senator from Delaware, and Albert Gallatin to St. Petersburg, where they arrived July 21, 1813. Lord Castlereagh had already declined the Czar's offer; but on November 4, 1813, he proposed a direct mediation. Madison's nomination of J. Q. Adams (Minister to Russia), Bayard, Henry Clay, and Jonathan Russell as peace commissioners was confirmed January 18, 1814. On February 8, Gallatin was confirmed as fifth commissioner. After much delay, the negotiations began at Ghent on August 8, 1814.

refrained from asserting the whole British demand, or making it an ultimatum.

The chief pressure on the Ministry came from Canada, and could not be ignored. The Canadian government returned to its old complaint that Canadian interests had been ignorantly and wantonly sacrificed by the treaty of 1783, and that the opportunity to correct the wrong should not be lost. The Canadian official "Gazette" insisted that the United States should be required to surrender the northern part of the State of New York, and that both banks of the St. Lawrence should be Canadian property. A line from Plattsburg to Sackett's Harbor would satisfy this necessity; but to secure Canadian interests, the British government should further insist on acquiring the east bank of the Niagara River, and on a guaranty of the Indian Territory from Sandusky to Kaskaskias, with the withdrawal of American military posts in the Northwest. A pamphlet was published in May to explain the subject for the use of the British negotiators, and the required territorial cessions were marked on a map. The control of the Lakes, the Ohio River as the Indian boundary, and the restitution of Louisiana were the chief sacrifices wished from the United States. The cession of a part of Maine was rather assumed than claimed, and the fisheries were to be treated as wholly English. A memorial from Newfoundland, dated November 8, 1813, pointed out the advantages which the war had already brought to British trade and fisheries by the exclusion of American competition, to the result of doubling the number of men employed on the Labrador shores; and the memorialists added,—

"They cannot too often urge the important policy . . . of wholly excluding foreigners from sharing again in the advantages of a fishery from which a large proportion of our best national defence will be derived."

British confidence was at its highest point when the Emperor of Russia and the King of Prussia visited London, June 7, and received an enthusiastic welcome. Gallatin[29] obtained an interview

[29] Gallatin heard, October 19, 1813, that the Senate had turned down his appointment as peace commissioner with Bayard. None the less, although now without official standing, he went with Bayard to London, hoping to keep the negotiation alive. They arrived April 9, 1814, having learned on the way that a new commission had been nominated. In London, they received the news that Gallatin was to be the fifth commissioner; and on May 17 they agreed that the negotiation should be held at Ghent.

with the Czar, June 17, and hoped that Russian influence might moderate British demands, but the Czar could give him no encouragement. Gallatin wrote home an often-quoted despatch, dated June 13, warning the President that fifteen or twenty thousand men were on their way to America, and that the United States could expect no assistance from Europe.

"I have also the most perfect conviction," Gallatin continued, "that under the existing unpropitious circumstances of the world, America cannot by a continuance of the war compel Great Britain to yield any of the maritime points in dispute, and particularly to agree to any satisfactory arrangement on the subject of impressment; and that the most favorable terms of peace that can be expected are the *status ante bellum.*"

Even these terms, Gallatin added, depended on American success in withstanding the shock of the campaign. He did not say that at the time he wrote, the *status ante bellum* would be scouted by public opinion in England as favorable to the United States; but his estimate of the situation was more nearly exact than though he had consulted only the apparent passions of the British press.

"Lord Castlereagh," wrote Gallatin to Clay, "is, according to the best information I can collect, the best disposed man in the Cabinet." Yet Castlereagh did not venture at that stage to show a disposition for peace. He delayed the negotiation, perhaps wisely, six weeks after the American negotiators had assembled at Ghent; and his instructions to the British commissioners, dated July 28, reflected the demands of the press. They offered, not the *status ante bellum,* but the *uti possidetis,* as the starting-point of negotiation. "The state of possession must be considered as the territorial arrangement which would revive upon a peace, except so far as the same may be modified by any new treaty." The state of possession, in view of the orders that had then been given, or were to be given, for the invasion of the United States, was likely to cost the Americans half of Maine, between the Penobscot and the Passamaquoddy; Plattsburg, and the northern part of New York, Vermont, and New Hampshire; Fort Niagara, Mackinaw, and possibly New Orleans and Mobile. Besides this concession of the *uti possidetis,* or military occupation at the date of peace, the Americans were required at the outset to admit as a *sine qua non,* or condition precedent to any negotiation, that England's Indian allies, the tribes of the Northwestern Territory, should be included in the pacification, and that a definite boundary should be assigned to them under a mutual guaranty of both Powers. Eastport, or Moose Island, and the fishing privileges were to be regarded as British. With these instructions of July 28, the British commissioners, early in August, started for Ghent.

Between Castlereagh's idea and those of Madison no relation existed. Gallatin and his colleagues at Ghent were provided with two sets of instructions. The first set had been written in 1813, for the expected negotiation at Petersburg. The second set was written in January, 1814, and was brought to Europe by Clay. Neither authorized the American commissioners to discuss such conditions as Castlereagh proposed. The President gave his negotiators authority to deal with questions of maritime law; but even there they were allowed to exercise no discretion on the chief issue in dispute. Monroe's latest letter, dated January 28, was emphatic. "On impressment, as to the right of the United States to be exempted from it, I have nothing to add," said the secretary; "the sentiments of the President have undergone no change on that important subject. This degrading practice must cease; our flag must protect the crew, or the United States cannot consider themselves an independent nation." The President would consent to exclude all British seamen, except those already naturalized, from American vessels, and to stipulate the surrender of British deserters; but the express abandonment of impressment was a *sine qua non* of treaty. "If this encroachment of Great Britain is not provided against," said Monroe, "the United States have appealed to arms in vain. If your efforts to accomplish it should fail, all further negotiations will cease, and you will return home without delay."

On territorial questions the two governments were equally wide apart. So far from authorizing a cession of territorial rights, Monroe instructed the American commissioners, both at St. Petersburg and at Ghent, "to bring to view the advantage to both countries which is promised by a transfer of the upper parts and even the whole of Canada to the United States." The instructions of January 1 and January 28, 1814, reiterated the reasoning which should decide England voluntarily to cede Canada. "Experience has shown that Great Britain cannot participate in the dominion and navigation of the Lakes without incurring the danger of an early renewal of the war."

These instructions were subsequently omitted from the published documents, probably because the Ghent commissioners decided not to act upon them; but when the American negotiators met their

British antagonists at Ghent, each party was under orders to exclude the other, if possible, from the Lakes, and the same divergence of opinion in regard to the results of two years' was extended over the whole field of negotiation. The British were ordered to begin by a *sine qua non* in regard to the Indians, which the Americans had no authority to consider. The Americans were ordered to impose a *sine qua non* in regard to impressments, which the British were forbidden to concede. The British were obliged to claim the basis of possession; the Americans were not even authorized to admit the status existing before the war. The Americans were required to negotiate about blockades, contraband and maritime rights of neutrals; the British could not admit such subjects into dispute. The British regarded their concessions of fishing rights as terminated by the war; the Americans could not entertain the idea.

The diplomacy that should produce a treaty from such discordant material must show no ordinary excellence; yet even from that point of view the prospect was not encouraging. The British government made a peculiar choice of negotiators. The chief British commissioner, Lord Gambier, was unknown in diplomacy, or indeed in foreign affairs. A writer in the London "Morning Chronicle" of August 9 expressed the general surprise that Government could make no better selection for the chief of its commission than Lord Gambier, "who was a post captain in 1794, and happened to fight the 'Defence' decently in Lord Howe's action; who slumbered for some time as a Junior Lord of the Admiralty; who sung psalms, said prayers, and assisted in the burning of Copenhagen, for which he was made a lord."

Gambier showed no greater fitness for his difficult task than was to be expected from his training; and the second member of the commission, Henry Goulburn, could not supply Gambier's deficiencies. Goulburn was Under-Secretary of State to Lord Bathurst; he was a very young man, but a typical under-secretary, combining some of Francis James Jackson's temper with the fixed opinions of the elder Rose, and he had as little idea of diplomacy as was to be expected from an Under-Secretary of State for the colonies. The third and last member was William Adams, Doctor of Civil Law, whose professional knowledge was doubtless supposed to be valuable to the commission, but who was an unknown man, and remained one.

Experience had not convinced the British government that in dealing with the United States it required the best ability it could command. The mistake made by Lord Shelburne in 1783 was re-

peated by Lord Castlereagh in 1814. The miscalculation of relative
ability which led the Foreign Office to assume that Gambier, Goulburn, and William Adams were competent to deal with Gallatin,
J. Q. Adams, J. A. Bayard, Clay, and Russell was not reasonable.
Probably the whole British public service, including Lords and
Commons, could not at that day have produced four men competent to meet Gallatin, J. Q. Adams, Bayard, and Clay on the
ground of American interests; and when Castlereagh opposed to
them Gambier, Goulburn, and Dr. Adams, he sacrificed whatever
advantage diplomacy offered; for in diplomacy as in generalship,
the individual commanded success. . . . (IX, i, 6-14)

The British note of August 19 and the American rejoinder of
August 24 brought about a situation where Lord Castlereagh's influence could make itself felt. Castlereagh had signed the British
instructions of July 28 and August 14, and himself brought the
latter to Ghent, where he passed August 19, before going to Paris
on his way to the Congress at Vienna. He was at Ghent when Goulburn and his colleagues held their conference and wrote their note
of August 19; and he could not be supposed ignorant of their language or acts. Yet when he received at Paris letters from Goulburn,
dated August 24 and 26, he expressed annoyance that the American
commissioners should have been allowed to place England in the
attitude of continuing the war for purposes of conquest, and still
more that the British commissioners should be willing to accept
that issue and break off negotiation upon it. In a letter to Lord
Bathurst, who took charge of the negotiation in his absence, Castlereagh suggested ideas altogether different from those till then advanced in England.

"The substance of the question is," said Castlereagh, "Are we prepared to continue the war for territorial arrangements? And if not,
is this the best time to make our peace, saving all our rights, and
claiming the fisheries, which they do not appear to question? In
which case the territorial questions might be reserved for ulterior
discussion. Or is it desirable to take the chance of the campaign, and
then to be governed by circumstances? . . . If we thought an immediate peace desirable, as they are ready to waive all the abstract
questions, perhaps they might be prepared to sign a provisional article of Indian peace as distinct from limits, and relinquish their
pretensions to the islands in Passamaquoddy Bay, and possibly to
admit minor adjustments of frontier, including a right of communication from Quebec to Halifax across their territory. But while I state

this, I feel the difficulty of so much letting down the question under present circumstances."

At the same time Castlereagh wrote to Goulburn, directing him to wait at Ghent for new instructions from London. Lord Liverpool shared his disapproval of the manner in which the British commissioners had managed the case, and replied to Castlereagh, September 2, that the Cabinet had already acted in the sense he wished:—

"Our commissioners had certainly taken a very erroneous view of our policy. If the negotiation had been allowed to break off upon the two notes already presented, or upon such an answer as they were disposed to return, I am satisfied that the war would have become quite popular in America."

The idea that the war might become popular in America was founded chiefly on the impossibility of an Englishman's conceiving the contrary; but in truth the Ministry most feared that the war might become unpopular in England.

"It is very material to throw the rupture of the negotiation, if it is to take place, upon the Americans," wrote Liverpool, the same day, to the Duke of Wellington; "and not to allow them to say that we have brought forward points as ultimata which were only brought forward for discussion, and at the desire of the American commissioners themselves. The American note is a most impudent one, and, as to all its reasoning, capable of an irresistible answer."

New instructions were accordingly approved in Cabinet. Drawn by Bathurst, and dated September 1, they contained what Liverpool considered an "irresistible answer" to the American note of August 24; but their force of logic was weakened by the admission that the previous British demands, though certainly stated as a *sine qua non,* were in reality not to be regarded as such. In private this retreat was covered by the pretext that it was intended only to keep the negotiation alive until better terms could be exacted.

"We cannot expect that the negotiation will proceed at present," continued Liverpool's letter to Castlereagh; "but I think it not unlikely, after our note has been delivered in, that the American commissioners will propose to refer the subject to their Government. In that case the negotiation may be adjourned till the answer is received, and we shall know the result of the campaign before it can be resumed. If our commander does his duty, I am persuaded we shall have acquired by our arms every point on the Canadian frontier which we ought to insist on keeping."

Lord Gambier and his colleagues communicated their new instructions to the American negotiators in a long note dated September 4, and were answered by a still longer note dated September 9, which was also sent to London, and considered in Cabinet. Bathurst felt no anxiety about the negotiation in its actual stage. Goulburn wrote to him that "as long as we answer their notes, I believe that they will be ready to give us replies," and urged only that Sir George Prevost should hasten his reluctant movements in Canada. Bathurst wrote more instructions, dated September 16, directing his commissioners to abandon the demands for Indian territory and exclusive control of the Lakes, and to ask only that the Indians should be included in the peace. The British commissioners sent their note with these concessions to the Americans September 19; and then for the first time the Americans began to suspect the possibility of serious negotiation. For six weeks they had dealt only with the question whether they should negotiate at all.

The demand that the Indians should be included in the treaty was one that under favorable circumstances the Americans would have rejected; but none of them seriously thought of rejecting it as their affairs then stood. When the American commissioners discussed the subject among themselves, September 20, Adams proposed to break off the negotiation on that issue; but Gallatin good-naturedly overruled him, and Adams would not himself, on cool reflection, have ventured to take such responsibility. Indeed, he suggested an article for an Indian amnesty, practically accepting the British demand. He also yielded to Gallatin the ungrateful task of drafting the answers to the British notes; and thus Gallatin became in effect the head of the commission.

All Gallatin's abilities were needed to fill the place. In his entire public life he had never been required to manage so unruly a set of men. The British commissioners were trying, and especially Goulburn was aggressive in temper and domineering in tone; but with them Gallatin had little trouble. Adams and Clay were persons of a different type, as far removed from British heaviness as they were from the Virginian ease of temper which marked the Cabinet of Jefferson, or the incompetence which characterized that of Madison. Gallatin was obliged to exert all his faculties to control his colleagues; but whenever he succeeded, he enjoyed the satisfaction of feeling that he had colleagues worth controlling. . . . (IX, ii, 24-29)

Liverpool, writing to Castlereagh September 23, said that in his opinion the Cabinet had "now gone to the utmost justifiable point in concession, and if they [the Americans] are so unreasonable as to reject our proposals, we have nothing to do but to fight it out. The military accounts from America are on the whole satisfactory." The news of the cruel humiliation at Blandensburg and the burning of Washington arrived at Ghent October 1 and caused British and Americans alike to expect a long series of British triumphs, especially on Lake Champlain, where they knew the British force to be overwhelming.

Goulburn exerted himself to produce a rupture. His letter of September 26 to Bathurst treated the American offer of an Indian amnesty as a rejection of the British ultimatum. Again Lord Bathurst set him right by sending him, October 5, the draft of a reciprocal article replacing the Indians in their situation before the war; and the British commissioners in a note dated October 8, 1814, communicated this article once more as an ultimatum. Harrison's treaty of July 22 with the Wyandots, Delawares, Shawanees, and other tribes, binding them to take up arms against the British, had then arrived, and this news lessened the interest of both parties in the Indian question. None of the American negotiators were prepared to break off negotiations on that point at such a time, and Clay was so earnest to settle the matter that he took from Gallatin and Adams the task of writing the necessary acceptance of the British ultimatum. Gallatin and Clay decided to receive the British article as according entirely with the American offer of amnesty, and the note was so written.

With this cordial admission of the British ultimatum the Americans coupled an intimation that the time had come when an exchange of general projects for the proposed treaty should be made. More than two months of discussion had then resulted only in eliminating the Indians from the dispute, and in agreeing to maintain silence in regard to the Lakes. Another great difficulty which had been insuperable was voluntarily removed by President Madison and his Cabinet, who after long and obstinate resistance at last authorized the commissioners, by instructions dated June 27, to omit impressment from the treaty. Considering the frequent positive declarations of the United States government, besides the rejection of Monroe's treaty in 1807 and of Admiral Warren's and

Sir George Prevost's armistice of 1812 for want of an explicit concession on that point, Monroe's letter of June 27 was only to be excused as an act of common sense or of necessity. The President preferred to represent it as an act of common sense, warranted by the peace in Europe, which promised to offer no further occasion for the claim or the denial of the British right. On the same principle the subject of blockades was withdrawn from discussion; and these concessions, balanced by the British withdrawal from the Indian ultimatum and the Lake armaments, relieved the American commissioners of all their insuperable difficulties.

The British commissioners were not so easily rescued from their untenable positions. The American note of October 13, sent as usual to London, was answered by Bathurst October 18 and 20, in instructions revealing the true British terms more completely than had yet been ventured. Bathurst at length came to the cardinal point of the negotiation. As the American commissioners had said in their note of August 24, the British government must choose between the two ordinary bases of treaties of peace,—the state before the war, or *status ante bellum;* and the state of possession, or *uti possidetis.* Until the middle of October, 1814, the *uti possidetis,* as a basis of negotiation, included whatever country might have been occupied by Sir George Prevost in his September campaign. Bathurst from the first intended to insist on the state of possession, but had not thought proper to avow it. His instructions of October 18 and 20 directed the British commissioners to come to the point, and to claim the basis of *uti possidetis* from the American negotiators:—

"On their admitting to be the basis on which they are ready to negotiate, but not before they have admitted it, you will proceed to state the mutual accommodations which may be entered into in conformity with this basis. The British occupy Fort Michillimackinaw, Fort Niagara, and all the country east of the Penobscot. On the other hand, the forces of the United States occupy Fort Erie and Fort Amherstburg [Malden]. On the government of the United States consenting to restore these two forts, Great Britain is ready to restore the forts of Castine and Machias, retaining Fort Niagara and Fort Michillimackinaw."

Thus the British demand, which had till then been intended to include half of Maine and the whole south bank of the St. Lawrence River from Plattsburg to Sackett's Harbor, suddenly fell to a demand for Moose Island, a right of way across the northern angle of Maine, Fort Niagara with five miles circuit, and the Island of Mackinaw. The reason for the new spirit of moderation was not far to seek. On the afternoon of October 17, while the British Cabinet was still deliberating on the basis of *uti possidetis*, news reached London that the British invasion of northern New York, from which so much had been expected, had totally failed, and that Prevost's large army had precipitately retreated into Canada. The London "Times" of October 19 was frank in its expressions of disappointment:—

"This is a lamentable event to the civilized world. . . . The subversion of that system of fraud and malignity which constitutes the whole policy of the Jeffersonian school . . . was an event to which we should have bent and yet must bend all our energies. The present American government must be displaced, or it will sooner or later plant its poisoned dagger in the heart of the parent State."   . . . (IX, ii, 31-35)

Castlereagh at Vienna found himself unable to make the full influence of England felt, so long as such mortifying disasters by land and sea proved her inability to deal with an enemy she persisted in calling contemptible.

On the American commissioners the news came, October 21, with the effect of a reprieve from execution. Gallatin was deeply moved; Adams could not believe the magnitude of the success; but as far as regarded their joint action, the overthrow of England's scheme produced no change. Their tone had always been high, and they saw no advantage to be gained by altering it. The British commissioners sent to them, October 21, the substance of the new instructions, offering the basis of *uti possidetis*, subject to modifications for mutual convenience. The Americans by common consent, October 23, declined to treat on that basis, or on any other than the mutual restoration of territory. They thought that the British government was still playing with them, when in truth Lord Bathurst had yielded the chief part of the original British demand, and had come to what the whole British empire regarded as essentials,— the right of way to Quebec, and the exclusion of American fishermen from British shores and waters.

The American note of October 24, bluntly rejecting the basis of *uti possidetis*, created a feeling akin to consternation in the British Cabinet. At first, ministers assumed that the war must go on and deliberated only on the point to be preferred for a rupture. "We still think it desirable to gain a little more time before the negotiation is brought to a close," wrote Liverpool to the Duke of Wellington, October 28; and on the same day he wrote to Castlereagh at Vienna to warn him that the American war "will probably now be of some duration," and treating of its embarrassments without disguise. The Czar's conduct at Vienna had annoyed and alarmed all the great powers, and the American war gave him a decisive advantage over England; but even without the Russian complication, the prospect for ministers was not cheering.

"Looking to a continuance of the American war, our financial state is far from satisfactory," wrote Lord Liverpool; ". . . the American war will not cost us less than £10,000,000, in addition to our peace establishment and other expenses. We must expect, therefore, to hear it said that the property tax is continued for the purpose of securing a better frontier for Canada."

A week passed without bringing encouragement to the British Cabinet. On the contrary the Ministry learned that a vigorous prosecution of hostilities would cost much more than ten million pounds, and when Liverpool next wrote to Castlereagh, November 2, although he could still see "little prospect for our negotiations at Ghent ending in peace," he added that "the continuance of the American war will entail upon us a prodigious expense, much more than we had any idea of." A Cabinet meeting was to be held the next day, November 3, to review the whole course of policy as to America.

Throughout the American difficulties, from first to last, the most striking quality shown by the British government was the want of intelligence which caused the war, and marked the conduct of both the war and the negotiations. If the foreign relations of every government were marked by the same character, politics could be no more than rivalry in the race to blunder; but in October, 1814, another quality almost equally striking became evident. The weakness of British councils was as remarkable as their want of intelligence. The government of England had exasperated the Americans to an animosity that could not forget or forgive, and every dictate of self-interest required that it should carry out its policy to the end. Even domestic politics in Parliament might have been more easily managed by drawing public criticism to America, while in no event could taxes be reduced to satisfy the public demand. Another year of war was the consistent and natural course for ministers to prefer.

So the Cabinet evidently thought; but instead of making a decision, the Cabinet council of November 3 resorted to the expedient of shifting responsibility upon the Duke of Wellington. The Duke was then Ambassador at Paris. His life had been threatened by angry officers of Napoleon, who could not forgive his victories at Vittoria and Toulouse. For his own security he might be sent to Canada, and if he went, he should go with full powers to close the war as he pleased.

The next day, November 4, Liverpool wrote to Wellington, explaining the wishes of the Cabinet, and inviting him to take the entire command in Canada, in order to bring the war to an honorable conclusion. Wellington replied November 9,—and his words were the more interesting because, after inviting and receiving so decided an opinion from so high an authority, the Government could not easily reject it. Wellington began by reviewing the military situation, and closed by expressing his opinion on the diplomatic contest:—

"I have already told you and Lord Bathurst that I feel no objection to going to America, though I don't promise to myself much success there. I believe there are troops enough there for the defence of Canada forever, and even for the accomplishment of any reasonable offensive plan that could be formed from the Canadian frontier. I am quite sure that all the American armies of which I have ever read would not beat out of a field of battle the troops that went from Bordeaux last summer, if common precautions and care were taken of them. That which appears to me to be wanting in America is not a general, or a general officer and troops, but a naval superiority on the Lakes."

These views did not altogether accord with those of Americans, who could not see that the British generals made use of the Lakes even when controlling them, but who saw the troops of Wellington retire from one field of battle after another,—at Plattsburg, Baltimore, and New Orleans,—while taking more than common precautions. Wellington's military comments showed little interest in American affairs, and evidently he saw nothing to be gained by going to Canada. His diplomatic ideas betrayed the same bias:—

"In regard to your present negotiations, I confess that I think you have no right, from the state of the war, to demand any concession of territory from America. . . . You have not been able to carry it into the enemy's territory, notwithstanding your military success and now undoubted military superiority, and have not even cleared your own territory on the point of attack. You cannot on any principle of equality in negotiation claim a cession of territory excepting in exchange for other advantages which you have in your power. . . . Then if this reasoning be true, why stipulate for the *uti possidetis?* You get no territory; indeed, the state of your military operations, however creditable, does not entitle you to demand any."

After such an opinion from the first military authority of England, the British Ministry had no choice but to abandon its claim for territory. Wellington's letter reached London about November 13, and was duly considered in the Cabinet. Liverpool wrote to Castlereagh, November 18, that the Ministry had made its decision; the claim for territory was to be abandoned. For this retreat he alleged various excuses,—such as the unsatisfactory state of the negotiations at Vienna, and the alarming condition of France; the finances, the depression of rents, and the temper of Parliament. Such reasoning would have counted for nothing in the previous month of May, but six months wrought a change in public feeling. The war had lost public favor. Even the colonial and shipping interests and the navy were weary of it, while the army had little to expect from it but hard service and no increase of credit. Every Englishman who came in contact with Americans seemed to suffer. Broke, the only victor by sea, was a life-long invalid; and Brock and Ross,[30] the only victors on land, had paid for their success with their lives. . . . (IX, ii, 36-42)

The treaty of 1783 coupled the American right of fishing in British waters and curing fish on British shores with the British right of navigating the Mississippi River. For that arrangement the elder Adams was responsible. The fisheries were a Massachusetts interest. At Paris in 1783 John Adams, in season and out of season, with his colleagues and with the British negotiators, insisted, with the intensity of conviction, that the fishing rights which the New England people held while subjects of the British crown were theirs by no grant or treaty, but as a natural right, which could not be extinguished by war; and that where British subjects had a right to fish, whether on coasts or shores, in bays, inlets, creeks, or harbors, Americans had the same right, to be exercised wherever and whenever they pleased. John Adams's persistence secured the article

[30] Isaac Brock was killed at Queenstown Heights, October 13, 1812, and Robert Ross was killed, September 12, 1814, before Baltimore.

of the definitive treaty, which, without expressly admitting a natural right, coupled the inshore fisheries and the navigation of the Mississippi with the recognition of independence. In 1814 as in 1783 John Adams clung to his trophies, and his son would have waged indefinite war rather than break his father's heart by sacrificing what he had won; but at Ghent the son stood in isolation which the father in the worst times had never known. Massachusetts left him to struggle alone for a principle that needed not only argument but force to make it victorious. Governor Strong did not even write to him as he did to Pickering, that Massachusetts would give an equivalent in territory for the fisheries. As far as the State could influence the result, the fisheries were to be lost by default.

Had Adams encountered only British opposition he might have overborne it as his father had done; but since 1783 the West had become a political power, and Louisiana had been brought into the Union. If the fisheries were recognized as an indefeasible right by the treaty of 1783, the British liberty of navigating the Mississippi was another indefeasible right, which must revive with peace. The Western people naturally objected to such a proposition. Neither they nor the Canadians could be blamed for unwillingness to impose a mischievous servitude forever upon their shores, and Clay believed his popularity to depend on preventing an express recognition of the British right to navigate the Mississippi. Either Clay or Adams was sure to refuse signing any treaty which expressly sacrificed the local interests of either.

In this delicate situation only the authority and skill of Gallatin saved the treaty. At the outset of the discussion, October 30, Gallatin quietly took the lead from Adams's hands, and assumed the championship of the fisheries by proposing to renew both privileges, making the one an equivalent for the other. Clay resisted obstinately, while Gallatin gently and patiently overbore him. When Gallatin's proposal was put to the vote November 5, Clay and Russell alone opposed it,—and the support then given by Russell to Clay was never forgotten by Adams. Clay still refusing to sign the offer, Gallatin continued his pressure, until at last, November 10, Clay consented to insert, not in the project of treaty, but in the note which accompanied it, a paragraph declaring that the commissioners were not authorized to bring into discussion any of the rights hitherto enjoyed in the fisheries: "From their nature, and from the peculiar character of the treaty of 1783 by which they were recognized, no further stipulation has been deemed necessary by the Government of the United States to entitle them to the full enjoyment of all of them."

Clay signed the note, though unwillingly; and it was sent, November 10, with the treaty project, to the British commissioners, who forwarded it to London, where it arrived at the time when the British Cabinet had at last decided on peace. Bathurst sent his reply in due course; and Goulburn's disgust was great to find that instead of breaking negotiation on the point of the fisheries as he wished, he was required once more to give way. "You know that I was never much inclined to give way to the Americans," he wrote, November 25. "I am still less inclined to do so after the statement of our demands with which the negotiation opened, and which has in every point of view proved most unfortunate."

The British reply, dated November 26, took no notice of the American reservation as to the fisheries, but inserted in the project the old right of navigating the Mississippi. Both Bathurst and Goulburn thought that their silence, after the American declaration, practically conceded the American right to the fisheries, though Gambier and Dr. Adams thought differently. In either case the British note of November 26, though satisfactory to Adams, was far from agreeable to Clay, who was obliged to endanger the peace in order to save the Mississippi. Adams strongly inclined to take the British project precisely as it was offered, but Gallatin overruled him, and Clay would certainly have refused to sign. In discussing the subject, November 28, Gallatin proposed to accept the article on the navigation of the Mississippi if the British would add a provision recognizing the fishing rights. Clay lost his temper, and intimated something more than willingness to let Massachusetts pay for the pleasure of peace; but during the whole day of November 28, and with the same patience November 29, Gallatin continued urging Clay and restraining Adams, until at last on the third day he brought the matter to the point he wished.

The result of this long struggle saved not indeed the fisheries, but the peace. Clay made no further protest when, in conference with the British commissioners December 1, the Americans offered to renew both the disputed rights. Their proposal was sent to London, and was answered by Bathurst December 6, in a letter offering to set aside for future negotiation the terms under which the old fishing liberty and the navigation of the Mississippi should be continued for fair equivalents. The British commissioners communicated this suggestion in conference December 10, and threw new dissension among the Americans.

The British offer to reserve both disputed rights for future negotiation implied that both rights were forfeited, or subject to
forfeit, by war,—an admission which Adams could not make, but
which the other commissioners could not reject. At that point
Adams found himself alone. Even Gallatin admitted that the claim
to the natural right of catching and curing fish on British shores
was untenable, and could never be supported. Adams's difficulties
were the greater because the question of peace and war was reduced
to two points,—the fisheries and Moose Island,—both interesting to
Massachusetts alone. Yet the Americans were unwilling to yield
without another struggle, and decided still to resist the British
claim as inconsistent with the admitted basis of the *status ante
bellum*.

The struggle with the British commissioners then became warm.
A long conference, December 12, brought no conclusion. The treaty
of 1783 could neither be followed nor ignored, and perplexed the
Englishmen as much as the Americans. During December 13 and
December 14, Adams continued to press his colleagues to assert the
natural right to the fisheries, and to insist on the permanent character of the treaty of 1783; but Gallatin would not consent to make
that point an ultimatum. All the commissioners except Adams resigned themselves to the sacrifice of the fisheries; but Gallatin
decided to make one more effort before abandoning the struggle,
and with that object drew up a note rejecting the British stipulation because it implied the abandonment of a right, but offering
either to be silent as to both the fisheries and the Mississippi, or
to admit a general reference to further negotiation of all subjects
in dispute, so expressed as to imply no abandonment of right.

The note was signed and sent December 14, and the Americans
waited another week for the answer. . . . (IX, ii, 44-50)

The extraordinary patience and judgment of Gallatin, aided by
the steady support of Bayard, carried all the American points without sacrificing either Adams or Clay, and with no quarrel of serious
importance on any side. When Lord Bathurst received the American note of December 14, he replied December 19, yielding the
last advantage he possessed: "The Prince Regent regrets to find
that there does not appear any prospect of being able to arrive at
such an arrangement with regard to the fisheries as would have the
effect of coming to a full and satisfactory explanation on that subject"; but since this was the case, the disputed article might be altogether omitted.

Thus the treaty became simply a cessation of hostilities, leaving every claim on either side open for future settlement. The formality of signature was completed December 24, and closed an era of American history. In substance, the treaty sacrificed much on both sides for peace. The Americans lost their claims for British spoliations, and were obliged to admit question of their right to Eastport and their fisheries in British waters; the British failed to establish their principles of impressment and blockade, and admitted question of their right to navigate the Mississippi and trade with the Indians. Perhaps at the moment the Americans were the chief losers; but they gained their greatest triumph in referring all their disputes to be settled by time, the final negotiator, whose decision they could safely trust. . . . (IX, ii, 52-53)

The prosperity that followed the Peace of Ghent suffered no check during the year 1816, or during the remainder of Madison's term. The exports of domestic produce, officially valued at $45,000,-000 for the year ending Sept. 30, 1815, were valued at nearly $65,000,000 for the following year, and exceeded $68,000,000 for 1817. The Southern States still supplied two thirds of the exported produce. Cotton to the amount of $24,000,000, tobacco valued at nearly $13,000,000, and rice at $3,500,000, contributed more than forty of the sixty-five millions of domestic exports in 1816. The tables showed that while South Carolina, Georgia, and Louisiana gained with unparalleled rapidity, New England lost ground, and New York only maintained its uniform movement. While the domestic exports of Georgia and Louisiana trebled in value, those of New York increased from eight to fourteen millions.

Notwithstanding the great importations from Europe which under ordinary conditions would have counterbalanced the exports, the exchanges soon turned in favor of the United States. Before the close of 1816 specie in considerable quantities began to flow into the country. Canada, being nearest, felt the drain first, and suffered much inconvenience from it; but during the summer of 1816 and 1817 Europe also shipped much specie to America. Every ship brought some amount, until the export began to affect the Bank of England, which at last found its bullion diminishing with alarming rapidity. The returns showed a drain beginning in July or August, 1817, when the Bank of England held £11,668,000, until August, 1819, when the supply was reduced to £3,595,000; and in the interval a commercial crisis, with a general destruction of credit, occurred. The reaction could not fail in the end to affect

America as it affected England, but the first result was stimulating beyond all previous experience. In England the drain of specie embarrassed government in returning to specie payments. In the United States the influx of specie made the return easy, if not necessary.

The recovery of internal exchanges kept pace with the influx of specie. At Boston, July 27, 1816, United States six-per-cent bonds were quoted at eighty-five, and Treasury notes at ninety-four to ninety-four and one-half; at New York six-per-cents stood at ninety, and Treasury notes at par; in Philadelphia six-per-cents were worth ninety-eight, and Treasury notes one hundred and seven; in Baltimore six-per-cents were selling at one hundred and two, and Treasury notes at one hundred and twelve. During the next five months the recovery was steady and rapid. The banks of New York, September 26, began to cash their one-dollar notes, thus relieving the community from the annoyance of fractional currency. October 26 the six-per-cents stood at ninety-two in Boston, at ninety-eight in Philadelphia, and at one hundred and one and one-half in Baltimore. November 28 they sold at ninety-six in Boston; November 30 they sold at ninety-six and one-quarter in New York, at one hundred and one and one-half in Philadelphia, and at one hundred and five in Baltimore. January 1, 1817, the Treasury resumed payments at Boston in Boston money, and no further discredit attached to government securities.

The banks of the Middle States were less disposed than the government to hasten the return of specie payments. In order to do so, they were obliged to contract their circulation and discounts to an extent that would have been unendurable in any time but one of great prosperity; and only the threats of Dallas overcame their reluctance, even under most favorable conditions. Both Dallas and the President were irritated by their slowness. July 22, 1816, the Secretary of the Treasury issued a circular warning them that, at whatever cost, the Treasury must carry into effect the order of Congress to collect the revenue, after February 20, 1817, only in specie or its equivalent. "The banks in the States to the South," he said, "and to the west of Maryland, are ready and willing, it is believed, to co-operate in the same measure. The objection, or the obstacle to the measure, principally rests with the banks of the Middle States." Dallas invited them to assist the Treasury in resuming specie payments with the least possible delay; and accordingly the banks of the Middle States held a convention at Philadelphia, August 6, to consider their course.

This convention, on discussing the possibility of resumption, agreed that the banks needed more time than the government was disposed to allow. Credit had been necessarily expanded by the unusual scale of commerce and enterprise. So sudden and violent contraction as was required for specie payments could not fail to distress the public, and might cause great suffering. Yet in some degree the new United States Bank[31] could relieve this pressure; and therefore, the resumption should not be attempted by the State banks until the National Bank should be fairly opened and ready to begin its discounts. The State banks in convention foresaw, or imagined, that the United States Bank could not begin operations so early as February 20, 1817, and they declined to risk resumption without its aid. Acting on this impression, they met Dallas's urgency by a formal recommendation that their banks should begin to pay specie, not on the 20th of February, but on the first Monday of July, 1817.

This decision, though unsatisfactory to Dallas and the President, could not be considered unreasonable. Credit was expanded beyond the limit of safety, and the government was largely responsible for the expansion. Many of the State banks were probably unsound from the first, and needed careful management. Between 1810 and 1830, on a total capital of one hundred and forty millions, the bank failures amounted to thirty million, or more than one fifth of the whole. In Pennsylvania the country banks reduced their issues from $4,756,000 in November, 1816, to $1,318,000 in November, 1819. The latter moment was one of extreme depression, but the former was probably not that of the greatest expansion. When the banks of the Middle States held their convention, August 6, 1816, contraction had already begun, and steadily continued, while specie flowed into the country to supply a foundation for bank paper. Under such circumstances the banks asked no extravagant favor in recommending that eleven months, instead of seven, should be allowed for resumption.

Dallas was not disposed to concede this favor. Having at last the necessary machinery for controlling the State banks, he used it with the same vigor that marked all his acts. No sooner had the convention announced its unwillingness to co-operate with the Treasury in executing the order of Congress, than Dallas issued instructions, August 16, hastening the preparations for opening the National Bank as early as January 1, 1817. Soon afterward, Sep-

[31] "New United States Bank": The Second Bank of the United States was chartered on March 14, 1816.

tember 12, he renewed his notice that the notes of suspended banks would be rejected by the Treasury after Feb. 20, 1817.

The Bank subscription was filled in August, a deficit of three million dollars being taken by Stephen Girard [32] in a single mass. In October the board of directors was chosen by the shareholders, and in November the directors met and elected as President the former Secretary of the Navy, William Jones. One of their first acts was much debated, and was strongly opposed in the board of directors by J. J. Astor. They sent John Sergeant, of Philadelphia, abroad with authority to purchase some millions of bullion; and his mission was calculated to impress on the public the conviction that specie payments were to be resumed as soon as the Bank could open its doors.

Hurried by Dallas, the Bank actually began its operations in January, 1817, and under the double pressure from the Treasury the State banks had no choice but to yield. Another meeting was held at Philadelphia, February 1, consisting of delegates from the banks of New York, Philadelphia, Baltimore and Richmond. The convention entered into a compact with the Secretary of the Treasury to resume payments, on certain conditions, at the day fixed by Congress. The compact was carried into effect February 20, a few days before the close of Madison's Presidency. Its success was magical. In New York, at ten o'clock on the morning of February 20, species was at two and one-half per cent premium. The banks opened their doors, and in half an hour all was once more regular and normal.

Thus the worst financial evil of the war was removed within two years after the proclamation of peace. A debt of about one hundred and thirty million dollars remained; but the people which only twenty years before had shrunk with fear and disgust from a debt of $80,000,000, gave scarcely a thought in 1816 to their funded obligations. The difference between the two periods was not so much economical as political. Population and wealth had increased, but the experience of the people had advanced more rapidly than their numbers or capital. In measuring the political movement shrewd judges might easily err, for the elections of 1816 showed little apparent change in parties; but in truth parties had outgrown their principles, and in politics, as in finance, the close of Madison's Administration obliterated old distinctions. . . . (IX, vi, 126-32)

[32] Stephen Girard: Philadelphia banker and philanthropist.

In returning to their early views of resistance to centralization,[33] Madison and Jefferson must have maintained the invalidity of precedents to affect the Constitution. The veto seemed to create a new classification of public acts into such as were Constitutional; such as were unconstitutional, but still valid; and such as were both unconstitutional and invalid. The admitted validity of an act, like the purchase of Louisiana, even though it were acknowledged to be unconstitutional, did not create a precedent which authorized a repetition of a similar act.

Viewed only from a political standpoint, the veto marked the first decided reaction against the centralizing effect of the war. Unfortunately for the old Republican party, whose principles were thus for a second time to be adopted in appearance by a majority of the people, sixteen years had affected national character; and although precedents might not bind Congress or Executive, they marked the movement of society.

The Veto Message of March 3, 1817, was Madison's Farewell Address. The next day he surrendered to Monroe the powers of government, and soon afterward retired to Virginia, to pass, with his friend Jefferson, the remaining years of a long life, watching the results of his labors. . . . (IX, vi, 153)

The result of the sixteen years, considered only in the economical development of the Union, was decisive. Although population increased more rapidly than was usual in human experience, wealth accumulated still faster. From such statistics as the times afforded, a strong probability has been shown that while population doubled within twenty-three years, wealth doubled within twenty. Statistics covering the later period of national growth, warrant the belief that a valuation of $1,742,000,000 in 1800 corresponded to a valuation of $3,734,000,000 in 1820; and that if a valuation of $328 per capita is assumed for 1800, a valuation of $386 per capita may be estimated for 1820.

These sixteen years set at rest the natural doubts that had attended the nation's birth. The rate of increase both in population and wealth was established and permanent, unless indeed it should become even more rapid. Every serious difficulty which seemed alarming to the people of the Union in 1800 had been removed or

[33] Having accepted a Second Bank of the United States, and the mildly protective Tariff of 1816, Madison refused to complete this nationalist program by signing a bill to create a permanent fund for internal improvements. He vetoed this so-called "Bonus Bill" on March 3, 1817.

had sunk from notice in 1816. With the disappearance of every immediate peril, foreign or domestic, society could devote all its energies, intellectual and physical, to its favorite objects. This result was not the only or even the chief proof that economical progress was to be at least as rapid in the future as at the time when the nation had to struggle with political difficulties. Not only had the people during these sixteen years escaped from dangers, they had also found the means of supplying their chief needs. Besides clearing away every obstacle to the occupation and development of their continent as far as the Mississippi River, they created the steamboat, the most efficient instrument yet conceived for developing such a country. The continent lay before them, like an uncovered ore bed. They could see, and they could even calculate with reasonable accuracy, the wealth it could be made to yield. With almost the certainty of a mathematical formula, knowing the rate of increase of wealth, they could read in advance their economical history for at least a hundred years. . . . (IX, vii, 172-74)

10.

American Character in 1816:
The Limits of Mechanical Evolution

Until 1815 nothing in the future of the American Union was regarded as settled. As late as January, 1815, division into several nationalities was still thought to be possible. Such a destiny, repeating the usual experience of history, was not necessarily more unfortunate than the career of a single nationality wholly American; for if the effects of divided nationality were certain to be unhappy, those of a single society with equal certainty defied experience or sound speculation. One uniform and harmonious system appealed to the imagination as a triumph of human progress, offering prospects of peace and ease, contentment and philanthropy, such as the world had not seen; but it invited dangers, formidable because unusual or altogether unknown. The corruption of such a system might prove to be proportionate with its dimensions, and uniformity might lead to evils as serious as were commonly ascribed to diversity.

The laws of human progress were matter not for dogmatic faith, but for study; and although society instinctively regarded small States, with their clashing interests and incessant wars, as the chief obstacle to improvement, such progress as the world knew had been coupled with those drawbacks. The few examples offered by history of great political societies, relieved from external competition or rivalry, were not commonly thought encouraging. War had been the severest test of political and social character, laying bare whatever was feeble, and calling out whatever was strong; and the effect of removing such a test was an untried problem.

In 1815 for the first time Americans ceased to doubt the path they were to follow. Not only was the unity of their nation established, but its probable divergence from older societies was also well defined. Already in 1817 the difference between Europe and America was decided. In politics the distinction was more evident than in social, religious, literary, or scientific directions; and the result was singular. For a time the aggressions of England and France forced the United States into a path that seemed to lead toward European methods of government; but the popular resistance, or inertia, was so great that the most popular party leaders failed to overcome it, and no sooner did foreign dangers disappear than the system began to revert to American practices; the national government tried to lay aside its assumed powers. When Madison vetoed the bill for internal improvements he could have had no other motive than that of restoring to the government, as far as possible, its original American character.

The result was not easy to understand in theory or to make efficient in practice; but while the drift of public opinion, and still more of practical necessity, drew the government slowly toward the European standard of true political sovereignty, nothing showed that the compromise, which must probably serve the public purpose, was to be European in form or feeling. As far as politics supplied a test, the national character had already diverged from any foreign type. Opinions might differ whether the political movement was progressive or retrograde, but in any case the American, in his political character, was a new variety of man.

The social movement was also decided. The war gave a severe shock to the Anglican sympathies of society, and peace seemed to widen the breach between European and American tastes. Interest in Europe languished after Napoleon's overthrow. France ceased to affect American opinion. England became an object of less alarm. Peace produced in the United States a social and economical revolution which greatly curtailed the influence of New England, and with it the social authority of Great Britain. The invention of the steamboat counterbalanced ocean commerce. The South and West gave to society a character more aggressively American than had been known before. That Europe, within certain limits, might tend toward American ideas was possible, but that America should under any circumstances follow the experiences of European development might thenceforward be reckoned as improbable. American character was formed, if not fixed.

The scientific interest of American history centered in national character, and in the workings of a society destined to become vast, in which individuals were important chiefly as types. Although this kind of interest was different from that of European history, it was at least as important to the world. Should history ever become a true science, it must expect to establish its laws, not from the complicated story of rival European nationalities, but from the economical evolution of a great democracy. North America was the most favorable field on the globe for the spread of a society so large, uniform, and isolated as to answer the purposes of science. There a single homogeneous society could easily attain proportions of three or four hundred million persons, under conditions of undisturbed growth.

In Europe or Asia, except perhaps in China, undisturbed social evolution had been unknown. Without disturbance, evolution seemed to cease. Wherever disturbance occurred, permanence was impossible. Every people in turn adapted itself to the law of necessity. Such a system as that of the United States could hardly have existed for half a century in Europe except under the protection of another power. In the fierce struggle characteristic of European society, systems were permanent in nothing except in the general law, that, whatever other character they might possess they must always be chiefly military.

The want of permanence was not the only or the most confusing obstacle to the treatment of European history as a science. The intensity of the struggle gave prominence to the individual, until the hero seemed all, society nothing; and what was worse for science, the men were far more interesting than the societies. In the dramatic view of history, the hero deserved more to be studied than the community to which he belonged; in truth, he was the society, which existed only to produce him and to perish with him. Against such a view historians were among the last to protest, and protested but faintly when they did so at all. They felt as strongly as their audiences that the highest achievements were alone worth remembering either in history or in art, and that a reiteration of commonplaces was commonplace. With all the advantages of European movement and color, few historians succeeded in enlivening or dignifying the lack of motive, intelligence, and morality, the helplessness characteristic of many long periods in the face of crushing problems, and the futility of human efforts to escape from difficulties religious, political, and social. In a period extending over four or five thousand years, more or less capable of historical treatment, historians were content to illustrate here and there the most dramatic moments of the most striking communities. The hero was their favorite. War was the chief field of heroic action, and even the history of England was chiefly the story of war.

The history of the United States promised to be free from such disturbances. War counted for little, the hero for less; on the people alone the eye could permanently rest. The steady growth of a vast population without the social distinctions that confused other histories,—without kings, nobles, or armies; without church, traditions, and prejudices,—seemed a subject for the man of science rather than for dramatists or poets. To scientific treatment only one great obstacle existed. Americans, like Europeans, were not disposed to make of their history a mechanical evolution. They felt that they even more than other nations needed the heroic element, because they breathed an atmosphere of peace and industry where heroism could seldom be displayed; and in unconscious protest against their own social conditions they adorned with imaginary qualities scores of supposed leaders, whose only merit was their faculty of reflecting a popular trait. Instinctively they clung to ancient history as though conscious that of all misfortunes that would befall the national character, the greatest would be the loss of the established ideals which alone ennobled human weakness. Without heroes, the national character of the United States had few charms of imagination even to Americans.

Historians and readers maintained Old World standards. No historian cared to hasten the coming of an epoch when man should study his own history in the same spirit and by the same methods with which he studied the formation of a crystal. Yet history had its scientific as well as its human side, and in American history the scientific interest was greater than the human. Elsewhere the student could study under better conditions the evolution of the individual, but nowhere could he study so well the evolution of a race. The interest of such a subject exceeded that of any other branch of science, for it brought mankind within sight of its own end.

Travelers in Switzerland who stepped across the Rhine where it flowed from its glacier could follow its course among mediaeval towns and feudal ruins, until it became a highway for modern industry, and at last arrived at a permanent equilibrium in the ocean. American history followed the same course. With prehistoric glaciers and mediaeval feudalism the story had little to do; but from the moment it came within sight of the ocean it acquired interest almost painful. A child could find his way in a river valley, and a hoy could float on the waters of Holland; but science alone could sound the depths of the ocean, measure its currents, foretell its storms, or fix its relations to the system of Nature. In a democratic ocean science could see something ultimate. Man could go no further. The atom might move, but the general equilibrium could not change.

Whether the scientific or the heroic view were taken, in either case the starting-point was the same, and the chief object of interest was to define national character. Whether the figures of history were treated as heroes or as types, they must be taken to represent the people. American types were especially worth study if they were to represent the greatest democratic evolution the world could know. Readers might judge for themselves what share the individual possessed in creating or shaping the nation; but whether it was small or great, the nation could be understood only by studying the individual. For that reason, in the story of Jefferson and Madison individuals retained their old interest as types of character, if not as sources of power.

In the American character antipathy to war ranked first among political traits. The majority of Americans regarded war in a peculiar light, the consequence of comparative security. No European nation could have conducted a war, as the people of America conducted the War of 1812. The possibility of doing so without destruction explained the existence of the national trait, and assured its continuance. In politics, the divergence of America from Europe perpetuated itself in the popular instinct for peaceable methods. The Union took shape originally on the general lines that divided the civil from the military elements of the British constitution. The party of Jefferson and Gallatin was founded on dislike of every function of government necessary in a military system. Although Jefferson carried his pacific theories to an extreme, and brought about a military reaction, the reactionary movement was neither universal, violent, nor lasting; and society showed no sign of changing its convictions. With greater strength the country might acquire greater familiarity with warlike methods, but in the same degree was less likely to suffer any general change of habits. Nothing but prolonged intestine contests could convert the population of an entire continent into a race of warriors.

A people whose chief trait was antipathy to war, and to any system organized with military energy, could scarcely develop great results in national administration; yet the Americans prided themselves chiefly on their political capacity. Even the war did not undeceive them, although the incapacity brought into evidence by the war was undisputed, and was most remarkable among the communities which believed themselves to be the most gifted with political sagacity. Virginia and Massachusetts by turns admitted failure in dealing with issues so simple that the newest societies, like Tennessee and Ohio, understood them by instinct. That incapacity in national politics should appear as a leading trait in American character was unexpected by Americans, but might naturally result from their conditions. The better test of American character was not political but social, and was to be found not in the government but in the people.

The sixteen years of Jefferson's and Madison's rule furnished international tests of popular intelligence upon which Americans could depend. The ocean was the only open field for competition among nations. Americans enjoyed there no natural or artificial advantages over Englishmen, Frenchmen, or Spaniards; indeed, all these countries possessed navies, resources, and experience greater than were to be found in the United States. Yet the Americans developed, in the course of twenty years, a surprising degree of skill in naval affairs. The evidence of their success was to be found nowhere so complete as in the avowals of Englishmen who knew best the history of naval progress. The American invention of the fast-sailing schooner or clipper was the more remarkable because, of all American inventions, this alone sprang from direct competition with Europe. During ten centuries of struggle the nations of Europe had labored to obtain superiority over each other in ship construction, yet Americans instantly made improvements which gave them superiority, and which Europeans were unable immediately to imitate even after seeing them. Not only were American vessels better in model, faster in sailing, easier and quicker in handling, and more economical in working than the European, but they were also better equipped. The English complained as a grievance that the Americans adopted new and unwarranted devices in naval warfare; that their vessels were heavier and better constructed, and their missiles of unusual shape and improper use. The Americans resorted to expedients that had not been tried before, and excited a mixture of irritation and respect in the English service, until Yankee smartness became a national misdemeanor.

The English admitted themselves to be slow to change their habits, but the French were both quick and scientific; yet Americans did on the ocean what the French, under stronger inducements, failed to do. The French privateer preyed upon British commerce for twenty years without seriously injuring it; but no sooner did the American privateer sail from French ports, than the rates of insurance doubled in London, and an outcry for protection arose among English shippers which the Admiralty could not calm. The British newspapers were filled with assertions that the American cruiser was the superior of any vessel of its class, and threatened to overthrow England's supremacy on the ocean.

Another test of relative intelligence was furnished by the battles at sea. Instantly after the loss of the "Guerrière" the English discovered and complained that American gunnery was superior to their own. They explained their inferiority by the length of time that had elapsed since their navy had found on the ocean an enemy to fight. Every vestige of hostile fleets had been swept away, until, after the battle of Trafalgar, British frigates ceased practice with their guns. Doubtless the British navy had become somewhat careless in the absence of a dangerous enemy, but Englishmen were themselves aware that some other cause must have affected their losses. Nothing showed that Nelson's line-of-battle ships, frigates, or sloops were as a rule better fought than the "Macedonian" and "Java," the "Avon" and "Reindeer." Sir Howard Douglas, the chief authority on the subject, attempted in vain to explain British reverses by the deterioration of British gunnery. His analysis showed only that American gunnery was extraordinarily good. Of all vessels, the sloop-of-war,—on account of its smallness, its quick motion, and its more accurate armament of thirty-two-pound carronades, —offered the best test of relative gunnery, and Sir Howard Douglas in commenting upon the destruction of the "Peacock" and "Avon" could only say,—

"In these two actions it is clear that the fire of the British vessels was thrown too high, and that the ordnance of their opponents were expressly and carefully aimed at and took effect chiefly in the hull."

The battle of the "Hornet" and "Penguin" as well as those of the "Reindeer" and "Avon," showed that the excellence of American gunnery continued till the close of the war. Whether at point-blank range or at long-distance practice, the Americans used guns as they had never been used at sea before.

None of the reports of former British victories showed that the British fire had been more destructive at any previous time than in 1812, and no report of any commander since the British navy existed showed so much damage inflicted on an opponent in so short a time as was proved to have been inflicted on themselves by the reports of British commanders in the American war. The strongest proof of American superiority was given by the best British officers, like Broke, who strained every nerve to maintain an equality with American gunnery. So instantaneous and energetic was the effort that, according to the British historian of the war, "a British forty-six-gun frigate of 1813 was half as effective again as a British forty-six-gun frigate of 1812"; and, as he justly said, "the slaughtered crews and the shattered hulks" of the captured British ships proved that no want of their old fighting qualities accounted for their repeated and almost habitual mortifications.

Unwilling as the English were to admit the superior skill of Americans on the ocean, they did not hesitate to admit it, in certain respects, on land. The American rifle in American hands was affirmed to have no equal in the world. This admission could scarcely be withheld after the lists of killed and wounded which followed almost every battle; but the admission served to check a wider inquiry. In truth, the rifle played a small part in the war. Winchester's men at the river Raisin may have owed their overconfidence, as the British Forty-first owed its losses, to that weapon, and at New Orleans five or six hundred of Coffee's men, who were out of range, were armed with the rifle; but the surprising losses of the British were commonly due to artillery and musketry fire. At New Orleans the artillery was chiefly engaged. The artillery battle of January 1, according to British accounts, amply proved the superiority of American gunnery on that occasion, which was probably the fairest test during the war. The battle of January 8 was also chiefly an artillery battle; the main British column never arrived within fair musket range; Pakenham was killed by a grapeshot, and the main column of his troops halted more than one hundred yards from the parapet.

The best test of British and American military qualities, both for men and weapons, was Scott's battle of Chippawa. Nothing intervened to throw a doubt over the fairness of the trial. Two parallel lines of regular soldiers, practically equal in numbers, armed with similar weapons, moved in close order toward each other, across a wide open plain, without cover or advantage of position, stopping at intervals to load and fire, until one line broke and retired. At the same time two three-gun batteries, the British being the heavier, maintained a steady fire from positions opposite each other. According to the reports, the two infantry lines in the center never came nearer than eighty yards. Major-General Riall reported that then, owing to severe losses, his troops broke and could not be rallied. Comparison of the official reports showed that the British lost in killed and wounded four hundred and sixty-nine men; the Americans three hundred and ninety-six. Some doubts always affect the returns of wounded, because the severity of the wound cannot be known; but dead men tell their own tale. Riall reported one hundred and forty-eight killed; Scott reported sixty-one. The severity of the losses showed that the battle was sharply contested, and proved the personal bravery of both armies. Marksmanship decided the result, and the returns proved that the American fire was superior to that of the British in the proportion of more than 50 per cent if estimated by the entire loss, and of two hundred and forty-two to one hundred if estimated by the deaths alone.

The conclusion seemed incredible, but it was supported by the results of the naval battles. The Americans showed superiority amounting in some cases to twice the efficiency of their enemies in the use of weapons. The best French critic of the naval war, Jurien de la Gravière said: "An enormous superiority in the rapidity and precision of their fire can alone explain the difference in the losses sustained by the combatants." So far from denying this conclusion the British officers complained of it. The discovery caused great surprise, and in both British services much attention was at once directed to improvement in artillery and musketry. Nothing could exceed the frankness with which Englishmen avowed their inferiority. According to Sir Francis Head, "gunnery was in naval warfare in the extraordinary state of ignorance we have just described, when our lean children, the American people, taught us, rod in hand, our first lesson in the art." The English textbook on Naval Gunnery, written by Major-General Sir Howard Douglas immediately after the peace, devoted more attention to the short American war than to all the battles of Napoleon, and began by admitting that Great Britain had "entered with too great confidence on war with a marine much more expert than that of any of our European enemies." The admission appeared "objectionable" even to the author; but he did not add, what was equally true, that it applied as well to the land as to the sea service.

No one questioned the bravery of the British forces, or the ease with which they often routed larger bodies of militia; but the losses they inflicted were rarely as great as those they suffered. Even at Bladensburg, where they met little resistance, their loss was several times greater than that of the Americans. At Plattsburg, where the intelligence and quickness of Macdonough and his men alone won the victory, his ships were in effect stationary batteries, and enjoyed the same superiority in gunnery. "The 'Saratoga,'" said his official report, "had fifty-five round shot in her hull; the 'Confiance, one hundred and five. The enemy's shot passed principally just over our heads, as there were not twenty whole hammocks in the nettings at the close of the action."

The greater skill of the Americans was not due to special training, for the British service was better trained in gunnery, as in everything else, than the motley armies and fleets that fought at New Orleans and on the Lakes. Critics constantly said that every American had learned from his childhood the use of the rifle, but he certainly had not learned to use cannon in shooting birds or hunting deer, and he knew less than the Englishmen about the handling of artillery and muskets. As if to add unnecessary evidence, the battle of Chrystler's Farm proved only too well that this American efficiency was not confined to citizens of the United States.

Another significant result of the war was the sudden development of scientific engineering in the United States. This branch of the military service owed its efficiency and almost its existence to the military school at West Point, established in 1802. The school was at first much neglected by government. The number of graduates before the year 1812 was very small; but at the outbreak of the war the corps of engineers was already efficient. Its chief was Colonel Joseph Gardner Swift, of Massachusetts, the first graduate of the academy: Colonel Swift planned the defences of New York harbor. The lieutenant-colonel in 1812 was Walker Keith Armistead, of Virginia,—the third graduate, who planned the defences of Norfolk. Major William McRee, of North Carolina, became chief engineer to General Brown, and constructed the fortifications at Fort Erie, which cost the British General Gordon Drummond the loss of half his army, besides the mortification of defeat. Captain Eleazer Derby Wood, of New York, constructed Fort Meigs, which enabled Harrison to defeat the attack of Proctor in May, 1813. Captain Joseph Gilbert Totten, of New York, was chief engineer to General Izard at Plattsburg, where he directed the fortifications that stopped the advance of Prevost's great army. None of the works constructed by a graduate of West Point was captured by the enemy; and had an engineer been employed at Washington by Armstrong and Winder, the city would have been easily saved.

Perhaps without exaggeration the West Point Academy might be said to have decided, next to the navy, the result of the war. The works at New Orleans were simple in character, and as far as they were due to engineering skill were directed by Major Latour, a Frenchman; but the war was already ended when the battle of New Orleans was fought. During the critical campaign of 1814, the West Point engineers doubled the capacity of the little American army for resistance, and introduced a new and scientific character into American life.

In the application of science the steamboat was the most striking success; but Fulton's invention, however useful, was neither the most original nor the most ingenious of American efforts, nor did it offer the best example of popular characteristics. Perhaps Fulton's torpedo and Stevens's screw-propeller showed more originality than was proved by the "Clermont." The fast-sailing schooner with its pivot gun—an invention that grew out of the common stock of nautical intelligence—best illustrated the character of the people.

That the individual should rise to a higher order either of intelligence or morality than had existed in former ages was not to be expected, for the United States offered less field for the development of individuality than had been offered by older and smaller societies. The chief function of the American Union was to raise the average standard of popular intelligence and well-being, and at the close of the War of 1812 the superior average intelligence of Americans was so far admitted that Yankee acuteness, or smartness, became a national reproach; but much doubt remained whether the intelligence belonged to a high order, or proved a high morality. From the earliest ages, shrewdness was associated with unscrupulousness; and Americans were freely charged with wanting honesty. The charge could neither be proved nor disproved. American morality was such as suited a people so endowed, and was high when compared with the morality of many older societies; but, like American intelligence, it discouraged excess. Probably the political morality shown by the government and by public men during the first sixteen years of the century offered a fair gauge of social morality. Like the character of the popular inventions, the character of the morals corresponded to the wants of a growing democratic society; but time alone could decide whether it would result in a high or a low national ideal.

Finer analysis showed other signs of divergence from ordinary standards. If Englishmen took pride in one trait more than in another, it was in the steady uniformity of their progress. The innovating and revolutionary quality of the French mind irritated them. America showed an un-English rapidity in movement. In politics, the American people betwen 1787 and 1817 accepted greater changes than had been known in England since 1688. In religion, the Unitarian movement of Boston and Harvard College would never have been possible in England, where the defection of Oxford or Cambridge, and the best educated society in the United Kingdom, would have shaken Church and State to their foundations. In literature the American school was chiefly remarkable for the rapidity with which it matured. The first book of Irving was a successful burlesque of his own ancestral history; the first poem of Bryant sang of the earth only as a universal tomb; the first preaching of Channing assumed to overthrow the Trinity; and the first paintings of Allston aspired to recover the ideal perfection of Raphael and Titian. In all these directions the American mind showed tendencies that surprised Englishmen more than they struck Americans. Allston defended himself from the criticism of friends who made complaint of his return to America. He found there, as he maintained, not only a growing taste for art, but "a quicker appreciation" of artistic effort than in any European land. If the highest intelligence of American society were to move with such rapidity, the time could not be far distant when it would pass into regions which England never liked to contemplate.

Another intellectual trait, as has been already noticed, was the disposition to relax severity. Between the theology of Jonathan Edwards and that of William Ellery Channing was an enormous gap, not only in doctrines but also in methods. Whatever might be thought of the conclusions reached by Edwards and Hopkins, the force of their reasoning commanded respect. Not often had a more strenuous effort than theirs been made to ascertain God's will, and to follow it without regard to weaknesses of the flesh. The idea that the nature of God's attributes was to be preached only as subordinate to the improvement of man, agreed little with the spirit of their religion. The Unitarian and Universalist movements marked the beginning of an epoch when ethical and humanitarian ideas took the place of metaphysics, and even New England turned from contemplating the omnipotence of the Deity in order to praise the perfections of his creatures.

The spread of great popular sects like the Universalists and Campbellites, founded on assumptions such as no Orthodox theology could tolerate, showed a growing tendency to relaxation of thought in that direction. The struggle for existence was already mitigated, and the first effect of the change was seen in the increasing cheerfulness of religion. Only when men found their actual world almost a heaven, could they lose overpowering anxiety about the world to come. Life had taken a softer aspect, and as a consequence God was no longer terrible. Even the wicked became less mischievous in an atmosphere where virtue was easier than vice. Punishments seemed mild in a society where every offender could cast off his past, and create a new career. For the first time in history, great bodies of men turned away from their old religion, giving no better reason than that it required them to believe in a cruel Deity, and rejected necessary conclusions of theology because they were inconsistent with human self-esteem.

The same optimism marked the political movement. Society was weary of strife, and settled gladly into a political system which left every disputed point undetermined. The public seemed obstinate only in believing that all was for the best, as far as the United States were concerned, in the affairs of mankind. The contrast was great between this temper of mind and that in which the Constitution had been framed; but it was no greater than the contrast in the religious opinions of the two periods, while the same reaction against severity marked the new literature. The rapid accumulation of wealth and increase in physical comfort told the same story from the standpoint of economy. On every side society showed that ease was for a time to take the place of severity, and enjoyment was to have its full share in the future national existence.

The traits of intelligence, rapidity, and mildness seemed fixed in the national character as early as 1817, and were likely to become more marked as time should pass. A vast amount of conservatism still lingered among the people; but the future spirit of society could hardly fail to be intelligent, rapid in movement, and mild in method. Only in the distant future could serious change occur, and even then no return to European characteristics seemed likely. The American continent was happier in its conditions and easier in its resources than the regions of Europe and Asia, where Nature reveled in diversity and conflict. If at any time American character should change, it might as probably become sluggish as revert to the violence and extravagances of Old World development. The inertia of several hundred million people, all formed in a similar social mold, was as likely to stifle energy as to stimulate evolution.

With the establishment of these conclusions, a new episode in American history began in 1815. New subjects demanded new treatment, no longer dramatic but steadily tending to become scientific. The traits of American character were fixed; the rate of physical and economical growth was established; and history, certain that at a given distance of time the Union would contain so many millions of people, with wealth valued at so many millions of dollars, became thenceforward chiefly concerned to know what kind of people these millions were to be. They were intelligent, but what paths would their intelligence select? They were quick, but what solution of insoluble problems would quickness hurry? They were scientific, and what control would their science exercise over their destiny? They were mild, but what corruptions would their relaxations bring? They were peaceful, but by what machinery were their corruptions to be purged? What interests were to vivify a society so vast and uniform? What ideals were to ennoble it? What object, besides physical content, must a democratic continent aspire to attain? For the treatment of such questions, history required another century of experience. . . . (IX, x, 219-42)

The Classics in History Series